Douglas Hyde

The Lad of the Ferule

Vol. 1

Douglas Hyde

The Lad of the Ferule
Vol. 1

ISBN/EAN: 9783337341046

Printed in Europe, USA, Canada, Australia, Japan

Cover: Foto ©Thomas Meinert / pixelio.de

More available books at **www.hansebooks.com**

Giolla an Ḟiuġa

OR,

THE LAD OF THE FERULE.

Eaċtra Cloinne Riġ na h-Ioruaiḋe

OR,

ADVENTURES

OF THE

CHILDREN OF THE KING OF NORWAY.

EDITED,

With Translation, Notes, and Glossary,

BY

DOUGLAS HYDE, LL.D., M.R.I.A.
(An Craoiḃín Aoiḃinn),
PRESIDENT OF THE IRISH TEXTS SOCIETY;
PRESIDENT OF THE GAELIC LEAGUE, ETC., ETC.

LONDON:
PUBLISHED FOR THE IRISH TEXTS SOCIETY,
BY DAVID NUTT, 270 & 271, STRAND.
1899.

PRINTED AT THE

DUBLIN UNIVERSITY PRESS

BY PONSONBY & WELDRICK.

PREFACE.

In addition to the information already given respecting the Society's foundation, aims, membership, and intentions, there is need only of a few words touching the work that lies before us, and the need of its being done.

It is of high importance that the great mass of MS. Irish literature of the sixteenth, seventeenth, and eighteenth centuries, now exposed to the risks of destruction, much of it being in single paper transcripts, should be rendered safe and accessible in print. Much of the inner history and thought of the Irish people for the last three centuries is enshrined in these frail papers.

To the student of language the publication of modern and middle Irish texts is a real and long-felt need, and it is one that only a Society such as ours can hope adequately to satisfy.

That those who speak and read Irish, as well as those that are interested in the tongue and history of Ireland, should have trustworthy and handy texts of the standard literature of that tongue placed within their reach, is surely a laudable and moderate object.

The work of the Irish Text Society is to fulfil these wants. It is a work of national importance, but it has been left to private hands to carry out. Still, with sufficient

support, and sufficient self-sacrifice and energy, it can be
carried out by a Society of workers and helpers.

If, in the next twenty-five years, with far more copious and
more interesting and more valuable material, we can do for
Irish Literature, new and old, what the Early English Text
Society has been able to do for old and medieval English
Literature in the last twenty-five years, we shall not have
existed in vain. We have also the encouraging examples of
the Scandinavian Texts Societies, and the Anciens Textes
Français. The good work done in a few volumes by the
too shortlived Ossianic Society, and by the Irish Archæological
Societies, is well known.

To our Irish members it is permissible to quote, once
more, Hugh M'Curtin's lines, they put the case from an
Irish point of view, perhaps, as well as it could be put:—

> A uaiſle 'Eiⱡeann áilne,
> A cⱡú na ʒ-céimeann combáⱡoe,
> Tⱡéiʒⱦ buⱡ ⱱ-tⱡomſuan ʒan ón;
> Céimⱦ lomluaⱱ buⱡ leabaⱡ.

> Tⱡom an céⱦm ſo ⱦaⱡláⱦ ⱱaoiⱱ,
> lⱱiⱡ mnáiⱱ aʒuſ macaoiⱦ,
> Aⱡ ſéanaⱱ ſeanⱡáⱱ buⱡ ſean,
> Cómⱡáⱱ ſoluⱡ buⱡ ⱡⱦſeaⱡ.

> ⱦioⱡ ⱱealⱱ an ⱱoⱦan uile,
> Teanʒaⱦ iſ milſe móⱡcuile,
> ⱱe bⱡacⱡaiⱱ iſ bⱡⱦocⱦſⱦuiⱦe blaſ,
> Caint iſ ciaⱦciⱦe cunⱦuⱡ.

> ⱦa cⱡaiʒⱦeaⱡ ⱦiobⱡuⱦ an ſiⱡ,
> leabaiⱡ uaⱦa a'ⱡ ⱦiⱡ,
> ſalaⱦ buⱡ ⱡʒeul ni ⱡʒⱡoⱡ ʒan,
> ʒan ſioⱡ buⱡ ʒ-céimeaⱦ coⱦⱡom.

The work before us is happily work that all who care for knowledge and literature, whether Irish, Welsh, or Breton, whether Celt or non-Celt, can join in. There is plenty of scope for scholars of all grades—those who cannot edit can photograph or copy, those that care not for copying may have special gifts as collectors of living songs and tales, those that cannot collect may help with indices, etc. The work will not be light, and the patience, temper, and devotion of the I. T. S. will be tried before its objects are adequately accomplished. At least a beginning has now been made, thanks to the energetic and patriotic historian of native Irish Literature; and, though in our case it is not quite true that Cúṗ máiċ leáċ ná h-oibṗe, still a good beginning is something to augur hopefully from.

F. YORK POWELL,

July, 1899. *Chairman, I.T.S.*

ᵹᴉoᴌᴌᴀ ᴀɴ ᵹ́ɪᴜᵹ́ᴀ

OR,

THE LAD OF THE FERULE.

ᴇᴀᴄ́ᴛᴘᴀ cᴌoɪɴɴᴇ ʀᴉᵹ́ ɴᴀ ʰ-ɪoʀᴜᴀɪᴆᴇ

OR,

ADVENTURES OF THE CHILDREN OF THE KING OF NORWAY.

INTRODUCTION.

THE two stories, printed in this first volume of the Irish Texts Society, are specimens of two different classes of tales which were, almost up to the present day, very popular with the native Irish, but of which scarcely a single specimen exists in print. For this reason I have chosen to edit them here, not, of course, as fair specimens of Irish literature, but as specimens of a peculiar class of story, which it is hoped will be of interest to folklorists, and which, on account of the good and idiomatic language in which they are couched, will offer a moderately easy reading-book to students. The first of these, "The Adventures of the Lad of the Ferule," has, in language and general character, a much closer relationship to the still-existing folk-tale as it survives, even yet, upon the mouths of old men, than has the second one, which is more antique in language, and more literary in expression. It will be well to say a few words about each story separately.

I.

"The Adventures of the Lad of the Ferule" was first mentioned by Mr. Standish Hayes O'Grady in a list of thirty or forty popular stories of the same kind, which he printed in his preface to the Fenian tale of "Diarmuid and Gráinne," published by him for the Ossianic Society in 1857. This particular tale, however, appeared to have been lost, for M. D'Arbois de Jubainville did not find a single copy of it in any of the libraries which he searched while

viii INTRODUCTION.

compiling his catalogue of the Epic Literature of Ireland. Old
John O'Daly, of Anglesea-street, had a copy, but when he died, his
invaluable collections of modern Irish manuscripts were not purchased
by the Royal Irish Academy, as they might have been for a few
pounds, but were allowed to be dispersed to the four winds of
heaven, and to be hopelessly lost to the country. I saw some of them
years later in Quaritch's. After this I was under the impres-
sion that this particular story was lost, and I was agreeably surprised
to come across an excellent copy of it in a well-written and voluminous manuscript, compiled during the first part of this century, by
one Michael O'Mongain or Mangan, which was lent me by my friend,
Mr. Thomas Houlihan, of Killard, a farmer in the County Clare.
Seeing that the story had so precarious an existence, I thought well
to save it by printing it. Soon afterwards my friend Mr. Robert
Stewart Macalister, by good luck, found another manuscript of the
same story, made by Mr. Daniel Mac Cabe, of Banteer, which was lent
him by Mr. J. G. O'Keefe, of the London Irish Literary Society. Of
this he very kindly made me a transcript, and I have edited from a
careful comparison between it, which I term B, and O'Mongain's
manuscript, which I have made the base of the text, and which I
allude to as A.[1]

To those who are unaccustomed to the ways of the traditional
Irish storyteller, "The Lad of the Ferule" will appear entirely
wanting in sequence, though it really is not altogether so. The story
is briefly as follows :—First a mysterious stranger comes with a
present of two wonderful hounds to Murough, son of Brian Boru—

---

[1] There is no very great difference between the two MSS., all the most salient
differences of reading are given in the notes. Outside of these, the most marked
distinction between them is the love of impersonal and passive forms in O'Mongain's
MS., which are almost always translated into the concrete in the other. Thus,
O'Mongain will write—(1) ᵇᵒ h-éιρᴄeaᵇ leιρ ; (2) ᵇᵒ ριαρρυιᵹeaᵇ ᵇe ᵹaᵇ
aon ; (3) ᵇᵃ ᵇᴄιoᴄρaoι, where MacCabe's MS. reads—(1) ᵇ'éιρᴄ aɴ ṁóρ-
ᴄυιᵇeaᴄᴄ leιρ ; (2) ᵇ'ριαρρυιᵹ ριaᵇ ᵇe ᵹaᵇ aon ; (3) ᵇᵃ ᵇᴄιoᴄρaᵇ ɴeaᴄ.
Since writing the above I discovered yet a third copy of this story in Maynooth

he who afterwards perished at Clontarf—saying "they were sent by the Queen of Pride as a present." He then disappears, and there is no more heard in the story about him, or the Queen of Pride, or her message. Next, Murough makes a great hunting with his two hounds, and all his people desert him, so that he is unable to carry home his game. In this dilemma another mysterious stranger approaches him, and offers to carry it home for him, and to become his servant for a year if Murough will give him what he asks for at the end of the year. Murough agrees. What he asks for is a ferule to fit his stick. The only ferule that will fit it turns out to be, along with a caldron of marvellous powers, at the bottom of a lake in the care of a serpent. Murough kills the serpent, and recovers ferule and caldron. Then the mysterious servant seizes the caldron, and dives under the lake with it. Murough follows to recover the caldron, and finds himself in another land below the lake, which the story-teller equates with Tír na n-Óg, the Land of the ever-young. This country he finds ruined by a giant. He slays the giant, sets free the country, recovers the caldron, and returns.

Now, the reader familiar with Irish story-telling will understand at once that all this machinery of the hounds, the hunting, and the ferule, was put in motion by a mysterious being, a god in fact (a similar being appears in some stories as Lugh, and in others as Manannán), to the end, that he might save Tír na n-Óg. It is he who appears as the messenger with the two hounds, and an untrue tale about the Queen of Pride. It is he again who, having by means of his hounds placed Murough in a dilemma, takes service with him as his gillie ; and it is he who finally entices him down into Tír na

College, with the following colophon—lap na ᵹᵹᴎoᵇaᴆ liomᵽa Coᵹan Coibín óum uᵽáιᴆe aᵹuᵽ aᵽ uᵽalaṁ eaᵽboiᵹ coᵽcaιᵹe .ι. an ᴄ-aᴄaιᵽ Seaᵹan O'Muᵽóaᴆ, an 6aᴆ lá ᴆon ṁι December annᵽa mblιaᵹaιn ᴆ'aoιᵽ aᵽ ᴆᴄιᵹeaᵽna 1817. My friend Dr. Hickey showed me this MS., which had been written for Dr. Murphy, Bishop of Cork. On a hasty perusal of it I could not see that it in any way materially differed from the copies I have used.

n-Óg, and makes use of him to set free the country. I feel quite certain that this is the way the story would be understood, and was meant to be understood, by all native Irish readers.

At what time this story was first composed, or at what time it was first committed to writing, there is no means of telling. But it is noticeable that, so far back as eight hundred years ago, Murough, son of Brian Boru, was credited with adventures in the fairy world. We read, in the Wars of the Gael with the Gaill, a work written in the end of the eleventh or the beginning of the twelfth century, that when Dúnlang, who had promised Murough never to abandon him, suddenly appears beside him on the very eve of the battle of Clontarf, Murough gently reproached him and said, "Great must be the love and attachment of some woman for thee which has induced thee to abandon me." "Alas!" answered Dúnlang, fresh from the embraces of his fairy sweetheart, "the delight which I have abandoned for thee is greater if thou didst but know it, namely, life without death, without cold, without thirst, without hunger, without decay, beyond any delight of the delights of the earth to me, until the judgment." "*Often,*" said Murough, "*was I offered, in hills and in fairy mansions, this world and these gifts,* but I never abandoned, for one night, my country nor mine inheritance for them." It is quite possible that stories may have been current about Murough's exploits, adventures, and courtships in the land of faërie, and the present tale may be a survival of them. As to the fight with the serpent in the lake, compare the story of the Death of Fergus in "Silva Gadelica," from a text of the fifteenth century, and the serpent in the Táin Bo Traich from a text of the twelfth century. The language of this tale is modern, and it does not differ very much from what may be heard from old story-tellers of the present day. I suspect that it had been told for ages before it was written down, and that, in fact, it may never have been committed to paper at all until perhaps a century or two ago.

II.

"The Adventures of the Sons of the King of Ioruaidh" [or Norway?] is a specimen of a different stamp of story. It does not deal with Ireland at all, nor with Irish people. It is not a growth of the soil, nor a distinct folk-lore development, in anything like the same sense as " The Lad of the Ferule " is. It probably did not pass through the mouths of many generations as a folk-tale before it was committed to writing. It smacks of pen and paper and cumbrous invention far more than the other story. It contains ten different poems inserted in the text, and from at least one of these poems—see the last one, p. 194—containing allusions to circumstances not mentioned in the text, it would appear as though the prose had been partly built up upon them. There are in all 188 lines of verse. Seven of the poems are in a rather loose metre, a mixture of Cassbhairdne and Little Rannaigheacht, an unusual verse-form, which makes me think that these poems originated from the same hand, especially as they do not observe alliteration and are careless in form. Two of the poems are in Deibhidh metre, and one in Great Rannaigheacht, but alliteration and the finer niceties of verse are not observed in any of them. For some reason or other this story has always been a great favourite with Irish scribes, and it is contained in quite a number of existing manuscripts. The manuscript which I have taken for the basis of the text was written by one Aodh Mac Dómhnaill of, I think, the County Down, for Tomás O'Luinigh or Lenin in 1714. Although faultily spelt and carelessly written, I found it to be perhaps the most voluminous and best-told version of the story, and there is not in it such a confusing mixture of ancient word-forms with modern ones as in some of the other MSS. I made a minute and careful comparison of Mac Dómhnaill's text (which I term A), copied for me by my friend Tadhg O'Donnchadha, with the copy of the same story preserved in the fine MS. H. 2. 6 in Trinity College, Dublin, which professes to be a copy of the Book of Brian Maguire, a copy made in 17⅟₄ by Seán Magabhráin. This fine manuscript contains 456 large pages, and the preface is sufficiently curious to give it here.

"αȝ ρο leαȝαρ Ḃριαm Ṁc Ȝυιȝιρ, mιc Concαȝαιρ moȝαρα, mιc ȝριαιn, mιc Seᾱιn, mιc Ḟcιȝ-leιnne ȝυιȝ, mιc Ȝιollαὁαccραιȝ, mιc Cαmυιnn nα Cúιle .ι. Ṁαȝ-υιȝιρ, mιc Ċomᾱιρ óιȝ, mιc Ṫomαιρ móιρ .ι. αon ceαnn coċυιȝċe αȝυρ conȝȝᾱlα ḟleαȝcα Ȝιollαὁαccραιȝ mιc Cmυιnn nα Cúιle, bιαcαὁ ιom-lᾱn, conȝȝυρ ceαὁ αοιȝeαȝ ρριnρι-ραlcα le hαȝαιȝ υαραl αȝυρ ιριol, eιȝρι αȝυρ ollαṁαn, αορ cιúιl αȝυρ οιρριce, οιȝe οιleαṁnα αȝυρ αlc-ρυιm nα noρȝccρᾱιȝċeαὁ αnαιmριρ ρeρρecυcιon, ȝeιρceαὁ αȝυρ cιoȝ-lαιceαὁ ȝo boċcαιȝ ȝo bαιncρeαȝ-υιȝ αȝυρ ȝo ȝιleαccυιȝ αȝυρ ȝo ȝeιȝlcιnnιȝ ȝeαρóιle Ḃe: ȝυιne ȝo cαιll moραn αιρȝιȝ le hαċnυαȝυ-ȝαȝ le ρȝριoȝα αȝυρ le ρυαρȝlαȝ ιomαȝ leαȝαρ o Ȝαllαιȝ αȝυρ o Ȝαeȝeαlαιȝ, ċυm mαιċιορα nα cυn-ȝαe, ȝo ṁeαȝυȝαȝ αnmα αȝυρ onoρα αn cιnc ȝα ȝρυιl Ḃé, αȝυρ ȝo cυm α ȝυl α leαρ αȝυρ α ρoċαρ ȝα αnαm, αȝυρ ȝo nȝeαcαιȝ.

"Jañy. ye 2, 17{48}."

" Here is the Book of Brian Maguire, son of Concabhar the surly, son of Brian, son of Seán, son of Feidhlim the black, son of Gillapatrick, son of Eám-onn *na Cúile,* namely, Maguire, son of Thomas óg, son of Thomas mór, namely, the one nourishing and upholding head of the race of Gillapatrick, son of Eámonn *na Cúile,* a complete hospitaller, who keeps a principal guest house for high and low, for poet and ollamh, for musicians and minstrels, the rearing and fostering teacher of the pious orders in time of persecution, giver and bestower of alms to the poor, to widows, and to orphans, and to the wretched impover-ished of God; a man who lost much money in renewing, in writing, and in ransoming many books, from the foreigners and from the Gaels, to the good of the county, to increase the fame and honour of the race from which he is, to increase the glory and honour of God, and for it to go to the good and profit of his soul, and that it may!

" January the 2nd, 17{46}."

This excellent MS. which contains many old forms disused in the other[1] I call H. If two people attempted for a wager to say exactly the same thing in different words, they could hardly succeed better than A and H. In comparing them it was a perpetual source of astonishment to me how, without any alteration in the sense, the two manuscripts picked out different words and phrases to express precisely the same thought. The prototypes from which they were written were perhaps penned from the dictation of different story-tellers who each used his own words, while neither of them took the slightest liberty with the story itself.

---

[1] As " αροιle " for " eιle," noὁα for nι, ριl for cᾱ, ol for αρ, lυιȝ for ċυαιȝ and verbal forms, αȝ concαȝαρ, ȝo ρonραc, noὁαρ ḟeαȝραȝ, leαnρυm ċυȝρυm, ρυιȝeαρcαρ, etc.

Besides these I used three other more recent MSS., 23. L. 39 of
the Royal Irish Academy [which I call L], a good Munster manuscript, written in a beautiful hand by one Seághan O'Domhnaill in
1778. Another marked 23. L. 27, written by Seághan O'Cinéide in
1738, and another, a northern manuscript, 23 A. 25, written by one
Séamus Mac Ciarnáin, in a small duodecimo volume, in a large bold
hand, in 1770. I have also, in my own possession, a fragment of the
story in a beautiful but imperfect manuscript by a northern scribe of
the last century, I think Patrick O'Prunty; but most of the pages
are unfortunately lost.

I had completed my comparison of these MSS., and prepared my
text from them, when, knowing that a copy of this story had been
mentioned as having been found in Colgan's cell at Louvain after his
death in 1658, I thought that I would search the Library of the
Franciscans on Merchants Quay, Dublin, to try if it still survived,
although neither D'Arbois de Jubainville, nor Sir John Gilbert who
catalogued their books for the Government, mention it as extant. I was
lucky enough, thanks to the kindness of the Librarian, Father O'Reilly,
to find this very MS. It is one of various contents on paper, bound up
in the remains of a beautifully-written old Irish vellum, under which
is a second cover consisting of an illuminated Latin vellum, and it
probably dates from the end of the sixteenth or the beginning of the
seventeenth century. The writing is in many places very indistinct,
through time and use, and it abounds so in contractions that it would
be absolutely impossible to edit the story from it alone.[1] In my

---

[1] Thus, the letter n with a stroke and dot over it stands not only for no but for
naċ and neaċ. A stroke over ꞇ stands not only for ꞇan but for ꞇíne. A stroke
over ꝑ stands not only for ꝑéin but for ꝑuil. A stroke over an ꞃ stands not only
for aċꞇ but for ꞃaoꞃ! Often only the initial letter of a word is given, and one
has to guess the word from the context, as cl. ᵹ ⁊ cl- ꝑ ⁊ cl- b, which stands for
cláꞃ ᵹoꞃm aᵹuꞃ cláꞃ ꝑionn aᵹuꞃ cláꞃ bub, a fact one could not have
guessed without another copy. This MS. also contains an imperfect copy of the
Death of Cuchulain, the Breach of Magh Muirtheimhne, the Fight at the Ford, the
Story of Cearbhall and Farbhlaith, and one hundred and nine pages of poems by
such bards as Tadhg Dall, and Tadhg Óg O'Higinn, O'Gnimh, O'Ruanadha
O'Hussey, Geoffrey *Fionn* O'Daly, Owen Magrath, Cearbhall *Buidhe* O'Daly,
Conor *Ruadh* Mac Coinmidhe, Miler Magrath, Flann Óg Magrath, etc.

notes I have called it ꝑ. The story of "The Sons of the King of Norway" commences at p. 23 of the MS., and is continued to p. 54, when
another and much later and poorer hand takes it up to p. 68. Then
the story is continued in the original hand to its end on p. 83. This
manuscript, which is, I believe, a northern one, abounds in curious
forms, and contains traces of a language far more archaic than any
spoken or written in 1600,[1] which makes me believe that this story
was a written one in perhaps the fourteenth century, a fact which,
except for the discovery of this MS., I should never have suspected.
So far as the story goes, it does not differ appreciably from the modern
manuscripts, and I have compared carefully with it a large portion
of my text.

As this story also may appear somewhat confused to the reader,
it will be useful to summarize it here, as follows :—The three sons of
the King of Ioruaidh are out hunting one day when they meet a
strange lady, Bright-eyed Féithlinn [Fay-lin], who, being herself
under *geasa* [gassa], or enchantment, is desirous of having it taken
off by the three warriors. She accordingly puts them under *geasa* to
search the world till they find her out. They do not find her, but
they meet an island and a palace, with a remarkable cat as its sole
inhabitant. Afterwards they fall in with the daughter of the King
of the White Men, whom they rescue. She tells them that the cat
they had seen is Féithlinn, who had put them under *geasa*, and that
she is her own half-sister. On learning this they sail away at once
to seek again the cat and the island, but cannot find them. They are
attacked by the son of the King of Sorcha,[2] but beat him off. They
sail then with a great fleet to Sorcha, to avenge themselves, but all
their men and two of themselves are slain there by treachery, the
eldest brother Cod alone surviving. Féithlinn, who had originally put
them under *geasa*, comes to Cod now in the form of a swan, and brings

---

[1] Thus, mıllꝑı ocuꝓ buꝓbo ꝓıono a mblaċa, *i.e.* their blossoms were sweeter
and harsher [stronger] than wine. ꝓ is generally put for b, as ꝁoıꝓ for ꝁoıb.
o is used frequently for a, as aıꝓċċeallo for aıꝓb-ċealla, ꝓıꝓ ébṁaꝓo for
ꝓıꝓ éabṁaꝓa, etc.

[2] Sorcha is often translated Portugal ; it is a name that occurs frequently in
folk stories, but I feel sure that it has no geographical significance.

him a mantle to put round his slain brothers, which will keep them for ever as fresh as though they had been only just slain. She departs, and Cod meets the enchanted Lady Bethuinè, who is a descendant of the previous reigning house in Sorcha, whose people had been dethroned by the ancestors of the King of Sorcha whom Cod had just slain. She accordingly befriends him, and puts him on the track of a salve that can bring his brothers again to life. Cod goes in search of it, and reaches the Forest of Wonders, where many adventures befall him; and Bright-faced Sun, the daughter of the King of the Forest, befriends him, and gives him a magic rod. While he is with her, Féithlinn brings away the salve, and restores to life his two brothers, and on his return to Bethuinè, in Sorcha, he finds them alive there before him. He and Gold-armed Iollan, a warrior whom he had saved in the Forest of Wonders, sail to Greece, to restore to Bright-faced Sun her lover, who had been enchanted by the daughter of the King of Greece. They do this after hard fighting, and Cod returns with her lover to Bright-faced Sun. In the meantime, his brothers have been conquering the world, but meeting with the City of the Red Stream, which is surrounded by a river of fire, they cannot conquer that, but are themselves taken prisoners by Eiteall [Ett-yăl], daughter of the King of the World, who is chieftainness of the city. Cod and his friends hear this, and beleaguer the city. They are aided by a magic mantle given them by the King of the White Men, whose daughter, Féithlinn's half-sister, they had saved. The King of the World hears this, and assembles all his feudatory kings to rescue his daughter. But Cod finds out the secret of the fire, and his friend Buinnè Roughstrong captures the stone which will dry up the flames. The King of the World dies, his army is defeated, the city captured, and Cod, son of the King of Norway, becomes King of the World.

This story, in which much of the stock-in-trade of the Celtic story-teller is employed, is one which, for the student of comparative folk-lore, would lend itself to frequent annotation, but I have rigorously refrained from the temptation to extend this volume by folk-lore notes, such not being properly within the scope of the

Irish Texts Society, which like the Early English Texts Society is, I believe, intended to somewhat subordinate the æsthetic and historical side of Irish Literature to the philological. It remains now to explain the freedoms I have taken with my texts.

III.

The two texts from which I edit the "Lad of the Ferule" were both Munster texts, and the story is a Munster story. Neither of them were very good texts, or in any way regular in orthography. There appeared to me to be no use in allowing mere orthographical and kindred errors to stand, and hence I reduced the text for the most part to the regular standard language of all Ireland by making a few consistent changes which I shall here particularize.

In the first place the most of the capitals, hyphens, and punctuations are mine. I have (*a*) consistently edited the preposition ꝺe, meaning 'of' or 'from' or 'off,' instead of the ambiguous form ꝺo, and the simple preposition aꞃ, 'on,' for aiꞃ, and ı, 'in,' for a, and aɴɴ a, for the various forms, ıoɴ a, ıɴa, ıoɴa, aɴɴa, &c.; and aɴɴ ꞅoıɴ for aɴɴꞅıɴ, 'there.'

(*b*) I have corrected the following misspellings and grammatical inaccuracies: cꞃıuꞤal for ꞅıuꞤal, a ɴ-aꞃmaıꞤ for a ɴ-aꞃma [nom. case], cúꞡaıɴɴ and ꞅúꞡaım for cuꞡaıɴɴ and ꞅúm, auꞤáꞡaıl for auꞤáıl, ꞅocꞃa for ꞅocꞃaıꞡ, ꝺe ꞅeóıꝺe for ꝺe ꞅeóıꞤıꞤ, buaꝺċaıl for buaċaıll, ıɴꞡíoɴ for ıɴꞡeaɴ, ꝺcaꞃa for ꝺaꞃa, ꝺeaɴcúṁaꞃ for ꝺéaɴcúꞃ, ꞡo mo for ꞡo mꞤuꝺ, cꞃe ɴa plucaꝺ for cꞃe ɴa plucaıꞤ, aꞡ ꞃꞡolcaꝺ coꞃꞤuıꞤ for aꞡ ꞃꞡolcaꝺ coꞃꞤ, ċoɴɴaıꞃceaꝺaꞃ for ċoɴɴcaꝺaꞃ, ꝺeıɴıꝺ for ꝺéaɴaıꝺ, ċaıꞃꞡıꞤıꞃ for ċaꞃꞃaıɴꞡıꞤíꞃ. If I had had a third manuscript I would probably have found the true forms.

(*c*) The more peculiarly Munster forms which I have ventured to change, and which are of much more importance, as they represent not mistakes or inaccuracies, but a real dialect, are Ʞeaꞃꞃa for Ʞeaꞃꞃ, ꞃíɴe and bꞃıꞃe for ꞃíɴeaꝺ and bꞃıꞃeaꝺ, ċáıɴe for ṫáinig, ná feacadar for nać bfacadar, ná biḋeać for nać mbiḋeać, feacar for facar, drom for druim, greiḋm (pronounced *grime*) for greim, and camm for cam.

(*d*) I have edited do ráiḋ for do ráḋ, guṫ for guiṫ, d'éiriġ for d'éirġe, uirri for uirṫe, márać for máireać, cosṁúil for cosaṁail, and the letter g for cc, and io for ea in such verbs as rinnear. The above is an almost complete list of the changes made to reduce the text to a uniform standard, and in some cases the forms I have adhered to were used alongside of the forms I rejected.

In the case of "The Children of the King of Norway," there were so many available MSS. of the story that if I found a misspelling or a provincial form in one of them I was sure to find the correct form in another. The manuscript which I took for the basis of the text, that of Aodh Mac Domhnaill, I take to have been written in the County Down, because, immediately after finishing the story of "The Children of the King of Norway," he either composes or copies a curious piece with the following heading:—"Here is a letter that was sent to a minister who came to us here in the parish of Drumarath, to deliver a sermon in Irish, in order to turn the people with him to the Protestant religion."[1] This parish is in the County Down, and I have little doubt that the scribe was a native of it. He frequently falls into dialectical peculiarities, which are of great interest, as they represent the farthest possible geographical and dialectical divergence from the language of the "Lad of the Ferule," which is that of south-west Munster, as this is that of north-east Ulster. The principal peculiarities of this scribe's dialect are as follows:—

(*a*) Frequent omission of f in the future and conditional, as béarad for béarfad, déandírt for déanfadaois. This shows that the f of these tenses had already begun to be dropped in the north nearly two hundred years ago.

---

[1] Ag so litir cuiraḋ dionsaiḋ ministir tainig deanam seanmoire a Gaoiḋilg cugain an so go pairais Druimarath cum daoine tiompo leis ar an creidioṁ Protestan, ⁊c.

xviii INTRODUCTION.

(*b*) The occasional shortening of the infinitive ending -uᵹaᵭ, as
coᵱuᵹ and meaᵱúᵭ for coᵱuᵹaᵭ and meaᵱuᵹaᵭ, which is exactly
what we find in central Connacht at the present day, where the ending
-uᵹaᵭ is pronounced as though it were the monosyllable úᵹ', or aᵭ.

(*c*) A tendency to strengthen the final ᵱ of the first and third
persons plural of the conditional active, by adding c to it, as
ċiᵹiᵭiᵱc and ċiᵹᵭiᵱc for ċiᵹiᵭiᵱ, ᵬéaᵱamuiᵱc for ᵬéaᵱᵱamaoiᵱ,
and ᵭéanᵭiᵱc for ᵭéanᵱaᵭaoiᵱ. This tendency to strengthen the
final ᵱ has been carried into the adverb aᵱiᵱ, which is frequently
written both ᵱiᵱc and aᵱiᵱc, as it is at this day pronounced
in most parts of Connacht.

(*d*) The forms of the pronouns and prepositional pronouns offer
some peculiar features, the most noticeable being the dialectic muᵱ
for ᵬuᵱ, not uncommon in Northern MSS., ᵬuaim and ᵬuaic, as in
Scotland, [ᵱuaim and ᵱuaic may be heard in Béara at the opposite
extreme of Ireland] for uaim and naic, ᵭioᵱ and ᵭioᵬċa [no doubt
pronounced ᵭioᵱa] for ᵭioᵬ, and ᵭúᵱa or ᵭúᵯᵱa for ᵭam-ᵱa or
ᵭaᵯ-ᵱa, a pronunciation which is at this day largely used in
Connacht. The final m in ᵭam is often aspirated, but I do not
know what the exact pronunciation may have been. There is a
great variety in the orthography of the pronouns, as ᵱaioᵬ-ᵱi for
ᵱiᵬ-ᵱe, ᵭioᵬᵱa for ᵭaoiᵬ-ᵱe, hioᵬ-ᵱi for hiᵬ-ᵱe, acú for aca [as
is the usage at present in Connacht], and naᵭa for uaiᵭ.

The principal irregularities in the text of this story with which
I have not interfered relate to (*a*) eclipsis by prepositions, (*b*) erratic
verbal forms, (*c*) the genitive plural of nouns, (*d*) duplicate forms of
words, (*e*) doubling of consonants.

(*a*) The prepositions ᵹo, "with," aᵱ, in, cᵱe, and ᵱo, do not
uniformly eclipse, as they do at the present day, for we meet such
forms as ᵹo cloċaiᵬ, inᵱ an cáċᵱaiᵹ, cᵱeᵱ an ceó, ᵱo an cloiᵭe,
aᵱ an ᵬᵱeiċeaᵯnaᵱ, side by side with the regular eclipsed forms.

(*b*) We meet the irregular verbal forms muna n-iaᵱᵱaiᵭ
ᵱiᵬ (p. 54), muna ᵭcuᵹaiᵭ ᵱiᵬ (pp. 102, 138), for the regular
n-iaᵱᵱann and ᵭcuᵹann. A ᵭo also slips in before the present

passive, apparently in the sense of a relative pronoun, in na ʒeaρa
ꝺo cuιρċeaρ, on p. 120 ; and before the future relative, ιρ cρío ꝺo
ċιucρaρ, on p. 144. We find ꝺeaꝺ, ꝺeιċ, and ꝺιaꝺ, for the 3rd
person sing., conditional, of ꝺeιċ.[1]

(c) The forms of the acc. plural are frequently used, as I
have noticed them used in conversation at the present day in
Connacht, for the regular genitive plural forms : as ꝺ' úρlannaιꝺ
a ρleaʒa, "off the handles of their spears," where the proper form
would be ρleaʒ; ꝺo ʒaꝺaιl a nꝺánca, p. 140; aʒ ρéaċaιn na
ceιċρe áρꝺa, p. 58; aʒ ceaρcuʒaꝺ a ʒcρanna, p. 76; aʒ
ιnnριn ρʒéala.

(d) We meet different forms or different spellings of certain
words, almost on the same page, as ρé and ρaé, na laoιꝺ and na
laoιꝺe, ꝼριċιꝺ and ꝼρíoċaιꝺ, ꝺρaoιʒeaċc and ꝺρaoιꝺeaċc, ꝺo'n
ċoꝺlaċ and ꝺo'n ċoꝺlaιʒ, ιριn and ιρan, coṁalcaιʒ and coṁalcuιꝺe,
ꝺealꝺa and ꝺeιlꝺe, ꝺún and ꝺúnaꝺ, eaρρaꝺ and eaρρa.

(e) There is, in a few words, some uncertainty in the doubling
of the liquids, especially n and ρ, as coρaċ, or coρċaċ, and coρρaċ,
ιnιρ and ιnnιρ, ρaιρʒe and ρaιρρʒe.

The principal survivals of forms now obsolete, which occur in
even the most modern MSS. of this story, are: nochaρ for náρ,
ꝺaꝺaρ for ꝺιꝺeaρ, ρuʒρac, ċiṁρeac, ρonρac, ʒeallρac, for
ρuʒaꝺaρ, ċiṁeaꝺaρ, ριnneaꝺaρ, ʒeallaꝺaρ, ρá for ꝺa or ꝺuꝺ,
ρaιρ for aιρ, ꝼρι and ꝼριa for le, ꝼριρ for leιρ, ꝼoρ for aρ,
ριa for léι, aꝺ ċιú for ꝺo ċιꝺιm, ρe aρoιle for le ċéιle.

The principal spellings which I have ventured to change are the
following:—I have consistently edited ρaιꝺ for ρoιꝺ, ꝺe [off] for ꝺo,
ιna for ιona, ιoṅa, and other forms; ꝼρeall for ιoρal, cρéan for

[1] The following irregular forms occur in the first story too :—"d'iarras tu",
and "go n-iarras tu", p. 12, "do dhéanfair", p. 30, "do sracfad", p. 42.
"Thangathas", p. 28, is an impersonal form not uncommon in Munster, meaning,
"it was come", "they came". Nouns wrongly inflected are "slinneáin", p. 12,
for "slinneánaibh", and "an uillphéist", p. 42, for "na h-uillphéiste". For
"buachaille", p. 20, and "buachaill", p. 44, read "buachalla": I extended the
contractions wrongly.

τρέη, and éα for é in a few other words, ιмċеаċτ for ιомċеаċτ, ιм-ὄéαηαṁ for ιoм-ὄéαηαṁ, ηίoρ for ηίρ, cρίċe [gen.] for cρίoċα, ὄαoιηιὄ for ὄαoιηoιὄ, ηιὄ [thing] for ηί, ὄéαηαṁ for ὄeιηαὄ, ὄί for ὄαoι, ʟⁱⁱὄeαηαιὄ [dat. plur.] for ʟⁱⁱὄιoηα, ċάηʒαὄαρ for ċάιηιʒeαὄαρ, ράηʒαὄαρ for ράιηιʒeαὄαρ; and I have used eα for ιo where it occurred in such words as ριηηeαρ. In all or almost all of these cases, other MSS. contained the forms which I have given. In every case I have given the standard forms of the prepositions and prepositional pronouns, about whose orthography there is in all the manuscripts a considerable laxity. I have not, I know, succeeded in thus preparing a perfectly uniform text, but I have certainly gone a long way towards it, and I feel sure that no learner will be disposed to quarrel with me for having done so. I have in every case given in the notes the more important variants exactly as I found them.

Rambling and disjointed as these stories appear—and there certainly is a sad lack of form about them,—they will yet be found, I think, to compare very favourably with many of the mediæval romances that are made the subject, at the present day, not only of philological but of literary study, and that in point of fact form the material upon which several hundreds of students all over Europe are working under some dozens of professors. I believe that these two texts, apart from any interest their subject-matter may have for the scientific folklorist, present, if nothing else, a fair specimen of the more modern Irish language from the two extremes of Ireland which, geographically, are most widely separated; and while the text of the first is modern in the sense that it may not have been committed to paper more than a century or two ago, the other represents the *modernised version* of a text which may have been written in the fourteenth or fifteenth century. It is to be hoped that they will thus make a useful and not too difficult book for those who desire to study in its different forms the modern written language.

DOUGLAS HYDE.

(Αη Cραoιὄίη Αoιὄιηη.)

ꞡɪoʟʟɑ ɑɴ ꝼɪuᵹɑ.

ADVENTURES OF THE LAD OF THE FERULE.

An ȝcualabaṛ an móṛ-clú, ainm, áiṛioṁ, aȝuṛ uṛṛaḋnoṛ¹

ḋo bí aṛ Ṁuṛċaḋ mac Ḃṛiain bóiṛṁe, ṁic Ċinéiḋe,

ṁic Loṛcain [ṁic Laċtna], ṁic Ċuiṛc, ṁic Anluain,

ṁic Ṁatȝaṁna, ṁic Toiṛḋealḃaiȝ, ṁic Ċatail,

ṁic Aoḋa Ċaoiṁ, ṁic Ċonaill, ṁic Eoċaċ²

Ḃaill-ḋeiṛȝ, ṁic Ċaṛtainn Ḟinn, ṁic Ḃlóiḋ³,

ṁic Ċaiṛ, ṁic Ċonaill eaċ-luaiṫ, ṁic

Luȝaiḋ Meann, [ṁic Aonȝuṛa Tiṛeaċ],

ṁic Ḟiṛcuiṛb, ṁic Ṁoȝa Ċuiṛb,

ṁic Ċoṛmaic Caiṛ, ṁic Oiliolla

Óluim, aȝuṛ an ċuiḋ eile

ḋe ṛíol Eiḃiṛ Ḟinn⁴.

¹ "Oṁós". A.   ² "Eachaidh". A.   ³ "Blaid". B.
⁴ A adds "mic Eibhir Fhinn uaibhrigh, chaomh-áluinn, glann-thapa, mear-

Have you heard of the great fame, name, renown, and reputation that belonged to Murough son of Brian Boru, son of Kenedy, son of Lorcan, son of Lachtna, son of Core, son of Anluan, son of Mahon, son of Turlough, son of Cathal, son of Aodh the gentle, son of Conall, son of Eochaidh Red-spot, son of Carthan the fair, son of Blód, son of Cas, son of Conall of the swift steeds, son of Lughaidh Meann, son of Aongus Tireach, son of Fercorb, son of Mogh Corb, son of Cormac Cas, son of Oilioll Olum, and the rest, of the race of Eber Finn.

---

mhíleata, do gléir (?) cheap na Craoibhe, os asgar na míle meanmach is laochda gníomh", which seems corrupt. The genealogy is correct except for the omission of two names which I have restored in brackets.

ᵹiolla an ḟiuᵹa.

Aᵹur ḟór, ve ḟíol Éiḃir ḃeimionn* inᵹean Arcaḋ ṁic Ṁurcaḋ ríᵹ iarṫair Connaċt, máṫair Ḃriain Ḃóirṁe[1], ᵹo mbuḋ é rin ḟéin an ríᵹ ᵹan uaḃar ᵹan ḟeall ᵹan impear. An ríᵹ le n-a ḋuḃraḋ na h-aiṫḟrinn aᵹur re n-ar beannuiᵹeaḋ na h-aḃlanna[2], re n-ar bairḃeaḋ na ḃaoine, re n-ar rlánuiᵹeaḋ ḟineaċar aᵹur ḟearann Críoċ Ḟáil[3], re n-ar croċaḋ rlaḃaiᵹṫe aᵹur ᵹaḃaiᵹṫe an ḃoṁain uile i n-aon ló, ᵹc[4].

Lá ḃár éiriᵹ an ríᵹ ḟéin amaċ ar an ḃḟáiṫċe óirḃearc[5] ḟeur-uaiṫne ḃo ḃí i nḊún Cinn-Coraḋ[6], ir iaḃ ḃo ḃí ann [a] ḟoċair an lá rin an ċuiḃ buḋ ḟine ḃ'á ċloinn, mar ḃo ḃí Ṁurċaḋ mac Ḃriain, Ḋonnċaḋ mac Ḃriain, Ḋóṁnall mac Ḃriain, Conċuḃair mac Ḃriain, Ḟlann, Taḋᵹ, Ḋuḃlainn[7] ᵹioḃail aᵹur ᵹiolla an ᵹaiḃ[8] mac Ḟinnḃearra mic ríᵹ Alḃanaiᵹ, an ḟear ḃo ḃ'ḟearr méin aᵹur mioċal, coiᵹċeríoċaiᵹ aᵹur clainne coiᵹċeríoċaiᵹ[9] ḃo ṫáiniᵹ riaṁ ᵹo h-Éirinn. Ḟeuċainc ḃá ḃcuᵹaḃar ṫarrra ann ran Ḃraiṫċe ḃo ċonarcaḃar ċuᵹṫa an ḃóṫar réiḃ[10] ró-ḟiúḃlaċ, an Ḋraoi aᵹur an ḃeaᵹ-ḃuine[11] ealaḃanta, aᵹur léine ḃo'n ṫrleaṁan-tríoḃa um a ċnear, aᵹur a Ḃrat ciúṁar-ḃuiḃe cró-ḃearᵹ cruinn-ċruaiḃ[12]. Ḋo ḃí ann ran mbrat[13] buine óir 'na ḃrollaċ, ḟiḃe óir ar ḟolc an ḃraoi, ḟlearᵹ aᵹ rileaḃ[14] ar an ḃḟolc aᵹ conᵹḃáil[15] an ḟuilt o n-a rorᵹ aᵹur o n-a raḋarc. Cu aᵹur ᵹaḃar aᵹur beann-buaḋṁuin[16] leir, ḟiḃ ḃe'n airᵹioḃ ḟinn-ᵹeal a mbarra croiḃ[e]

---

* Her name was ḃeḃinn, according to Keating.   [1] Both copies usually leave ḃoirṁe unaspirated, but not always.   B omits the above passage.   [2] B "abhlainigheadh".   A "ollainighe".   [3] A reads "re ar sloineadh na cindhicha re a ndearnathas Crioch Fáil fearainn agus fionnadhus." A reads re ar always, while B inserts an n, re n-ar.   [4] B omits "ᵹc".   [5] B "fordharch", A "fordhréamh".   [6] Both mss. write "Dún ceann coradh" and "Dún Cinn" or "Chinn", "Coradh" or "Choradh" indifferently.   [7] B "Daoibhlinn".   [6] A adds "Fladharta".   [9] A has after coiᵹċeríoċaiᵹ the words "taoisigh

ADVENTURES OF THE LAD OF THE FERULE.

And of the race of Eber, moreover, was Beimionn, daughter of Arcadh, son of Murough, king of the West of Connacht, mother of Brian Boru—and it was he himself was the king without pride, without treachery, without quarrelling; the king by whom the masses were said, and by whom the wafers were blessed, by whom the people were baptized, by whom the tribeship and the land of Inisfail were saved; by whom the plunderers and thieves of the whole world were hanged in a single day—and the rest of it (¹).

Of a day that the king himself rose [and went] out on the splendid grass-green lawn that was at Kincora, those who were that day in his company were the eldest of his children, Murough Brian's son, Donough Brian's son, Donal Brian's son, Conor Brian's son, Flann, Teig, Dubhlainn *giobail*, and the Lad of the Gad, son of Finbhearr, son of a Scotch king, the man of best mien and mettle—of a stranger or of a stranger's children—who ever came to Ireland. Of a look that they cast round them in the lawn, they beheld [coming] to them [along] the smooth easily-travelled road, the druid and the good man of science, and a shirt of the smooth silk around his skin, and his mantle yellow-bordered, blood-red, tightly-gathered (²). There was in the mantle a golden pin in its front, a golden circlet [was] on the druid's hair, a fillet [was] stretched upon his locks, keeping the hair from his eyes and from his sight. A hound and a stag-hound and a horn with him; a ring of fine-white silver on the top of his left hand, the rest of the chain aloft above the neck of the

agus clann taoiseach sar clann ar bhfear n-Eireann, fearlaoigh Ciarraidhe Midhe agus Laighean," which seems corrupt.   ¹⁰ A "socma socsiubhlach".   ¹¹ A "deaghdamhan ealadhan".   ¹² B "cruinne cruadh". A "cruinne truadh".   ¹³ A adds "go húr a bruinne ar feadh lán laoch no curadh".   ¹⁴ A "filleadh".   ¹⁵ A "cruinneamhail".   ¹⁶ B "buabhall", *passim*.

(¹) This apparently means that this "run" or alliterative passage on the virtues of Brian was cut short by the writer.   (²) Literally "round-hard."

a láṁ[e] ċlí, an ċuiḃ eile ḃe'n ᴄrlaḃra a n-áirḃe aᵹur ḟá
ṁuinéal na con. Ann rúḃ ir é ḃ'ḟill a ᵹlún, ḃo ċrom a ċeann
aᵹur ḃ'ḟeac a ċollan¹, ḃo ḃeannaiᵹ aᵹur ḃ'úṁlaiᵹ ḃo ṁac
árḃ-riᵹ Éireann.

"Le ᴄri réaḃaiḃ ruiriᵹe ċuᵹaḃ-ra ᴄánᵹar o ḃainríoᵹain
an uaḃair, re cu aᵹur re ᵹaḃar aᵹur re beann-ḃuaṁuin.
Ir é rin cuiḃ an ᵹaḃair ḃo'n ḃuaḃ-ḃuaṁuin² binn [.i.] ni
ċuirreaḃ lonᵹ aᵹur ni ḃéanraḃ riaḃaċ no ᵹo ᵹcluinreaḃ ré
an ḃeann ḃ'á reinm³. Ann rin an uair ḃo ċloirreaḃ ré an
ḃeann ḃ'á reinm ᵹluaireóċaḃ ré ḟá ḟoraiᵹir lonᵹ⁴ aᵹur ḟá
ᵹraiḃlri⁵ riaḃᵹuiḃeaċᴄa, ionnur naċ ḟáᵹᴄar leir riaḃ i
ḃriaḃuiᵹeaċᴄ⁶, ná broc i mḃruċlaraiḃ, ná rionnaċ i ḃᴄalaṁ,
ná beiᴄiᵹeaċ ró-ḟaicrionaċ ná[ċ] ḃúirᴄiᵹᴄear leir. Ann rin
leiᵹᴄear an ċu anḃiaiᵹ na reilᵹe ionnur naċ léiᵹriᵹear léi
beiᴄiᵹeaċ ḃíoḃ roir ná riar, ó ḃear ná ó ᴄuaiᵹ, naċ marḃᴄar
aᵹur náċ ḃiᴄ-ċeanntar léi iaḃ, ḃo láᴄair aon áiᴄe."

"Ni h-ionᵹnaḃ liom-ra rin," ḃo ráiḃ Murċaḃ, "réaḃa
ruiriᵹe ḃ'ḟáᵹail ó ḃainrioᵹain an uaḃair, aᵹur ó ᵹaċ mnaoi
eile, maiḃir léi, ḃá ċóṁaċᴄa ḃá ḃḟuil ran ḃoṁan-ro ḟéin,
aᵹur ir ionᵹanᴄaċ liom cá ᵹcualaᴄar⁷ le bainríoᵹain an
uaḃair, clú nó ainm nó áireaṁ nó mór-urraḃnór⁸ ḃo ḃeiᴄ
orm ḟéin."

"Aiċrirreaḃ rin ḃuiᴄ a ṁic an riᵹ. Lá ḃ'á raḃamar-ne
ran nᵹréaᵹ⁹, aᵹ ḃéanaṁ lúiᴄ aᵹur liaċróiḃe, aᵹ ḃéanaṁ
malairᴄ uraḃ¹⁰ aᵹur airm aᵹur éaḃaiᵹ, aᵹ caiᴄeaṁ fleaḃ
aᵹur feurᴄa i mór-ċeallaċ riᵹ Ḡréiᵹe ḟéin an ló ran. Ḃo
finniḃeaᵹ¹¹ ar na borḃaiḃ na rᵹoraiḃiḃ¹² reannaṁla¹³ raiᵹ-
reaṁla¹⁴ ḃe ᴄoᵹa ᵹaċa baiᴄ ḃo ḃul ar ᵹaċ éaḃaċ, ḃe ḃuiḃe ḃe
bán ḃe ḃearᵹ ḃe ᵹorm aᵹur [ḃe] ᵹlar-uaiᴄne. Ḃo ḃáileaḃ ar
na bórḃaiḃ úḃ biaḃna ro-ċaiᴄᴄe, ḃeoċa ró-ólᴄa, ró-ṁillre,
aᵹur fíonᴄa uairle ro-ḃaora, ionnur ᵹuraḃ lia fleaḃ aᵹur
feurᴄa ḃo ḃí i mór-ċeallaċ riᵹ Ḡréiᵹe, an lá rin, 'ná mar ḃo

---

¹ A adds " thug poroiste (?) d'oillibh, umhla agus urma". ² B "don bheann".
³ A "sing" and "sinng". ⁴ A "fa oiraidhlsi " (?). ⁵ B "gradhailsigh".
⁶ B "nduireadha". ⁷ ᵹcualaᴄar, in both MSS. ⁸ A "órnós". ⁹ A reads "i
ngréig bheag meodhanach, agus an gréag eile comhsanntur dóibh sin seacht
n-ealaighe deug na gréige agus oiread Eireann na Albain an gach tuaith diobh
san," which is corrupt. ¹⁰ A "iorradh". ¹¹ A "finneadhag".

hound. Then it was he bent his knee, bowed his head, and stooped his body, saluted and made reverence to the son of the High-king of Erin.

"With three treasures of courtship, to thee have I come, from the Queen of Pride, with a hound and with a stag-hound and with a horn. And this is how the stag-hound is connected with the melodious horn, namely, he will neither run on a track nor make a hunting until he hear the horn sounding. Then, when he hears the horn sounding, he will proceed through forests with tracks [of beasts] and thickets (?) for hunting deer, so that there is not left by him deer in deer-ground, badger in badger-resort, fox in earth, or [other] visible beast, but is roused by him. Then is the hound let loose after the game, so that she will not leave a beast of them, east or west, south or north, but is slain and pulled-down (¹) by her in one place."

"I wonder not at this," said Murough, "to get treasures of courtship from the Queen of Pride, and from every other woman as well as from her, no matter how powerful, of all who are in this world itself; but what I wonder at is where it was heard by the Queen of Pride that I possessed either fame or name, renown or reputation."

"I shall relate thee that, O Prince. We were of a day in Greece, (²) playing at games of activity and ball, exchanging garments and arms and armour, consuming feasts and banquets in the great household of the King of Greece on that day. There were whitely-laid upon the tables the exquisite plentiful table-cloths, with a choice of every colour to go upon every cloth, of yellow, of white, of red, of blue, and of green. There were placed upon those tables foods easily-eaten, drinks easily-drunk, very-sweet, and wines noble, very-costly; so that more abundant was the feast and banquet that was in the great mansion of the King of Greece on that day than

---

¹² B "scordaibh". ¹³ B "fineálta". ¹⁴ B "réidhseamhla". B omits the passage about the colours.

(¹) Literally "beheaded." (²) Literally "a day that we were in Greece," but this is an anacoluthon, unless a comma be placed after "an ló san", and "do finnidheag" be taken as the relative clause.

ḃí ḟeaṟ ná buıḋeann ċum a ċaıċċe[1], ḃe ċoıṇ, ḃe ჳaḋaıṟ, ḃe ṁná[ıḃ], ḃe ċoıleáın, aჳuṟ ḃ'aċalaıṟჳ uṟláıṟ, ıonnuṟ ჳuṟ buḋ ċoṁ-ḟoluṟ ċeaჳlaċ ṁóṟ na Rıȯıṟeaċċa[2] an lá ṟıṇ aṟ an ḃcaoıḃ amuıჳ aჳuṟ aṟ an ḃcaoıḃ aṟcıჳ. Ann ṟúḃ ıṟ eaḋ ḃ'éıṟıჳ ḃollṟaıṟe na bṟuıჳne ann a ḟeaṟaṁ aჳuṟ ḃo ċṟaıċ ṟé ṟlaḃṟa-éıṟceaċca ḃo ḃí aıჳe. Ḋo h-éıṟceaḋ leıṟ, ṟaoı maṟ ḃo ḃí ṟoıṟ ṟıaṟ ó ċuaıჳ[3] aჳuṟ ó ḃeaṟ, aṟ ṟeaḋ an ṟéıḃ-ċeaჳlaıჳ ṟın. Iṟ ann ṟın ḃ'ḟıaṟṟaıჳ ḋıoḃ cıa aca ıoıṟ áıṟḃ-ṟıჳ, ṗṟıonnṟa, ṟıჳ-ḃaṁna, ṗṟıoṁṗáıḋ, cıჳeaṟna, no ıaṟla, ḃo ḃí ı móṟ-ċeaჳlaċ ṟıჳ Ⴟṟéaჳ an lá ṟın, ıṟ mó ḃo ḃṟonnaḋ ḃ'óṟ aჳuṟ ḃ'aıṟჳıoḃ, ḃe ċalaṁ aჳuṟ ḃe ċıჳeaṟnaṟ, ḃ'eıċ aჳuṟ ḃ'éaḋaıჳıḃ, ḃe ṟჳoṟaıḃıḃ ṟınneaṁla[4] ṟéıჳṟaṁla[5], ḃe ċoჳa ჳaċa ḃaıċ ḃo ḃul aṟ ჳaċ h-éaḃaċ, ḃe ḃuıḋe ḃe ḃán ḃe ḃeaṟჳ ḃe ჳoṟm aჳuṟ ḃe ჳlaṟ-uaıċne[6], aჳuṟ ḃo ჳeaḃaḋ ann ṟéın ceaċċ aჳ ṟuıṟıჳe ṟe baınṟıoჳaın an uaḃaıṟ.

" Ḃ'éıṟıჳ ჳaıṟჳıḃeaċ éolჳaıṟeaċ ḃe'n ceaჳlaċ ann a ḟeaṟaṁ, aჳuṟ aḃuḃaıṟc ṟé ჳuṟaḃ eaḋ ṟéın é, aჳuṟ nı móıḃe ḃeıḃeaḋ ṟe aṁla, é ṟéın ḃá ṟáḃ ṟıṟ ṟéın[7].

" Ḋo ḟuıჳ ṟın ṟíoṟ aჳuṟ nı ḃuḃaıṟc nı ḃuṟ mó. Ann ṟoın ıṟeaḋ ḃ'éıṟჳíoṟ-ṟa ṟéın am' ḟeaṟaṁ, a ṁıc an ṟıჳ, aჳuṟ aḃuḃaıṟc mé ჳuṟ ჳaıṟჳıḃeaċ éolჳaıṟeaċ mé ḃo ḟıuḃal an ḃoṁan ṟo[8] ṟaoı aჳuṟ oṟ a ċıoṇ, ṟá maṟ ḃo ḃí o Uṟaḃ ჳo h-Uṟṟaḃ, o Lıṟe ჳo Loċlaınn, ó Loċlaınn ḃo'n Spáın, ó'n Spáın ḃo'n Eaṟḃáın, ó'n Eaṟḃáın ჳo h-Eıṟınn, ჳo Cıoḃṟaıḃ ḃo maoıle ṟınne, ჳo Ⴟáṟḃaıḃ na hlıṟḃeıṟce aṟ an ḃcaoḃ ṟıaṟ, ჳo cıჳ an cṟean ḃaıle. Ḃ'ınnıṟ mé náṟ ḃ' aıċne aჳuṟ náṟ ḃ' eólaċ ḃam aṟ an Ḃṟaḃ[9] ṟın mac ṟıჳ ná cuṟaḋ ná ṗṟoıṁınṟıl[10] ḃo ḃ' ḟeaṟṟ 'ná Muṟċaḋ mac Ḃṟıaın ḃóıṟṁe aჳuṟ an ċuıḃ eıle ჳc, aჳuṟ ḃ'ınnıṟ mé ḃóıḃ ჳo mbuḋ cu ṟéın an ṟıჳ ჳan uaḃaṟ ჳan ḟeall ჳan ımṟeaṟ, an ṟıჳ ṟe n-a ḃuḃṟaḋ na h-aıċṟṟınn ṟe n-aṟ beannuıჳeaḋ na h-aḃlanna[11], ṟe n-aṟ baıṟceaḋ na ḃaoıne, ṟe n-aṟ ṟloınneaḋ na ṟıneaṁaċa, ṟe n-aṟ ṟlánuıჳeaḋ ṟıneaċaṟ

---

[1] B omits from the word " caithte " to end of sentence.   [2] " Radharaigh-eacha ", MS.   [3] B " soir agus siar, thuaidh agus theas ".   [4] B "fineálta".
[5] B " reídhseamhla ".   [6] B omits again about the colours.   [7] B reads "ach nach móide go dtiucfadh an bhainrioghain ar aontughleis ", *i.e.* " but not the more for that would the queen come to consent to him ".   [8] B reads " an domhan so mórtimchioll go dtangas tar ais aris go h-Eirinn ", omitting the curious

were the men and companies to eat it—of hounds and stag-hounds and
women and puppies and the rabble of the floor ; so that the great mansion of the knights on that day was equally bright on the outside and on
the inside.   Then it was that the herald of the palace arose, standing
up, and he shook a chain-of-hearing that he had.   Hearing was
accorded him both east and west, north and south, throughout that
smooth mansion.   It was then he inquired of them which of
them all, be he high-king, prince, heir-apparent, primate, lord, or
earl, who was in the great household of the King of Greece that day,
used most to bestow gold and silver, land and lordship, steeds and
raiment, white plentiful cloths, with a choice of every colour to go
upon every cloth, of yellow, of white, of red, of blue, and of green,
—and who would find it in himself to come and court the Queen of
Pride.

"There arose standing a knowledgeable hero of the household,
and he said that he himself was that man, and not the more for
that would it be done, because he himself said it of himself (¹).
"That man sat down, and he said no more.   Then it was that I
myself rose and stood up, O Prince, and I said that I was a knowledgeable hero who had travelled this world both above and below (²), all
that was from Uradh to Urradh, from Liffey to Lochlann, from Lochlann to Spain, from Spain to Easpain, from Easpain to Erin, to the
Well of the Bald White Cow, to the Garden of Hesperides on the
western side [of the world], to the house of the old town.   I told
them that I was neither acquainted with nor knew in all that length
[of ground] a king's son, or a hero, or a provincial who was better
than Murough, son of Brian Boru, and the rest of it, and I told them
that you yourself were the king without pride, without treachery,
without quarrelling,—the king by whom the masses were said, by
whom the wafers were blessed, by whom the people were baptized, by
whom the races were surnamed, by whom the tribeship and land of

---

list of places.   ⁹ B "ar an bhfeadh sin ".   ¹⁰ B "iarla na laoch ".
¹¹ B "abhlainigheadh", A "hollainighe ".

(¹) *I.e.* Though he could say for himself that he fulfilled all necessary qualifi-
cations, yet not the more for that would he win the queen.   (²) The Tuatha
De Danann travelled underneath the earth as well as overhead, apparently. See
"Caoilte na gCos fada" in my "Sgeuluidhe Gaodhalach ", part iii.

agus fearann Críoċ Fáil, re n-ar croċaḋ fiaḋaiġṫe agus
gaḋuiġṫe an ḃoṁain uile i n-aon ló. Dá ḃfíġ sin cuirim i
gcoṁġaḃáilṫear¹ agus i ḃfiaḋnuise a ḃfuil ann so ḋo láṫair,
go nḋearna mé mo ċóṁall agus mo ṫeaċtaireaċt."

Ris sin ceileaḃar ḋo ṁac an ríġ, agus buḋ ṡaṁail se
h-uirge ceóiḋ geiṁriḋ no ríolla ḋe ġaoiṫ liárṫa ó ag imṫeaċt
ċum siuḃail, ionnus gur imṫiġ sé gan coraḋ gan tuarasgḃáil.
Ann sin ḋo ċuaiḋ Murċaḋ mac Ḃriain agus gaċ n-aon ḋ'á
raiḃ 'na ḟarraḋ ḋ'á ḋeiġ-ċeaglaċ, aḃaile.

D'éiriġ sé go moċ ḋe ló agus ḋe lán-trolus ar na ṁáraċ.
An uair ḋo ḋearcaḋar a réiḋ-ċeaglaċ, sin, ḋ'éirġeaḋar féin
ag comóraḋ² feilge an laoi sin leis, agus ḋo ṡeinn an ríġ
féin an ḃeann ḃuaḋṁainn³; ann sin gluairigear an gaḋar
fá forruiriḃ lorg, agus fá ġarrailriġ fiaḋguiḋeaċta, fá
ṫorc ór loċ⁴, agus fa críoċ ḃḞearmorc⁵ agus fá ḋá ṡliaḃ
ḃéag Ḟéiḃlime, ionnus nár fágaḋ leis fiaḋ i ḃfiaḋaċ⁶ na
broc i mbroiċinirg⁷ ná beiċiḋeaċ rói-feicrionaċ, ná rionnaċ⁸
i ḋtalaṁ, nár ṁúrglaḋ sir, ionnus go g-cuirreaḋ se broic ar
coilltiḃ, geilt ar gleannta[iḃ], faolċoin faoi áraiḃ, rionaiġ
ar reaċrán.   Ann sin ḋo leigeaḋ an ċu anḋiaiġ na feilge
ionnus nár leig sí beiċiḋeaċ ḋíoḃ-ran soir ná siar, ó ċuaiġ
ná ó ḋear, naċ raiḃ treargarta agus nár biṫ-ċeannaḋ léi ḋo
láṫair aon áite, ionnus go mbuḋ i sin an treas feilg is mó
ḋo rinneaḋ i n-Éirinn riaṁ ar na Creatalaċaiḃ⁹, or cionn
loċ Ḋeargtar¹⁰.   Aḋuḃairt Murċaḋ mac Ḃriain se gaċ n-aon
ḋ'á luċt-leanaṁna, eireaḋ a ḋroma agus a ḋ'á ḟlinneán ḋo
ḃreiṫ leis ḋe'n ṫreilg go ḋún Ċinn Ċoraḋ, ḋ'á innrint agus
ḋ'á ṡairnéir gur éiriġ a leiṫċóiḋ sin ḋe ṡeilg laċ leó.

"Dar bóga agus dar briaṫar," ḋo ráiḋ iaḋ-ran¹¹, "giḋ bé
niḋ ḋo ḋéanfamaois-ne se rgabal gairge, no se tular caṫa
no [se] éaḋaċ mic ríġ no tiġearna ḋ' iomċur, ni raċfamaoiḋ
ag iomċur ḋo ṡeilg-laoi-se linn ar ár nḋromaiḃ no ar ár

---

¹ A "o chomhaldeis".   ² B "a gcomórtus leis chum seilge".
³ B "buabhall".   ⁴ B "fa thorch oslach".   ⁵ B "na bhfearmborc".
⁶ B "fiaguidheacht".   ⁷ B "brochdanuis".   ⁸ B "seanach".
⁹ B omits.   ¹⁰ B reads "Deirgdheirc", *passim*.   ¹¹ B omits from

Inisfail were saved, by whom the robbers and thieves of the whole world were hung in one day.   For that reason I call all who are here present to substantiate (?) and bear witness that I have accomplished my fulfilment [of my task] and my message."

Therewith he takes his leave of the king's son, and he was like the water of a winter fog, or the whiff of a March wind, as he departed on his journey, so that he went away without tale or tidings of him.   Thereupon Murough, son of Brian, and everyone of his good household that was in his company went home.

He arose early in the day and full light of the morrow.   When his standing household beheld that, they themselves arose to prepare with him the hunt of that day, and the king himself blew the bugle-horn; thereupon the staghound proceeds through forests with tracks and thickets for hunting deer, through *Torc ós loch* and the country of the Fearmore, and through the twelve mountains of Felim, so that there was not left by him a deer in deer-ground, or a badger in badger-resort, or a visible beast, or a fox in earth, that was not roused by him, so that he would put badgers out of woods, *geilts* (¹) out of glens, wolves under heights, and foxes astray.   Then was the hound let loose after the game, so that she never left a beast of them east or west, north or south, that was not pulled down and slain by her in one place, so that that was the third greatest hunt ever made in Erin, on the Cratloes above Loch Derg.   Murough son of Brian told each one of his following to bring with him the load of his back and his two shoulders of the game, to the palace of Kincora, to tell it and proclaim it that they had succeeded in making such a day's hunting.

"By our bow and our word," said they, "whatever we might do about the carrying of a warrior's (²) shoulder-piece, or a head-piece of battle, or the garments of a prince or a lord, we will not go to carry your day's hunting with us on our backs or on our shoulders"; and

---

ıað-ṗan to nı ṗaċṗamaoıð.

(¹) *Geilt* usually means a "lunatic" or "wild man".   (²) Literally "a
shoulder-piece of valour".

rlinneáin," aᵹur rír rin ꝺ'ḟearᵹaꝺar a péiꝺ-ċeaᵹlaċ ᵹo ró ṁór rír, ionnur nár ḟan¹ aon ꝺuine ꝺíoꝺ láiṫreaċ, aᵹur ᵹur ḟáᵹꝺaꝺar Ɦurċaꝺ mac Ḃríain 'na uaċa aᵹur 'na aonar or cionn na reilᵹe.

Ḟeuċain ꝺ'á ꝺtuᵹ ré ann ran áirꝺ buꝺ ċuaiᵹ ꝺo ċonnairc ré ċuiᵹe ꝼear ꝼallainᵹe² loime léiċe, aᵹur léimtín ᵹarꝺ ꝺuꝺ [air], tri h-óirneaċ iuꝺair ar a ḃaclainn, ionnur ᵹo mbuꝺ ꝺóiᵹ le Ɦurċaꝺ ᵹo mbain[ꝼ]eaꝺ plaitín a ꝺá ᵹlún a innċinn ar ċúl a ċinn. Ɦar rin ꝺó, ᵹo roċtain an riᵹ. ann roin ꝺo ċúb³ a ᵹlún, ꝺo ċrom a ċeann, ꝺ'ḟeac a ċollan, aᵹur ꝺo ḃeannuiᵹ ᵹo h-úṁall ꝼómóraċ ꝺo ṁac riᵹ Éireann⁴. Ir ann roin ꝺ'ḟiaꝼruiᵹ mac áirꝺ-riᵹ Éireann ꝺé caꝺ é an ꝺuine é. aꝺuꝺairt ré ᵹur buaċaill é ꝺo ꝺí aᵹ lonᵹ máiᵹirtir.

" Ir maiċ mar ċárla," ꝺo ráiꝺ Ɦurċaꝺ, " cearꝺuiᵹear buaċaill uaim-re, aᵹur caꝺ é an tuararꝺal ꝺ'iarrar tu orm ᵹo ceann bliaꝺna?"

" ꝺreiċ mo ḃéil ꝼéin ꝺe ċuilleaṁ aᵹur ꝺe ċuararꝺal," ꝺo ráiꝺ an buaċaill.

" Ᵹo mbuꝺ ṁeara i ᵹcioñ bliaꝺna ċu," ꝺo ráiꝺ Ɦurċaꝺ, " caꝺ é an ꝺeantúr maiċeara aꝺeir tu a ḃeiċ ionnat mar ᵹo n-iarrar tu ꝺreiċ ꝺo ḃéil ꝼéin ꝺe ċuilleaṁ aᵹur ꝺe ċuararꝺal?"

" aꝺair ᵹuraꝺ mé aon rᵹeuluiꝺe búirꝺ aᵹur leapċan ir ꝼearr ꝺ'á ꝺtiocꝼaiꝺ ná ꝺ'á ꝺtáiniᵹ, ꝺ'á ruᵹaꝺ ná ꝺ'á mbéarꝼar ᵹo bruinne an ḃráċa."

" ꝺuꝺ ꝺoilꝺ⁵ ꝺaṁ-ra na maiċe móra ꝺo ċaꝺairt ꝺuit-re aᵹur ᵹo raiꝺ Ꝼlaċaꝺ⁶ an rᵹéaluiꝺe ꝺo ḃꝼearr ann, re linn Ꝼiaċa Ꝼionnluiꝺe ꝺo ḃeiċ i ḃꝼlaiċear Éireann."

" ꝺo ḃuꝺ eólaċ ꝺaṁ-ra ꝼéin Ꝼlaċaꝺ aᵹur buꝺ ró eólaċ, aᵹur ꝺam buꝺ eólaċ é. Ní inꝼreaꝺ ré rin aċt an rᵹéal ꝺo ḃí ann riaṁ aᵹur an rᵹéal ꝺo ḃeiꝺeaꝺ ann ċoiꝺċe. Ní mar rin ꝺaṁ-ra. Inneóraꝺ an rᵹeul naċ raiꝺ ann riaṁ, aᵹur an rᵹéal naċ mbéiꝺ ann ċoiꝺċe, ionnur luċt ꝺaor-oċair aᵹur earláinte an ꝺoṁain ᵹo ᵹcoꝺlaꝺaoir uile iar ᵹclor mo rᵹéalta-ra."

---

¹ B reads "ionus nár fhágbhadar aon duine d'uaith ná d'iongna air".
² A " fallainnigne ", B " falluinnin ".   ³ A ꝺ[ḟ]ill.   ⁴ A reads as

with that his household grew very greatly enraged with him, so that not a man of them remained in his presence, and they left Murough son of Brian in solitude and alone over the game.

Of a look that he cast towards the north he beheld coming towards him a man of a long bare cloak, and a little rough black shirt on him, three billets of yew in the hollow of his arm, [coming] so that Murough thought that the caps of his two knees would knock the brains out of the back of his head.   Thus he was till he reached the king.   Then he bent his knee, bowed his head, stooped his body, and saluted humbly and submissively the son of the King of Erin.   Then the son of the High King of Erin inquired of him what manner of man he was.   He said that he was a lad who was in search of a master.

"It has happened well," said Murough; "I want a lad, and what are the wages you will ask of me [from now] till the end of a year?"

"The award of my own mouth, of stipend and of wages," said the lad.

"That you may be worse at the end of a year!" said Murough; "what is the peculiar excellence you say is in you that you are asking the award of your own mouth, of stipend and of wages?"

"Say then, that I am the one best storyteller by table and couch of all that shall come or that have come, that were born or that shall be born, to the womb of judgment."

"It would be hard for me to concede those great excellences to you, seeing that 'Flathadh the best storyteller' existed during the period that Fiacha Fionnluidhe was in the sovereignty of Ireland."

"I myself knew Flathadh, and well I knew him, and it is I that did know him.   That man used never to tell except the story that was always in it, and the story that would be in it for ever.   Not so with me.   I will tell the story that never was in it, and the story that never shall be in it, so that the exceeding sick and ailing of the world would all sleep after hearing my stories."

---

before "thug poróiste dollamhumhla [*i.e.* d'ollamh, umhla] agus urma".
⁵ A "dála".   ⁶ A "an flatha".

" Caḋ iaḋ na ḃeancúip maiċeapa eile ḃéappap mé ḃeiċ ionnac, map ᵹo ḃḟuil cu aᵹ iappaiḋ ḃpeiċ ḋo ḃéil ḟéin ḋe ċuilleaṁ aᵹup ḋe ċuapapḋal?"

"Aḃaip ᵹup mé aon ᵹiolla cupaip¹ ip ḟeapp ḋ'á ḋciocpaiḋ ná ḋ'á ḋcáiniᵹ, ḋ'á puᵹaḋ no ḋ'á mḃéappap."

"Buḋ ḋoiliᵹ ḋaṁ-pa na maiċe mópa pin ḋo ċaḃaipc ḋuic-pe, aᵹup ᵹo paiḃ Luaiċluᵹa² Cam an ᵹiolla cupaip ḋo ḃ'ḟeapp pe linn piᵹ Ulaḋ ḃeiċ ann pan ᵹCpaoiḃ Ruaḋ."

"Do buḋ eólaċ ḋaṁ-pa Luaiċluᵹa Cam pe linn piᵹ Ulaḋ, aᵹup buḋ pó eólaċ, aᵹup ip ḋam buḋ eólaċ é. Do ḃeipeaḋ pé caipciol na cpíċe i ᵹcúiᵹ lá, ḃo ḃíoḋ cpi ᵹeapcaiᵹ ap a ṁuin aiᵹe i ᵹcliaḃán, ni ḃíoḋ aon ḃean ap an ḃpaiḋ pin naċ cóᵹpaḋ poᵹa ḃuilᵹ lae uaiċe³, ni map pin ḋaṁ-pa, ḃo ḃéappaiḋ mé caipcioll na cpíċe i n-aon ló, aᵹup ni ċóᵹpaiḋ me poᵹa ḃuilᵹ aon laoi ó aon ṁnaoi ap an ḃpaḋ pin aċc [ó] aoin ṁnaoi aṁáin, 'p ip cuma liom e ḟáᵹail uaiċe pin ḟéin no ᵹan ḟáᵹail!"

"Maipeaḋ an ḃcuᵹann cu ḃo ḃpiaċap ᵹup cuiṁin leac piᵹ Ulaḋ ḃeiċ ann pan ᵹCpaoiḃ Ruaḋ?"

"Dap mo ḃpiaċap," ap pan ᵹiolla, "ip cuiṁin, aᵹup piᵹċe poiṁe, .i. Eoċaiḋ Feiḋlime⁴ mac Ḟinn ṁic Ḟionnlóᵹa ṁic Roᵹnáin Ruaḋ, ⁊c⁵ ḋe ḟíol Eipeaṁóin."

"Dap mo ḃpiaċap," ḃo páiḋ Mupċaḋ, "ip oᵹánaċ⁶ aopca ċu, aᵹup caḋ é an ḃpeip ṁaiċeapa ḃéappap mé ḃo ḃeiċ ionnac ᵹo ḃcaḃaippinn ḃpeiċ ḃo ḃéil ḟéin ḋe ċuilleaṁ aᵹup ḋe ċuapapḋal ḃuic?"

"Aḃaip ᵹup mé aon ᵹiolla ceine ip ḟeapp ḋ'á ḋciocpap ná ḋ'á ḋcáiniᵹ, ḋ'á puᵹaḋ ná ḋ'á mḃéappap."

"Buḋ ḋoilḃ ḋaṁ-pa na maiċe mópa pin ḃo ċaḃaipc ḋuic, aᵹup ᵹo paiḃ mac Leipᵹ an ualaiᵹ ċpuim pe linn Copmaic ḃo ḃeiċ i ḃTeaṁaip, aᵹup ni paiḃ ᵹiolla ceine pe ḟáᵹail ḃo ḃ'ḟeapp 'ná é."

"Do buḋ eólaċ ḋaṁ-pa mac Leipᵹ an ualaiᵹ ċpuim, aᵹup buḋ pó eólaċ, aᵹup ip ḋam ḃo buḋ eólaċ é. Do ċuᵹaḋ pé

---

¹ B "an giolla-truis". ² B "an luaithligheadh". ³ A adds "agus do tugadh foillach da gearrcaigh". ⁴ B "Feidhlge". ⁵ B omits "⁊c". ⁶ A "og gan grádh aosta".

" What other forms of excellence shall I say to be in you, seeing you are asking the award of your own mouth of wages and of stipend ? "

" Say that I am the one best travelling lad of all who shall come or who have come, of all who were born or who shall be born."

" It were hard for me to concede those great excellences to you, seeing that Luathlugha the Crooked, 'the best travelling lad,' existed when the King of Ulster was in the Red Branch."

" I knew Luathlugha the Crooked in the time of the King of Ulster, and well I knew him, and it is I who did know him. He used to make the round of the country in five days. He used to have three chickens on his back in a basket. There used not to be one woman in all that length that he would not plunder a meal (¹) from her. Not so with me. I shall go the round of the country in one day, and I will not plunder a meal from any woman during all that way, but from one woman only, and I do not care whether I get it from her itself (²), or whether I do not get it."

" Musha! do you give your word that you remember the King of Ulster being in the Red Branch ? "

" By my word," said the gillie, " I do remember; and kings before him, namely, Eochaidh Feidhlime son of Finn, son of Fionnlogha, son of Roghnán the Red, and the rest, of the race of Eremon."

" By my word," said Murough, " it's an aged youth you are; and what more excellence shall I say is in you that I should give you the award of your own mouth of wages and of stipend ? "

" Say that I am the one best fire-gillie of all that have come or that shall come, that were born or that shall be born."

" It were hard for me to concede those great excellences to you, seeing that ' Mac Leisg of the heavy burden ' lived at the time Cormac was in Tara, and there was not a fire-gillie to be found better than he."

" I knew Mac Leisg of the heavy burden, and well I knew him, and it is I who did know him. He used to bring with him from the woods

---

(¹) Literally, "raise the belly-plunder of a day ".   (²) "Itself" is used, in Anglo-Irish, after the analogy of the Gaelic, in the same sense as the French *même*.

ḟuir[1], ó na coillṫiḃ, eireaḋ a ḋroma aᵷur a ḋá ḟlinneán
ḋ'áḋmaḋ. Do ḃiḋeaḋ ré aᵷ ḃruiṫ aᵷur aᵷ ḃeirḃiuᵷaḋ ρe
reaċṫ lá aᵷur reaċṫ n-oiḋċe, aᵷur ḋo ḃeiḋ' ḟéin na ċoḃlaḋ
reaċṫ lá aᵷur reaċṫ n-oiḋċe eile. Ní mar rin ḋaṁ-ra. Ní
ḋéanraiḋ mé aċṫ mo ṫri h-oirneaċ iuḃair ḋo ċur ríor, aᵷur
ᵷaċ a ḋṫiucraiḋ 'r a ḋṫáiniᵷ ḋ'á ruᵷaḋ no ḋ'á mḃéarρar,
ḋo ᵷeoḃaiḋír ᵷoraḋ aᵷur ṫear aᵷur ḃeirḃiuᵷaḋ biḋ ḋ'á
ḋṫairḃe, aᵷur ni lúᵷaiḋe aᵷur ni móiḋe aᵷam ḟéin i ᵷceann
bliaḋna iaḋ."

"Ir ṫu aon[2] ḃuaċaill aṁáin ir ḟearr ar biṫ," ar Murċaḋ,
"má 'r ríor a n-abrann[3] ṫu."

"Ir ríor ᵷo ḋeiṁin," ḋo ráiḋ an buaċaill.

Do réiᵷṫíᵷeaḋar ar an móḋ rin.

"Ir mór an ṫreilᵷ í reó ḋ'éiriᵷ leaṫ a ṁic an riᵷ," ar
an buaċaill.

"Maireaḋ ir mór," ḋo ráiḋ Murċaḋ.

"Créaḋ ḟáṫ nár ḋúḃrair ρe ᵷaċ n-aon ḋe ḋ' ṁuinnṫir
eireaḋ[4] a nḋroma aᵷur a ḋá ḟlinneán ḋe'n ṫreilᵷ ḋo ḃreiṫ
leó, ḋ'á innrinṫ aᵷur ḋ'á ċóiṁ-innrinṫ[5] ᵷur éiriᵷ a leiṫéiḋ
reo ḋe ḟeilᵷ laoi leó?"

"Maireaḋ aḋuḃarṫ," ar Murċaḋ, "aᵷur ṫuᵷaḋar ρuaṫ
a'r éaraḋ orm mar ċiḋeann ṫu mé[6]."

Leir rin ṫarrainᵷear an buaċaill ḃroirnín ḋe ċórḋaiḃ
beaᵷa ċruaiḋ-ċnáiḃe amaċ ó ḃeann a ḃruiṫ, aᵷur ḋo léiριᵷ[7]
ré ċuiᵷe iaḋ ar árḋ an ṫalaṁ aᵷur ḋo ċruinniᵷ ċuiᵷe, ρaoi
mar ḋo ḃí ann, ριaḋna méiṫe meiṫ-ṁuinċalaċa, aᵷur eilṫe
beaρaċa baρρaċluaραċa, ionnur nár ḟáᵷ ρé oireaḋ maiḋe
ρᵷeine ḋe'n ṫreilᵷ ᵷo léir nár líon ρé arṫeaċ ann a ċórḋa.
Do ḟnaḋmaiᵷ ρé ρe inᵷniḃ a ċor aᵷur a láiṁ[8] é. "Ṫar ρá
ḋeire an ualaiᵷ a ṁic an riᵷ," ar ρé, "aᵷur árḋaiᵷ é orm."

"Ní ḟaṁlóċainn[9] a leiṫéiḋ rin ḋ'ualaċ ρe h-aon óᵷ-laoċ
'ran ḋoṁan," ḋo ráiḋ Murċaḋ.

"Ρá mar ir ṫura an máiᵷirṫir aᵷur ᵷur mire an buaċaill

---

[1] A reads "na coillte creatalacha d'eire agus d'aon ualach. Do bhi sé", etc.
[2] B "an buadhchail". [3] "a nabair tu". MSS. [4] A "arradh".
[5] B "cómhall". [6] A reads "agus nior fhagbhadar aon duine
d'fhuaith na d'iongna orm acht mar chidh tusa mé". See above, p. 12, note.

the burden of his back and his two shoulders of timber. He used to be seething and boiling [food] for seven days and seven nights, and he used to be himself asleep another seven days and seven nights. Not so with me. I shall do nothing but lay down my three billets of yew, and all who shall come or who have come, who were born, or who shall be born, they could get warmth and heat and boiling of food through their means, and I myself shall have them at the end of a year neither the greater nor the smaller for it."

"You are the one best lad at all," said Murough, "if it is true all you say."

"It is true indeed," said the lad.

They settled in that manner.

"This is a great hunting you succeeded in making, O Prince," said the lad.

"Indeed, great it is," said Murough.

"Why did you not tell every one of your people to bring with them the load of their back and their two shoulders of the game, to tell and proclaim it that such a day's hunting had succeeded with them?"

"Why, I did tell them," said Murough, "and they gave me hatred and refusal [and left me] as you see me."

With that the lad draws a little bundle of small cords of hard hemp out from the corner of his mantle, and ranged them for himself in order, on the ground's height, and he collected to himself all that was there, fatted fat-necked deer, and spit-like, pointed-eared fawns, so that he did not leave so much as a whitling of the entire hunt that he did not fill into his cord. He knotted it with the nails of his feet and hands. "Come under the bottom of the load, Prince," said he, "and hoist it on me."

"I would not compare such a load as that with any young hero,"(¹) said Murough.

"Well, as you are the master and I the boy, it is right for myself to

---

⁷ B béipiჳ.   ⁸ "a chosa agus a lámha", MSS.   ⁹ B "shámlúghan".

(¹) *I.e.* I would not connect that load and any man in my own mind, that load is impossible for any man.

ir cóir bam péin é árbúʒaó." Do ċuʒ ré úrċoʒbáil¹ ꝼaoi an
ualaċ ionnur ʒur árbaiʒ ré ar ḃeirc a ḃroma aʒur a ḃá
ḟlinneán é. "Anoir car² rómam amaċ, a ṁic riʒ," ar ré,
"aʒur múin an c-eólar bam."

"Ni ḃeiḋ mé i m' ʒiolla aʒ ꝼear an ualaiʒ rin," ar Murċaḋ.
Cóʒann ré [.i. an ʒiolla] péin ar na bonnaiḃ biana beaʒ-
reaċa, bo na coircéimiḃ culcanca calcanca créan-ṁóra, ionnur
ʒo ʒcuirꝼeaḋ ré cnoc be léim be, aʒur ʒleann be ċrorlóiʒ, mar
rin bó ʒo raiḃ aʒ béanaṁ ʒo céim-bíreaċ ar ċeaċ Cinn Coraḋ.

Ꝼéaċain b'á bcuʒ an boirreóir ċairir, bo ċonnairc ré ċuiʒe
anuar bo ċaoḃ an crléiḃe aṁail rin é. Riċear arceaċ, aʒur
bo ċonnairc an cócaire é, aʒur abubairc, "bo ʒoin³ a'r bo
ʒuair orc," ar rí, "bo ḃubabar c'ꝼiacla, bo bánabar bo
ꝼúile, bo ċuaiḋ bo ʒlór ċum riʒꝼriʒeaċc[a]⁴ iḋ' ċeann, bo ċáiniʒ
brón báir aʒur buan-éaʒa orc, no créaḋ ruaiċeancar no
ionʒnaḋ bo ċonnairc cu?"

"Do ḃuḃraḋ c' ꝼiacla-ra aʒur bo ḃánꝼaḋ bo ꝼúile, bo
ċiucꝼaḋ brón báir aʒur buan-éaʒa orc aʒur bo raċꝼaḋ
bo ʒlór ċum riʒꝼriʒeaċca iḋ' ċeann bá ḃꝼeicꝼeá-ra an
c-ionʒancar bo ċonaꝼc-ra."

Ann roin bo ċuala an ꝼean riʒ .i. brian bóirṁe iaḋ, aʒur
b'ꝼiarꝼaiʒ ḋioḃ caḋ bo ċonncabar. Abubairc an boirreóir
ʒur ab é aon óʒlaoċ aṁáin mi-líoċaċ, maol-riabaċ, bí aʒ ceaċc
be ḃruim an crléiḃe, a raiḃ na reacc ʒcoillce Creacalaċa
no bá ꝼliaḃ béaʒ Ꝼéiḃlime no a ṁacraṁail eile rin b'ualaċ
ar a ṁuin aiʒe, aʒur má leanann ré bo'n críubal acá ꝼaoi
ir beiṁin ʒo rʒuabꝼaiḋ ré ceaċ Cinn Coraḋ ann a ċoraiḃ
ꝼaoi an ḃꝼairrʒe leir.

"Cárrċaiʒ, cárrċaiʒ!" ar an Ríʒ, "cuiriḋ rʒéala ċuiʒe
ʒan ár múcaḋ ná ár mbáċaḋ, aʒur má ré rioċʒaoiċe Cuaċa
Dé Danann péin acá ann, ʒiḃé niḃ acá uaiḋ ʒo ḃꝼáʒaḋ é."

Ar nbul amaċ bo'n ceaċcaire bo leaʒ an c-óʒlaċ an c-ualaċ
aʒur bo ċuir ré an calaṁ ʒo léir aʒur ceaċ Cinn Coraḋ
ar ronnaċriċ. Do ċáiniʒ ré arceaċ aʒur bo ꝼocruiʒ ré ríor
a ċrí oirneaċ iubair. Aʒur níor ꝼáʒ ré oireaḋ maibe rʒeine

<hr>

¹ B uraḋ cóʒbála.   ² B "tear".   ³ A has "do

hoist it." He gave a vigorous lift to the load, so that he hoisted it on the end of his back and his two shoulders. "Now come out before me, king's son," said he, "and show me the way."

"I won't be a servant to the man who carries that load," said Murough.

The lad raises himself on powerful quick-running footsoles, with vigorous, valorous, mighty-great steps, so that he would leave behind him a hill of one leap, and a valley of one hop, and thus he went making off straight for the House of Kincora.

Of a look that the porter cast round him, he beheld him in that guise coming down the side of the mountain towards him. In he runs, and the cook saw him and said—"Wounds and danger on you," says she, "your teeth have blackened, your eyes have whitened, your voice has turned to a ghastly sound in your head, the pains of death and everlasting dissolution have come upon you, or what token or wonder have you seen?"

"Your own teeth would blacken, your eyes would whiten, and your voice would turn to a ghastly sound in your head, if you were to see the wonder I have seen."

Then the old king, namely, Brian Boru, heard them, and he asked them what they had seen. The porter told him that it was a single, ill-visaged, bald-grey warrior, who was coming down the back of the mountain, who had the seven woods of Cratloe, or the twelve mountains of Felim, or some such other load upon his back, and if he continues the course he is going in, it's certain that he'll sweep the House of Kincora with his feet under the sea with him.

"Save, save [us]," says the king. "Send him word not to smother us or drown us, and even if it be a fairy sprite of the Tuatha De Danann that he is, whatsoever thing he wants [tell him] that he'll get it."

As the messenger went out, the youth [arrived, and] threw down his load, and set the entire ground and the House of Kincora in a mighty shaking. He came in then and laid down in order his three billets of yew, and he never left as much as a whitling of the game

dhona agus do dhuais ort", *passim.*   ⁴ B "siobhraidheacd."

c 2

ᴅe'n ᴄᴘeilᵹ naċ ᴘaiᴅ ᴘiaᵹᴘᴄálᴄa[1] ᴘuaᴘ aᴘ ᴅoᴘᴅaiᴅ, ᴘul ċáiniᵹ
Muᴘċaᴅ mac Ḃᴘiain ná aon ᴅuine ᴅ'á ᴘeiᴅ-ċeaᵹlaċ a-ᴅaile.

An niᴅ ᴅo ᴘinn ᴘé an lá ᴘan, ᴅo ᴘinn an niᴅ céaᴅna ᵹaċ
lá ᵹo ceann bliaᴅna no níoᴘ ᴘeaᴘᴘ. Ní ᴘaiᴅ aon lá naċ
ᴘiuᴅalᴘaᴅ ᴘé[2] ó Uᴘaᴅ, ᵹo h-Uᴘᴘaᴅ, ó Liᴘe ᵹo Loċlainn, ó
Loċlainn ᴅo'n Spáin, ó'n Spáin ᵹo h-Eaᴘᴅáin, ó Eaᴘᴅáin ᵹo
h-Éiᴘinn, ᵹo Ꞇioᴅᴘaiᴅ ᴅó ṁaoile ᴘinne, ᵹo Ꞡaᴘᴅa na h-Iᴘᴅiᴘᴄe
aᴘ an ᴅᴄaoiᴅ ᴘiaᴘ ᴘíoᴘ ᴅ' Aᴘainn maᴘ a ᴅᴄéiᴅeann an ᵹᴘian
ċum leaᴘᴄan, ó ᴅoċán na ᴅuaile ᵹo Ꞇeaċ an ᴄᴘean-ᴅaile. Ní
ᴅíoᴅ ᴘᵹeul nuaᴅ ná ionᵹnaᴅ aᴘ an Ḃᴘaᴅ ᴘin naċ mᴅíoᴅ aiᵹe
ᴘe h-innᴘinᴄ ᴅo Muᴘċaᴅ mac Ḃᴘiain ᴅóiᴘṁe ᵹaċ aon oiᴅċe
ann a leaᴅaiᴅ.

Ꝺo ᴅí aᵹ caiᴄeaṁ na h-aimᴘiᴘe maᴘ ᴘin ᵹo ceann bliaᴅna
aᵹuᴘ aᵹ ᴅéanaṁ ᵹnóᴄa buaċaille aᵹuᴘ cailín ᵹaċ aon nómenᴄ
aᴘ an ló ᴅ'á n-iaᴘᴘaiᴅe aiᴘ é, ᵹo ᴘonnṁaᴘ[3]. " bliaᴅain
aᵹuᴘ lá anᴅiú," aᴘ ᴘé, " a ṁic an ᴘiᵹ, ᴅo ᴘéiᴅᴄiᵹeaᴘ ᴘéin
leaᴄ aᴘ Ḃᴘeiċ mo ᴅéil ᴘéin, ᴅe ċuilleaṁ aᵹuᴘ ᴅe ċuaᴘaᴘᴅal
ᴅ'ᴘáᵹail uaiᴄ."

" Iᴘ é ᵹo ᴅeiṁin," aᴘ mac an ᴘiᵹ, " aᵹuᴘ beiᴘ ᴅo Ḃᴘeiċ oᴘm."

" beiᴘim-ᴘe ᴅe Ḃᴘeiċ oᴘᴄ, a ṁic an ᴘiᵹ," aᴘ ᴘé, " ᴘiuᵹ ᴅo
ċuᴘ aᴘ an ᴘaᵹᴘaiᵹ[4] ᴘeo ᵹan ᴘuiᵹioll ᵹan eaᴘᴅaiᴅ ᵹan iomaᴘca,
ionnuᴘ naċ Ḃᴘáᵹaᴅ loċᴄ uiᴘᴘi."

" Ꝺo ᵹoin aᵹuᴘ ᴅo ᵹuaiᴘ[5] oᴘᴄ," ᴅo ᴘáiᴅ Muᴘċaᴅ, " cᴘéaᴅ
ᴘáċ naċ milliún óiᴘ no aiᴘᵹiᴅ no ᴘuaᴘᵹ ailᴄ ᴘiᵹ no Ríᴅiᴘe[6]
ᴅ'iaᴘᴘaiᴘ oᴘm, ᴘul aᴘ iaᴘᴘaiᴘ an ᴘᴘᴘioᴘánᴄaċᴄ ᴘin?"

" Ní beaᵹ liom ᴘúᴅ ᴘéin oᴘᴄ," ᴅo ᴘáiᴅ an buaċaill.

Ꞡluaiᴘeaᴘ Muᴘċaᴅ aᵹuᴘ céiᴅ ᵹo ᴅᴄi an ᵹaᴅa ᴅo ᴅí aᵹ
obaiᴘ ᴅó, aᵹuᴘ aᴅuᴅaiᴘᴄ ᴘiᴘ ᴘiuᵹ ᴅo ċuᴘ aᴘ an ᴘaᵹᴘaiᵹ[7] ᴘin
ᵹan ᴘuiᵹioll ᵹan eaᴘᴅaiᴅ ᵹan iomaᴘca. Ꝺo ᴘinn an ᵹaᴅa
an ᴘiuᵹ, aᵹuᴘ níoᴘ ᴘoiᴘ ᴘí ᴅó. Ꝺéanaᴘ[8] ᴘiuᵹ aᵹuᴘ ᴘiuᵹ eile
ᴅí, aᵹuᴘ ᴅá mbeiᴅeaᴅ a ᴅáᴘ aiᴘ, ni ᴅéanᴘaᴅ aon ᴘiuᵹ naċ
Ḃᴘáᵹaᴅ ᵹiolla an ᴘiuᵹ loċᴄ uiᴘᴘi[9]. Ꞡluaiᴘiᴅ ᴘómᴘa ann

---

[1] B "riastaidhthe". [2] B reads "nach siubhalfadh sé ó tiobraid bo
mhaoile finne, go gáruidhe na hisbirte air an dtaoibh shiar shíos do arran mar a
dtéighean an ghrian cum leapthan go bhuathán na buaille go teach an tsean-
bhaile." A reads *mhíle* for *maoile*. [3] A "dhá ngearthaoi ar farais sin (?)".
[4] B ᴘáṁaċ. [5] A "Donn agus duais ort". [6] A "ᴘuᴅaiᴘe", which is the

that was not served up on tables before Murough son of Brian or anyone of his household came home.

The thing which he did that day he did the same thing to the end of a year [as well], or better.   There was never a day that he would not travel from Uradh to Urradh, from Liffey to Lochlann, from Lochlann to Spain, from Spain to Easpain, from Easpain to Erin, to the well of the bald white cow, to the garden of Hesperides on the west side down from Aran, where goes the sun to its couch, from the hut of the Booley to the house of the old town.   There used never be any new story or wonder throughout all that [ground] that he would not have to tell to Murough son of Brian Boru every single night on his couch.

He was spending the time in this way to the end of a year, and doing willingly the business both of a boy and a serving girl, every single moment of the day that it would be required of him.   "A year and a day to-day," says he, "king's son, since I settled with you to get the award of my own mouth of wages and of stipend from you."

"It is, indeed," said the king's son, "and give your award against me."

"I award as my award against thee, O king's son," says he, "to put a ferule on this staff without either lack, or want, or excess, so that I shall find no fault with it."

"Your wound and your peril on you!" said Murough, "why was it not a million of gold or silver, or the release of a king or a knight that you asked of me, before you asked such a ridiculous trifle as that ? "

" Even that I do not think a small claim against you," said the lad.

Murough departs, and he goes to the smith who was working for him, and he told him to put a ferule on that staff, and not to make it too big or too small or too great(¹).   The smith made him the ferule, and it did not fit it.   The smith makes another ferule, and another, but if he were to be put to death for it he could not make a single ferule that the Lad of the Ferule would not find fault with.   They

usual pronunciation.   B reads " Righ a ngeibhionn ".   7 ꝛaṁaċ, *passim.*
8 A "deinios".   B "Rinneas".   9 Both texts make ꝼiúȝ masculine and feminine indifferently, writing an ꝼiuȝ and an ꝼiuȝ, and in the gen. "an fhiugh" and "na fiugh ".

(¹) Literally, "without leavings, without want, without too much."

ᵱoin, aᵹuᵱ níoᵱ ḟáᵹḃaḋaᵱ aon ᵹaḃa aᵱ ḟeaḋ na cᵱíce naċ nḋcaᵱnaıḋ ḟıúᵹ óóıḃ, aᵹuᵱ níoᵱ ḟoıᵱ[1] aon ċeann ḋíoḃ ḋo'n cᵱaᵹᵱaıᵹ. Maᵱ ᵱın óóıḃ ᵹo ḋcánᵹaḋaᵱ aᵱ an ḃᵱaıċċe oᵱ cıonn loċ Ḋcaᵱᵹcaᵱ[2] maᵱ aᵱ ᵱéıḋcıᵹeaḋaᵱ le ċéıle an ċeuḋ lá ᵱıaṁ. "A ṁıc an ᵱıᵹ," aᵱ ᵱé, "nı ḃᵱuıl maıċ ḋuıc ḃeıċ aᵹ ḟáᵹaıl ḋuaḋ na ḟıúᵹ ᵱo, nı ḃuᵱ ḟaıḋe, óıᵱ nı ḃᵱuıl aon ᵹaḃa ḟaoı an nᵹᵱéın ḋo ḃéanᵱaḋ ḟıúᵹ ḋ' ḟoıᵱᵱeaḋ ḋo'n cᵱaᵹᵱaıᵹ[3] ᵱeo, aċc an ḟıúᵹ ḋo ḃí uıᵱᵱı ḟéın ᵱoıṁe ᵱeo."

"Cá ḃᵱuıl ᵱí ᵱın anoıᵱ?" ḋo ᵱáıḋ Muᵱċaḋ.

"Muna mḃeıḋeaḋ [a] ḟaıḋ lıom-ᵱa, a ṁıc an ᵱıᵹ," aᵱ ᵱé, "ḋo ċonᵹḃáıl aᵱ ḃonn ḋo óá ċoıᵱ an ḟaıḋ ḋo ḃeıḋınn ḋ'á ınnᵱınc, ḋ'ınneóᵱaınn ḟéın ᵱın ḋuıc."

"O! nı ḟaḋa lıom-ᵱa é," aᵱ Muᵱċaḋ.

Ḋo ḟuıᵹeaḋaᵱ aᵱaon ᵱíoᵱ aᵱ óá ċolmán[4] ᵹlaᵱa. "Ann ᵱo, a ṁıc an ᵱıᵹ, maᵱ a ḃᵱuılmıḋ aᵱaon ann áᵱ ᵱuıḋe, ḋo ḃí cúıᵱc ᵱó ḃᵱeáᵹ ı n-alloḋ. Ċáᵱla ᵹo ᵱaıḃ an Rıᵹ ᵱá ċuınn[5], Aıᵱḋ-ᵱıᵹ Éıᵱeann, aᵹuᵱ ᵱıᵹ Ḟéınne, a n-aoıᵱ ᵹᵱáḋ, aᵹuᵱ a luċc leanaṁna, aᵹ caıċeaṁ ḟleaḋ aᵹuᵱ ḟeuᵱca ı ḃᵱoınn-ceaċ na cúıᵱce an lá ᵱın, ıonnuᵱ ᵹo mḃuḋ[6] lıa ḟleaḋ aᵹuᵱ ḟeuᵱca ḋo ḃí aᵹaınn 'ná maᵱ ḋo ḃí buıḋean ċum a ċaıċce. Ann ᵱúḋ a ṁıc an ᵱıᵹ, ıᵱ ᵱeaḋ ḋ'éıᵱıᵹ bollᵱaıᵱe an ceaᵹlaıᵹ 'na ḟeaᵱaṁ aᵹuᵱ ḋo ċᵱoıċ ᵱé ᵱlaḃᵱa éıᵱceaċca ḋo ḃí aıᵹe. Ann ᵱoın ḋo ḟıaᵱᵱuıᵹeaḋ ḋe ᵹaċ aon neaċ ḋíoḃ an ḃᵱacaḋaᵱ ᵱıaṁ bóᵱḋ bıḋ ḋo ḃ'ḟeaᵱᵱ no buḋ ḟaıḋḃᵱe aᵹuᵱ buḋ ᵱaıᵹᵱeaṁla[7] 'ná an bóᵱḋ bıḋ ᵱın ḋo ḃí láıċᵱeaċ. Aḋuḃᵱaḋaᵱ ᵱın uıle naċ ḃᵱacaḋaᵱ aᵹuᵱ naċ ᵱaıḃ a leıċéıḋ ann ᵱıaṁ. Nı ḋuḃaᵱc ḟéın aon ḟocal. Ḋo cuᵹaḋ ᵱá nḋeaᵱa mé, maᵱ náᵱ ṁolaᵱ aᵹuᵱ náᵱ ċáıneaᵱ an bıaḋ. Aḋuḃᵱaḋaᵱ má 'ᵱ leaċ-ıomaᵱca[8] bıḋ no bıᵹe ḋo ᵱınneaḋ oᵱm ᵹo ᵹcaıċᵱıḋe a ċoıṁlíonaḋ lıom. Aḋuḃaᵱc naċ molᵱaınn aᵹuᵱ naċ cáınᵱınn an bıaḋ, aᵹuᵱ naċ molᵱaınn aon bıaḋ aċc an bıaḋ ḋo ċıucᵱaḋ aᵱ an ᵹcoıᵱe ḋo ḃí ı ᵹcᵱíoċaıḃ Loċlaınn, naċ mbıḋeaḋ uaıċe aċc cᵱı cloċa éıḃıᵱ aᵹuᵱ cᵱı h-oıᵱneaċ[9] ıúḃaıᵱ ḋo ċuᵱ ᵱá n-a ċóın, aᵹuᵱ a

---

[1] A has *níor úir* and *níor ir*. B "níor oir". I have restored the usual ḟ.
[2] B "Deirgdheirc". [3] B ᵱáṁaċ. A sometimes aspirates the final ᵹ in ᵱaᵹᵱaıᵹ, and sometimes not. [4] A ċalán. [5] A ċuınᵹ. [6] A "gur budh". B "gur ab". [7] B "réighseamhla". [8] B "leith iomairce". [9] B "thoirneach".

depart on their way after that, and they never left a single smith throughout the country who did not make a ferule for them, and not a single one of them fitted the staff. Thus they were until they came upon the lawn above Loch Derg, where they settled with one another the first day ever. "King's son," said he [then], "it's no good for you to be having trouble about this ferule any longer, for there's not one smith under the sun who could make a ferule that would fit this staff, except the ferule that was on itself before."

"Where is that one now?" said Murough.

"If I did not think it too long, King's son," said he, "to keep you on the soles of your two feet while I would be telling you, myself would tell you that."

"Oh! I don't think it long," said Murough.

They sat down together on two green tussocks. "In this place, O King's son, where we are seated together, there was a very fine court in ancient times. It chanced that the King of Under-Wave ([1]), the High-king of Ireland, and the King of the Fenians, their friends and their followers, were partaking of a banquet and feast in the refectory of the court that day, so that more plentiful was the banquet and feast that we had than the band we had to eat it. Then it was, O King's son, that the herald of the mansion rose, and stood up, and shook the chain-of-hearing that he had. Then it was asked of every one of them did they ever see a table of food that was better or richer or more abundant than that table of food there present. All of those said that they had not seen [such a thing] and that such a thing never existed. Myself said no word. It was observed of me that I neither praised nor dispraised the food. They said if it was any deficiency of food or drink that was given me, that it must be made good to me. I said that I would neither praise nor dispraise the food, and that I would praise no food except the food that would come out of the caldron that was in the lands of Lochlann, that wanted only to have three fairy stones and three billets of yew put under its bottom, and all that shall come or that have come, that they would get any food they might desire ready

---

([1]) The Country-under-wave is the Irish name for Holland and the Low Countries, and the "King [of] under-wave" is a common character in Irish folk-tales; but the name has absolutely no geographical significance in the folklore, and has nothing to say to the Low Countries.

24 ᵹιoꝈꝈa αɴ ꝼιυᵹα.

ᴅᴄιυᴄꝼaᴅ aᵹuꞃ a ᴅᴄáιɴιᵹ ᵹo ᴜꝼáᵹᴅaoιꞃ aoɴ ᴜιaᴅ ᴅ'ιaꞃꞃꞃaιᴅíꞃ, oꝈꝇaṁ, ᴜꞃuιᴄᴄe¹, aꞃ aɴíoꞃ, aᵹuꞃ ᵹaɴ aoɴ ᵹꞃeιꝿ ᴅo ᴄuꞃ aɴɴ ᴅé ᵹo ᴜꞃáᴄ. Cᴅouᴜꞃaᴅaꞃ ɴaᴄ ꞃaιᴜ aṁaιꝇ ꞃιɴ aɴɴ ꞃιaṁ, aᵹuꞃ aᴅuᴜaιꞃᴄ ꞃιᵹ Ꝼéιɴɴe ɴaᴄ [ɴ-]ιɴɴꞃeóꞃaιɴɴ² ꝼéιɴ ᴜꞃéaᵹ. Cɴɴ ꞃoιɴ aᴅuᴜꞃaᴅaꞃ ɴa ꝇaoᴄꞃa ɴáꞃ ᴜꝼuꝇáιꞃ ᴅuꝇ aꞃ ᴄóιꞃιᵹeaᴄᴄ aɴ ᴄoιꞃe. Cɴɴ ꞃoιɴ ᴅo h-oꝈꝇaṁɴuιᵹeaᴅ³ ꝇιoꝿ ꝼéιɴ ꞃeaᴄᴄ ᵹᴄéaᴅ ꝇaoᴄ ꝇáɴ-ᴄaꝇꝿa ᴅe ᴄaoιꞃeaᴄaιᴜ ɴa Ꝼéιɴɴe⁴ ι ɴ-aιꞃꝿ 'ꞃ ɴ-euᴅaᴄ. Ꝺo ᵹꝇeuꞃaᴅ ᴅúιɴɴ ᴄuꞃaᴄáɴ ᴄeaɴɴ-áꞃᴅ ᴄꝇiaᴜ-ꝼaιꞃꞃꞃιɴᵹ ꝇoɴᵹꝇuᴄᴄꝿaꞃ, ꝇáιɴ-íꞃιoꝈꝈ⁵. Ꝺ'éιꞃιᵹ ᵹaoᴄ ιᴅιꞃ ᴅá ꞃᵹóᴅ oꞃꞃaιɴɴ, aᵹuꞃ ᴅ'éιꞃᵹeaꝿaꞃ aꞃ ᴄaιꞃᴅιoꝈꝈ ᵹaoιᴄe, ιoɴɴuꞃ ɴáꞃ ꝼáᵹaᴅ ꞃeóꝇ⁶ ᵹaɴ ꞃíɴeaᴅ, ɴá ꞃᴄιúꞃ ᵹaɴ ꝇeóɴaᴅ,⁷ ιoɴɴuꞃ ᵹo ꝿᴜíᴅeaᴅ ᴄúᴜaꞃ ɴa ꝼaιꞃꞃᵹe ᴅ'á ᴄuꞃ ι ɴ-íoᴄᴄaꞃ aᵹuꞃ aɴ ᵹaιɴeaṁ ᴅ'á ᴄuꞃ ι ɴ-uaᴄᴄaꞃ. Ꝇaꞃ ꞃιɴ ᴅúιɴɴ ᵹo ꞃoᴄᴄaιɴ ᴄuaιɴ ᴄꞃíᴄe Ꝉoᴄꝇaιɴɴ. Cɴɴ ꞃoιɴ ᴄuᵹaꝿaꞃ ᴄeaɴᵹaꝇ ꝇaé aᵹuꞃ ꝇáιɴ-ᴜꝇιaᴅɴa aꞃ áꞃ ᵹᴄuꞃaᴄáɴ, ιoɴɴuꞃ ɴaᴄ [ꝿ]ᴜeιᴅꝿíꞃ uaιᴅ aᴄᴄ uaιꞃ a ᴄꝇuιᵹ. Ꞃíoꞃ ᴜꝼaᴅa aɴɴ ꞃoιɴ ᵹo ᴜꝼaᴄaꝿaꞃ uaιɴɴ ᴄɴoᴄ áꞃᴅ aɴɴ a ꞃaιᴜ ᴄeιᴄꞃe ᴜóιᴄꞃe ᴅ'á ιoɴɴꞃaιᴅe⁸, ó ᴄeιᴄꞃe h-áꞃᴅaιᴜ aɴ ᴅoṁaιɴ ṁóιꞃ, aᵹuꞃ ɴι ꞃaιᴜ aoɴ ᴜóᴄaꞃ ᴅιoᴜ ɴaᴄ ꞃaιᴜ ᴄéaᴅ ꝇaoᴄ ꝇáɴ-ᴄaꝇꝿa aᵹ ꝼaιꞃe aᵹuꞃ aᵹ ᴄoṁéaᴅ aɴ ᴄɴuιᴄ. Ꝺo ᴄoɴɴaꞃᴄꝿaꞃ aɴ ᴄoιꞃe ι ꝿuꝇꝇaᴄ aɴ ᴄɴuιᴄ, aᵹuꞃ ꞃeaᴄᴄ ᵹᴄéaᴅ ꝇaoᴄ ꝇáɴ-ᴄaꝇꝿa aᵹ ᵹaᴄ aoɴ ᴄúιɴɴe⁹ ᴅé, ι ɴ-éaᵹꝿaιꞃ a ꞃaιᴜ ᴅe ꝇuᴄᴄ ꝼꞃeaꞃᴅaιꝇ aᵹuꞃ ꝼꞃιᴄaꝇaṁ aɴ ᴜιᴅ ᴜeιꞃιᵹᴄe aꞃ ꝇuᴄᴄ ɴa ᴄꞃíᴄe uιꝇe. Cᵹuꞃ aꞃ a ᴜꝼaιᴄꞃιɴ 'ꞃaɴ oꞃᴅuᵹaᴅ ꞃιɴ ᴅo ꝿ' ꝇaoᴄꞃaιᴜ ꝼéιɴ ᴅo ᵹꝇaᴄ ꝿeaᴄaᴄᴄ aᵹuꞃ ꝿι-ṁeιꞃꞃeaᴄ ιaᴅ, ιoɴɴuꞃ ᵹuꞃ ᴄuιᴄeaᴅaꞃ a ɴ-aꞃꝿa aꞃ a ꝇáṁaιᴜ, aᵹuꞃ ɴáꞃ ꝼaɴ ᴜꞃιᵹ ɴá ᴄaꞃa ιoɴɴᴄa, aᵹuꞃ aᴅuᴜꞃaᴅaꞃ ᴅá ᴜꝼuιᵹᴅíꞃ ꝼꝇaιᴄeaꞃ ᴄꞃíoᴄ Ꝉoᴄꝇaιɴɴ ɴaᴄ ꞃaᴄꝼꞃaᴅ ɴeaᴄ ᴅíoᴜ ᴄaιꞃιꞃ ꞃιɴ. Ꞃι ꞃaιᴜ aᵹaꝿ ꝼéιɴ, a ṁιᴄ aɴ ꞃιᵹ, aᴄᴄ ᴜeaꞃꞃaᴅ óιɴꞃιᵹ ɴo aꝿaᴅáιɴ¹⁰ ᴅo ᴄaᴅaιꞃᴄ oꞃꝿ ꝼéιɴ aᵹuꞃ ᴅuꝇ ꞃuaꞃ ꝿaꞃ a ꞃaιᴜ aɴ ᴄoιꞃe, aᵹuꞃ ᴜeιᴄ aᵹ ιᴄe aɴ ᴜιᴅ ꝿaꞃ ᴄáᴄ, ᵹo ᴜꝼuaιꞃeaꞃ aꝿaꞃ aꞃ ɴa ᴄꞃι ᴄꝇoᴄaιᴜ éιᴜιꞃ ᴅo ᴜí ꝼa 'ɴ ᵹᴄoιꞃe ᴅo ᴄaιᴄᴄaṁ aɴɴ aꞃᴄeaᴄ, aᵹuꞃ ɴa ᴄꞃι h-óιꞃɴeaᴄ ιuᴜaιꞃ ꝿaꞃ aɴ ᵹᴄéaᴅɴa: ꞃιꞃ ꞃιɴ ᴄuᵹ [me] úꞃ-ᴄóᵹᴜáιꝇ¹¹ ꝼaoι aɴ ᵹᴄoιꞃe,

---

¹ B "brighte". A "beirghthe". ² "na neósíainn" in both MSS.
³ B "hollmhuigheadh". ⁴ A adds "fó na lán sróil, fo na gceasaibh [?] síoda agus iarshnáith óir". ⁵ B omits this word which seems to mean that they were low in the water. ⁶ A reads "fala". ⁷ ¹ A adds here "na bearna gan briseadh na tairne gan tuathadh gan consgludh (?) go d . . . lamar i n-iomarbháidh dian-diograiseach na fairrge, no srotha saidhbhre seamsanta na gciosaghorm

boiled, up, out of it, and without their ever putting a single bit of it in the caldron. They said that there never existed such a thing, but the Fenian King said that myself would not tell a falsehood. Then the heroes said that they must go in pursuit of the caldron. Then there was prepared, along with myself, seven hundred full-valiant heroes of the chiefs of the Fenians in arms and armour. A high-headed, broad-breasted, ship-laden, full-low bark was prepared for us. There arose a wind upon us between two scuds, and we rose travelling the wind so that there was left not a sail unstretched nor a steer un-strained, so that the foam of the sea used to be sent down below, and the sand sent up on high. Thus we were until we reached the harbour of the country of Lochlann. Then we gave our bark the fastening of a day and a full year, even though(¹) we should not be absent from her but an hour of the clock. It was not long then till we saw at a distance from us a high hill, in which there were four roads, which led to it from the four airts of the great world, and there was never a road of them but had a hundred full-valiant warriors watching and guarding the hill. We beheld the caldron on the top of the hill and seven hundred full-valiant heroes at each corner of it, not to speak of those who attended and dealt out the boiled meat to the people of the entire country. And on my own warriors seeing them in this array, cowardice and dispiritedness seized them, so that their arms fell from their hands, and there remained neither strength nor activity in them, and they said that if they were to get the sovereignty of the lands of Lochlann that not a man of them would go past that. I had nothing to do myself, King's son, but to take on myself the shaving of a fool or an idiot,(²) and to go up to where the caldron was, and to be eating the food like everyone else, until I got a chance to throw the three fairy stones that were under the caldron into it, and the three billets

uaithne agus dos na bróinte borba braonacha, na genoic geinnfhliucha cogadhsacha di-chéillidhe na fairrge", which, like most of A's interpellations, is corrupt.
⁸ A "ag déanamh mar a bheidheadh ceithre áird ar an domhan mór".
⁹ A reads "cuinge". B omits.   ¹⁰ B "oinmide no aimid".
¹¹ A reads "uradh thógbhla", as before.

(¹) The text, which is evidently corrupt, reads "so that we should not be", &c.
(²) *I.e.*, to get my head shorn in the way in which the mad and demented were shorn. This seems to have been an old custom, perhaps to set people on their guard against them. I have met the phrase elsewhere.

ɪonnuр ᵹuр ᵽuaᵭaɪᵹ mé lɪom é ɪ nᵹlɪnnᴄɪᵬ an aᴄᴅɪр a ᵬᵽaᵭ aр рaᵭaрᴄ an oɪрeaᴄᴄaɪр. ᑫnn рoɪn ᵹluaɪрɪᵭ luᴄᴄ na cрɪᴄe aᵹuр an ᵬuɪᵭean ᴄalma ᵭo ᵬɪ aᵹ coɰᵭeaᵭ an ᴄoɪрe aр a loрᵹ, aр ᵽuᵭ ᵹleannᴄa aᵹuр cnocⁱ, no ᵹuр ᴄáрlaᵭaр рe m' ᵽeaᴄᴄ ᵹᴄéaᵭ laoᴄ ᵭe ᴄaoɪрeaᴄaɪᵬ na ᵽéɪnne, ᵹo nᵭéanaɪᵭ рɪaᵭ oррa², ᵹo рaᵬaᵭaр ᵭá n-ᵭɪᴄ-ᴄeaɰaᵭ aᵹuр ᵭ'á n-éɪрleaᴄ; ᵹo nᵭuᵬaрᴄ ᵽéɪn ᵹuр ᴄрuaᵹ lɪom ᴄaoɪрeaᴄa na ᵽéɪnne ᵭo ᵬeɪᴄ ᵭ'á ᵭᴄрeaрᵹaɪрᴄ maр ᵹeall aр an рррealaɪрe coɪрe рɪn, ᴄoɪᵭᴄe, aᵹuр caɪᴄɪm uaɪm ᵽaᵭ m' uрᴄaɪр é, aᵹuр ɪonnрaɪᵹɪm oрра, ɪonnuр ᵹo mᵬuᵭ ᴄoɰ-ᴄloр ᵭuɪᴄ anᵭɪú aᵹuр an lá рɪn, an léɪрᵹрɪoр ᵭo ᴄuᵹamaр aр ᵽluaɪᵹᴄɪᵬ Loᴄlaɪnn. ᗫá éɪр рɪn ᴄuᵹamaр lɪnn an coɪрe, aᵹuр ᵭo ᵽocрuɪᵹeamaр, ann áр ᵹcuрaᴄán ᴄuᵹaɪnn é, ɪonnuр náр рᴄaᵭaᵭ lɪnn ᵹo рoᴄᴄaɪn Éɪрe[ann] ᵭúɪnn aᵹuр ᵹo ᵭᴄuᵹamaр lɪnn an coɪрe ᵹuр an рéɪᵭᴄeaᵹlaᴄ³ ᵭo ᵬɪ ann рo. ᵹɪᵭeaᵭ nɪoр ᵬᵽéɪᵭɪр a ᴄuр ɪ nᵭoрuр na cúɪрᴄe aрᴄeaᴄ, aᵹuр ɪр aɰlaɪᵭ ᵭo ᵬ'éɪᵹɪn a ᵽocрuᵹaᵭ рe h-aɪр bɪle⁴ ᵭo ᵬɪ ɪ nᵹaр ᵭo'n loᴄ. ᗫo cuɪрeaᵭ na ᴄрɪ cloᴄa éɪᵬɪр ᵽaoɪ na ᴄoрaɪᵬ aᵹuр na ᴄрɪ h-oɪрneaᴄ ɪuᵬaɪр ᵽaoɪ n-a ᴄóɪn, ɪonnuр ᵹo ᵬᵽрɪᴄálᵽaᵭ bɪaᵭ bрuɪᴄᴄe, ollaɰ, aр ᵽeaрaɪᵬ aᵹuр ɰnáɪᵬ Éɪрeann, aᵹuр ᵹan aon ᵹрeɪmⁱ ᵭo ᴄuр ann ᵭé ᵹo bрáᴄ—ᵹuр ᵽá h-éɪᵹean ᵭóɪᵬ aᵭᵬáɪlⁱ ᵹuр ᴄanaр ᵽéɪn ᵽɪрɪnne leó. Nɪoр ᵬрaᵭa ᵭ' aɪmрɪр ann рoɪn, ᵹo рaᵬaᵭaр ᵽɪр Éɪрeann cрom ɪ ᵬᵽeóɪl, ᵹan lúᴄ ná ᵹaɪрᵹe, рe neaрᴄ рocaрaᴄᴄ, ɪaр ᵬᵽáᵹaɪl a mbeaᴄa ᴄoɰ рaoр рɪn, ollaɰ ɪ ᵹcóɰnuɪᵭe, aр an ᵹcoɪрe; ᵹo lá ᵭ'áр éɪрɪᵹ uɪllᵽɪaрᴄⁱ aр an loᴄ, ɪaр ᵬᵽáᵹaɪl ᵬolaɪᵭ an ᵬɪᵭ ᵬeɪрɪᵹᴄe, ᵹo nᵭeaрррna⁸ рɪ ᵹo céɪɪ-ᵭɪрeaᴄ aр an ᵹcoɪрe, aᵹuр ᵭo ᴄoрnaɪᵹ aр an bɪaᵭ ᵭo ᵬɪ ɪnnᴄɪ ᵭo alрaᵭ. ᗫo ᵬɪ рɪ ᴄoɰ uaᴄᵬáрaᴄ рɪn ᵭe ᵽéɪрᴄ ᵹuр ᵹlac ᵹráɪn aᵹuр eaᵹla ᵽɪр Éɪрeann рoɪmрɪ, ᵹuр ᴄeɪᴄeaᵭaр uaɪᴄe, aᵹuр ᵭo ᵬɪ рɪ aᵹ ɪᴄe an bɪᵭ aр an ᵹcoɪрe ᵹo nᵭuᵬaрᴄ ᵽéɪn ᵹuр boᴄᴄ an рᵹéal lɪom ᴄaр éɪр a ᵬᵽuaɪрeamaр ᵭe ᵭuaᵭ an ᴄoɪрe, a ᵽoᴄaр ᵭo ᵬeɪᴄ aᵹ an uɪllᵽéɪрᴄ рɪn. ᗫo рɪnneaр uɪррɪ, aᵹaр ᵹan ᵭ'aрm aᵹam ᵽéɪn aᴄᴄ an рáᵹрaᴄⁱ рo, aᵹuр le рóɪрneaрᴄ na [m]buɪllɪᵭeaᵭ, ᵹuр рᵹeɪnn an ᵽɪuᵹ ᵭe'n ᴄрaᵹᵽaᴄ

---

of yew also. With that I gave a vigorous lift to the caldron, so that I rushed it away with me in the glens of the air, far away out of the sight of the assembly. Then the people of the country and the valorous band that was guarding the caldron, proceed on the track of it, through glens and hills, until they met my seven hundred warriors of the chiefs of the Fenians, and they make at them, so that they were beheading them and slaying them, till I said myself that I thought it a pity the chiefs of the Fenians ever to be a-slaughtering on account of that wretch of a caldron, and I throw it from me the length of my shot (¹), and I attack them so that you could hear as well to-day as that day(²) the destruction we inflicted on the hosts of Lochlann. After that we took with us the caldron, and we settled it with us in our bark, so that no halt was made by us until our reaching Erin, and until we took with us the caldron to the household that was here. However, it was not possible to bring it in through the door of the court, and consequently we had to fix it beside a big-tree near the lake. The three fairy stones were put under its feet and the three billets of yew under its bottom, so that it would supply meat boiled and ready to all the men and women of Ireland, without ever putting one morsel of it into it—so that they were obliged to acknowledge that myself spoke the truth to them. It was no long time after that till the men of Erin grew heavy in flesh, without activity or valour, by reason of easy-times, on getting their food so cheaply, always ready, out of the caldron ; until a day that there arose a serpent out of the lake, finding the scent of the cooked meat, so that she made direct for the caldron ; and she began to swallow-down the food that was in it. She was such a dreadful [monster] of a serpent that horror and fear seized on the men of Erin before her, so that they fled from her, and she was eating the food out of the caldron until myself said that I thought it a poor story after all the hardship we had with the caldron, that this serpent should reap the advantage. I made at her, and I had no weapon myself but this staff, and with the vehemence of the blows, if the ferule didn't fly away from me, off the staff and

---

⁷ A " ollapiast ".   ⁸ B " gur aimsigh sí ".   ⁹ B " an tsámhach."

(¹) *I.e.* " as far as I could throw it."   (²) This apparently means that the story of the defeat of the men of Lochlann was as vividly remembered as ever.

uaım aʁteaċ ʁan ᵹcoıʁe¹. Rıʁ ʁın ċuᵹaʁ úʁ-ċóᵹḃáıl² ḟúm
ḟéın ᵹo nḃeaċa[ʁ] ı mḃaʁʁa an ḃıle úḃ ċall, ʁuaʁ, aʁ ceıċeaḃ
uaıċı. Ann ʁoın, aʁ ḃʁáᵹaıl ʁuaıṁnıʁ ḃo'n ḟéıʁc ó na
buıllıöıḃ, aᵹuʁ ʁe ʁaınc ċum an ḃıö, ḃo ċaʁ ʁí a h-úıʁ-ᵹéaᵹ³
cımċıoll an ċoıʁe ᵹuʁ ʁᵹuaḃaö léı ʁíoʁ ḟá'n loċ é, ıonnuʁ
ᵹuʁ ımċıᵹ uaınn ᵹan copaö ᵹan cuapaʁᵹḃáıl, aᵹuʁ acá an
uıllṗıaʁc, an coıʁe aᵹuʁ an ḟıuᵹ ḟá'n loċ ʁíoʁ ḟóʁ."

Ann ʁoın cıᵹeaʁ Muʁċaö mac Ḃʁıaın a-ḃaıle, aᵹuʁ éıʁᵹeaʁ
ᵹo moċ ḃe ló aᵹuʁ ḃe lán-cʁoıllʁe aʁ n-a ṁáʁaċ, aᵹuʁ ḃo
ʁocʁaıᵹ aıʁ a ċulaıö aıʁm aᵹuʁ éaḃaıᵹ ᵹo h-ıomlán, aᵹuʁ ḃo
ċuıʁ ʁé aıʁ a ċcannʁaʁc ᵹlaıne⁴, aᵹuʁ ḃo ʁınn aʁ an loċ, é
ḟéın aᵹuʁ a ʁ' lean é, ḃ'á aoıʁ ᵹʁáö aᵹuʁ ḃ'á luċc leanaṁna.
Ann ʁoın ḃo ċuᵹ ʁuċaᵹ⁵ ḃó ḟéın ᵹo nḃeaċa ḃe léım ı ᵹceaʁc-
láʁ an loċa, aᵹuʁ níoʁ ḃʁaḃa ᵹo ḃʁacaıö an uıllṗıaʁc, aᵹuʁ ı
'na lúıb, ʁıllce⁶ cımċıoll an ċoıʁe, ᵹuʁ⁷ leıᵹ é ḟéın aʁ a öʁuım
ʁan cʁnáṁ ᵹuʁ ċaıċ uʁċaʁ ḃ'á ḟıeıᵹ léı, ᵹuʁ aımʁıᵹ ann a
láʁ í, ᵹo nḃeaʁʁnaıö öá óʁöán⁸ öí. Leıʁ ʁın ḃo öʁuıö léı ᵹo
cʁóöa ᵹuʁ ḃaın an ceann ḃe'n uıllṗéıʁc.

Ḋ'éıʁıᵹ ʁe n-a lınn ʁın báʁʁ ḃeaʁᵹ aʁ an loċ. Ann ʁoın
ḃo ċánᵹaċaʁ aʁ ᵹaċ caoıḃ ḃe'n loċ, aᵹuʁ aḃuḃaıʁc ᵹaċ n-aon
ᵹuʁ aḃ é Muʁċaö ḃo ḃí maʁḃ.

"Iʁ coʁṁúıl ʁe ᵹlóʁ óınḃıöe no amaöáın ḃuʁ nᵹlóʁ," ḃo
ʁáıö ᵹıolla an ḟıuᵹ, "óıʁ ıʁ ḃeıṁın [ḃá mḃeıöeaö] a ḃʁuıl
ann ʁo ḃe ḃaoınıḃ, aᵹuʁ Muʁċaö, aᵹuʁ a ʁeaċc n-oıʁeaö maʁḃ
naċ öcaḃaʁʁaıöíʁ uıle ʁnóö ċoṁ ḃeaʁᵹ aʁ an loċ, aᵹuʁ nı h-é
aċc an uıllṗıaʁc acá maʁḃ." Re n-a lınn ʁın ḃo ċonncaḃaʁ
ċuca ᵹo ʁéımeaṁaıl Muʁċaö aᵹuʁ an ḟıúᵹ, aᵹuʁ ceann na
h-uıllṗéıʁce ann a öá láṁ aıᵹe, aᵹuʁ ḃo ʁocʁaıᵹ ʁé an ḟıúᵹ
ʁe n-a öá láṁ aʁ an ʁaᵹʁaıᵹ⁹ ᵹan ʁuıᵹıoll ᵹan eaʁḃaıö ᵹan
ıomaʁca; aᵹuʁ ċuᵹ ḃo Ᵹıolla an ḟıúᵹ é.

"Ꞇá mo ċuaʁaʁöal aᵹam anoıʁ," aʁ ʁé, "ᵹıöeaö ıʁ ʁeaʁʁ
an c-ʁeóıö ḃ' ʁáᵹḃaıʁ ıö' öıaıᵹ 'ná [a] öcuᵹaıʁ leac."

---

¹ A " do thugamar gorra dá chéile gur sgeinn," etc.   ² A reads "uradh
" thógbhála," as before.   ³ A "a h-úróg."   ⁴ B "chuir sé ar a cheann
clogad gloine ".   ⁵ B "thug baoithléim asteach agceartlár an locha ".

into the caldron. Then I gave a vigorous-lift to myself so that I went up into the top of yon big-tree, flying from her. Then when the serpent got some rest from the blows, and with greed for the meat, she twisted her members round the caldron, so that it was swept away by her down under the lake; so that she went away from us without tale or tidings, and the serpent, the caldron, and the ferule are down under the lake still."

Then Murough son of Brian comes home, and he rises up early on the day and full light of the morrow, and he arranged on himself completely his suit of arms and armour, and he put on him his helmet of glass, and he made for the lake, himself and all of his friends and followers who followed him. Then he made a rushing-race till he went of a leap into the very heart of the lake; and it was not long until he beheld the serpent, and she in a coil, twisted round the caldron ; so that he laid himself on his back, swimming in the water, till he threw a cast of his spear at her, so that he hit her in the middle, so that he made two pieces of her. Thereupon he approached her valiantly, till he smote the head off the serpent.

There arose, while that was going on, a surface of red upon the lake ; then the people came together on each side of the lake, and everyone said that it was Murough who was dead.

"Your speech is like the speech of a simpleton or a fool," said the Lad of the Ferule ; "for it's certain that if all the people who are here, and Murough, and seven times as many others were dead, that they all [together] would not bring so red an appearance upon the lake, and it is not he but the serpent which is dead." And with that they beheld Murough coming proudly towards them, and the ferule and the head of the serpent with him in his two hands, and he fixed the ferule with his two hands on the staff, without anything-over, without lack, without excess, and he gave it to the Lad of the Ferule.

"I have my wages now," said he ; "howsoever, better is the treasure that you have left behind you than all that you have brought with you."

---

⁶ A "feidhilte". B omits.   ⁷ B omits from "gur" to "snámh".
⁸ B "leath".   ⁹ B "sámhach". A "samhfaigh".

"Ⅿaiℓeaḃ," aℓ Ⅿuℓċaḃ, "iⱄ ḟeaℓℓ an ṫ-eólaⱄ aṫá aᵹam anoiⱄ 'ná ḃí aᵹam ℓoiṁe ⱄeó." Leiⱄ ⱄin ṫéiḃ Ⅿuℓċaḃ an ḃaℓa ḟeaċṫ ḟá'n loċ, aⱄíⱄ, ᵹuⱄ ċuaⱄṫaiᵹ é ᵹo mion minic, ᵹuⱄ ṫeanᵹṁaiᵹ an coiⱄe leiⱄ, ᵹo ḃṫuᵹ leiⱄ ᵹo calma aⱄ poⱄṫ é.

Ⅽnn ⱄoin caiṫeaⱄ ᵹiolla-an-ḟiuᵹ an ḟiuᵹ aᵹuⱄ a ċⱄi óiⱄneaċ iuḃaiⱄ, aᵹuⱄ a ċⱄi cloċa éiḃiⱄ aⱄṫeaċ ⱄan ᵹcoiⱄe, aᵹuⱄ aḃuḃaiⱄṫ, "Iⱄ anoiⱄ, a ṁic an ⱄiᵹ," aⱄ ⱄé, "aṫá mo ċuilleaṁ aᵹuⱄ mo ṫuaⱄaⱄḃal aᵹam," aᵹ ḟuaḃaċ an ċoiⱄe ⱄiⱄ ḟá'n loċ ᵹan ṫoⱄaḃ ᵹan ṫuaⱄaⱄᵹḃáil.

Ⅽnn ⱄoin ḃuaileaⱄ Ⅿuⱄċaḃ a ċli aᵹuⱄ a ċoⱄⱄ ḟá láⱄ, ᵹan ⱄṫaḃ, aᵹuⱄ ḃo ḃí ḟéin aᵹuⱄ a ṁuinnṫiⱄ ᵹo ḃuaiḃeaⱄṫa ṫⱄe imṫeaċṫ na ⱄeóiḃe ⱄin ḃo ⱄaoċⱄaiᵹeaḃ leiⱄ, aⱄ an móḃ ⱄin, uaṫa. Ṫéiḃeaⱄ Ⅿuⱄċaḃ a-ḃaile aᵹuⱄ noċṫaⱄ an ṫoiⱄᵹ[1] ⱄin ḃ'á aṫaiⱄ, ᵹuⱄ ⱄaoⱄṫaiᵹeaḃ leiⱄ a ḟaṁail ⱄin ḃe ⱄeóiḃiḃ aᵹuⱄ ᵹo ⱄuᵹ ᵹiolla-an-ḟiuᵹ leiⱄ aⱄ an móḃ ⱄin iaḃ.

"Ⅽaḃ ḃo ḃéanⱄaiⱄ-ⱄe aiⱄ ⱄin, a ṁic?" ḃo ⱄáiḃ an ⱄiᵹ aoⱄṫa[2].

"Ḃéanⱄaḃ-ⱄa," ḃo ⱄáiḃ Ⅿuⱄċaḃ, "ᵹo nᵹeoḃaḃ ḃe ᵹeaⱄaiḃ oⱄm ḟéin ᵹan ḃá oiḃċe ḃo ċoḃlaḃ aⱄ aon leaba, ná ḃá ḃéile biḃ ḃ'iṫe aⱄ aon ḃoⱄḃ, no ᵹo ḃṫuᵹⱄam-na ᵹiolla-an-ḟiúᵹ aᵹuⱄ an coiⱄe aᵹuⱄ na ṫⱄi cloċa éiḃiⱄ aᵹuⱄ na ṫⱄi h-oiⱄneaċ iúḃaiⱄ ṫaⱄ aiⱄ aⱄíⱄ ᵹo Ḃún Ċinn Ċoⱄaḃ."

"Ḃeiⱄ ḃuaiḃ aᵹuⱄ beannaċṫ a ṁic, aᵹuⱄ ᵹuⱄab maiṫ an ṁaiⱄe ḃuiṫ-ⱄe ⱄin," ḃo ⱄáiḃ Ḃⱄian.

Ḃo ċuaiḃ Ⅿuⱄċaḃ a ċoḃlaḃ an oiḃċe ⱄin, aᵹuⱄ éiⱄiᵹeaⱄ ḃe ló aᵹuⱄ ḃe lán ṫⱄoillⱄe aⱄ na ṁáⱄaċ[3] aᵹuⱄ ḃo ċoiⱄⱄiᵹ é ḟéin, ḃo ċiaⱄ a ċeann aᵹuⱄ ḃ'ionnlaiᵹ a láṁa aᵹuⱄ [a] aᵹaiḃ. aᵹuⱄ ḃo ċaiṫ a ḟⱄoin, aᵹuⱄ iaⱄ ⱄin ḃ'iaⱄⱄ beannaċṫ a aṫaⱄ aᵹuⱄ a ṁáṫaⱄ aᵹuⱄ a ᵹaolṫa, aᵹuⱄ ḃo ḟeaⱄaḃ ⱄin [ḃó].

Ḃo ᵹleuⱄ an ⱄiannuiḃe ⱄúl-ᵹoⱄm ó ḟéin 'na éiḃeaḃ aᵹuⱄ aiⱄm ᵹaiⱄᵹe, .i. a lúiṫⱄeaċ leaṫan lán-ḃainᵹionn, a lann ⱄaḃa niṁḟaoḃⱄaċ, a ċloᵹaḃ cuⱄáiḃeaċ lán ḃe cloċaiḃ caⱄḃúncail ⱄéalṫannaċ[a], a ḃá ċⱄaoiⱄeaċ cⱄann-ⱄaṁⱄa caṫa ann a ḃóiḃiḃ ḃainᵹne ḃó-ⱄᵹaoilṫe, a ⱄᵹiaṫ ċoⱄcoⱄṫa ḃoinn-ḃeaⱄᵹ aⱄ ⱄṫuaiᵹ-leiⱄᵹ a ḃⱄoma, meaḃⱄaċ ⱄᵹeinne ᵹéiⱄe ḟá n-a ṫaoiḃ ċlí, aᵹuⱄ ṫⱄi liṫⱄe ḃe liṫⱄeaċaiḃ óⱄḃa, ⱄᵹⱄíoḃṫa aⱄ an ⱄᵹéiṫ aᵹuⱄ aⱄ

---

[1] A "an t-aithisg". B "an taithis, i.e. "the shame," "affront."   [2] "Beríona".

" Well, then," said Murough, " I know the way better now than I did before." With that Murough goes the second time under the lake again, till he searched it closely and often, till he chanced on the caldron, and till he brought it valiantly with him to the shore.

Then the Lad of the Ferule throws the ferule and his three billets of yew and its three fairy stones into the caldron, and said, "It is now, King's son," said he, "I have [indeed] my wages and my stipend," as he swept the caldron with him beneath the lake, [disappearing] without tale or tidings.

Then Murough smites his breast and his body upon the ground, unceasingly, and he himself and his people were in trouble through that treasure which had been gained by him going from them in that manner. Murough goes home [then], and makes known those tidings to his father, how he had gained such treasures, and how the Lad of the Ferule had brought them away with him in that manner.

" What will you do about that, my son?" said the aged king.

" I will do this," said Murough; "I will take *geasa* [mystic bonds] upon myself, not to sleep two nights on one couch, or to eat two meals of meat at one table, until we bring the Lad of the Ferule and the caldron and the three fairy stones and the three billets of yew back again to the Castle of Kincora."

" Take a victory and a blessing, my son, and sure it is well that became you!" said Brian.

Murough went to sleep that night, and he rises up with the day and the full light on the morrow, and he blessed himself, combed his head, laved his hands and his face, ate his meal, and after that asked the blessing of his father and his mother and his kin, and that was accorded him.

The blue-eyed hero dressed himself in his armour and arms of valour, his broad full-firm mail-coat, his long venom-edged blade, his champion's helmet full of starry carbuncle stones, his two thick-hafted battle-javelins in his firm unlooseable hands, his empurpled brown-red shield upon the arched-expanse of his back, a sharp knife-dagger on his left side, and three letters, of golden letters, written on

---

³ B omits from mᴅᴘᴀċ to ιᴀᴘᴘιn, and reads simply " do iarr beannacht a athar agus a mháthar, agus fuair se beannachadh ó chroidhe uatha."

an ríġ, b'á ḟuiḋeaṁ ġur ab é féin bo ċearbaḋ na laoċra san bṫreas¹. Ann soin bo ġabaḋ eaċ bo .i. eaċ mín meara-ġánta lom-luaċ léir-léimneaċ ġo n-a ċeiṫre crúḃaiḃ² b'airġiob ḟionnġeal³ fé, aġus srian béal-órḋa, aġ a raiḃ bá ġníoṁ béaġ ċum na⁴ maiċeara innti, faoi mar bo ḃí trí ġníoṁ o ṁnaoi ar bṫúir, com caol, toll raṁar, aġus meanmna uallaċ, trí ġníoṁ o ċarb, fúil ċeann, muinéal raṁar, aġus éaban leaṫan, trí ġníoṁ ó ḟionnaċ, .i. síuḃal fannġaċ aġus cluar bearaċ aġus earball sġoṫaċ⁵, trí ġníoṁ ó ṁíol-buiḋe .i. léim árb, filleaḋ ġrob, aġus riṫ anaġaiḋ cnuic. Ann soin bo ċuaiḃ sé ar ṁuin an eiċ⁶ ġorm-sġuabaiġ ṁór-eólair beóḋa ċlirte, ionnus naċ [in]ḃfíoḋ be nór orra aċt mar a beiḃ' lon aġ bul le ġaoiṫ⁷, no, faoileann be ṁaoilin sléiḃe, no roṫ aġ bul [le] mór-ḟánaḋ⁸, no ġaoċ aġ⁹ bul i nġleanntaiḃ, no Céabaċ mac ríġ na Sorċa¹⁰ aġ bul a' bífróireaċt se ríġ-ṁac Ċ[a]oillte ṁic Ronáin i n-uaṫaiḃ mic Airreaċt uí Ċonċuḃair, i ġcóṁġár Éire[ann] aġus Alban, aġus ġur ab é sin an saon¹¹ síuḃail aġus síor-imċeaċt[a] bo ḃí fá'n nġairġiḃeaċ an tan sin. Ionnus ġo ġcuirreaḋ sé broic ar ċoilltiḃ, aġus ġeilt ar ġleanntaiḃ, faol-ċoin faoi árbaiḃ, aġus sionnaiġ ar seaċrán, riaṁ, ġo bṫáiniġ sé ar bruaċ loċa Ḋearġtar.¹²

Ann sin bo ċuir se uime a ċloġab ġloine¹³, aġus ċuġ úr-ċóġbáil¹⁴ bó féin ġo nbeaċaiġ i ġceart-lár an loċa, ġo raiḃ aġ síuḃal ann ar feaḋ trí lá aġus trí oiḋċe, no ġur sloiġeaḋ é fá ḋeireaḋ ġo tír fá ċuinn, mar a fuair iomab boġaiġċe aġus coillte aġus ġleannta biaṁaire, ġan buine ġan beaċaiġeaċ aġ áitreaṁ ann. Bo ḃí Murċaḋ aġ imċeaċt

---

¹ A reads as follows: "Do chómhruidh se air corpannacha éide fé mar do bhi aige, léine don tsleamhain' tsíoda, uime a gheal chnis, a thruis chaol bruithineach nuadh-chóraighthe seaca saidhbhre socruighthe go h-iomalach eugsamhla, comhraic cuifeach chuinneach choilearach caitineach mor-uchtrach brad brádh baramhail, a dhá bhróig miona clúdaighthe dheasa dhubha ghaodhalacha, togh gar drisbéalacha thiorma theanna shasda: a spuir gheara ghreannta de'n airgiod cearrbhálta go na n-iallachaibh i n-iomall órdha dá n-iaig agus dá n-osgailt go hainmeach, faoi an mbeilgín mbreac mbróigh, agus do chuir sé a chrios tharis, .i. crios conallach buadhach buadhchlach bhándearg lán do chnaipidhe dísle, de shioda na h-Arabia, da iadh agus dá osgailt, a sgaball phollach phéarlach o uachtar luingheach a chloidhimh fada re feidh imuinge a bheinn chúmhdaighe clochórdha córta arm an Fhianaidhe shochma shulgorma, a lann neimhe choinn-láidir corportha ag an laoch gan eagla comhraic, a chlogad cuirrceach cusógach lán de chlochaibh carrabuncail faoi na hata ceart-

the shield and on the knife, setting-forth that it was he himself who used to lop the heroes in the battle.   Then there was found a steed for him, a smooth, high-spirited, very-fast, clear-leaping steed, with four shoes of fine-white silver beneath him, and a golden bitted bridle, which [steed] had in itself twelve accomplishments of excellence, first, three excellences of a woman, a narrow waist, a full hip, and a proud spirit, three excellences from a bull, a stout eye, a thick neck and a broad face, three excellences from a fox, a bounding gait and a pointed ear, and a bushy tail, three excellences from a hare, a high leap, a rapid turning, and a run up-hill.   Then he got upon the back of his blue-sweeping, very-knowing, lively expert steed, so that they went in no other fashion than as it were a *lon* going before the wind, or a seamew off a bald mountain-head, or a wheel down a great incline, or a wind going through the valleys, or *Céadach* (¹), the son of the king of Sorcha, going to dispute with the king-son of Caoilte mac Ronain in the desert-places of Airreacht O'Conor on the near confines of Erin and Alba, so that such was the career of travel and constant-going which this hero made at that time, so that he would rout badgers out of woods, *geilts* out of glens, wolves under heights, and [put] foxes a-wandering, ever, until he came to the brink of Loch Derg.

Then he put round him his glass helmet, and gave a vigorous lift to himself, till he went into the very middle of the lake, so that he was travelling in it for three nights and three days, until he was swallowed up at last to the Country-under-wave, where he found many bogs and woods and mysterious glens without a person or a beast inhabiting it.

---

bheannach airgid, agus a luireach leathan Lochlannach lán-daingionn réaltanach o Chaisléan Chonaill Craoibh-ruadha, agus éide Chonaill ceann-ruadh, a dhá chraoiseach ceann-ramhra chatha ann a dhornaibh dhaingionna do-sgaoilte," most of which is so corrupt as to be almost unintelligible.   ² A " crúithe ".   B " cruite ". ³ A " diarnuidhe ".   ⁴ B omits na.   ⁵ A " sgathach ".   ⁶ A " air mhuin an tseara bheanna bhéilisioll taobh aoigear ".   ⁷ A " ag lomadh gaoithe ro " (?). ⁸ A " re faillte ".   ⁹ B omits from *no gaoth* to *Alban*.   ¹⁰ " Sorrach," MS. ¹¹ A " ag sin comh-thionól siúbhail ".   ¹² B " Deirgdheirc ", as before. ¹³ A " ceannfair glaine ".   ¹⁴ A "urradh togbhala," as before.

(¹) This refers to a story, now I fear lost, but of which I once heard an oral version.   It was one of the stories in the MSS. stolen from Denis Buckley n 1803, for which he issued the "warrant" printed by Mr. Macalister in "Gaelic Journal," vol. ix., p. 324.

aʀ ᵱeaḋ an laoi ʀin ʒuʀ caʀaḋ é ḋo ċaillíʒ ṁáiʀ-liaṫ ṁaʀlaṫaċ[1] buḋ ʒʀánna ḋeilḃ aʒuʀ ḋéanaṁ ḋá'ʀ ḃʀaca ʀúil ḋaonna ʀiaṁ, ionnuʀ ʒo ḃʀanʀaḋ mion-úḃall no móʀ-áiʀne aʀ ḃáʀʀ ʒaċ ʀibe ḋe'n ṁuinʒ ʒaʀḃ-liaṫ ḋo ḃí maʀ ʒʀuaiʒ uiʀʀi. Ḋo óiʀiʒ an ᵱéiʀc caillíʒe ʀeo i ʒcoinne Ṁuʀċaḋ ċum caṫa ḋo ṫaḃaiʀc ḋó.

"Ḋo ʒoin aʒuʀ ḋo ʒuaiʀ oʀc," ḋo ʀáiḋ an ċailleaċ, "a Ṁuiʀიċín ʒʀánna o Éiʀinn! iʀ mion liom maʀ ʒʀeim ḋo ċuiḋ ᵱeóla aʒuʀ iʀ lúʒa ḃeoċ ḋe ḋ' ċuiḋ anaiʀċe aʒam[2]," aʀ ʀí.

"Ḋo ʒoin aʒuʀ ḋo ʒuaiʀ oʀc," ḋo ʀáiḋ Muʀċaḋ, "ḋo ċuiʀ m'aṫaiʀ ḋe ʒeaʀaiḃ oʀm ʒan cóṁʀac caillíʒe ḋo ḋéanaṁ no ʒo ḋċéiḋinn a-ḃaile, aʒuʀ má ċuiʀ, níoʀ ċuiʀ ʀé ḋe ʒeaʀaiḃ ʒan ḋo leiṫéiḋ-ʀe ḋe ċaillíʒ ʒʀánna ḋo ċeanʒal."

Ann ʀoin beiʀeann aʒuʀ ʒuʒann ceanʒal na ʒcúiʒ ʒcaol uiʀʀi ʒo ḋaoʀ aʒuʀ ʒo ḃoċc aʒuʀ ʒo ḋainʒionn, ᵱá maʀ ḃí caol a ḋá ċoiʀ, caol a ḋá láiṁ aʒuʀ caol ʀaṁaʀ a muinéil[3], aʒuʀ ni ḋuḃaiʀc ʀí "oċón[4]." Ċéiḋeaʀ anonn an ḃaʀa ᵱeaċc aʒuʀ ċuʒ leiʀ caʀʀaiʒ ċloiċe 'na ʀaiḃ ʀoc uiʀʀi coṁ ʒeuʀ le baʀʀa ʀnáṫaiḃe aʒuʀ ʒaḃaʀ míle buille ᵱá ċaʀʀán an ʒé . . . . an ʒcaillíʒ ḃí, aʒuʀ ni ḋuḃaiʀc ʀí "oċón." Ann ʀoin buaileaʀ míle buille . . . . na luʀʒan uiʀʀi aʒuʀ ni ḋuḃaiʀc ʀí "oċón"[5].

"Anoiʀ," aʀ ʀí, "ni ḃᵱuil aon niḋ aċc ʒo ḃᵱuil luaʀ andla oʀm ó'n ualaċ." Ᵽáʒḃaʀ an ċailleaċ ann ʀoin aʒuʀ ʒluaiʀeaʀ ċum ʀiúḃail, aʒuʀ níoʀ ḃʀaḋa ḋó ʒo ḋċáʀla buaċaill bó aiʀ, aʒuʀ ʒaʀ éiʀ beannuʒaḋ ḋá ċéile aḋuḃaiʀc an buaċaill ʀe Muʀċaḋ ʒuʀ ḋóiʒ leiʀ ʒo ʀaiḃ an ʒaiʀʒiḋeaċ ċuiʀʀeaċ ḋéiʀ an laoi, aʒuʀ ʒo ḋċiúḃaiʀᵱeaḋ ʀé ᵱéin ḋʀeaʀ[6] maʀcuiʒeaċta ḋó. "Ʒlacᵱaḋ ʀin uaic aʒuʀ ᵱáilte," ḋo ʀáiḋ Muʀċaḋ. Ċóʒḃaʀ aʀ a ʒualainn aʀ ᵱeaḋ ʀeaċc míle é. Ann ʀoin ċuʒaʀ Muʀċaḋ mám óiʀ aʒuʀ aiʀʒiḋ ḋó aʒuʀ buiḋeaċaʀ; aʒuʀ níoʀ ḃʀaḋa ḋó ann ʀoin ʒo ḋċáʀla an ḃaʀa buaċaill bó aiʀ, aʒuʀ beannuiʒeaʀ ḋo Muʀċaḋ ʒo na bʀiaṫʀaiḃ ʀoiʀḋineaċa

---

[1] B reads, after "maslathach", " iona raibh corda fighimín fá na cúilfhiacail agus cor d'á chúilfhiacail fá na chrios agus seacht slata do chlúmha pisembusgánach ag treabhadh 's a fuirse na diaigh agus an chúilfhiacail 'san gearbad eile mar mhaide chroise na láimh." [2] B " agus is milis sóghail liom deoch dod chuid anbhruith ". [3] B "a sgrogall". [4] B "giog". [5] The omitted

Murough was going throughout that day until he met a grey-hipped abusive hag, the most ugly of shape and make that human eye ever beheld, so that a little apple or a big sloe would remain upon the point of every hair of the coarse-grey mane that she had in place of hair. This serpent of a hag rose up before Murough to give him battle.

" Your wound and your peril on you!" said the hag; "ugly little Morougheen from Ireland! I think your flesh small for a mouthful, and a drink of your broth still less for me," said she.

" Pains and peril on you," said Murough.   "My father put me under *geasa* not to fight with a hag until I should return home ; but, if he did, he never put me under *geasa* not to bind such a hideous hag as you."

With that he catches her, and gives her the binding of the five smalls, severely and rigidly and firmly, namely, the small of her two legs, the small of her two hands, and the thick small of her neck, and she never once said " ochone."   He goes over the second time, and he took with him a rock of a stone on which there was a point as sharp as the top of a needle, and he strikes a thousand blows on the hag, and she never said " ochone."   Then he strikes a thousand blows on her shins, and she never said " ochone."   [He then piles the load of stones on her.]

" Now," says she, " there is nothing [the matter with me] but that there is shortness of breath on me from the load."   He leaves the hag there and proceeds upon his journey, and it was not long until there met him a cow-boy; and after they had saluted one another, the boy said to Murough that he was sure the hero was tired after the day, and that he would give him a spell of riding.   " I shall take that from you, and welcome," said Murough.   He lifts him on his shoulder [and goes] for seven miles.   Then Murough gives him a handful of gold and silver, and thanks.   And it was not long then till the second cow-boy met him, and he salutes Murough with courteous prophet-like words

---

words are torn away in A. B reads, for the above : " Do fhéach Murchadh thairis 7 chonnaic carn cloch do thug leis iad agus chuir anuas air a druim iad uile, as dubhairt an tan sin ' braithim luathas anála a teacht orm o mhéid an unlach so orm ', do rádh an chailigh ".   ⁶ B reads " greis " for " dreas " in each case.

ṗáɪġeaṁla[1] ḋo ḃí ann ḋo péɪp na h-aɪmpɪpe pɪn, aɡup ḋo
ḟpeaɡaɪp Mupċaḋ an beannaċaḋ map an ɡcéaḋna.

"Ip ḋóɪġ lɪom ɡo ḃpuɪl ṫu ṫuɪppeaċ, a ġaɪpɡɪḃɪġ," ḋo páɪḋ
an buaċaɪll, "aɡup buḋ ṁéɪn lɪom ḋpeap mapcuɪġeaċṫ[a] ḋo
ċaḃaɪpṫ ḋuɪṫ." "Ɡlacpaḋ pɪn uaɪṫ aɡup páɪlṫe," ḋo páɪḋ
Mupċaḋ. Rɪp pɪn ṫóɡḃap ap a ġualaɪnn é, aɡup pɡɪobap
leɪp ap peaḋ peaċṫ míle é. Rɪp pɪn ṫuɡap Mupċaḋ mám aɪpɡɪḋ
aɡup óɪp ḋó, aɡup buɪḋeaċap.

Níop ḃpaḋa ḋó aɡ pɪúḃal no ɡup ṫápla an ṫpeap[2] buaċaɪll
ḃó aɪp, aɡup ḋo beannaɪġ ḋo Mupċaḋ 'pan móḋ peaṁ-páɪḋṫe,
aɡup ḋo ḟpeaɡaɪp Mupċaḋ é map an ɡcéaḋna, aɡup ḋo ġlac
an ṫpeɪp ṁapcuɪġeaċṫa ap peaḋ an ḟaɪḋ ċéaḋna ḋo ɪomċaɪp
[ɡaċ] aon ḋe'n ḋíp buaċaɪllɪḋ eɪle é, aɡup ṫuɡ mám óɪp
aɡup aɪpɡɪḋ ḋó pe móp-buɪḋeaċap. Níop ḃpaḋa ḋó ann poɪn,
no ɡup aɪpɪġ pé bean aɡ caoɪ ɡo paoɪḋeaċ[3] aɡup aɡ ɡol ɡo
ṫpuaġ. Ann poɪn aḋuḃaɪpṫ Mupċaḋ ɡup 'ḋ béap ḋ'á béapaɪḃ
náp éɪpṫ pɪaṁ pe ɡol mná 'na h-aonap ɡan pɪop a cúɪpe
ḋ'ḟáġaɪl, aɡup ḋo pɪnn uɪppɪ ɡo céɪm-ḋípeaċ, aɡup ḋ'ḟɪappuɪɡ
ḋí cpéaḋ é ḟáṫ a ɡuɪl. Aɡup aḋuḃaɪpṫ pɪpe, "cá cpíoċ no cá
h-oɪléan ḋuɪṫ no cá ḋúɪċċe ann ap puɡaḋ ṫu[4] map naċ ḃpuɪl
pɪop mo ċúɪpe-pe ná mo ġeapdɪn aɡaḋ-pa?" ap pí.

"Ip [Éɪpe ɪp][5] ḋúṫa aɡup ɪp oɪleán ḋam, aɡup nɪ ḃpuɪl pɪop
ḋo ġeapdɪn ná ḋo ġuɪl aɡam," ap pé.

"Ɪnneópaḋ[6] pɪn ḋuɪṫ a ġaɪpɡɪḃɪġ," ap pí; "an píoġaċṫ po
ɡo léɪp ḋo ḃí aɡ Ríġ Ṗá Ṫuɪnn, no ɡup baɪn paṫaċ na ɡcúɪɡ[7]
ɡceann na ɡcúɪɡ mbeann, aɡup na ɡcúɪɡ muɪnéal aɡup a
ṁáṫaɪp .ɪ. an uɪllṗéɪpṫ ċaɪllɪġe, úṁla ḋ'á aɪṁḋeóɪn ḋé, aɡup
ḋá ḋṫpɪan a píoġaċṫa, aɡup ɡo paɪḃ pé ḋ'áɪpḋ-ċíop aca aɪp,
ɡaċ aon uaɪp ḋo ġeoḃaḋ pé ċapppṫa amaċ no apṫeaċ,
maɪġḋean ḋo ċaḃaɪpṫ ḋó ɡaċ aon oɪḋċe ċum a leapṫan aɡup
a beɪṫ aca [aɪɡe] a mápaċ ċum ppoɪnne[8]; aɡup aṫá," ap pí,
"an píoġaċṫ uɪle ḋípɡɪġṫe ó ṁnáɪḃ óɡa, aċṫ ɪnġean an pɪġ
péɪn, aɡup aon ɪnġean aṁáɪn aṫá aɡaɪn-pa, aɡup aṫá pí ap
mnáɪḃ bpeáġa an ḋoṁaɪn, aɡup ɪp ɡeapp anoɪp, beaɡ[9], o ġaḃ

---

[1] B "le briathradh faistineach fáigeamhail do bhi mar nós 'san tir do réir na
h-aimsire sin".   [2] A omits the third ride.   [3] B "go fhaodhbhadh".
[4] A reads "cá leabaidh codalta cuis leathan duit", which is not clear to me.

of the sort that they had in use at that time, and Murough answered the greeting in like manner.

"I am sure you are tired, O hero," said the boy, "and I would desire to give you a spell of riding." "I shall take that from you and welcome," said Murough. Therewith he raises him upon his shoulder and sweeps him along with him for seven miles. Thereupon Murough gives him a handful of silver and gold, and thanks.

He was not long walking until the third cow-boy met him, and he saluted Murough in the aforesaid manner; and Murough answered him in the same, and accepted the spell of riding for the same distance that each of the other two boys had carried him, and he gave him a handful of gold and silver with much thanks. He was not long then until he perceived a woman weeping bitterly and crying lamentably. Then Murough said [to himself] that it was a habit of his habits that he never yet listened to the cry of a lone woman without getting knowledge of her case, and he made straight for her, and he asked her what was the cause of her crying. And she said: "What country or island are you from, or what land were you born in, that you do not know my case and my complaint?" said she.

"Erin is my land and island, and I have no knowledge of your complaint or of your weeping," said he.

"I shall tell you that, O hero," said she. "The whole of this kingdom belonged to the King-under-Wave, until the giant of the five heads, the five bens, and the five necks, and his mother, the monster of a hag, exacted submission from him in spite of himself, and took two-thirds of his kingdom; and the high-tribute they had on him was that every time the giant would go past them either out or in, they had to bring him a maiden every single night to his couch, and he had to have her in the morning for breakfast; and," said she, "the kingdom is altogether emptied of young women, except the daughter of the king himself, and one only daughter that I have, and she is [counted] amongst the handsome women of the world; and it is only just a short

---

5 B reads "is as oileán dam".   6 "neósad", mss.

7 A omits from "na cúig" to "muinéal."   8 A reads "breacfaist"!

9 B "anois beag-nach."

ré ann ro arᴄeaċ, aᵹur coiꞃe aꞃ a ṁuin aiᵹe, aᵹur o'ṗáᵹ ꞃe ꞃóᵹꞃaó¹ aᵹam-ꞃa m' aon inᵹean bo ċuꞃ ċuiᵹe i ᵹcóṁaiꞃ na h-oióċe anoċᴄ, aᵹur ꞃin aᵹao-ꞃa a ᵹaiꞃᵹióiᵹ ꞃáċ mo ᵹuil aᵹur mo ᵹeaꞃáin."

"Ꞇaḃaiꞃ baṁ-ꞃa," bo ꞃáió Muꞃċaó, "an óiᵹbean aᵹur ꞃaċꞃaó ꞃéin aꞃ maioin ċum an ṗaċaiᵹ aꞃ a ꞃon."

" Oo ᵹeoḃaiꞃ aᵹur míle ꞃáilᴄe," aꞃ ꞃí.

Ann ꞃoin o'ṗiaꞃꞃaiᵹ óí an ꞃaió ꞃáᵹail ꞃuaꞃᵹalᴄa ᵹo bꞃáċ aꞃ an ꞃíoᵹaċᴄ.

"Ni ḃꞃuil," aꞃ ꞃí, "aċᴄ ᵹo ḃꞃuil ꞃé ann ꞃan ᴄaꞃꞃain-ᵹeaꞃaċᴄ ᵹo oᴄiucꞃaió Muꞃċaó mac Uꞃiain Uóꞃoiṁe ó Éiꞃinn ann, aᵹur ni ꞃioꞃ an ꞃuᵹaó é ꞃin ꞃóꞃ², ná a aᴄaiꞃ ná a ṗean-aᴄaiꞃ, no cao é an ᴄ-am ᵹo ceann míle bliaóain 'na oᴄiucꞃaió ꞃé ann ꞃó ó Éiꞃinn³," aꞃ ꞃí, "aᵹur iꞃ leiꞃ ꞃaoꞃꞃaꞃ an ċꞃíoċ."

"Iꞃ miꞃe an ꞃeaꞃ ꞃin," aꞃ Muꞃċaó, "aᵹur⁴ ni iaꞃꞃꞃao-ꞃa o'inᵹean aꞃ ꞃeiꞃ láiṁe na leapᴄan, oíꞃ níoꞃ ꞃinn ꞃíoꞃ-laoċ ó Éiꞃinn maiᵹóean bo ċꞃuailleaó ꞃiaṁ, aᵹur má ᴄá ꞃé aꞃ mo ċumuꞃ, le neaꞃᴄ ᵹail aᵹur ᵹaiꞃᵹe ꞃaoꞃꞃaió me ḃuꞃ ꞃíoᵹaċᴄ ó ꞃmaċᴄ bꞃúibeaṁail an ṗaċaiᵹ."

Ann ꞃin bo ṗꞃeaꞃ an bean ꞃuaꞃ le luċᵹáiꞃ aᵹur beiꞃeaꞃ aꞃ Muꞃċaó, aᵹur iꞃ ionᵹnaó náꞃ ṁúċ ꞃí ꞃe ꞃóᵹaió é, aᵹur náꞃ báiċ⁵ ꞃí ꞃe beóꞃaió e, aᵹur ċioꞃmaiᵹ ꞃí ꞃe bꞃaᴄaió ꞃíoꞃ-uaiꞃle ꞃíoba aᵹur ꞃꞃóil é, aᵹur ᴄuᵹ ꞃí óó be blaꞃ ᵹaċ bió, ꞃean ᵹaċ oiᵹe, beoċa ᵹeuꞃa ᵹaḃála i ᵹcoꞃánaió ᴄioꞃma ᴄeó, mil ᵹꞃeuᵹaċ, aᵹur beóiꞃ Loċlannaċ, ᵹo ꞃaió⁶ ꞃé meaóaꞃ-ᵹlóꞃaċ ᵹan meiꞃᵹe. Ꞇuᵹ⁷ ꞃí léi a-baile an oióċe ꞃin Muꞃċaó ċum a ᵹꞃianáin ᴄaiċneaṁaiᵹ ᵹoꞃm-ṗuinneóᵹaiᵹ ꞃéin, aᵹur bo ċonnaiꞃc ꞃé ꞃoiṁe aꞃᴄiᵹ an ṗionna-bean ċaoṁ áluinn óꞃ-ṗolᴄaċ ᵹoꞃm-ꞃoꞃᵹaċ ᵹeal-béaóaċ. buó ᵹile a cneaꞃ 'ná ꞃneaċᴄa aoṗuaꞃ aon oióċe, aᵹur buó óeiꞃᵹe a ᵹꞃuaó 'ná 'n ꞃóꞃ ꞃíoᵹóa, aᵹur aꞃ ꞃeicꞃinᴄ an ᵹaiꞃᵹióiᵹ óí bo b'ṗeaꞃꞃ beilḃ aᵹur oꞃeaċ ionall aᵹur éaᵹcoꞃᵹ o'á bꞃacaió ꞃí ꞃiaṁ ꞃoiṁe, bo b' ionᵹnaó

<hr>
¹ A "bhárnáil"! In the next sentence A adds after "óigbhean" the words "chum leapthan na hoidhche anocht". ² After "fós" B reads "ná a mbéarfar choidhche", omitting what follows, down to "críoch". ³ "Eire," ᴍss. ⁴ A omits this from "agus" to "fhathaigh."

time ago since he came in here and a pot with him on his back, and
he left notice for me to send my only daughter to him for to-night,
and there is for you, O hero, the cause of my weeping and my
complaint."

" Grant the young woman to me," said Murough, "and I shall
go myself to the giant in the morning on her behalf."

" You shall get her and a thousand welcomes," said she.

Then he inquired of her was there any possibility of relief for
the kingdom for ever.

" There is not," said she, " except that it is in prophecy that
Murough son of Brian Boru will come into it from Ireland, and we
do not know if that man is born yet, or his father or his grandfather,
or at what time, to the end of [the next] thousand years, he will come
here from Ireland," says she, "and it is by him the country shall be
saved."

" I am that man," said Murough, "and I shall not ask your
daughter of you by force, for no true hero from Ireland ever hurt a
maiden, and if it is in my power by might of valour and heroism I
shall free your kingdom from the brutal sway of the giant."

Then the woman leaps up for joy, and seizes Murough, and it was
a wonder but she smothered him with kisses and drowned him with
tears ; and she dried him with precious cloths of silk and satin, and
gave him of the tasty of every meat, and the old of every drink—sharp
distilled beverages in dry warm cups, Greek honey and Danish beer,
until he was pleasant-voiced, without intoxication. She brought
Murough home with her that night to her own pleasant blue-windowed
grianan [sunny-house], and he beheld before him, inside it, the gentle,
beautiful, golden-haired, blue-eyed, white-toothed fair woman. Her
skin was whiter than the cold snow of one night, and her cheek was
redder than the royal rose ; and when she beheld the hero, best of
form and person, make and appearance, that she had ever beheld

---

⁵ B " bádhaig ".   A " badhaicc ".   ⁶ A omits from " go raibh " to " meisge,"
and gives the preceding passage somewhat differently.

⁷ B omits the next eighteen lines, from here to " do rinneadar tri treanna de'n
oidhche ".

ᴌéⁱ cⁱa 'ᴘ ḃ'é ḟéⁱɴ, ɴo caḃ [é] ḟáċ a ċuᴘaⁱᴘ ḃo'ɴ cíᴘ ᴘⁱɴ. Ḋo
ᴌaḃaⁱᴘ a máċaⁱᴘ aᵹuᴘ ⁱᴘ é aḃuḃaⁱᴘc, "Aᵹ ᴘo aɴ ᵹaⁱᴘᵹⁱḃeaċ
ḟíoᴘ-uaᴘaᴌ 'ɴ a ᴘaⁱḃ ᴘé ⁱ ɴḃáɴ ḃúⁱɴɴ ḟuaᴘᵹaⁱᴌc oᴘᴘaⁱɴɴ ḟéⁱɴ,
aᵹuᴘ aᴘ aɴ ᴘíoᵹaċc uⁱᴌe."

Aɴɴ ᴘⁱɴ ḃo ᴌaḃaⁱᴘ aɴ ⁱɴᵹeaɴ ḃe ᵹuċ áᴘḃ ᴘoᴌaᴘ-ᵹᴌaⁱɴ :
"Ḟíoᴘ-ċaoⁱɴ ḟáⁱᴌce ᴘóⁱṁaḃ, a Ṁuᴘċaḃ ṁⁱc Ḃᴘⁱaⁱɴ Ḃóᴘoⁱṁe ó
Éⁱᴘⁱɴɴ. ⁱᴘ ᴘaḃa ᴘⁱɴɴ aᵹ ḟeⁱċeaṁ ᴘe ḃo ċeaċc ḃo'ɴ cíᴘ ᴘeó ḃá'ᴘ
ḃḟuaᴘᵹaⁱᴌc ó'ɴ ᵹcᴘuaḃ-ċáᴘ 'ɴa ḃḟuⁱᴌṁⁱḃ ᴌe ᴘaḃa ḃ'aⁱmᴘⁱᴘ."

Aɴɴ ᴘoⁱɴ ḃo ᴌeaᵹ aɴ ⁱɴᵹeaɴ ḃⁱaḃa ᴘaoᴘa ᴘo-ċaⁱċṁe aᵹuᴘ
ḃeoċa ᵹaᴘᵹa ᵹaḃáᴌa, aᵹuᴘ ᴌeaɴɴca ᴘéⁱḃ ᴘóⁱ-ṁⁱᴌᴌᴘc ⁱ ᴌáċaⁱᴘ
ṁⁱc ᴘⁱᵹ Éⁱᴘeaɴɴ. Aᵹuᴘ ḃo ḃⁱoḃaᴘ ᴘúᵹaċ ᴘóⁱ-ṁeaɴmɴaċ caᴘ
éⁱᴘ ɴa ᴘᴘoⁱɴɴe ḃo ċaⁱċeaṁ ḃóⁱḃ. Aɴɴ ᴘoⁱɴ ḃo ᴘⁱɴɴeaḃaᴘ cᴘⁱ
cᴘeaɴɴa ḃe'ɴ oⁱḃċe, cᴘⁱaɴ ċum ḟⁱaɴɴuⁱᵹeaċca aᵹuᴘ ċum ᴘᵹéaᴌuⁱ-
ᵹeaċca, aᵹuᴘ cᴘⁱaɴ ċum ḟᴌeaḃ aᵹuᴘ ḟeuᴘca, aᵹuᴘ a cᴘíoṁaḃ
cᴘⁱaɴ ċum ᴘuaⁱɴ aᵹuᴘ ᴘíoᴘ-ċoḃaᴌca[1]. Aɴɴ ᴘoⁱɴ ḃo ċóⁱᴘⁱᵹ aɴ
ⁱɴᵹeaɴ ⁱomḃa aᵹuᴘ áⁱᴘḃ-ᴌeaḃa ḃo ṁac ᴘⁱᵹ Éⁱᴘeaɴɴ, ᵹuᴘ éⁱᴘⁱᵹ
aɴ ṁaⁱḃⁱɴ ᴌáɴ-cᴘoⁱᴌᴌᴘeaċ aᴘ ɴ-a ṁáᴘaċ.

Ḋ'éⁱᴘⁱᵹ Ṁuᴘċaḃ ᵹo moċ, aᵹuᴘ ḃo ċⁱaᴘ[2] a ċeaɴɴ, ḃ'ⁱoɴɴaⁱᴌ
a ᴌáṁa aᵹuᴘ [a] aᵹaⁱḃ aᵹuᴘ ḃo ċaⁱċ ḃⁱaḃ. Aᵹuᴘ ⁱᴘ uaⁱᵹɴeaċ
ḃo ḃí aɴ ḟaċaċ aᴘ ḃⁱċ ᴘúᵹᴘaḃ ɴa h-oⁱḃċe aᵹuᴘ aᴘ ḃⁱċ ᴘᴘoⁱɴɴ'
ɴa maⁱḃɴe. Ḋo ᵹᴌeuᴘ[3] aɴ ḟⁱaɴɴaⁱḃe ᴘúᴌ-ᵹoᴘm é ḟéⁱɴ aɴɴ a
ċuᴌaⁱḃ éⁱḃeaḃ aᵹuᴘ aⁱᴘm-ᵹaⁱᴘᵹe .ⁱ. aɴ ᴌúⁱcᴘeaċ ᴌeaċaɴ ᴌáɴ-
ḃaⁱɴᵹⁱoɴɴ, a ᴌaɴɴ ᴘaḃa ɴeⁱṁ-ḟaoḃᴘaċ, a ċᴌoᵹaḃ cuᴘaⁱḃeaċ
ᴌáɴ ḃe ċᴌoċaⁱḃ caᴘḃúɴcaⁱᴌ ḟéaᴌcaɴɴaċ[a], a ḃá ċᴘaoⁱᴘeaċ
cᴘaɴɴ-ᴘaṁᴘa caċa, aɴɴ a ḃóⁱḃⁱḃ ḃaⁱɴᵹɴe ḃó-ᴘᵹaoⁱᴌce, a ᴘᵹⁱaċ
ċoᴘcᴘa ḃoⁱɴɴ-ḃeaᴘᵹ aᴘ ᴘcuaⁱḃ-ᴌeⁱᴘᵹ a ḃᴘoma ; meaḃᴘaċ
ᴘᵹeⁱɴɴe ᵹéⁱᴘe ḟá ɴ-a ċaoⁱḃ ċᴌⁱ, aᵹuᴘ cᴘⁱ ᴌíɴe ḃe ᴌⁱcᴘeaċaⁱḃ
óᴘḃa ᴘᵹᴘíoḃca aᴘ ⁱomaᴌᴌ-ḃóᴘḃaⁱḃ ɴa ᴘᵹéⁱċe, aᵹuᴘ aᴘ aɴ ᴘᵹíɴ,
ḃá ḟuⁱḃeaṁ ᵹuᴘaḃ é ḟéⁱɴ ḃo ċeaᴘḃaḃ ɴa ᴌaoċᴘa ᴘaɴ ḃcᴘeaᴘ ;
caᴘ éⁱᴘ[4] ceóᴘa ᴘóᵹa ḃo ċaḃaⁱᴘc ḃo'ɴ ⁱɴᵹⁱɴ, aᵹuᴘ ḃ'ḟáᵹ beaċa
aᵹuᴘ ᴘᴌáⁱɴce aⁱcⁱ ḟéⁱɴ aᵹuᴘ aᵹ a máċaⁱᴘ. Aᵹuᴘ buḃ ḃuḃaċ
ḃeaᴘaċ ḃoḃᴘóɴaċ ḃo ḃí aɴ ⁱɴᵹeaɴ aɴɴ a ḃeoⁱᵹ. Aɴɴ ᴘoⁱɴ
ḃéaɴaᴘ[5] aᴘ ċúⁱᴘc aɴ ḟaċaⁱᵹ ᵹo céⁱm-ḃíᴘeaċ aᵹuᴘ buaⁱᴌeaᴘ
cᴘⁱ ḃuⁱᴌᴌe aᴘ aɴ ᵹcuaⁱᴌᴌe cóṁᴘaⁱc. Aɴɴ ᴘoⁱɴ ċáⁱɴⁱᵹ ċuⁱᵹe

---

[1] B omits the next sentence also, down to "márach". A adds after
"Éireann" the words "agus do luigh féin ann fhochair an oidhche sin".
[2] B omits and reads instead "do uadh a chéadphronn go grinn ard mheannmnach".
[3] From here to "san dtreas" is from B. A reads "annsan do shocruigh air a

before, she wondered who he was, or what was the cause of his journey to that country. Her mother spoke, and 'twas what she said : "Here is the truly-noble hero who has been appointed for us by fate to relieve ourselves and the whole kingdom."

Then the daughter spake with a loud voice, clear as light, "A truly-gentle welcome to thee, O Murough son of Brian Boru from Erin. Long are we waiting for thy coming to this land to release us from the hard fate in which we have been for this long time."

Then the daughter laid noble foods easily-eaten, and rough distilled drinks, and ready very-sweet ales before the King of Ireland's son. And they were merry and high-spirited after partaking of their meal. Then they made three thirds of the night, a third for Fenian tales and story-telling, a third for feast and banquet, and the third third for slumber and continuous sleep. Then the daughter arranged a bed and high couch for the son of the King of Ireland, and he slept that night until the full-shiny morning arose upon the morrow.

Murough arose early, combed his head, laved his hands and his face, and ate food. And it was lonesome the giant was lacking the night's pleasure and lacking the morning's food. The blue-eyed hero clothed himself in his suit of armour and arms-of-valour, the broad full-firm mail-coat, his long venom-edged blade, his champion's helmet full of starry stones of carbuncle, his two thick-hafted battle javelins in his firm unlooseable hands, his purple brown-red shield on the arched expanse of his back, a sharp knife-dagger on his left side, and three lines of golden letters written on the edge-boards of the shield and on the knife, affirming that it was he himself who used to lop the heroes in the battle—after giving the daughter three kisses, and he left farewell and good-wishes (¹) with herself and her mother. And it was sad, tearful, and sorrowful the girl was after him. Then he makes straight for the court of the giant, and strikes three blows upon the Pole of Combat. Then the great sour-visaged unlovely giant

---

chlogad chuirceach chuasógach lán do clochaibh carmogaile faoi na hata ceart bheannach airgid, a lúithreach leathan Lochlannach, ⁊c."   ⁴ B omits from here to "ann a dheóigh ".   ⁵ "deinios", MSS.

(¹) Literally, "life and health ".

an ḟaċaċ móp moḃapċa mí-pᵹiaṁaċ na¹ ᵹcúiᵹ ceann na ᵹcúiᵹ
mbeann aᵹup na ᵹcúiᵹ muinéal : "Náp aḃ é ḃo ḃeaċa ná ḃo
ṁóp-ḟláinċe, a Ṁuipċín ᵹpánna ó Éipinn, aᵹup ip mion ḃo
ḟpacpaḃ²-pa ap a ċéile ċu ap an mball³."

Ann poin ḃ'ionnpaiᵹeaḃap a ċéile ᵹo ḟpaoċṁap ḟeapᵹaċ
ḟíop-náiṁḃeaṁail ḃána ḃápaċċaċ, map ḃo ḃeiḃeaḃ ḃá ċapḃ
buile, no map ḃá leóṁan ḟpaoċ-ċuċaiᵹ⁴, ionnup ḃá ḃċiucpaoi
o ioċċap an ḃoṁain ᵹo h-uaċċap an ḃoṁain aᵹ ḟéaċain ap
ċaċ no ap ċpuaḃ-ċóṁpac ᵹup aḃ oppa apaon buḃ ċóip ceaċc
aᵹ ḟéaċain. Aᵹup ḃo ḃ'é pin an cóṁpac ḟuilceaċ ḟaoḃpaċ
ḃo ḃí eaċoppa ᵹan ḟiop cime ná cláp aᵹ ceaċċap ḃíoḃ ap a
ċéile⁵. Ḃo cloipci ann pna cpi cpiúċaiḃ buḃ ᵹoipe ḃóiḃ béiceaċ
an ḟaċaiᵹ aᵹup bloipᵹḃéimeanna an ċupaiḃ ċalma aᵹ leaḃpaḃ
an uillḟéipc. Ḃo ċuipiḃíp ceiċpe ceaċa ḃíoḃ, ciċ ceine ḃ'á
n-apmaiḃ, ciċ cailce ḃ'á pᵹiaċaiḃ, ciċ ḟola ḃ'á ᵹcneaḃaiḃ, aᵹup
ciċ ḟoiḃpeaċ⁶ ḃe'n calaṁ, ionnup ᵹo nḃéanaiḃíp ball boᵹ ḃe'n
ḃall cpuaiḃ aᵹup ball cpuaiḃ ḃe'n ḃall boᵹ, ípleán ḃe'n ápḃán,
aᵹup ápḃán ḃe'n ípleán. Ḃo ċappainᵹiḃíp coiḃpeaċa ḟíop-
uipᵹe cpe leacpaċaiḃ cpuaḃ-ċloċ, ionnup ᵹup impiᵹeaḃap na
ḟip ḃána a móip-ċleapa ap a ċéile ann a ḃḟeipᵹ aᵹup ann a
neaṁ-ḟéiᵹceaċċ⁷ ap ḟeaḃ lá aᵹup oiḃċe⁸.

Ḃo ḃí Ṁupċaḃ aᵹup an ḟaċaċ aᵹ pníoṁ cloᵹaḃ aᵹup ceann
aᵹ pᵹolcaḃ copp aᵹup meanᵹ, aᵹ iappaiḃe buaiḃe ap a ċéile
no ᵹo paiḃ an ḟaċaċ aᵹ cup ᵹaḃáil na mbuilliḃe[aḃ] ap
Ṁupċaḃ ᵹup laḃaip ᵹuċ map a ḃeiḃ' buine aopca⁹, ᵹo nḃubaipc
ᵹup móp an náipe ḃo ᵹaipᵹiḃeaċ ċoṁ maiċ leip cuicim ḟe
n-a ḟaṁail púḃ ḃe ḟéipc ᵹpánna ċoṁ ḟaḃa pin ó baile "aᵹup

---

¹ A omits this down to "muinéal".　² B "stracad".　³ B "ar ball".
⁴ A reads simply "annsan deanaid an dias laoch ar a chéile".　⁵ A adds
here, "ni bhidheadh de nós orra acht mar da druig ar fásach, no dá tharbh
dána dásachta, no dá leómhan ar leacain no dá seabhac ruadh i n-uachtar faille,
londarracha sgiatha dá mbriseadh", which is not clear ; "druig" is probably
dragon, and " raithe" for "reithe," a ram.　⁶ B "feidreacha."
⁷ " naimhreighteach " in A.　B omits it.　⁸ B has "tri lá agus teora oidhche ".
⁹ B reads "gur cirigh an spideóigin bheannuighthe ar an gcraoibh budh neasa dhó
agus dubhairt si leis ".

of the five heads, the five bens, and the five necks came to him :
" May it be neither life nor health to you, ugly little Murough-*een*
from Ireland, and it 's in small bits I 'll presently tear you
asunder."

Then they attacked one another, fiercely, furiously, full-hostilely,
boldly, ragingly, as it were two angry bulls or two furious mad lions,
so that if people were to come from the bottom of the world to the top
of the world to view a battle or hard-combat, surely it was to view
them both they ought to have come. And that was the bloody keen-
edged fight that was between them, without either of them knowing
terror or timorousness before the other. They were like nothing but
two dragons in a wilderness, or two fierce furious bulls, or two lions
on a rock (?) or two rams rushing, or two red falcons on the top of a
cliff, . . . their shields breaking. The roaring of the giant and the
furious blows of the valiant hero smiting the monster might be heard
in the three cantreds nearest to them. They used to send forth from
them four showers (¹), a shower of fire from their weapons, a shower
of chalk from their shields, a shower of blood from their wounds, and
a shower of sods from the ground, so that they would make a soft
spot of the hard spot, and a hard spot of the soft spot, a hollow of the
height and a height of the hollow ; they used to draw wells of spring
water through flags of hard-stone, and so the fearless men plied their
great arts-of-combat against one another in their anger and in their
animosity throughout a day and a night.

Murough and the giant were wrenching helmets and heads,
splitting bodies and necks, striving for the victory each over the other,
until the giant was sending the heaviest shower of the blows on
Murough, when a voice spake as it were the voice of an aged person (²),
and said that great was the shame for so good a hero as he to fall by

---

(¹) Compare the verse in the Ossianic poem, " The Battle of Gabhra " :

b' éiɲɪჳ τɲɪ ceaτa
oɲ a ჳcɪonn ann ɲna clɪaτaɪb,
cɪoτ ɲola, cɪoτ τeɪne,
'ɲ cɪoτ caɪlce b'á ɲჳɪaτaɪb.

I.e. " there arose three showers over their heads in the encounter (?), a shower of
blood, a shower of fire, and a shower of chalk from their shields ".   (²) B reads
" until the blessed little robin arose upon the bough nearest to him and said:
' without a woman to lay you out or keene over you, unless I were to throw a little
wisp of moss upon you.' "

ɢαn αon ḃeαn ċαoιnτe αɣαḃ αnn ꝛo, α ṁιc αn ꝛιɢ υαꝛαιl ιꝛ ꝼeαꝛꝛ méιn¹."

Rιꝛ αn nɢꝛíoꝛυɣαḃ ꝛιn ḃ'éιꝛιɣ αn ꝼuιl υαꝛαl ι n-υαċταꝛ α υċτα αɣ Mυꝛċαḃ, ɢo ḃτυɣ coꝛ τꝛéαn-ꝼoιꝛτιl ꝼíoꝛ-αꝛꝛαċταċ ḃo'n ꝼαċαċ ḃo ċuιꝛ αꝛ α ḃá ɣlúιn é, αɣυꝛ ċυɣ αn ḃαꝛα coꝛ ḃó ɢuꝛ ċuιꝛ αꝛ α ḃꝛuιm αꝛ αn ταlαṁ é.

"Ɗo ċeαnn ḃíoτ α ꝼαċαιɣ," αꝛ Mυꝛċαḃ.

"Iꝛ ꝛé α ṁιc², má'ꝛ τoιl leατ-ꝛα é, αɣυꝛ ná ḃéαn-ꝛα ꝛιn αɣυꝛ ɢeoḃαιꝛ móιꝛ-ɣꝛéιċꝛe υαιm .ι. ꝛleαɣ³ ḃυαḃ αɣυꝛ beαnnαċτ, αn τ-eαċ clυαιꝛ-leαċαn ḃeαꝛɣ-ḃonn ḃo ḃéαꝛꝼαḃ αꝛ αn nɢαoιċ ḃo ḃí ꝛoṁe, αɣυꝛ nαċ béαꝛꝼαḃ αn ɣαoċ ḃo ḃí 'nα ḃιαιɣ αιꝛ, ḃαllán ꝛlánυιɣċe αɣυꝛ móꝛán ḃe ꝼeóḃαιḃ eιle, αɣυꝛ ḃéαnꝼαḃ ꝼéιn ιonαḃ ḃυαċαιll αɣυꝛ cαιlín ḃuιτ, αɣυꝛ ḃá ḃτꝛιαn nα ꝛíoɣαċτα ꝛo ó lá mo ḃáιꝛ αmαċ."

"Béιḃ ꝛιn uιle αɣυꝛ ḃo ċeαnn⁴ αɣαm," αꝛ Mυꝛċαḃ. Leιꝛ ꝛιn ḃo ċαꝛꝛαιnɣ αmαċ α lαnn leαḃαꝛċα nα ḃτꝛí⁵ ḃꝼαoḃαꝛ nαċ ḃꝼáɣꝛαḃ ꝼuιɣιoll buιlle ná béιme—ḃá ḃꝼáɣꝛαḃ ḃe'n ċéαḋ-ḃuιlle ɢo nɢeαꝛꝛꝼαḃ αɣυꝛ ɢo mbéαꝛꝼαḃ leιꝛ ḃe'n ḃαꝛα buιlle. Leιꝛ ꝛιn ḃo ċóɣ le ḃáꝛαċτ náꝛ lαɣ αn αꝛm nιṁe αɣυꝛ ḃo ḃuαιl ι ɢcóṁɣαꝛ ċιnn αɣυꝛ mυιníl é, ɢuꝛ ꝛɢιoḃ ꝛé nα cúιɣ cιnn ḃé αꝛ αonḃαċτ⁶. Ͼαꝛꝛαιnɣeαꝛ ɣαḃ ꝼá n-α ꝼlυcαιḃ, αɣυꝛ τυɣαꝛ leιꝛ ιαḃ ɢo cúιꝛτ Rιɣ ꝼá ċuιnn. Aɣυꝛ ιꝛ αṁlαιḃ ḃo ḃí αnn ꝛoιn αꝛτιɣ ꝛoιṁe ɢιollα αn ꝼιuɣ, ι ɢcáċαoιꝛ óꝛloιꝛɢċe αɣυꝛ cúιꝛín αιꝛɣιḃ ꝼαoι n-α ċoꝛαιḃ, α ċꝛí h-oιꝛnιɣ⁷ ιúḃαιꝛ oꝛ α ċóṁαιꝛ αꝛ lαꝛαḃ ḃó. Éιꝛɣíoꝛ ι ɢcoιnne Mυꝛċαḃ αɣυꝛ ιꝛ ιonɢαnταċ náꝛ ṁúċ ꝛé le ꝛóɣαιḃ é αɣυꝛ náꝛ ḃáḃαιɣ ꝛé lé ḃéoꝛαιḃ é, αɣυꝛ ċιoꝛmαιɣ ꝛé le ḃꝛαταιḃ ꝼíoꝛ-υαιꝛle ꝛíoḃα αɣυꝛ ꝛꝛóιl e. Ͼυɣ⁸ ḃó blαꝛ ɣαc bíḃ, ꝛeαn ɣαċ ḃιɣe, mιl ɣꝛéαɣαċ αɣυꝛ beóιꝛ Loċlαnnαċ.

"Anoιꝛ," αꝛ αn ɢιollα, "α ṁιc Ḃꝛιαιn, ɢuꝛαb é ḃo ḃeαċα αɣυꝛ ḃo ṁóꝛ-ꝼlánτe ċυɣαm, αɣυꝛ ιꝛ ꝛαḃα αn ꝛíoɣαċτ ꝛo ꝼαoι αnḃꝛuιḃ αɣ ꝼeιċeαṁ leατ, αɣυꝛ αnoιꝛ ó ατá αn ċꝛíoċ uιle ꝛαoꝛ," αꝛ ꝛé, "nι ḃꝼuιl αon eαꝛḃαḃ oꝛꝛαιnn, αɣυꝛ ꝼαn 'náꝛ ḃꝛoċαιꝛ αɣ cαιċeαṁ ꝼleαḃ αɣυꝛ ꝼéαꝛτα ꝛeαlαḃ αιmꝛιꝛe."

---

¹ B reads "agus gan bean sínte na caointe agad muna gcaithfinnse soipin caonach ort".   ² B "'seadh go deimhin a mhuirnín".   ³ B "slata".   ⁴ B " ceannaibh".   ⁵ B omits from "na dtri" to "dara buille."   ⁶ A reads "an ceann d'aon bhuille dhe."   ⁷ A "hoirnimh". B omits.

such a hideous monster so far away from home, " and without a single woman to keene over you here, O son of the noble king of best mien."

Upon that incitement, the noble blood rose in the upper part of Murough's breast, so that he gave the giant a tremendous-strong truly-powerful twist which sent him on his two knees, and he gave him the second twist so that he set him on his back on the ground.

"Giant, your head off you!" said Murough.

"It is indeed, my son (¹), if you desire it, but do not do it, and you will get great things-of-price from me, a spear of victories and benisons, the broad-eared reddish-brown steed that would overtake the wind that was before it, and whom the wind that was behind it would not overtake, a bowl of healing and many other jewels, and I myself will fill the place of servant-boy and servant-maid, and [you shall have] two-thirds of this kingdom from the day of my death, forward."

" I shall have all that and your head," said Murough. With that he drew out his smiting blade of the three edges that would not leave [behind it] the remnant of a blow or a stroke—if it did leave it of the first blow, sure it would cut it, and take it with it, of the second blow. Therewith he raised with a fury not feeble the venomous weapon, and smote him at the joining of the head and the neck, so that he swept the five heads off him at once. He draws a gad through his cheeks, and takes them [the heads] with him to the court of the King-under-Wave. And this is what he found (²)—the Lad of the Ferule was in there before him, in a gold-overlaid chair, and a silver cushion beneath his feet, his three billets of yew in front of him, burning for him. He rises to meet Murough, and it was a wonder if he did not smother him with kisses and drown him with tears, and he dried him with noble cloths of silk and of satin. He gave him the tasty of every meat, the old of every drink, Greek honey and Danish beer.

"Now," said the lad, "that there may be your life and your health to you, son of Brian [who comest] to me, and this kingdom is for a long time under tyranny waiting for you, and now," says he, " since the whole land is free we lack for nothing, and stay thou with us for a space of time, enjoying feast and banquet."

---

⁸ B reads : " Thug do toghadh gach bigh agus rogha gach seandighe go rabhadar a dtriur .i. an righ Murchadh agus giolla an fhiugh meadharghlorach gan mheisge ".

(¹) In the other MS. the giant calls him " a vourneen ", "my dear".
(²) Literally " it is thus it was."

Do ḃáḃaꞃ aᵹ ca1ċeaṁ an ḟle1ḃ ꞃeal a1mꞃ1ꞃe aꞃ an móḋ ꞃ1n no ᵹuꞃ ḟ1aꞃꞃu1ᵹ an ᵹ1olla óé cá ḟa1ḃ ḃo ḃí ꞃé 'ꞃan ᵹcꞃíċ ꞃ1n.

"Ⱌá mó le ꞃeaċċṁa1n no ḃó," aꞃ ꞃé.

"Naċ ḃꞃu1l ḟ1oꞃ aᵹaḃ ᵹuꞃ aḃ é ꞃeó Ⱌíꞃ na n-Óᵹ, aᵹuꞃ naċ n-a1ꞃeóċá¹ an a1mꞃ1ꞃ aᵹ 1mċeaċċ ċaꞃc. Ⱌcá cu ann ꞃo le lá aᵹuꞃ bl1aḃa1n," aꞃ an ᵹ1olla.

"O! n1 ṁa1ꞃeann aon 1 m' ḃ1a1ᵹ 1 n-Ê1ꞃ1nn ḃe m' ṁu1nnc1ꞃ!" aꞃ Muꞃċaḃ."

"Ⱌá 'ꞃ aᵹaḃ náꞃ ḃ' olc an ᵹ1olla cuꞃa1ꞃ m1ꞃe, aᵹuꞃ ní ḃꞃu1l aon lá o ċánᵹa1ꞃ ann ꞃo naċ ḃꞃu1l ꞃᵹéala aᵹam-ꞃa óḃ' ṁu1nnc1ꞃ, aᵹuꞃ bí ꞃáꞃca ꞃua1ṁneaꞃaċ 'na ḃcaoḃ, ó1ꞃ cá1ḃ ꞃlán. Aᵹuꞃ ꞃóꞃ, cá ḟ1oꞃ aᵹam-ꞃa caḃ 1aḃ na ᵹeaꞃa ḃo ḃí oꞃc-ꞃa, aᵹuꞃ níoꞃ ḃꞃ1ꞃ cu aon ᵹeaꞃ ḃíoḃ², ó1ꞃ ḃo ḃí ḃ'ḟ1aċa1ḃ oꞃc ᵹan ḃá o1ḃċe ḃo ċoḃlaḃ aꞃ aon leaba ná ḃá ḃé1le ḃ'1ċe aꞃ aon ḃoꞃḃ no ᵹo ḃc1ucꞃá aᵹuꞃ ᵹo mbéaꞃꞃá m1ꞃe aᵹuꞃ an co1ꞃe o ċꞃíoċa1ḃ Loċla1nn ᵹo h-Ê1ꞃ1nn caꞃ a1ꞃ leac aꞃíꞃ. Ma1ꞃeaḃ, a Ⱡluꞃċaḃ, ḃo ᵹeoḃa1ꞃ ano1ꞃ 1aḃ aᵹuꞃ ꞃá1lce."

"Ⱡla1ꞃeaḃ! muna mbe1ḃ' ꞃ1n n1 1aꞃꞃꞃa1nn oꞃc é ᵹo bꞃáċ," [aꞃ Muꞃċaḃ].

"Ⱡla1ꞃeaḃ!" aꞃ an ᵹ1olla, "ḃá nᵹeallꞃá-ꞃa an co1ꞃe ḃo ċaḃa1ꞃc ḃaṁ-ꞃa caꞃ a1ꞃ aꞃíꞃ, ḃ'1omċóꞃa1nn³ an co1ꞃe le c-a1ꞃ ᵹo h-Ê1ꞃ1nn."

"Ⱡla1ꞃeaḃ ᵹealla1m ᵹo ḃcaḃaꞃ-ꞃa ḃu1c é caꞃ a1ꞃ aꞃíꞃ, le caḃa1ꞃc leac ᵹo cꞃíoċa1ḃ Loċla1nn."

Ann ꞃo1n cóᵹḃa1ḃ ꞃ1aḃ leó aꞃ n-a ṁáꞃaċ an co1ꞃe, aᵹuꞃ 1omċaꞃann⁴ an ᵹ1olla ꞃe h-a1ꞃ Ⱡluꞃċaḃ ᵹo h-Ê1ꞃ1nn é, ᵹo ḃún Ċ1nn Ċoꞃaḃ. Ann ꞃo1n cu1ꞃceaꞃ cꞃu1nn1uᵹaḃ aᵹuꞃ co1ṁċ1onól aꞃ ua1ꞃl1ḃ Ê1ꞃeann u1le, ḃ'á 1nnꞃ1nc aᵹuꞃ ḃ'á ḟa1ꞃné1ꞃ ᵹuꞃ é1ꞃ1ᵹ⁵ a le1ċé1ḃ ḃe áċaꞃ le Muꞃċaḃ mac Ḃꞃ1a1n aᵹuꞃ ᵹo ḃcá1n1ᵹ ꞃé ꞃaoꞃ ꞃlán ꞃoláln caꞃ a1ꞃ aꞃíꞃ ᵹo h-Ê1ꞃ1nn, aᵹuꞃ ᵹo ḃcuᵹ le1ꞃ ᵹ1olla an ḟ1uᵹ [aᵹuꞃ] an co1ꞃe. Do ḃí an cóṁċ1onól ᵹo ᵹá1ꞃḃeaċ aᵹ ca1ċeaṁ ꞃleaḃ aᵹuꞃ ꞃeuꞃca aꞃ ꞃeaḃ cꞃí lá aᵹuꞃ ceóꞃa o1ḃċe. Ann ꞃo1n ḃo ꞃá1ḃ

---

¹ B " níor bhraithis an aimsir ag dul thart ".   ² B " do chóimhlionais iad go fíorlaochdha ro-chalma, agus do shaorais an rioghacht so o anbhroid an fhathach bhruideamhuil 's a mháthar an phéist ghránda adhfhuathmhar ".   ³ A " d'iompreóinsi," and this is the common pronunciation, "iomchar" being generally

They were enjoying the banquet for a space of time until the lad asked him how long was he in that country.

" I am a week or two," said he.

" Do you not know that this is Tir na n-Óg (¹) 'the country of the ever-young,' and that you would not feel the time passing by ? You are here for a day and a year," said the lad.

" Oh ! not one of my people survives me in Ireland," said Murough.

" You know that I was not a bad travelling lad, and there is not a single day since you came here that I have not tidings from your people, and be satisfied and at ease about them, for they are well. And I know, too, what the *geasa* are that were on you, and you have not broken one of them, for you were bound not to sleep two nights in one bed, or to eat two meals at one table until you should come and bring me and the caldron from the lands of Lochlann to Ireland back again with you. Well, then! O Murough, you shall get them and welcome."

" Well, indeed, were it not for that, I should not ask it of you for ever," said Murough.

" Well," said the lad, " if you were to promise to give me the caldron back again, I would carry it alongside you to Ireland."

" Well, I promise that I shall give it to you back again to bring with you to the lands of Lochlann."

Then on the morrow they take with them the caldron, and the lad carries it alongside of Murough to Ireland to the palace of Kincora. There the nobles of all Ireland are gathered and convened together, to announce and publish to them that Murough, son of Brian, had succeeded with such fortune, and that he was come back again, safe and sound and whole, to Ireland, and that he had brought with him the Lad of the Ferule and the caldron.   The assembly was joyously consuming feast and banquet for three days and three nights.   Then

---

pronounced as *iompar*, as *timchioll* is pronounced *timpioll*.   ⁴ A " iompruighion ".
⁵ B " gur comhilladh re Murchadh, a leitheid sin do eachtra ".

(¹) Pronounced " Teer " or " T'yeer na nogue ", " nogue " rhyming to " rogue."

ᵹiolla an ḟiuᵹa.

Muɼċaḋ "Cá na ᵹeaɼa ḋo ḃí oɼm cóiṁ-líonta ᵹo h-uile, aᵹuɼ, ó ċáiḋ, ḃéaɼɼaiḋ mé an coiɼe taɼ aiɼ aɼíɼ ḋo Ⅎiolla an ḟiuᵹ, ᵹo ḃuiḋeaċ ḃeannaċtaċ, óiɼ ḃuḋ ɼó ṁaiċ an ḃuaċaill é, aᵹuɼ iɼ cóiɼ a ċeaɼt ḋliɼteanaċ ḋo ċaḃaiɼt ḋó, aᵹuɼ ḋo ḃí ɼé ḋ'ḟiaċaiḃ¹ oɼm ḃɼeiċ a ḃéil ḟéin ḋe ċuilleaṁ aᵹuɼ ḋe ċuaɼaɼḋal ḋo ċaḃaiɼt ḋó, aᵹuɼ ó'ɼ cuiḋ ḋíoḃ ɼo an coiɼe ḃeiɼeaḋ ɼé ɼiɼ é." Ḋo ḃí an Ⅎiolla ᵹo ḃuiḋeaċ ḃeannaċtaċ aᵹ imċeaċt, aᵹuɼ tá ɼé ḟéin aᵹuɼ an coiɼe i ḋtíɼ ḟá ċuinn ó ɼoin a leiċ, aᵹuɼ ḃéiḋ ᵹo ḋeó.

Ⅎuɼaḃ í ɼin cɼíoċ imċeaċta Ⅎiolla an Ḟiuᵹ aᵹuɼ an coiɼe aᵹuɼ taiɼḃioll Ṁuɼċaḋ ᵹo cɼíóċaiḃ Loċlainn, ᵹo nuiᵹe ɼin, ⁊c.

ḞOIⱤĊEANN ḊE'N SᵹEUL SO.

Síɼaim ᵹuiḋe an leiᵹteoɼa eaᵹnaiḋe aɼ ɼon Ḋé ⁊ ᵹan mé imḃeaɼᵹa ná ḋíomolla má ċáɼla ḋam ḋul aɼ an ɼlíᵹe ċóiɼ am ɼᵹɼíḃin ḋo ḃɼíᵹ ᵹuɼ cóiṁ-ṁeaɼaċal ḋo leanuɼ miɼe, ⁊ an láṁ iɼ ḟeaɼɼ ḋo ɼuᵹ aɼ ḟeann ɼiaṁ, .i. náċ ḟuil a ᵹ-cóṁaċta aon ḋon aḋaiṁ ċloin é ḟéin ḋo ċoɼaint ḋo ḟíoɼ ᵹan ḃeaɼmaḋ ⁊c.

Ḋo ḟeiɼḃíɼeaċ ḃiċḋíliɼ a leiᵹċóiɼ ionṁuin.

MIĊEáL UA MONᵹáIN.

---

¹ "do dhinchaibh", MSS.   ² Aᵹuɼ tá an ᵹiolla aᵹuɼ an coiɼe i ᵹcɼíoċaiḃ Loclain ɼóɼ ᵹo ɼlán aᵹuɼ ḃéiḋ ᵹo ḃɼáċ.

said Murough, "the *geasa* that were on me are altogether fulfilled, and since they are, I shall give the caldron back again to the Lad of the Ferule, with thanks and blessings, for a very good servant he was, and it is due to give him his lawful rights; and it was incumbent on me to give him the reward of his own mouth of wages and of stipend, and since the caldron is a part of them, let him take it with him." The lad was full of thanks and blessings going away, and he himself and the caldron are in the Land-under-Wave from that day to this, and shall be for ever(¹).

So that is the end of the goings of the Lad of the Ferule, and the caldron, and the journey of Murough to the lands of Lochlann up to this, &c.

CONCLUSION OF THIS STORY.

I desire the prayer of the wise reader, for the sake of God, and that he may not reproach nor dispraise me if it has happened to me to go out of the just way in my writing, because a confusion follows me and [even] the best hand that ever seized on pen, namely, that it is not in the power of any of the clan-Adam to guard himself constantly without a mistake, &c.

Your ever faithful servant, O beloved reader,

MICHAEL O'MONGAIN.

(¹) The other MS. reads "and the Lad and the caldron are in the lands of Lochlann yet, safely, and shall be for ever."

eaċtra cloinne Ríġ na h-ioruaiḋe.

Aṗb-Ríġ uaral óirḋearc ḟír-ġlic ḟír-eólaċ calma cupaca ceartḃriaṫraċ, ro ġaḃ ḟlaiṫior aġur ḟorláṁar aġur ḟorrmaċt ar ėríoḋaiḃ ġlan-áille cnuar-ṫoraċ[a] na h-ioruaiḋe, ḋar ba ċóṁ-ainm IORUAIḊ mac Ḋealḃa, ṁic Ḋaṫaoin, ṁic Ḋaire Ḋeirġ-ġlair, ṁic Ioruaiḋe, ⁊c. Ba laċtṁar loilġiḋeaċa¹, ba ċnuar-ṫorraċ coillte, ba h-iarġ-líonṁar² aiḃne, ba ėrom-ṫorraċ ḟearoinn, ba ḃuiḋeanṁar ḃrúġa, ba ṫoiceaċ oireaċta, ba ċonaiġeaċ áṗb-ċealla, aġur ba h-ioṛḃaiġċe ollaṁuin le linn an tréin-Ríġ rin³.

Ir aṁlaiḋ iomorro ṗo ḃí an Ríġ rin, ní raiḃ ḋe ċloinn aiġe aċt triar mac móir-ṁeanmnaċ mór-ṗḋálaċ, eaḋon Coḃ aġur Ceaḋ aġur Míceaḋ. Aġur ní raiḃ cearṗa⁴ ġaile no ġairġe ṗo ėrí ṗoġail⁵ rannaiḃ an ḃeaċaḋ naċ ḃcuġaḋar real éiġin ḃ'a n-aimrir i ḋcír ionnta, aġ mín-ṁeaḋṗaḋ⁶ ġaċa ġlan-ġairġe ionnur ġo nġoiriḋír cáċ ġo coitċeann trí h-uaiċne coranca an ḃeaċaḋ ḋíoḃ, óir ḃo ċuaiḋ a n-ainm⁷ aġur a n-áṗb-nóir ar⁸ ḟearaiḃ an ḋoṁain ġo h-iomlán ina ġcoṁ-aimrir ḟéin⁹.

Lá ḃ'á nḋeaċaḋar na ḟir óirḋearca-ra ḃo ḟeilġ ar oileán na n-éan, ḃe'n caoḃ ba ċuaiḋ ḃe'n Ioruaiḋ: Ir aṁlaiḋ atá an t-oileán rin aġur ḟíoḋ clúṫar ġlan coille ḃe ċaoḃ ḃé, aġur muir ḃe'n caoḃ eile ḋé. Seallaḋ¹⁰ éiġin ḃ'á ḃcuġaḋar ar muir ḃo ċonncaḋar lonġ luċtṁar leaḃar-ḟairpring¹¹ ḃ'á n-ionnraiḋe, ġo reólta iomḋa éaġraṁla uirri, aġur ráiniġ i ġcuan na h-inre rin ġan ṁoill; aġur nuair ḃo ḟíleaḋar neart rlóiġ aġur roċaiḋe

---

¹ Thus H. A reads "bo táinte". ² P reads "h-iascemhar".
³ I have extended the contracted adjectives as *conaigheach* and *iosdaighthe*, but they may be *conaighthe* and *iosdaigheach*. H omits. P reads, "ba toicteach tromconaig tromaireacht agus ba hiosrdreic airttcheallo, ba hiosdamhoil", etc.
⁴ Thus H. P reads "cearttcha". A "sgoill". ⁵ Thus H. A has "foidhail".
⁶ P reads "mion meaphrughadh". A "meadhrudh". ⁷ P and H read "analla". ⁸ P reads "os" for "ar." ⁹ P adds "agus do bhadar fir

THE ADVENTURES OF THE CHILDREN OF THE KING OF NORWAY.

THERE was a High-king, noble, illustrious, knowledgeable, very pru-
dent and very wise, valiant and valorous, of righteous words, who
assumed sovereignty, possession, and authority over the fair-clean
cluster-fruited regions of Norway,([1]) whose name was IORUAIDH
[Irrua *or* Irroo-ȳ] son of Dealbha, son of Dathaoin, son of Daire Red-
green, son of Ioruaith, etc. Milkful were milch-cows, cluster-fruited
were woods, fishful were rivers, heavy-fruited were lands, populous
were mansions, wealthy were assemblies, rich were high-churches,
and entertained were ollamhs during the time of that strong king.

Now this is how that king was : he had no children except three
spirited, proud sons, Cod, Cead, and Micead.([2]) And there was never a
forge of valour or heroism in the three plunder divisions of life but
they had spent some while of their time in them, in [each] country
closely acquiring every perfect heroism, so that all in common used to
call them the three protecting columns of the world ;([3]) for their name
and high fame excelled that of the men of the whole world in their
own time.

Of a day these([4]) famous men went to hunt upon the isle of birds
on the north side of Norway. This is how that isle is situated.
It has a clear, close forest wood on one side of it, and the sea
upon the other side of it. Of a look that they cast towards sea, they
beheld a laden broad-spread bark coming towards them, with many and
variegated sails upon it, and it put in without delay to the island's
harbour ; and when they deemed that a number of warriors and people

---

edmharo an bheatha lan ded agus diomoidh riusan agus mna ionnraca an domhain
accomgradh doib na ttriur.''   [10] H reads ''silleadh''.   [11] Thus H. A 25
reads ''lán-aidhbhseach '', and A has an abbreviation meant, I think, for the same
thing.

([1]) I have translated ''Ioruaidh'' by ''Norway'', but this is doubtful.   ([2]) Pronounced '' Kudd '', '' Kadd '', and '' Meekadd ''.   ([3]) Literally ''of life '', ''the
three plunder divisions of life '', or '' of the world '' is a common phrase in this
story.   ([4]) Literally '' of a day that these '', &c., which is an anacoluthon.

ṫo ċeaċc airci, ní ċáiniₓ airci aċc aon bean[1], ba ḋilne cruċ
ṫealb aₓur ṫéanaṁ, ineall aₓur éaₓcorₓ, ṫe ṁnḋib an ṫoiṁain
ₓo h-iomlán.   Ir aṁlaiṫ ṫo bí an inₓean rin aₓur callaṫ[2]
ṫ'ór ḋluinn Ḋirrice ra n-a ceann[3] aₓur é ar n-eaₓraṫ ₓo
cearṫaṁail ṫe ċloċaib buaṫa Pḋrċair Ḋṫaiṁ[4], aₓur rolc
raṫa ror-órṫa ror a ceann, anuar car ₓuaillib na h-óₓ-ríoₓna
rin.   ba ṫeirₓe no bláċ na parcuinₓe a béal[5], aₓur aṁail
rór ro-ċorcar ar laraṫ 'na ₓruaiṫ, aₓur aṁail ba frar ṫe
neaṁanaib a béaṫ ina ceann, aₓur rorₓ ₓorm ₓaireaċcaḋ
aici, aₓur í ciúin[6] miocaire ṫeaₓ-ċóṁráiṫceaḋ milir-briacraḋ,
aₓur brac ṫe'n crról na cimċioll[7], aₓur ṫealₓ ṫearₓ-óir ar
lorcaṫ i mbrollaċ an braic fír-ṫeannaiₓ rin.   Aₓur an méaṫ
ruₓ an Ṁuir Ruaṫ or na maraiṫ, aₓur Sliab Síon or na
rléibcib, aₓur an ioruaiṫ[8] or an éanlaiċ, ruₓ an ċaoin-bean
rin ṫe bárr ṫeire aₓur ṫeaₓċumċa ar ṁnḋib na cruinne
ₓo h-iomlán.

Ir annrin ṫo beañuiₓeaṫar Clann Ríₓ na h-Ioruaiṫe ṫo'n
óₓṁnaoi il-ṫealba rin, ₓo milir briaċra aₓur ₓo caoinear
cóṁrḋiṫ[9], aₓur ṫo fiarraiṫ rior a h-eaċcraṫ aₓur a h-ḋirṫ-
imċeaċca féin ṫí.   Ro freaₓair an inₓean aₓur ir eaṫ ro
rḋiṫ, "acá m' eaċcra-ra raṫa ror-rₓaoilce re innrin," ar
rí, "aₓur ir córa ṫaoib-re bur rₓéala féin ṫo ċaḋairc
ṫaṁra a ccúir, óir ir lia ṫe ṫaoinib rib-re 'nḋ mire : aₓur
ḋṫbar eile, muna[10] ṫuₓaim-re mo rₓéala féin ṫaoib-re ṫo m'
ṫeóin ir éiṫir lib-re a mbuain ṫo m' aṁṫeóin[11] ṫíom."   Ir
ann rin ċuₓaṫar a rₓéala ó ċúr ₓo ṫeireaṫ ṫo'n ríoₓain[12]
iolbuaṫaiₓ rin.

Ir annrin, a h-aiċle na rₓéal ṫ'fḋₓail ṫi-re, ṫo laḃair
an inₓean rin aₓur ir eaṫ aṫuḃairc, "Raċaṫ-ra ṫo ċarraiₓ
mo luinₓe i ṫcír aₓur ṫo béarraṫ mo rₓéala féin ṫaoib-re
ṫḋ éir rin."

Ceaṫuiₓiṫ-rean rin ṫi, ionnur ₓur ₓluair ₓo h-aċlḋṁ

<hr>

[1] H adds "ma má".   [2] H "calla".   P "callo".   [3] H "uasda".
[4] H omits "Parthais Adhaimh."   [5] Thus H. A reads "nior dheirge
Parthlann na [a] béal".   P reads "ba deircce nobartloind a bel".   [6] P "ciuin
cionchoin comraiteach."   [7] H "ar tonguil na timchioll".   P "ar
tondghoil".   L 39 "ar tonngaile".   [8] A reads "moruaith".
[9] P "go naineas niomagulla".   [10] A "muradh".   [11] Thus H. A has

would come out of her, there only came out of her a single woman, the most beautiful of form, shape, and make, of mien and appearance, of the women of the entire world. This is how that girl was : she had a hood of beautiful gold of Africa upon her head, cunningly lined with precious stones of Adam's Paradise, and on her head was long hair, very golden, [falling] down upon the young queen's shoulders. Redder than the flower of the *partuing* was her mouth, and there was like a purple rose burning in her cheek, and like to a shower of pearls her teeth in her head, and a blue laughing eye she had, and gentle, courteous, well-spoken, sweet-toned she was, and there was a mantle of satin around her, and there was a red gold pin blazing in the breast of that symmetrically-peaked mantle. And as much as the Red Sea excels the seas, and Mount Sion the mountains, and the *ioruaidh* the birds, so much did that fair lady excel for beauty and for good mien the women of the entire world.(¹)

Then the children of the King of Norway saluted this shapely damsel with sweet words, and with gentleness of discourse, and asked of her to tell them her adventures and her goings. The girl made answer, and 'twas what she said: "My adventures are lengthy and various to be told," said she, "and it is meeter for you to give me your tidings first, for ye are more numerous than I; and another reason! if I do not give you my tidings of my own good-will, ye are able to extract them from me against my will." Thereupon they told their tidings from beginning to end to that variously-accomplished queen.

Then, after her getting their news, that damsel spake, and 'twas what she said: "I shall go draw my ship to land, and I shall relate you my tidings after that."

They permit her to do this, so that she moved quickly, spiritedly,

---

"go hiom-deonach" for "go h-aimh-dheónach".   ¹² Thus A 25.
A has "oigdeir"[?].

(¹) This constant harping on the word "world" appears monotonous in English, but there are numerous Irish words employed for it, as "beatha", "saoghal" "domhan", and "cruinne".

úrṁairneaċ croiċ-ċarġa ḃo ċum a luinġe aġur a luaċ-ḃairc, aġur ḃo ċuġ a h-aġaiḋ orra iar nḃul innci roċċaḋóir ḃí, aġur ircaḋ aḃuḃairc¹. "Na cri ranna ċuġ Ṁarcur Crarur Ꝑomp. maiġc² aġur luliur Serar ar an ḃoṁan, .i. na crí ranna³ ḃo rinneaḃar ḋé .i. an rann Euróir, an rann Airric aġur an rann Aria, cuirim-re riḃre ꝑá ċrom-ġearaiḋ ḃoilḃċe ḃraoiḋeaċċa muna n-iarraiḋ riḃ ġaċ áirḃ a'r ġaċ íreall ḃe na crí rannaiḃ rin ḃo m' iarraiḋ-ri, no ġo ḃꝑáiġiḃ riḃ an ġnáċ-áic ḃunaiḃ⁴ ina mḃím-re."

A h-aiċlc na h-iom-aġallṁa⁵ ḃo ċóġ an ríoġan reólca na reanġ-luinġe ġo h-aċláṁ im-éarġaiḋ, ionnur ġur ġluair roimpi ar ḃruim-ċlaḃaiḃ na ḃíleann aġur ar ċreaċan-connaiḃ na créan-ḃóċna, ġaċa n-ḃíreaċ, aġur ḃo ḃí ḃe luar aġur ḃe luċṁaireaċċ lán-imċeaċċ[a] na luinġe, aġur ḃ'eólċa na h-ainnire ar a h-árḃ-rciuraḋ, naċ cian ḃo ḃí aġ ḃul ar raicrin aġur ar ꝑíor-raḃarc Cloinne riġ na h-ioruaiḋe⁶, ionnur naċ ꝑior ḃóiḃ cá críoċ ḃe ċríoċaiḃ an ḃoṁain i n-ar ġaḃ rí uaċa. Aġur annrin ḃo claoċluiġeaḋ cruċ ḃealḃ aġur ḃéanaṁ Cloinne Ríġ na h-ioruaiḋe; aġur ḃo ġluaireaḃar rompa, aġur ní h-aiċrirċear a n-imċeaċċa no ġo ránġaḃar Ḋún na ḃáiḃċe⁷ ḃeirġe .i. baile ḃe ḃailciḃ Ríġ na h-ioruaiḋe, aġur ḃo ḃaḃar ġo ḃúḃaċ ḃoḃrónaċ.

Ḃ'ꝑiarruiġ Ríġ na h-ioruaiḃe áḃḃar a nḃóḃróin ḃíoḃ ġo ḃíċċiollaċ⁸ aġur ċuġaḃar⁹ rġéala ó ċúr ġo ḃeireaḋ ḋó. Annrin ḃo laḃair Ríġ na h-ioruaiḃe aġur ir eaḋ aḃuḃairc, "A Ċlann," ar ré, "na ḃíoḃ na ġeara rin ḃe ċeirc orraiḃ-re," ar ré, "óir cuirꝑeaḃ-ra loinġear lán-ṁór liḃ, ċoranar ceannar ġaċa críċe ġo coiċċeann aġur ríġeaċċ ġaċa h-oileáin ġan impearan¹⁰ no ġo riúḃlaiḃ riḃ an ḃoṁan."

"Ní hí rin an ċóṁairle ḃ'á ḃcuġamar ꝑéin ár ḃcoil," ar Coḃ mac Ríġ na h-ioruaiḃe, "aċc rinn ꝑéin ár ḃcriar ḃo ḃul ḃo ꝑúr an ḃoṁain no ġo ḃꝑáġam ár n-iarraiḋ, aġur ġaċ

---

¹ The last thirty words are from H, which gives the best reading, but I have changed the "sium" of H into "sean", for the sake of uniformity. ² H reads "Crasus agus Pomp. maigh agus J. Caésar". Ꝑ reads "Marais Grasus agus Poimp. maidhe agus nercesoir ar an doṁan". ³ H "hoirne". Ꝑ "hoirdne". ⁴ Ꝑ reads "go bfinntar libsi antarusbuna [= árus bunaidh] ambimsi". ⁵ Thus L 39. A has "h-iomghala". ⁶ Thus H the

and with rapid feet to her ship and swift bark, and she faced towards them, after first getting into it, and 'twas what she said : "The three divisions that Marcus Crassus, Pompey of the plain, and Julius Cæsar brought upon the world, that is, the three divisions they made of it, the division of Europe, the division of Africa, and the division of Asia, I put you under heavy deadly *geasa* of enchantment, unless ye search all that is high and all that is low of those three divisions to seek for me, until ye find the usual residing-place in which I be."

After this address the queen raised actively and nimbly the sails of the slender ship, so that she moved forward over the back-ridges of the flood, and the powerful waves of the strong ocean, straight before her ; and what with the speed and buoyancy of the full-going of the vessel, and the skill of the damsel in the exact steering of it, it was not long she was in passing out of sight and vision of the children of the King of Norway, so that they did not know to what region of the regions of the world did she go from them. Then were the form, shape, and make of the children of the King of Norway changed, and they moved away, and their goings are not told until they reached the Dún of the Red Vessel, that is a town of the towns of the King of Norway, and they were sad and sorrowful.

The King of Norway asked them anxiously the reason of their sorrow, and they related to him their tidings from first to last. Then the King of Norway spake and said : "Children," said he, "be not troubled over those *geasa*, for I shall send with you a full-great fleet to defend your authority over every country in common, and the kingship of every island without dispute, until ye travel the world."

"That is not the advice on which we ourselves have set our desires," said Cod, the King of Norway's son, "but for the three of ourselves to go and search the world, until we find what we seek, and

last fifty-two words. A reads "do thógis a seolta a mbarraibh na seol-chrann bhfada bhfuighbharsi agus do leig an ghaoth na gadanaibh glóracha a nglothar na seol suathrighin néagsamhail niongantach agus tug sithe séigheamhail sruth luaimach ins an aidhbheis". 7 Thus L 39. A reads "dabhtba", Ᵽ "dobhcha". 8 A has ᴅ́ıoᵹalᴄaċ, the others omit. 9 A confounds two different forms and reads "thugsadar" ! 10 A "iomraisin".

nuaḋ-ċreire b'á [n]ʒeaḃam ba móiḋc alla aʒur óirḋearcar
búinn, ʒan bo ḃeiċ linn aċc rinn féin aṁáin." Níor
ċoirmearʒ an Ríʒ an ċóiṁairle ar ar ċinneaḋar.
Ar n-a ṁáraċ bo ḋearuiʒeaḋar lonʒ luċċṁar lán-aiḋḃreaċ
bóiḃ, aʒur bo ḃí ʒaċ re clár ran luinʒ rin .ı. clár ʒorm
aʒur clár ḋearʒ, clár uaiċne, clár buḃ, clár buiḋe, aʒur
clár rionn, aʒur cuireaḋ crí pobaill ınnce .ı. pobal ʒeal 'na
corac, pobal ḋearʒ 'na meaḋon, aʒur pobal buḃ 'na ḋeireaḋ;
aʒur bo cuireaḋ crí cionnċaire¹ loinʒe ınncı .ı. biaḋ ı n-ıonaḋ
a caiċṁe², airm ı n-ıonaḋ a [n]ḋıuḃraice³ aʒur ór ı n-ıonaḋ
a ḃronnca. Do ċuaḋar clann Ríʒ na h-lopuaiḋe bo ċum a
loinʒe lán-ṁói[re] féin aʒur bo leıʒeaḋar urlanna a
ʒcraoireaċ re lár aʒur re lán-calṁain aʒur bo éirʒeaḋar
be ċrí léim lúċṁar lán-aıʒeancaċ b'urlannaıḃ a rleaʒa aʒur
be ċrannaıḃ a ʒcraoireaċ ʒur ʒaḃaḋar leaċaḋ a mbonn be'n
ṗríoṁ-luinʒ rin, aʒur ċuʒaḋar aʒaıḋ ar ċreaḃaḋ⁴ na bóċna
ḃrac-uaiċne, aʒur bo rinneaḋar an laoıḋ eacorra⁵:—

Cóʒċar reól na caol-ḃairce
Daṁ-ra 'r bo m' ḋiar ḋearḃrátair
Ceaċc beó ʒıon ʒo raoilim-re
Noċa an buḃaċ acáċair.

Déancar búinn an c-ımċeaċc-ra⁶
Fá mbiaḋ riḃre ʒo rúḃaċ,
Má rí ro bur ʒcéaḋ-eaḋcra
Ná bíoḋ bur meanmna búḃaċ⁷.

buaıḋ neóıl ar na céaḋaıḃ-rı
Ʒé cá na cuirre ar óʒ-ṁnáıḃ,
Seól na bairce béal-ṗairrınʒ
Ⅿo ċeann rearca b'á ċóʒḃáıl.

A h-aıċle na laoıḋe rin ba rorʒ-ḟliuċ beaʒ-laoıċ⁸ aʒur ba
ḋearʒ-ḃaraċ maıʒḋeanna⁹ aʒur ba ṗúıl-ḟliuċ bainríoʒna,

---

¹ H = "Tionchaire". F = "tioncur". A 25 "tioncuire". L 39 "Teanncaire".
² A "caithfe" which shows the usual pronunciation of *mh* after *th*. ³ This
passage was so familiar to the scribe of F, that he abbreviates it thus, "⁊ a. anıoñ.
a. nḋ". ⁴ Thus L 39. A has "treibh". ⁵ Both F and H omit
this lay. ⁶ A "t-iomceachta". A 25 "t-iomceacht-sa". ⁷ A reads
"na bi mur meanmna go dubhach". ⁸ A "deaghlaoidh".
⁹ A "mindeire": compare its "óigdeir" for "óigbhean", above.

every fresh victory([1]) we get, our fame and glory shall be the greater for there being nobody with us but ourselves alone." The King did not forbid the plan on which they had resolved.

On the morrow they fitted out a capacious full-fair vessel for them, and every other board in that bark was a blue board, a red board, a green board, a black board, a yellow board, and a white board ; and there were set in it three tents, a white tent in its prow, a red tent in its midst, and a black tent in its poop ; and a ship's three requisites([2]) were placed in it, food in its place of eating, weapons in their place of throwing, and gold in the place of its bestowing.   The children of the King of Norway went to their full-great ships, and they set the handles of their javelins on the soil and on the ground, and they rose of three active high-couraged leaps off the handles of their spears and the hafts of their javelins, till they attained the breadth of their soles of that prime bark, and they faced for the flowing of the green-mantled ocean, and they composed between them this lay :—

> Raise our sails, broad, venturous
> For me and for my brothers.
> Wild our course and perilous,
> Our sorrow be for others.([3])

> Let this expedition be made by us,
> For which ye shall be merry.
> If this is your first adventure
> Let not your mind be sorrowful.

> Victory of cloud on these ropes,([4])
> Although they be a grief to young women,
> The sail of the wide-mouthed bark
> My desire from henceforth is to hoist it.

After that lay, moist-visioned were good heroes, and red-palmed[5] were maidens, and wet-eyed were queens, and sigh-ful was High king,

---

([1]) Literally " each new-might ".   ([2]) Literally " pincers " (?).
([3]) Literally " Let the sail be raised of the narrow bark | for me and my two brothers | although I think not to return alive | not very sorrowful are we."   The verse in the text is in the metre of the last two verses of original, the first verse of which is in the metre called " cass-bairdne," while the last two are a " cumasc of cass-bairdne and Rannaigheacht Beag," without any observance of alliteration. ([4]) *I.e.* " may good weather attend these tacklings" (?).   [5] *I.e.* from clapping their hands together in their grief.

aġup ba h-opnaiöcaċ Apö-Ríġ, ba ċainteaċ pile, aġup ba
bpónaċ ban-ċuipe, tap éip na ʒcupaö ʒcalma pin.

Öála Cloinnc Ríġ na h-lopuaiöc innipteap¹ pin peal eile.
Ó páinʒaöap a nölúċap² na öconn aġup ap pál na peaṅ-ṁapa
baöap aʒ péaċain na ceiċpe Ápöa na [ö]cimċioll, map atá
poip piap ba öcap aġup ba ċuaiʒ. Níop ċian öóiö map pin
ʒo bpacaöap aon ṁapcaċ ö'á n-ionnpaiöc, aġup pċéaö lúċṁap
lán-ṁaipcaċ³ ceann-beaʒ cop-éaötpom ionʒan-ċpuinn⁴ pnuaö-
ṗoltaċ paoi. Beannuiʒcap an macaoṁ pin ʒo milip-ḃpiatapaċ⁵
öo Ċloinn Ríġ na h-lopuaiöc, aġup [öo] ṗpeaʒpaö[ap]-pan é
map an ʒcéaöna, aġup an peaö öo báöap aʒ iomaʒallaṁ⁶
le céile, öo ċeanʒail pé polt an eiċ öpaoiöcaċta pin öo ċop
topaiʒ⁷ loinʒe Ċloiṅe Ríġ na h-lopuaiöc, aġup ʒluaipcap an
t-eaċ poimpe ʒo péiṁ-öípeaċ aġup an lonʒ 'na leanṁúin, na
öiaiö, ʒaċa nöípeaċ⁸.

Cíoö tráċt öo ṗíopaöap iol-ṁapa na cpuinnc inöiaiö an eiċ,
ap an ópöuʒaö pin, ʒan ap a ʒcumap pʒapaö na loinʒe pip an
eaċ⁹. Öo báöap bliaöain on callean¹⁰ [ʒ]o céile, aṁlaiö pin,
aġup ní ʒeapppaö lann ná¹¹ paoöap aon poinne ö'ṗolt an eiċ
öpaoiöcaċta pin. Ba ċoṁ-luaċ öí ap ṁuip aġup ap típ aʒ
piúöal. La éiʒin öóiö map pin aʒ taipöioll na öconn öo ċonn-
caöap boöap-ċú niṁe ö'á n-ionnpaiöe, aġup iolpa ʒaċa öaċa
innte, aġup a púile le lapaö ina ceann, aġup caop teintiöe
teiniö aʒ teaċt tap a béal aġup tap a ṗóin amaċ, aġup map öo
ċonnaic an Macaoṁ an cú niṁe ö'á ionnpaiʒe öo pʒaoil pé polt
an eiċ ó'n lunʒ ṁóip pin Ċloinne Ríġ na h-lopuaiöc, i múimiʒin a
ċpéan-luaċaip, aġup leanap an cú neiṁe an mapcaċ aġup ní
puʒ paip, aġup öo pʒapaöap apaon map pin le Cloinn Ríġ na
h-lopuaiöc.

Aġup öo ċuaiö peap öe Ċloinn Ríġ na h-lopuaiöc i ʒcpann-
peóil¹² na loinʒe, aġup ċuʒ pé púil ċuaipim ap na ceiċpe
h-áipöiö 'na timċioll, aġup öo ċonnaipc toipc iaċa aġup
im-öéanaṁ oileáin i Úpaö uaċa, aġup ċuʒ pé [na] pʒéala pin
ö'á öeapbpáiċpiö, aġup peólaiö aʒaiö na luinʒe ö'aon-ċóṁaiple

---

¹ A has "instear".   ² A has "ndluis"; A 25 "ndlús"; L 39 "teas".
³ Thus H, but I have inserted the second a in "maiseach." A has "fuireachair
fiorluthmhar".   ⁴ Thus A 25. A has "ioghan"; thus, in West Galway,
"teanga" is pronounced "teaga".   ⁵ H has "go hormaisneach".

talkative was poet, and sorrowful the bands of ladies after those valiant heroes.

As for the children of the King of Norway, that is told another time. After they had reached the closeness of the waves and the heel(¹) of the old sea, they were regarding the four quarters of the globe around them, both east and west and south and north. And they were not long in this wise until they beheld a single horseman approaching them, and an active full-fair, small-headed, light-footed, hard-hoofed, handsome-haired steed beneath him. That youth salutes with fair words the children of the King of Norway, and they answered him in the same way; and while they were in conversation with one another he bound the hair of that enchanted steed to the prow of the ship of the children of the King of Norway, and the steed goes straight on, with the ship following straight behind him.

Howsoever, they searched the various seas of the world behind the steed, in that order, without its being in their power to separate the ship from the steed. They were a year, from one kalends to another, in this way, and neither blade nor edge would cut a single hair of the hair of that enchanted steed. He travelled equally swiftly by sea and by land. On a certain day as they were thus voyaging the waves, they beheld a venomous otter coming towards them, and a variety of every kind of colour on her, and her eyes flaming in her head, and a blazing ball of fire coming forth out of her mouth and nose. And when the youth beheld the venomous hound approaching him, he loosed the hair of his steed from that great ship, trusting to his extreme speed [to escape], and the venomous hound follows the horseman, and it overtook him not, and in this way they both parted from the children of the King of Norway.

And one of the sons of the King of Norway climbed upon the mast of the ship, and he cast an eye about, on the four points of the compass round him, and he saw the bulk of a land, and the make of an island far from them, and he brought his brothers those tidings, and they face the prow of the vessel with one consent towards that

---

⁶ A has "iomgala", as usual.   ⁷ Thus H. A has "cuir tosuidh"; A 25 has "corr thosaidh"; L 39 "cúrthosaicc".   ⁸ Thus H from "gluaiseas", A omits.   ⁹ Thus H from "gan" to "each".   ¹⁰ H omits. A 25 reads "on calainn a chéile".   ¹¹ A "inaidh" for "ionâ".   ¹² H reads "i gerannóig".

(¹) *Sál*, "heel", is perhaps a scribal error for *sáile*, "brine."

ḋo ċum an oileáin rin, aġur ḋo ḃaḋar rroċa uai(ċ)ne éaġraṁla ċre ċearċ-láṙ¹ an oileáin rin, aġur ḋo ḃ' iomḋa ċoraḋ apuiḋ ionċaiċṁe ar ċrannaiḃ ceann-ċroma na h-innre rin, aġur eánlaiċ éaġraṁla ann². Ir ann rin ḋo ċonncaḋar cáċair ċeann-árḋ uċċ-ḃláiċ uai[ċ]ne il-ġearaċ uaċa.

Aċċ aċá níḋ ċeana, ḋo ċuaḋar ḋo'n ḋúnaḋ rin i ġcéaḋóir aġur ḃa h-áluinn an ḋún rin re aṁarc, óir ḋo ḃaḋar ġaċ re clár ann .i. clár rion(n), clár ġorm, clár ḋearġ, clár ḋuḃ, aġur clár uaiċne, aġur ní ḟéaḋraḋ ċeanġa ḋá ġlioca no úġḋar ḋá ḟearaiġe leiċ no ċrian aoiḃnear[a] an ḋúna rin ḋ'innrin, óir ḋo ḃaḋar móráin ḋe clóċaiḃ criorċail aġur coirmoġaill aġur ḋe leaġaiḃ loġṁara na h-Aria, aġur na h-Eórra³ aġur a lán ḋe ḃraċaiḃ rróil aġur ríoḋa aġur ḋ'éaḋaiḃ uairle onóraċa ar ḃórḋaiḃ biċ-áille ir an Ríoġ-ḃruiġin rin.

Aġur ní ḃfuaraḋar neaċ beó no marḃ innċi aċċ aon ċaċ mór-áḋḃall mór-ionġanċaċ, aġur ḋo ḃí an caċ rin féin aġ ḋéanaṁ luine aġur lúċġaire ina ċimċioll, aġur ḋo ḃí cruiċ ċeól-ḃinn ċaoin-ċéaḋaċ ḋ'á rrar-ḟeinm ġo healaḋanta binn-ġoċaċ aiġe⁴, aġur eóin áille Airrice aġ cóiṁ-ḟeinm ciúil rir an ġcaoin-ċruiċ rin⁵, aġur ḋo ḃaḋar clann Ríġ na h-Ioruaiḋe ċrí la aġur ċeóra oiḋċe inr an uaral-ḃruiġin rin.

Ir annrin aḋuḃairt Coḃ mac Ríġ na h-Ioruaiḋe, "ir miċiḋ ḋúinn ċriall anoir, óir ní maiċ cóṁnuiġe ġan coṁ-ḟlaiċior⁶, aġur ir ḋoirḃ ḋoiliġ linn an ċ-imċeaċċ rin ḋo ḋéanaṁ, óir ḋá mbeiḋ⁷ aon riġ ar ċrí rannaiḃ an ḋoṁain ir ḋíol ḋúna ḋó an Ríġ-ḋún ro, aġur ir ḋoiliġe ḋúinn iná rin an ċ-imċeaċċ rin ḋo ḋéanaṁ aġur ġan níḋ éiġin ḋe rġéalaiḃ an ċaiċ ionġanċaiġ reo beiċ aġainn." A h-aiċle rin ḋo ḃeanaḋar móráin ḋe ċorċaiḃ an oileáin aġur ċánġaḋar ḋ'á luinġ, aġur ḋo ċuaḋar innċi, aġur ḋo ċaiċeaḋar aimrir ḟaḋa aġ arġnaḋ an aiġéin, aġur aġ rrar-iomraḋ na ċréan-ḃóċna⁸.

Lá éiġin ḋóiḃ aṁlaiḋ rin aġur ḋo ċonncaḋar oileán ró ionġanċaċ eile uaċa, aġur ḋo ḟeólaḋar aġaiḋ a loinġe i ḋċír

---

¹ Thus A 25. A reads "cealtar". ² H adds about the "éanlaith"; ᵱ reads "bahalain ria amorc an criochsin oir fa hiomdha bláth abhall iongantach innti, agus millsi iomorro agus burbo fiono amblátha naccrand soimheasga sin". ³ H adds "lecuis Lochlann", which is not clear. ⁴ H adds these six words. ⁵ Thus H. A reads "i gcombaighe agus i gcomhdháil ceól na cruite sin".

isle. And there were green lovely streams through the centre of
that island, and many were the ripe edible fruits upon the heavy-
headed trees of that isle, and variegated birds therein. And there
they saw a high-headed, fair-breasted, green, much-adorned mansion
(*cathair*) at a distance from them.

Howsoever, they proceeded at once to that dún, and a beautiful
dún it was to behold, for every other board in it was a white board,
a blue board, a red board, a black board, and a green board, and no
tongue, no matter how skilful, and no author, no matter how knowing,
could tell one-half or one-third of the delight of that mansion, for
there were many crystal stones and carbuncles, and precious gems of
Asia and of Europe, and many mantles of satin and of silk, and
many noble cloths of honour upon ever-fair tables in that kingly
fort.

And they found in it no one either alive or dead, except one
awful-great very-wondrous cat, and that cat was herself frolicking
round about and amusing itself, and there was a melodious gentle-
stringed harp playing expertly and musically, and handsome birds of
Africa making music in concert with that gentle harp; and the
children of the King of Norway were for three days and three nights
in that noble steading.

It was then Cod, son of the King of Norway, said : "It is time for
us to voyage now, for not good is sojourn without co-authority,(¹) yet
we are sad and sorry to thus depart, for if there were one king over
the three divisions of the world, this royal mansion were a sufficient
one for him, but we are sadder still at taking our departure thus,
without our knowing anything of the story of this wondrous cat."
After that they plucked many of the fruits of the island, and they
came to their ship and they entered it, and spent a long time sailing
the deep, and actively-rowing over the strong ocean.

Of a certain day, as they were thus, they beheld at a distance
from them(²) another very wonderful island, and they directed the

⁶ Thus H. L 39 reads "ni maith comhnuidhe gan tiagharnas". A is corrupt;
Ƿ omits.   ⁷ L 39 reads "dá mbeadh", "beith" is the usual northern
and western pronunciation of the modern "beidheadh".   ⁸ H adds the
last fourteen words.

(¹) A proverb.   (²) Literally "they saw from them."

ann, aġur do ḃí cáṫaír ċeann-árd ṗoċaír-ḃláíṫ ṗuinneóġaċ[1] ı ġceaptláp an oilcáin pin[2], aġur puapaḃap poṙġaılte an Ríoġ-ḃpuıġean pin, aġur do ċuaḃap arteaċ ınntı, aġur ní ḃpuapaḃap neaċ ınntı, aċt aon ṁacaoıh mallporġaċ ṁná do ba ċopṁúıl cpuċ aġur ḃeılḃ, ınneall aġur orḃuġaḋ ṗıp an ınnaoı do ċuıp na ġeapa pin oppa. Aġur an tan do ċonncaḃap an ınġean, do leıġ na ppapa ḃıana ḃeóp uaıċı.

Ap a h-aıċle pin po ṗıappuıġ an ınġean pġéala ḋíoḃ, aġur ċuġaḃap-pan a pġéala ṗéın ġan ımpeapán ḃí, aġur do ṗıappuıġ Coḃ pġéala ḃe'n ınġın, aġur annpın do ċuaıḃ ı ġceann pġéala ḃ'ınnpın ḋóıḃ, aġur aḃuḃaıpt: "Ríġ copónta ceapt-ḃpeıċeaċ do ḃí ı ḃtíp na ḃ̃eap ḃ̃ıonn ḃ'ap ba ċoṁ-aınm Eoċaıḋ apmıġéap mac Maıḃıon[3] aġur ní paıḃ ḃe ċloınn aıġe aċt ḃıap ınġean aṁáın, aġur níop ḃ'ıonnan máċaıp ḃo'n ḃíp ınġean pin ṗéın. Inġean Ríġ na h-Antuaıġe, an ċéaḃ ḃean do ḃí aġ Ríġ na ḃ̃eap ḃ̃ıonn, aġur ní puġ pí ḃe ċloınn pıaṁ aċt aon ınġean aṁáın, aġur ḃá mbeaċ aon pí ap ċpí pannaıḃ an ḃoṁaın ba ḃıonġṁála map ṁnaoı ḃó í, óıp ní paıḃ ına cóṁ-aımpıp ṗéın bean ba ṗeápp ḃpeaċ ḃealḃ ḃéanaṁ aġur éaġcopġ 'ná í, eaḃon, ṗeıċlınn ṁongṗúıleaċ ınġean Ríġ na ḃ̃eap ḃ̃ıonn, aınm na mná pin. Aġur a h-aıċle báıp na céaḃ-ṁná pin, ċuġ an Ríġ pin bean eıle .ı. ınġean Ríġ na Ḋpeólaınne aġur puġ an bean pin ınġean eıle ḃó aġur nı puġ níop mó, aġur ınıpe ṗéın an ınġean pin. Ḋála mo ṁáċap, ap ḃteaċt ġo típ na ḃ̃eap ḃ̃ıonn ḃí, ċuġ puaċ aġur ṗíop-ṁıopġap ḃ'ṗeıċlınn ṁongṗúılıġ .ı. ḃ'á leıp-ınġın,[4] aġur do ḃpeuġ[5] léıċe do ṗnám ap eap do ḃí láıṁ leıp an ġcáıċpıġ í,..ı. eap ḃomaıne[6] aınm an eapa, aġur ıap n-a ṗáġaıl ap an uıpġe í, ımpeap ḃpaoıḃeaċt uıppı, aġur[7] cuıpeap ṗó ġeapaıḃ í ḃeıċ bliaḃaın 'na cat aġur bliaḃaın 'na h-eala[8] aġur bliaḃaın 'na ḃoḃap-ċú[9] nıṁe. Aġur bí pí lá ġaċa bliaḃna 'na cpuċ ṗéın, aġur

---

[1] Thus H. A reads "clogasach uchtbhláith uineoga". [2] A adds "agus ni lamhdis sluagh no sochaidh da h-iomdheoin". [3] Thus A. H reads "armdearg mac Scadna Suiligh mac Lughaidh Lamhfhada"! F reads "mac namhadon". L 39 omits. [4] The last twenty-six words are from H, whose reading I prefer here to that of A. [5] Thus H. A reads "rug". [6] H reads "bobhuinne"; F "bobuinne". [7] The last twelve words are from H. [8] H reads "halainn". [9] H inflects, "dobharchoin".

prow of their vessel towards its land; and there was a high-headed, flower-bordered,([1]) windowed *cathair* or mansion in the very centre of that island, and they found that royal mansion open, and they went into it, and no one did they find in it except one slow-eyed([2]) damsel of a woman, who, in shape and form, mien and make, was like to the woman who had put the *geasa* upon them, and when they beheld the girl she shed desperate showers of tears.

Thereafter, the damsel asked them their news, and they gave her their own news without disputing; and Cod asked tidings from the girl, and thereupon she began to tell them her story, and said: "A crowned king of righteous judgments there was in the Land of the White Men, whose name was Eochaidh [Yohy] the Sharp-armed, son of Maidin, and he had no children except two daughters only, and even those two daughters had not the same mother. The daughter of the King of Antuaigh was the first wife that the King of the White Men had, but she never bore any children except one daughter only; and if there were to be a single king over the three divisions of the world she were his match, of a wife; for there was not in her own time a woman of better form, beauty, make, and appearance than she; Feithlinn [Faylin], the bright-eyed,([3]) the daughter of the King of the White Men, was that woman's name. And after the death of that first wife this king took another one, the daughter of the King of Dreólann, and that woman bore him another daughter, and bore no more, and I myself am that daughter. As for my mother, upon her coming to the country of the White Men, she conceived a hatred and a real enmity against bright-eyed Feithlinn, that is, her step-daughter, and she enticed her with her to swim by a waterfall that was near the mansion—Eas Bomaine is the name of the water-fall—and on her getting her in the water she works enchantment on her, and puts her under *geasa* to be a year a cat, and a year a swan, and a year a venomous otter. And she is for one day in every year,

---

([1]) I take *fochair* to be the same as *eochair*, "border". "Bláith" does not necessarily mean "flower", but may mean "smoothness" or sometimes even "fame", as in the proverb "is buaine bládh [fame] 'na saoghal".

([2]) A common epithet in Irish, almost always applied, however, to a married woman in contradistinction to the "brisk eye" of a girl; hence it seems here misplaced.

([3]) Could "mongshúileach" mean "with long eyelashes"?

§ıö bé peap do luıᵹpeaö léı an can ba cac í, pᵹaoılpeaö
a ᵹcapa öí, aᵹup nı h-ıon-luaıöce deılö ban an doṁaın¹ aᵹ
péaċaın deılö na h-ınᵹıne pın," aᵹup aöubaıpc² ᵹup b' í pın
do ċonncadap 'na cac ınp an oıleán pın ᵹan aṁpap, aᵹup
"Saop-ınnıp" aınm na h-ınnpe pın péın, aᵹup "cac na Saop-
ınnpe" ᵹoıpċeap dı-pe do ᵹpeap.

Do labaıp an ınᵹean apíp aᵹup ıp eaö aöubaıpc, "Ip
mıpe an ınᵹean eıle do bí aᵹ Ríᵹ na bFeap bFıonn, aᵹup
do ᵹabaö lá aonaıᵹ aᵹup ápd-oıpeaċcaıp leıp an Ríᵹ, aᵹup
do ṗuıᵹ an Ríᵹ ı ᵹcáċaoıp áluınn ópöa ı ᵹceapcláp na
pluaᵹ ıomapcaċ pın, aᵹup do bí bpeaċa³ píp-ᵹlıoca píp-eólaċa
da bpoıllpıuᵹaö döıb aᵹup do eáċ ı ᵹcoıċċınne, an uaıp pın.
Sıolla b'á dcuᵹadap na plóıᵹ ıomapcaċ[a]⁴ pın cap muıp aᵹup
cap móp-ṗaıpᵹe do ċonncadap lonᵹ luċcmap lán-aıöpeaċ aᵹ
ceaċc ı dcíp⁵ ı ᵹcuan na cáċpaċ pın aᵹup an can do ṗíleadap
ıomad plóıᵹ aᵹup poċaıöe do ċeaċc aıpdı, ní ċáınıᵹ aċc
pomóp⁶ úp-ᵹpánda ıl-ṗıapcaċ, aᵹup ba öuıöe 'ná ᵹual poıleaċ
ap na báċaö ı n-uıpᵹe ṗuap oıᵹpeaċa ᵹaċ alc aᵹup ᵹaċ
aᵹaıö de 'n ṗeap ṁóp pın, aᵹup ní paıb ᵹeal dé aċc [a] öá
ṗúıl, aᵹup ba ᵹıle ıad 'ná pneaċca aon-oıöċe, aᵹup beapc de
ċpoıcnıö pıaö-ṁaol aᵹup peapbóᵹ uıme, aᵹup do leıᵹ 'na paon
pó-peaċa cpíd na plóıᵹcıb é, aᵹup do baöup-pa ı ᵹcáċaoıp óıp
óıp-loıpᵹe pan aonaċ an uaıp pın, ı bpoċaıp m'aċap, aᵹup ní
oıpeapaṁ nó cóṁnuıöe⁷ do pınne an c-óᵹlaċ móp pın no ᵹup
ċuıp⁸ a öá láṁ am' ċımcıoll, aᵹup ᵹup ċuıp ap a ᵹualaınn ᵹo
h-úıp-éadcpom mé, aᵹup ċuᵹ aᵹaıö ap aıp ċum a loınᵹe.
Aᵹup map do ċonnaıpc an c-aonaċ pın ba náıp [leo] ó, aᵹup
cíoöcpáċc nodap ṗan peap ıomcap[ċ]a aıpm do na h-ıolṁaoınıb
[ıol-buıönıb] do babap ıp an báıl pın náp éıpᵹıö ᵹo h-aċlaṁ
ım-éapᵹa aᵹup náp lean eıpean, aᵹup ba öíoṁaoın döıb, óıp
nı puᵹpac aıp ᵹo ndeaċaıö b'á luınᵹ aᵹup ċuᵹ a copaċ do
ṁuıp aᵹup a deıpeaö do ċíp, aᵹup peólap poıṁe ᵹaċa nöípeaċ

---

¹ Thus II.   A reads "ni haon measadh naith*ne* deilbh mná san domhan", which
seems corrupt.   ² P reads "do ráidseat c. r. n. hIor. daitheasg aenfir gur be
an cat", etc.   ³ Thus H. A has "briathra".   ⁴ A reads
"niomarcach"; the others omit. I have often heard "niomarcaidh" used for
"iomarcaidh".   ⁵ H reads "ag soitheadh an chuain".   ⁶ H has
"fomhoir"; L 39 has "foghmhar".   ⁷ Thus L 39; but A reads

in her own shape, and whatever man would be beside her when she is a cat, would loose her *geasa* off her ; and the beauty of the women of the world is not worth mentioning on beholding that damsel's beauty " ; and she said that beyond doubt it was she they beheld as a cat upon that island, and Free Island is the name of that island itself, and she is always called the cat of Free Island.

The girl spoke again, and 'twas what she said : " I am the other daughter that the King of the White Men had, and a day for a fair and for a great assembly was appointed by the king, and he sat on his splendid golden throne in the very midst of those numerous hosts ; and truly-prudent, truly-wise judgments were being exhibited to them and to all in common at that time. Of a glance that those numerous hosts gave over the sea and great ocean, they beheld a capacious full-fine bark coming to land in the city's harbour, and when they thought that many warriors and people would come out of her, there came not but one fearful-ugly monstrous Fomor,([1]) and blacker than a coal of sally([2]) drowned in cold iced water was every joint and feature of that great man, and there was nothing of him white but his two eyes, and they were whiter than the snow of one night, and there was a garment of skins of hornless deer and roebuck about him, and he launched himself in a racing-rush through the hosts, and I was on a golden-gilt throne in the assembly at that time, close to my father, and neither halt nor stop did the great warrior make until he threw his two hands round about me and set me lightly on his shoulder, and faced back for his ship. And when the assemblage beheld that, they were shamed ; howsoever never a man who carried weapon of the many bands who were in that assembly but rose up quickly and speedily and followed him ; but vain it was for them, for they never overtook him until he went aboard his bark, and gave its prow to sea and its stern to land, and he sails away to this island, and he has me ever since ; and I have never seen of the people of the

---

"Toirneamh no tairisim ". H omits.   ᴮ H reads "iadhastar".

([1]) I do not like to render this word "Fomor" by "giant", which is usually "athach", or "fathach", so I have retained it in the translation. It seems to mean here nearly the same as "fathach", "giant".   ([2]) Sally, or sallow charcoal, is often used by the Irish, amongst other things, for bringing back the hair on an animal where it has been rubbed off.

F

ġuſ an oileán ſo, aġuſ aċáim-ſe aiġe ó fin a leiċ. Aġuſ ni
facaſ ꝺo ḃaoiniḃ an ꝺoṁain an eċᵬin aċá[im] ſunn aċᵬ ſiḃ-ſe
aṁáin, aġuſ an lá ċuġ loiſ mó ꝺo ġaḃaſ aġ caſſaiṅġ m'fuilᵬ
aġuſ m'ſionnſaḋ, aġuſ an ᵬan ꝺo ċonnaiſc an ſomóſ ſíoſ-
ġſánna ſin, aꝺuḃaiſᵬ liom-ſa meanmna maiᵬ ꝺo ḃeiᵬ aġam
aġuſ naċ ſaiḃ aᵬċuingiḋ aſ ḃiᵬ ꝺo iaſſſainn aiſ naċ
ꝺᵬiúḃſaḋ ſé ꝺam, aġuſ iſ ó aᵬċuinġe ꝺo iaſſaſ aiſ ġan
millceaḋ ꝺo ḃéanaṁ oſm ġo ceann bliaḋna, aġuſ aᵬáim aiġe
le bliaḋain ġuſ a[n] lá amáſaċ¹: aġuſ a ċáiſḃe ġſáḃaċ[a],"
aſ ſí, "ꝺéanaiḃ-ſe imᵬeaċᵬ ġo luaᵬ ó'n ḃſeaſ móſ, óiſ ní
ᵬéiꝺ cſéan no cſuaġ ġan báſuġaḋ uaiḃ²."

Iſ annſin aꝺuḃaiſᵬ Coḃ naċ nġeaḃaḋ ſé óſ na cſuinne
aġuſ ġan anṁain ſe cuaſaſġḃáil an fiſ móiſ ſin. Iſ ġeaſſ
ꝺo ḃáꝺaſ a h-aiᵬle an ċóṁſáḋa ſin ġo ḃſacaꝺaſ an ſomóſ
ſíoſġſánꝺa ċuca, aġuſ loṅġ im-ſeaṁaſ iaſnuiḋe ina láiṁ
ċioſcla ċiaſꝺuiḃ, ġo ſeaċᵬ ſleaſaiḃ uiſſi, aġuſ ſaoḃaſ ſġeine-
ḃeaſſᵬa³ aſ ġaċ ſlioſ ꝺíoḃ ſin, ſeaċᵬ ſlaḃſaiḋe oſ cionn na
ſiġ-luiſġe ſin, aġuſ uḃall-ṁeall iaſainn aſ ġaċ ſlaḃſaḋ ꝺíoḃ
ġo ſo-ḃealġaiḃ uime, aġuſ níoſ fáġḃaiġ ſí ſuaᵬ⁴ no ſiᵬeiḃe
allᵬa no aſſaċᵬ éiġcéille i ġcſeiġ no i ġcuaiſ no i ġcaſſaiġ
no i n-inbeaſ náſ ꝺúiſiġ ſé le ſuaim na ſſíoṁ-luiſġe ſin.
Aġuſ an ᵬan ꝺo ċonnaiſc an ſeaſ móſ clann Ríġ na
h-Ioſuaiḋe ꝺo ſinne ġloṁaſ ġaſḃ ġáiſe⁵ ionnuſ ġo ḃſéaꝺſaiḋe
a ionaᵬaſ⁶ uile ꝺ'áiſeaṁ aſ ṁéaꝺ an foſġailce ċuġ ſé aſ a
ḃéal⁷. Cíoꝺᵬſaċᵬ ċuġ an inġean cſuᵬ maiᵬ aſ éaġcſuᵬ, aġuſ
maiſe aſ ṁi-ṁaiſe aṅ ſin, ſe h-uaṁan aġuſ ſe h-imeaġla na
n-óġ niaṁ-ċſoᵬaċ ſin ꝺo ċuᵬim ſiſ an ḃſomóſ ḃſíoſġſánna⁸.
Iſ aṅ ſin ꝺo ſáiḃ Coḃ mac Ríġ na h-Ioſuaiḋe, "náſ ba ṁaiᵬ
aġuſ náſ ba ſoiſḃ an ſaoġal ꝺuiᵬ, aġuſ náſ ba ſoſ-fáilᵬeaċ
ceaċ niṁe no ᵬalṁan ſóṁaꝺ no ꝺo ḃiaiḃ ꝺuiᵬ a ſaᵬaiġ
ġſánꝺa" aſ ſé. Iſ annſin ꝺ'éiſiġ an bſaᵬ ᵬaſ bſuaċ⁹ aġuſ

---

¹ The last one hundred and forty-eight words are from H, which reads "eiseiomh"
and "taraing", for which I have substituted "eisean" and "tarraing" in the text.
A and the other mss. omit her request and the giant's promise. The word "fomór"
is very variously spelt even in the same ms., as "fomór", "fomhór", "fómhair",
"foghmor", and "foghmhor". I have kept to the first form for the sake of
uniformity.   ² H "Is gearr go ttuibhradh timgibh(?) saoghuil dhíbh."
³ Thus I₁. A has "bith aile saoir", which I do not understand.   ⁴ H has

world, all the time that I am here, but you alone. And the day he took me with him I began tearing my tresses and my hair, and when the truly hideous Fomor beheld that, he told me to have good courage, and that there was no petition I would ask of him that he would not grant me; and the petition I asked of him was to do me no harm until the end of a year, and he has me for a year all but to-morrow; and, beloved friends," said she, "depart ye quickly from the Great Man, for neither the powerful nor the puny escape from him without death."

It was then Cod said that he would not take the gold of the world and not wait for tidings of that Great Man. Short time they were after this discourse, until they beheld the hideous Fomor approaching them, and a thick iron club in his circular jet-black hand, with seven sides upon it, and an edge like a razor upon every side, seven chains above that great staff,(¹) and an iron apple-knob on every chain of them, with spikelets round about, and he never left horror or wild creature or senseless spectre in crag or hollow or rock or river-mouth that he did not rouse with the noise of that huge club. And when the Great Man beheld the children of the King of Norway he gave a coarse yell of laughter, so that it was possible to inspect(²) the whole of his inside, with all the opening that he gave his mouth. The girl, however, thereupon changed shapeliness for misshape, and loveliness for unloveliness, with horror, and with fear of those bright-formed youths falling by the awful Fomor. Then spake Cod, son of the King of Norway : " May life be neither good nor pleasant to you, and may the house neither of heaven nor of earth give welcome either before or behind you, hideous giant," said he. It was then arose the mantle

---

" uath ", " athaide ", and " arracht ". Ᵽ has "feithide no ealta no arocht ". A has " aireachta ". H " Ionnus go bhfaicfidh an pútato is lugh do bheith ar íoctur a ghuile ".   ⁵ Thus H. A has " glaodh mór garbh ionamhail gháire ". ⁶ Ᵽ has "iochtar ainathar ". A has " innichir ".   ⁷ H reads " ar a mhant chraos móradhbhal ".   ⁸ The last twenty-seven words are from H.   ⁹ Thus Ᵽ and L. H reads " brat tair bhruachas ". A 25 reads " brathair buadhach ". A reads " brathair bruacha ".

(¹) Literally " King-staff ". " Righ " is often used even to this day as a mere intensitive, and need not always be translated " king " or " royal ". (²) Literally " count ".

an cuile gan cráġaḋ¹ agus an buinne gan bpireaḋ agus an
cé naċ ocuġ aon croiġ ar ġcúl piaṁ re h-uaċaḋ no re
h-iomaḋ i ġcaċ go i ġcóṁlainn piaṁ .i. Coḃ mac Ríġ na
h-Ioruaiḋe, i ġcoinne agus i ġcóṁḋáil an ḟaċaiġ². Ir annrin
ḃo cromaḋ na pleaġa ceann-ġéara caċa eatorra le buirbe
an cóṁ-ḃuailte, gur lúbaḋ na crainn pir na rgiaċaiḃ, agus
ḃo ḃéiceaḋar na pirmaminte re h-ḋòḃal [a] n-im-ḃuailte, gur
lúbaḋar agus gur ġearraḋar³ na lúiṫreaċa ḋ'á luaċ-ġearraḋ
agus gur leaḃraḋ na cinn caċa ḋe na craoireaċaiḃ⁴, agus
gur h-aiṁréiḋeaḋ a ḃfuilt ḋe na lannaiḃ, agus gur ḃallaḋ
a rúile leir na linnciḃ pola plannruaiḋe⁵ ag cuicim go
porleaċan iḋir an ḋiar ġairgiḋeaċ rin, agus ni ḋearna[ḋ] po'n
TRAOI⁶ no po ċaċ caċarḋa, cóṁrac ḋeire ḋeaġlaoḋ ba ḟearr
'ná cóṁrac na ḋeire ḋeaġ-laoḋ ro. Iar rin ḟineaḋar na ḃóiḋe
riġne réiḋe car taoḃaiḃ agus car corraiḃ a ċéile, gur ṁaoiḃ
loċ tobar ḃílionna pó n-a ġcoraiḃ le peaḃar na ġleice agus
na corruiġeaċt[a] ḋo ḃaḋar ḋ'á ḋéanaṁ : agus ni h-annro
ḋo ḃeónaiġ an ḟír-Ḋia por-órḋa⁷ báir no oiḋe ṁic Ríġ na
h-Ioruaiḋe, agus, ó naċ ann, ċuġ ré raoḃ-ċor raoḃ-ċaṁ⁸ ḋo'n
ḃraċaḋ, gur ċuir na ceiṫre gaḃla go pó ċlirce i h-áirḋe pair,
agus ḋo laḃair an t-óglac mór agus ir eaḋ aḋuḃairc:
" Toraḋ ḋo ġaile agus ḋo ġairġe orc a ṁic Ríġ na h-Ioruaiḋe
i mbéal ruaġ agus reanċuiḃ agus luċt léiġte liag agus
leaḃar, agus ná cuir mé péin cum báir."

"Luiġim-re i ḃfiaḋnuire m'arm," ar Coḃ, "ḋá ocuġraiḋe⁹ ór
na cruinne ḋam naċ geaḃainn é agus gan ḋo ceann ḋo
ḃuainc ḋíoc," agus ḋo ċarraing a lann líoṁċa leaḃarċa, ar
a ċruaill ċirim tairgċe agus ḋo ḃuail a ġcóṁrac a ċinn¹⁰
agus ṁuinéil é, gur ċeilg a ċeann ḋ'á ċolainn ḋe'n ḃéim rin.
Agus ċáinig ḋo'[n] mbruiġin iaraṁ, agus ċuġ lorg an ḟir
móir leir, agus leigear ar lár í, i ḃfiaḋnuire na h-inġine, agus·

---

¹ Thus P. H has "traothughadh". A "traoithe". ² H has "an
torathar fomhordha". ³ A reads "gairidar" and "luathgairadh"; the
others omit. I read "lúbadar" for "lúbadh". ⁴ Thus A 25; but
A has "na ceann acu tres na cathbhairibh". ⁵ Thus H 25. A reads
"falruaide". ⁶ A adds "no fathanna"(?). P omits part of this
description. ⁷ A reads "forgadh"(?). ⁸ A 25 reads "taobhchor
taobhcham". ⁹ A has "da ttucigh". A 25 "da ttugthadh"; the

beyond border,(¹) and the flood without ebb, and the torrent without breaking, the man who never gave back one single foot before few or before many, in battle or in conflict, Cod, son of the King of Norway, to meet and oppose the giant. It was then the sharp-headed spears of battle were couched between them for the furiousness of the mutual striking, so that the hafts were bent against the shields, and the firmament roared with the awfulness of the smiting, so that they cut with quick-cutting their breastplates, and the battle heads were beaten off the javelins, and their locks were disordered by the blades, and their eyes were blinded with the pools of crimson blood falling copiously between those two heroes : and there was not performed at Troy, or in the *Cath Cathardha*,(²) a combat of two good heroes better than the combat of those two good heroes. After that they stretched their tough smooth hands across one another's sides and bodies, until a well-lake of a flood out-burst beneath their feet, with the excellency of the struggle and the wrestling they were making. But it was not here that the very-golden true-God permitted the death or the tragic-end of the son of the King of Norway; and, since it was not, he gave the giant a fierce twist, fiercely crooked, so that he sent the four forks(³) very cleverly over him, and the Great Youth spake, and 'twas what he said : " The fruits of your vigour and valour to you, son of the King of Norway, in the mouths 'of sages and shanachies and readers of flags(⁴) and books, and do not put myself to death."

" I swear in the presence of my weapons,"(⁵) said Cod, "if the gold of the world were to be given me that I would not accept it, if I were not to take the head off you," and he drew his polished smiting blade out of its dry protecting-sheath, and he struck him at the joining of the head and the neck, so that of that stroke he cast his head from his body. And after this he came to the palace and brought the club of the Great Man with him, and he lays it on the

---

others omit.   ¹⁰ A has "cheann". A 25 "cheainn"; the others omit.

(¹) This seems corrupt.   (²) I think that this is the Irish name for the battle of Pharsalia.   (³) This apparently means that he threw him on his back with his arms and legs in the air.   (⁴) This is an evident allusion to Ogams. It occurs again in the version of "Deirdre" which I published in the "Z. für Celt. Phil.", II. 1, p. 142.   (⁵) This expression also occurs in the "Deirdre" story. Naoise swears to her, "i bhfiadhnuise a arm".

ⅾo ráiḋ ʃe n-a ḋearḃráiṫriḃ a aiɼm ⅾo ᵹaḃáil uaiḋ[1], aᵹuʃ ⅾo ʃinne an laoiḋ :—

"ᵹaḃ na h-aiɼm-ʃe ann ⅾo ḋoɼn
A ṁic Ioɼuaiḋ na n-óɼlann,
ᵹo ḃʃaicim iaⅾ-ʃan ᵹo beaċt
Mo cɼeaċta uile ó'n ḃʃaiṫeaċ.

"Iʃ miʃe Coⅾ mac an ɼíoᵹ
ᵹe tá m'ḟuil na coḃaiɼ cɼíon,
Ⅾo caoinɼiḋe ʃinne ᵹan ʃuaċ
I ᵹcɼíoċaiḃ caoiṁe Ioɼuaiḋ.'

"Cuiɼiḋ luiḃe le mo óneaɼ
Má ʃeaɼɼbe liḃ mo leiᵹeaɼ,
Mo óneaḋa[2] ʃul ʃeaɼʃaɼ m'ḟuil
Aɼ ᵹɼaḋ ḃuɼ n-inᵹ ᵹaḃaiᵹ."[3]

A h-aiċle na laoiḋ ʃin ⅾo cuiɼeaḋ luiḃe íce aᵹuʃ léiᵹiʃ i ᵹcneáḋaiḃ aᵹuʃ a ᵹcɼéactaiḃ mio Ríᵹ na h-Ioɼuaiḋe, aᵹuʃ ⅾo ḃaḃaɼ tɼí lá aᵹuʃ teóɼa oiḋċe inɼ an ḃúnaḋ ʃin, aᵹuʃ iaⅾ aᵹ iomɼáḋ aɼ ċat na Saoɼ-innʃe ⅾe ᵹnáċ. Óiɼ ba ḋeiṁin ɼiu ᵹuɼab í an inᵹean ⅾo ċuiɼ iaⅾ ʃéin ʃo ʃeaɼaiḃ ⅾo ḃí ann, i ᵹcɼuċ caic. ᵹiḃeaḋ iɼ aiɼ ⅾo ċinnɼeat, an lonᵹ ⅾo ḃi aᵹ an ḃɼomóɼ ⅾo ċuɼ le hinᵹin Ríᵹ na ḃɼeaɼ ḃʃionn ᵹo [a] h-aċaɼⅾa ʃéin. Aᵹuʃ cɼíoċnuiᵹċeaɼ an ċóṁaiɼle ʃin leó. Aᵹuʃ iaɼ ᵹceileaḃɼaḋ ⅾo'n inᵹin ⅾóiḃ ᵹaḃaiⅾ aᵹ aɼᵹnaṁ[4] na ɼɼuċ-ʃaiɼɼᵹe aᵹuʃ aᵹ caiɼⅾeall na ⅾtonn ⅾtiuᵹ-ɼuaḋ aɼ ʃeaḋ

---

[1] The last twenty words are added from H, but I change "dearbhráithre" and "uadh" into "dearbhráithribh" and "uaidh."

[2] H reads— "M'arma sul silfeas mfuil."

A 25 reads—

"Mo chneadha sul fo thiucfas mfuil
Ar ghrádh bhur uinnia amaca."

[3] H reads—

"Gabhaidh na h-airm as mo láimh
A chlann Ioruaidbe gan miobháigh,
Go bfaicidh sibh um o seach
Créacht mo chuirp on aitheach.

"Caoinfighear Cod mac an righ
Ge ta mfhuil na chubhar críon
Re mor nainnire go mbuaidhe
I gcriochaibh caoimhe Ioruadhe."

ground before the girl, and told his brothers to take from him his weapons, and he made the lay :—

> " Take from me my arms, I práy,
> Sons of the King of Nórway.
> Let me see (my blood is scánt)
> The wounds made by the gíant.([1])

> " I am Cod, son of the king,
> Although my blood is [now] a withered foam,
> We would be lamented without hatred
> In the gentle lands of Norway.

> " Set ye herbs to my skin
> If ye desire to cure me,
> My hurts, before my blood ebbs away,
> For the love of your generosity, attend to."

After that lay, herbs of balm and healing were put into his hurts and wounds. And they were three days and three nights in that palace, and they discoursing constantly about the cat of the Freo Island, for they were certain that it was the girl who placed themselves under *geasa* who was in it, in the shape of a cat. Howsoever the thing they resolved on was, to send the ship that the Fomor had, with the daughter of the King of the White Men, to [take her] to her own patrimony. And that plan is carried out by them. And after bidding farewell to the maiden, they proceed to voyage over the stream-of-the-sea, and to journey through the thick-red waves for five

---

I read " Ioruaidh' " for " Ioruaidhe " in the second line to make it scan. L reads the third and fourth lines thus—

> " Go bhfághthar amuigh 's amach
> Mo chreachta uile o'n atach."

and the seventh and eighth—

> " Caoinfear sinne go nuadh
> A ccríochaibh áille na hiorruaidhe."

⁴ The last fifty-three words are from H, which gives the passage more fully than A ; but I have changed " ba dhéin" to "féin", for the sake of uniformity.

([1]) Literally, " Take these weapons in thy hand, | Son of Norway of the golden blades, | until I view them exactly | all my wounds from the giant." The translation of this verse in the text is in the metre of the original " Deibhidh ", without observance of alliteration. For an explanation of this metre see my " Literary History of Ireland ", p. 483.

cúiġ mbliaḋan¹ ḃ'á n-aimrir, aġ iarraiḋ na Saor-innre, aġur ní ḃruaraḋar. Aġur lá éiġin ḃóiḃ mar rin aġur iaḋ aġ óirceaċc le roġail² an ċuain ċainciġ ċúḃarḃáin, ḃo ċonncaḋar lonġ luċcṁar lán-aiḋḃreaċ ġo reólcaiḃ iomḋa eχaiṁla ḃ'á n-ionnraiḋe, aġur aon óġlaċ ríoḃġa³ porġ-leaċan calma curaca croiḋeaṁail i ġcor-ċoraiġ na luinġe rin, aġur ir aṁlaiḋ ḃo ḃí an c-óġlaċ-ran aġur mion óir ór-loirġe ro n-a ċeann, aġur corrán ḃ'iarann im-riġin ina láiṁ láiḋir luaċ-ġoṁaiġ. Cioḋcráċc ar noruḋ a n-aċroġur ḃo ċloinn Ríġ na h-loruaiḋe óḋ, ríncar an láiṁ ġur an loinġ a raḃaḋar, aġur cuircar an corrán uirri ġo h-aċlaṁ úrmaircaċ aġur cóġḃar i n-áirḃe ar an ḃrairrġe í⁴, aġur ċuġ aġaiḋ inr na h-iol-ṁaraiḃ : aġur ir é óġlaċ ḃo ḃí annrin .i. an Macaoṁ Mór mac Ríġ na Sorċa, aġur ir é áḋḃar rá raiḃ ré ḃóiḃ⁵ ġur le Ríġ na h-loruaiḋe ḃo ċuic Ríġ na Sorċa i ġcaċ eaċrac an cSroċa Ḋeirġ⁶ roiṁe rin.

Ċuġaḋar Clann Ríġ na h-loruaiḋe a ḃerí cloiḋṁċe amaċ aġur ḃuaileaḋar crí ḃuille ġaċ rear ḃíoḃ i ġcrann-reóil luinġe an ṗir ṁóir, ġur ġearraḋar an crann i ġceaḃóir, ionnur ġur ċuic an lonġ ċum an cráile ṗearḃ-ruaiḋ arír. Ir annrin aḋuḃairc an Macaoṁ Mór, "Mo ċeann rá ḃur mbeiċ annrin a ċlann Ríġ na h-loruaiḋe," ar ré, "ḃá nġeaḃaḋ riḃ cóṁrac aoinṗir uaim." "Ġeoḃam ġo ḃeiṁin," ar Coḃ, "óir ní ṗaicriḋ aon ḃuine rinn ġo bráċ aġ cuarġain aoinṗir aṁáin." Aġur ċuġ Coḃ aġur an ġairġiḋeaċ ḃá rġiaċ rġiaṁḋa rġoċḋearġ ḃreac buan-licreaċ, aġur ḃá ċloiḃeaṁ coṁ-ṗaḋa cóiṁ-ġéara ceirḃeaṁla, ḃ'á n-ionnraiḋe, aġur ḃo ċóṁraic riaḋ ar an láċair rin, aġur ba ḃuan-áiḃḃéil⁸ barluaċ béim-láiḋir cóṁrac na ḃeire ḃeaġ-laoċ rin, ġo ḃcuġ an Macaoṁ Mór crí croiġċe ar a ċúl iran cóṁrac rin, ar ġclaoċlóḃ croċa ḃeilḃe aġur céaḋraḋ óḋ. Ir annrin ḃo

---

¹ II omits this. ² P "re cíorgoil na ccuan cciomhasghorm". L has
"re ciorghuile an chuain". A 25 has "re fodhail ghuirm". ³ This is
the usual pronunciation of "ríoghdha". P has "a ccuir thosaigh na *leabhar loinge sin*". A "a ccuir thochta". ⁴ The last thirty-two words are from
H, which gives the sense best. ⁵ P "adhbhar fa raibhe doibh". H omits
this whole passage. The idiom is an unusual one. ⁶ A 25 reads "agcath
catharga na traoithe deirge". ⁷ The last forty-three words are

years of their time, seeking the Free Island, and they found it not. Of a certain day that they were thus, and they listening to the noises of the talkative white-foamed sea, they beheld a laden full-fair bark with many variegated sails coming towards them, and a single, royal, broad-eyed, valiant, valorous, vigorous([1]) youth in the prow of that ship, and this is how that youth was : he had a gold-gilt diadem upon his head, and a sickle of thick iron in his strong, swift-wounding hand. However, on his approaching near to the children of the King of Norway, he stretches his hand towards the ship in which they were, and puts forth his sickle, readily and boldly, and lifts the ship on high out of the sea, and faced for the multiple waters. And the youth who was there was the Macaomh([2]) Mór, the son of the King of Sorcha, and the reason he went for them was that it was by the King of Norway the King of Sorcha fell before that, in the battle of the city of the Red Stream.

The children of the King of Norway drew forth their three swords, and smote three blows, each man of them, on the sail-mast of the Great Man's ship, so that they cut the mast upon the spot, and the ship fell off again to the bitter red brine. Then said the Great Macaomh : " My joy it is, ye to be there, sons of the King of Norway," said he, " if ye would accept single combat from me." " Indeed we will accept it," said Cod, " for no one shall ever see us smiting a single man [together]." Then Cod and the Champion brought against one another two handsome flower-red, speckled, last-ingly-lettered shields, and two highly-wrought swords, of like length and sharpness, and they fought upon the spot. And constant-awful palm-quick stroke-strong was the combat of those two good heroes, until the Great Macaomh gave three steps backwards in that battle, his form, appearance, and senses being changed [with fear]. It was

---

from Ƿ and L.   A and A 25 omit them.   [8] A has " buanmall ".

  ([1]) Literally " hearty ".   ([2]) Pronounced " mokkave " ; it often occurs in the romantic tales, but seldom outside of them.   It seems to often mean a mysterious unknown youth of a particular age, and I think also of illustrious birth.   ([3]) Literally " the reason that he was for them," a curious and most uncommon idiom in Irish.

poillriġcaꝺ¹ ꝺo'n liláinaċ (.i. oiꝺe iiiic Ríġ na Sorċa), a ꝺalca ꝺo ḃeiċ inr an Ġiʒcan, map rin. i. Mac Ríġ na Sorċa, aʒur ꝺo ḃ'ó an Manaċ rin ṗéin² ṗear ba ṁó ꝺoilḃċe ꝺraoiʒeaċca ꝺ'á ꝺcáiniʒ ina ċoṁ-aimrir ṗéin⁹, aʒur ċuʒ liaʒ ceiċir-ḃeannaċ caorċainn⁴ ċuiʒe, aʒur ꝺo ċuaiꝺ uirri, aʒur ꝺo ꝺiriʒ le na ċúṁaċc ꝺraoiʒeaċca i ḃṗriéiḃ na ṗirmancí, aʒur ꝺo ċuir ceó ꝺorċa ꝺraoiʒeaċca cimċioll luinʒe an Iilacaoiṁ Iilóir, no ʒur ʒoiꝺ an Manaċ a ꝺalca leir crer an ceó nꝺuaiḃreaꝺ nꝺorċa rin, aʒur ar rʒaoileaꝺ ꝺo'n ꝺoḃar-ċeó ꝺraoiʒeaċca rin uaċa, ṗuaraꝺar Clann Ríġ na h-Iopuaiꝺe an lonʒ ṗollaiṁ. A h-aiċle an Iilacaoiṁ Iilóir ꝺ'imċeaċc uaċa ba h-im-ṗníomaċ aċ-cuirreaċ Clann Ríġ na h-Iopuaiꝺe, óir níor ʒnác leó a ʒcéile cóṁraic leiʒin uaċa ʒan ḃáruʒaꝺ. Ir annrin riarruiʒear Coꝺ ḃ'á ḃráiċriḃ créaꝺ an ċóṁairle ꝺo ꝺéan[ṗ]aꝺaoir. Ꝺubhraꝺar-ran an cSaor-innir ꝺ'iarraiꝺ real eilc. "Ní h-í rin mo ċóṁairle ṗéin ꝺaoiḃ," ar Coꝺ, "aċc ꝺul ʒo crioċaiꝺ na Sorċa aʒur rlóiʒ na h-Iopuaiꝺe ꝺo ḃreiċ linn, aʒur caċ ꝺo ċaḃairc ꝺo'n Iilacaoiṁ Mór, óir ir ꝺeiṁin liom ʒurab é ꝺo ċáiniʒ ꝺo ꝺíoʒailc marḃċa [a] aċar orrainn-ne, aʒur ni ba ruaiṁneaċ ʒo ꝺcuʒam iarraiꝺ air arír⁵." Ꝺo ṁolaꝺar-ran an ċóṁairle.

Ir ann rin ꝺo ceanʒlaꝺar Clañ Ríġ na h-Iopuaiꝺe lonʒ an ṗir ṁóir ꝺo rciúr a luinʒe ṗéin, aʒur ꝺo ṗeólaꝺar a h-aʒaiꝺ car ꝺrom-ċla ʒaċa ꝺoṁan-ṗairrʒe aʒur ní h-aiċrircear rʒéalaiꝺeaċc orra ʒur ʒaḃaꝺar cuan aʒur calaꝺ-ṗorc i ʒcrioċaiꝺ cré-ʒlan[a] cnuar-ċorċaċa ʒlan-áilne na h-Iopuaiꝺe, aʒur ranʒaꝺar ʒo ꝺún a n-aċar ṗéin an oiꝺċe rin. Aʒur ꝺo ḃaꝺar 'na n-aoiꝺeaċaiḃ⁶ ann, aʒur níor canaꝺ ceól no oirriꝺe no ealaꝺan ꝺóiḃ an oiꝺċe rin, aċc aʒ éirceaċc re rʒéalaiꝺ na ʒcuraꝺ ṗéiṁ-ráiꝺce rin ó ċúr ʒo ꝺeiriʒ.

Aʒur ar na ṁáraċ cuireaꝺ ṗeara aʒur ceaċca uaċa ar ṁaiċiḃ na h-Iopuaiꝺe, aʒur ċuʒaꝺar a ḃṗilꝺe aʒur a ḃṗal-raṁna ċuca, aʒur ċuaꝺar i ʒcóṁairle créaꝺ ꝺo ꝺéan[ṗ]aꝺaoir.

---

¹ L reads "taibhseadh".   ² Thus L. A reads "aon".   ³ H reads "neach do dhiochair agus do dhearsgnaigh dfearaibh dhomhain andraoidheacht agus andiabhlaigheacht".   ⁴ Ꝑ reads "cliath roth caorthainn".   ⁵ The last twenty-one words are added from H, whose "do ris" I have changed into "aris", to be uniform.   ⁶ L reads "na noidheadhaibh".   Ꝑ "na haoidiḃ",

then it was revealed to the Mánach (that was the tutor of the King of Sorcha's son) that his pupil was in such distress, and that Mánach was himself the man of most desperate enchantment of all who came in his own time, and he took to himself a four-cornered flag of holly,(1) and he got upon it, and he rose by his enchanted power in the ex- panse of the firmament, and he put a dark fog of enchantment round about the ship of the Great Macaomh, until he stole away his pupil with him through that desperate dark fog. And on the dispersing from them of that enchanted water-mist, the sons of the King of Nor- way found the ship empty, after the Great Macaomh thus going from them ; and disappointed, dispirited were the sons of the King of Nor- way, for it was not their wont to allow their fellow combatant to escape from them without his dying. Then Cod asked his brothers what plan would they advise. They answered : "To look for the Free Island for another while." "That is not my own advice to you," said Cod, "but to go to the lands of Sorcha and to take with us the hosts of Nor- way, and to give battle to the Great Macaomh, for I am certain that it is he who came to avenge on us the slaying of his father, and he will not be at rest until we again make an attempt at him." They approved of that counsel.

It was then the children of the King of Norway bound the Great Man's ship to the rudder of their own, and they faced her over the back-ridge of every deep sea, and no tidings are told of them until they took port and harbour in the clay-clean, cluster-fruited, clear-fair lands of Norway; and they arrived at their own father's palace that night. And there they were guests. And neither music was sung, nor minstrelsy, nor feats-of-science [played] for them that night, but [everyone] listening to the stories of the aforesaid heroes from beginning to end.

And, on the morrow, tidings and messengers were sent from them to the chiefs of Norway, and their poets and philosophers came to them, and they took counsel as to what they should do.

---

and H adds " nochar leigeadh ceol na oirfide d'éisteacht isan dunadh no gur bhéigin doibhsiomh a nachtra féin dfoillsiughadh don righ agus do na maithibh ar cheana, o imtheacht go filleadh dhóibh ".

---

(1) ꝑ, the oldest MS., reads a "harrow-wheel of holly".

Cᵹur ir í cómairle¹ ro cinneaö leó, an mór-eaccra rin bo
öéanaṁ; aᵹur ᵹabaö lá aonaᵹ aᵹur oireaccair leó i ᵹceann
míora, aᵹur cánᵹabar rlóiᵹ na h-Ioruaiöe uile cum aon lácair
i ᵹceann na ré rin, aᵹur bo ᵹababar an céaö lá aᵹ ᵹormaö
rleaᵹ, aᵹur aᵹ ᵹlanaö lúicreac, aᵹur aᵹ ᵹéirlíoṁaö colᵹ cror-
órba, aᵹur aᵹ colᵹ-öiriuᵹaö a roiᵹeaö², aᵹur aᵹ ᵹléar ᵹeal-
cuaᵹ, aᵹur aᵹ accailceaö rᵹiac, aᵹur bo ᵹababar an bara
lá aᵹ luacaö a lonᵹ aᵹur aᵹ riocaö a bpríoṁ-lonᵹ, aᵹur aᵹ
cearcuᵹaö a ccranna aᵹur aᵹ bearuᵹaö a nbonn-barc, aᵹur
aᵹ rocruᵹaö a ráṁ aᵹur aᵹ rnaömaö a rcólcrann. Aᵹur
babar an crear lá aᵹ cur lóin inr na lonᵹaib rin, aᵹur an
ceacraṁaö lá le h-imceacc.

Ir annrin bo cuabar an rluaᵹ iomarcac rin ina lonᵹaib
aᵹur iar roccain an cuain car ciúṁraib na mara öóib bo
leiᵹeabar ᵹáir áöbal uacbárac róiṁór or áirb, ᵹo ᵹclor i
bpríocaib na rirmamence an crom-ᵹáir rin, aᵹur níor lúᵹa
ᵹáir na mban aᵹur na macaoṁ, na bprileaö aᵹur na n-ollaṁan,
aᵹ éaᵹcaoine a ṗcriac aᵹur a bciᵹearna.

Ir annrin bo éiriᵹ an ṁuir³ 'na ᵹlar-connaib ᵹarba
ᵹáireaccaca ᵹo ᵹclor rá na críocaib rá cóiṁneara öóib
ᵹarb-conᵹáir na blacṁaoilmuire⁴, roöail ᵹearanac na rairrᵹe
rri rlear⁵ aᵹur rrí buirb na luinᵹear rin. Ba öian aᵹur
ba ṗaba bo bí an cuan crioc-braonac⁶ criᵹalac cainceac
conᵹaireac aᵹ ᵹleic aᵹur aᵹ impearán rrir na cruaölonᵹaib

---

¹ II reads "agus is i comairle air ar chinnseat leath ar leath an cath do
chomóradh láimh ar láimh, agus gan a cur ar cáirde, acht an gcéin do beiddis ag
dul gus an Sorcha".   ² H reads "ag colg diriughadh a soidhead searrgtha
sithruinnighthe agus ag glanadh agus ag daingniughadh a samhthach ria saor
thuaghaibh agus ag cailceadh agus ag caomh bhreachtnughadh a sgiath sgeal-
bolgach [L reads ' ccomharthach '] agus for córughadh agus for comhgleus gach cinel
airm archena".   ³ All the mss. gives this "run" somewhat differently.
H reads "ciodhtracht ar rochtain formna na fairge dona feinigheadh ro at agus ro
inbhuilg an mhuir milradharcach motharthonnach futha agus na ttimchioll, rompa
agus na ndiaigh, ionnus gur bhrúchtadar borbthonna na bóchna re crannaib a
mbarc mbronn-fairsing, gur doirtseat an díle duamhaibh dubhaidhbhseacha diana
aigmhéala rompa agus dia néis, gur bho samhail do thulach aibhsigh áirdshléibhe
gach aon chnoc mheall anfa da 'neirgeadh na nurtimchioll, gonar cuingbaighsat
locht an cobhlaigh suaimhnios no saidhileacht, cómhnuidhe no comhsanadh do
dheanamh, acht a beith ag fromhadh a bféamann go fiorchalma doifhreastal anfa
an aigéin olladhbail anfunnaig an ccéin do bhi ag imirt a bhrigh agus a bharrainne

And the plan that was resolved on by them was to fulfil that great adventure. And a day for a fair and an assembly was appointed by them at the end of a month. And the hosts of Norway all came to one place at the end of that time, and the first day they proceeded to blue their spears, and to clean their mail, and to sharply-polish their golden-hilted swords, and to make their arrows sword-straight, and to fix their bright axes, and to re-chalk their shields; and the second day they set about speeding their ships and calking(¹) their prime-ships, and righting their masts, and arranging their brown barks, and settling their oars, and hewing their sail-masts. And they were the third day [engaged] in putting provisions in those ships, and the fourth day [they were] for going.

It was then that this exceeding-great host went aboard their ships, and after reaching the open ocean across the borders of the sea they uttered an awful, terrific, very-great shout on high, so that that loud cry was heard in the expanse of the firmament, and no less was the cry of the women and the youths, of the poets and of the ollavs, lamenting their chieftains and their lords.

It was then the sea arose in green waves, rough and laughter-making, until the harsh shoutings of the . . . and the complaining noises of the sea, along the sides and boards of the fleet, were heard in the regions nearest them. Desperate and long was the tremulous-dropping, tremulous-vapoury, talkative, shouting sea, wrestling and disputing with those tough-ships; and since the sea found no weakness

---

urra, acht cheana o nach bfuair," etc. L reads "d'eighrig an mhuir na maol-thonnaibh mothar-ghlasa mall-ghlóracha agus na caomh-chuasaib cainteacha cladh-líonmhara cruadh-gháithfeacha agus ar ndórta na dílion d'á drom-chladhaibh, agus ar ndath [n-at] na haibhéise da hosnaidhibh, agus ar mbriseadh na bochna agus ar ndlúthughadh na dílion da tromanfadh do bhi an cuan cainteach ciorchladhach ag gleic ris na curraidhe sin, agus o nach fuair an mhuir laige ar na laochaibh ná treise ar na tréinfhearaibh na cróilidhe ar na curradhaibh do éirge féithchiúin ar na huisgidhibh agus do roinneadar neoil eadarbhuasacha an aedhir re cheile gur ba féithchiúin ciubhsaibh na ccuanta daithle na mór olc sin, agus ni rángadar a leas iomramha do dheanamh", etc. ⁴ Thus A 25; but A reads " mbladmaoill muiridh agus fodhil ". ⁵ A reads " frith shleacht agus frith buirne ". A 25 reads "frith leas agus frith bruith", from which I have doubt-fully edited as above. ⁶ A 25 reads " criot cobhrannach cogadalach ". A "criot brionach ", which I have edited as above.

(¹) Literally " pick," or perhaps it comes from " pic ", " pitch ", i.e. to tar.

rín, aɤur ó naċ ḃruaır an ṁuır laıɤe ar na laoċaıḃ no cıme
ar na crḋanḟearaıḃ no crıċ-eaɤla ar na curaḃaıḃ ḋo éırıɤ
bláċ ríoċċána ar an muır aɤur ar na connaıḃ. Ir ann rın ḋo
rınneaḋar neóıl uaċcraċa an acıḋır aɤur ḃúl na rırmamenc
rıċ aɤur róıṁríoċċána re ċéıle, ɤur ba ríċ-ċıúın coıḃruıḋ na
cuanca conɤaıreaċa rın. A h-aıċle rın ní ránɤaḋar a lear
a láṁa ḋo ċur ınr na ráṁaıḃ aɤur ḋo rınneaḋar an laoı :—

　　Ir maırɤ ċéıḃ ran curur-ra
　　Nı ḃóıɤ a ḃrorḃóɤ ḟearca[1]
　　Ríoṁ a n-uılc[2] ní hurura,
　　Crı h-uaıċne ɤaċa ɤaırɤıḃ.

　　Nı h-ıaḋ naċ ḃruıl ɤo meanmnaċ[3]
　　Cıa acáıḃ na n-ealcaın[4] aıneoıl
　　Fá cuar rola ḋ'aırm-reanḃoıḃ[5]
　　Ḋ̇ream ḋ'ar buıḋeaċ braıneoın[6].

　　Luċc [ıaḋ] nár ċleaóc ceól ḋ'obaḋ[7]
　　Ḋar cóır ceannur ɤaċ cıre
　　Fır ba nḋéancar[8] ór-ṗoball
　　Crí ṁananaın[9] na ṁíleaḃ.

　　Crí reaḃaıo na h-Ioruaıḃe
　　Faḃa ɤur rɤuır a móır-ḟearɤ[10]
　　Acá crıall ḋo'n[11] ċaċṙluaıɤ-re,
　　Ḋ̇ream ba ḋcıocraıḃ ró-ṁaırɤ.

---

[1] H omits lay altogether.　A reads "ni bfhuill sin ar caoi fostoigh".　F and L
as above.　　[2] F reads "rimh".　L "roimh anuilc".　A 25 "reim a n-uilc".
[3] A reads "in ceanna".　F has "inceann".　A 23 "go meanmnach".　L "nach
ann fhanaig".　　[4] Thus F and L.　A reads "nalte".
[5] Thus F.　A reads "tuar fola na fior linntibh".　L reads "da bhfrithléanaibh".
[6] L reads " dana buidheach brantuin".　　[7] Thus F.　A reads "nach
gcleachtan ceól dubhach".　L "ceolabhadh"; perhaps the right reading is "ceól-
obadh" : I have inserted "iad" to make the line scan.　　[8] F "iarthoir
oirfpoball".　　[9] Thus F and A.　L has "tarmhanuin".　　[10] F reads
"a bhfaidh fearg".　L "a bhfáldearg".　　[11] L reads "an"; the others
have "atá ag triall don", which makes better sense, but spoils the metre.

(¹) The MS. in Trinity College gives this sea "run" as follows :—"Howsoever
on these heroes reaching the shoulder of the ocean, the huge-waved, monster-eyed
sea swelled and bellyed, beneath them and about them, before them and behind
them, so that the fierce waves of the ocean belched around the masts of their
broad-wombed barks, so that they poured forth the flood from the dismal caverns
of the abyss, so that like to the fair top of a high mountain was every stormy hill-
lump that used to up-rise round them, so that the people of the fleet could have

in the heroes, nor terror in the strong-men, nor timorousness in the
champions, there arose a blossom of peace upon the sea and upon the
waves. It was then the upper clouds of the air and the elements of
the firmament made peace and gentle-accord with one another, so that
those shouting seas became peaceful-calm and settled. After that it
was no longer necessary for them to put their hands to the oars,([1]) and
they made the lay :—

> Over wild waves furious
>   They sail but not in pallor,
> Great their ills and numerous
>   Three pillars they of valour.([2])

> It is not they who are not spirited (?),
>   Although they are an unknowing flock,
> A presage of blood to weapon-points,
>   A band to whom ravens are thankful.

> A people who use not to refuse music,
>   To whom is due the sovereignty of every land,
> Men for whom are made golden-tents,
>   Three Mananáns([3]) of the heroes.

> Three falcons of Norway
>   Long until ceases their great anger,
> There are voyaging to this battle-host
>   People from whom shall come great woe.

---

neither rest nor peace, stay nor stop, but trying their sinews, to attend to the
storm of the awful-great deep, whilst it was working its power and oppression
upon them, etc."   The Munster MS. reads differently:—"The sea arose in bald
billow-green blunt-voiced waves, and in fair talkative many-ditched hard-
dangerous hollows, and on the pouring the flood from its back-ridges, and on the
swelling of the abyss from its sighs, and on breaking of the ocean, and on thickening
of the flood of its heavy storm, the talkative encircling water was wrestling with
these heroes ; but when the sea found no feebleness in the heroes nor [want of]
power in the strong men, nor feebleness in the heroes, there arose a great calm
over the waters, and the upper clouds of the air divided together, so that
calmful were the hollows [?] of the waters after those great evils, and they found
it no longer necessary to row, etc."   ([2]) Literally : " Alas for who goes on
this journey, | no expectation of holding them back henceforth ! | to enumerate their
evil [i. e., the evils they do] is not easy— | three pillars of every valour."   The
verse in the text is in the metre of the original, which was meant to be a "cumasc
of Cass-bairdne and Rannaigheacht Beag," but has been corrupted into something
like mere Rannaigheacht Beag in the 2nd and 3rd verses.   The 1st line of the 2nd
verse evidently originally ended with a trisyllable, and the true reading of the 1st
line of the 3rd verse is probably "ceól-obadh".   ([3]) Mananán is the Irish Neptune.

a h-aiṫle na laoiḋ ṛin ḋo ċonncaḋaṛ loinġeaṛ ḋóḃal-ṁóṛ ionġantaċ aṛ ċíṁṁṛaiḃ an ċuain ġaċa nḃíṛeaċ ṛompa, aġuṛ aṛ na ṗaiċṛin ṛin ḃóiḃ ḋo ṫóġaḋaṛ Clann Ríġ na h-loṛuaiḋe a meiṛġe aġuṛ a mḃṛaṫaċa maoṫṛóil[1] aġuṛ a n-aiṛm coṛanta 'na láṁaiḃ luaṫ-ġonaċa. Aṛ na ṗaiċṛin ṛin ḃo'n ċoḃlaċ eile ḋo loaġaḋaṛ a ṛeólta aġuṛ a meiṛġe ṗéin maṛ ċoṁaṛṫa ṛíoṫċána ḃóiḃ. Iṛ annṛin ḃ'éiṛiġ callaiṛe Cloinne Ríġ na h-loṛuaiḋe aġuṛ ḋo ṗiaṛṛuiġ ṛé ḋe ġuṫ áṛḋ ṗolluṛ-ġlan ḋe luċt an ċoḃlaiġ eile cia h-iaḋ; aġuṛ ṛo ṗṛeaġṛaḋaṛ é aġuṛ aṛeaḋ aḋuḃaiṛt ġuṛ b' iaḋ ṗéin clann Ríġ lnnṛe h-Oṛc, .i. Ġṛuaġaċ na cṛaoiḃe, Ġṛuaġaċ an ḃóḋa aġuṛ Ġṛuaġaċ an ḋoṛḃáin, iaṛ ḋtiaċtain ḋe ḃáiḋ aġuṛ ḋe ċonailḃe aġ conġnaṁ[2], ṛe Cloinn Ríġ na h-loṛuaiḋe.

Iṛ annṛin ṫánġaḋaṛ maiċe aġuṛ móṛ-uaiṛle na ġcoḃlaċ n-iomaṛcaċ aġuṛ ḋo ċuaḋaṛ i ġcaoineaṛ coṁṛáiḃ[3] aġuṛ iomaġallṁa ṛe ċéile. Aġuṛ aṛ ṛnaḃṁaḋ aġuṛ aṛ ceanġal a ġcáiṛḋiṛ ṛe ċéile, ḋo ḃaḋaṛ ṛeal eile aġ ṗéaċain ionġantuiṛ na ḋtonn tiuġ-ṛuaḋ taoḃ-ġoṛm tulġanaċ. Aġuṛ níoṛ ċian ḃóiḃ aṛ na h-iomṛáiḃtiḃ ṛin ġo ḃṛeacaḋaṛ cṛíoċa aġuṛ caiṛleáin iomḃa uaċa, aġuṛ aonaċ ḋóḃal-ṁóṛ aṛ ṗaiċċe an Ríġ-ḋúnaḋ, aġuṛ ba ḃóiġ leó oiṛeaḋ a ḃṛeacaḋaṛ ḋe ḋaoiniḃ ṛiaṁ ġo ṛaiḃ baṛaṁail ḃóiḃ ṛan aonaċ ṛin.

Aġuṛ iaṛ ḃṛaiċṛin an ċoḃlaiġ ḋóḃal-ṁóiṛ ṛin ḋo luċt na cṛíċe ḋo leiġeaḋaṛ 'na ṛuaċaṛ ṛo-ṛeaċa ġo h-úṛ an ċuain iaḋ. Iṛ annṛin ṫánġaḋaṛ Clann Ríġ na h-loṛuaiḋe maṛ a ṛaiḃ Clann Ríġ lnnṛe h-Oṛc .i. Ġṛuaġaċ na Cṛaoiḃe aġuṛ Ġṛuaġaċ an ḋoṛḃáin[4], aġuṛ ḋ'ṗiaṛṛuiġ ḋíoḃ aṛ ḃ'aiṫne ḋóiḃ an t-oileán no an ċáċaiṛ ṛin, ṗá ṛaiḃ an t-aonaċ ḋóḃal-ṁóṛ ṛin. Aḋuḃṛaḋaṛ-ṛan naṛ ḃ'aiṫne ḋóiḃ ṗéin iaḋ. Iṛ annṛin ḋ'ṗiaṛṛuiġ Coḃ ḋe ṁaiċiḃ na ṛlóġ, cṛéaḋ an ċóṁaiṛle ḋo ḋéanṛaḋaoiṛ. Ḋo laḃaiṛ Ġṛuaġaċ na Cṛaoiḃe aġuṛ iṛ eaḋ ṛo ṛáiḋ, "luċt ṛġéala iṛ cóiṛ ċuṛ ċuca ó ċíṛ," aṛ ṛé.

"Cia líon ṛaċaṛ ann[5]", aṛ Coḃ.

---

[1] L reads "ballbhreaca".   [2] A omits these names, which I give from H. Ꝑ reads "mogha" for "bhoda", and "dornain" for "dordáin".   [3] H adds here "agus a náineas". L "agus aighnis". A 25 "agus aninnealt laimhe". [4] L adds " agus gruagach na gaoithe".   [5] Thus A 25; but A reads "ca bhiad na líon rachis an bhúan [*i.e.* ann uainn]".

After this lay they beheld a terrific-great wonderful fleet on the edge of the ocean straight before them, and on their beholding that, the sons of the King of Norway raised their flags and ensigns of soft-satin, and [took] their defensive weapons in their swift-wounding hands. And on the other fleet's beholding this, they lowered their sails and their own flags as a token of peace to them. It was then the herald of the sons of the King of Norway arose, and he asked the people of the other fleet, with a loud clear voice, who they were. And they answered him, and what they said was that they themselves were children of the King of the Orkneys, the Gruagach(¹) of the Branch, the Gruagach of the Bow, and the Gruagach of the Humming,(²) who were after coming, out of love and affection, to help the children of the King of Norway.

It was then the chiefs and great nobles of the numerous fleets came, and went into gentle discourse and dialogue with one another. And on their having knit and bound their friendships with one another, they were for another while beholding the wonders of the thick-russet blue-sided clamorous waves. And they were not long at such entertainment until they beheld many lands and castles at a distance from them, and a tremendous-great assembly upon the lawn of a royal mansion, and they deemed that all the people they had ever seen—there were as many in that assembly.

And when the people of the land beheld that tremendous-great fleet, they launched themselves in a rushing race down to the border of the harbour(³). It was then the sons of the King of Norway came to where the sons of the King of the Orkneys were; that is to say, the Gruagach of the Branch and the Gruagach of the Humming, and asked them did they know that island or that city in which was that enormous assembly. They answered that they themselves did not know. Then Cod asked the chiefs of the hosts what plan should they adopt. The Gruagach of the Branch spake, and 'twas what he said : " We ought first to send to them messengers-to-bring-tidings," said he.

" How many shall go there?" said Cod.

(¹) " *Gruagach* " is usually translated " wizard ".   (²) " *Dordán* " seems to mean a humming or musical sound of some sort, but the oldest MS. reads *dornan*, "fist".   (³) " *Cuan* ", "harbour", is often used also for the open sea.

"Luċt rзéal ȯo ḃuain amaċ ȯ'aiṁȯeoin, ir fearr ȯo ċur
ann," ar riaȯ, "ȯ'caзla naċ ȯtiuḃraȯ rзéal зo h-úiṁal; aзur
cuirċear ríce céaȯ uaiḃ-re¹ aзur ȯeiċ зcéaȯ uainn-ne," ar
Ӡruaзaċ na Craoiḃe, "óir ȯo ḃéarraiȯ riaȯ rin rзéala leó,
ȯe ȯeóin no ȯ'aiṁȯeóin." Ir ann rin ȯo leiзeaȯar na ȯeiċ
зcéaȯ fiċċeaȯ rin iaȯ ȯ'ionnraiȯe an aonaiз, aзur ȯo зaḃaȯar
luċt na críċe ȯ'á leaȯraȯ aзur ȯ'á luaċ-ṁarḃaȯ; aзur ir iaȯ
muinntir Ċloinne Ríз Innre h-Orc ir mó ȯo ṁarḃ ȯe ṁuinntir
Ċloinne ríз na h-Iopuaiȯe, mar ir orra ir lúзa ȯo ḃaȯar ar
зcoiṁéaȯ, óir ir tre ṁeinз aзur tre ṁeaḃail-ċeilз an
Ꝉꝉacaoiṁ Ꝉꝉóir ȯo ċuaȯar clann Ríз Innre hOrc a зcoinne
aзur a зcóiṁȯáil Ċloiṅe Ríз na h-Iopuaiȯe ȯo ȯéanaṁ cumainn
aзur caraȯraȯ riu aiṁlaiȯ rin. Cíoȯtráċt² ni ċáiniз neaċ ḃeó
no marḃ ȯe ṁuinntir Ċloinne Ríз na h-Iopuaiȯe.

Ḃa faȯa re Coȯ ȯo ḃí ré зan rзéal a ṁuinntire ȯ'fáзail.
Ir annrin ȯo laḃair Ӡruaзaċ na Craoiḃe aзur ir eaȯ
aȯuḃairt, зur cóir ȯronз eile ȯo ċur ȯ'iarraiȯ rзéala na
críċe ċuca.

"Cá líon raċar ann?" ar Coȯ.

"Raċaiȯ rinn-ne aзur na rlóiз uile aċt luċt na trí lonз
ina ḃfuil riḃ-re, a Ċlann Ríз na h-Iopuaiȯe." Aȯuḃairt
Coȯ зur cóir rin³ ȯo ȯéanaṁ; aзur iar зclor rin ȯo'n ċoḃlaiз
ȯo leiзeaȯar an[n a n]ȯronзaiȯ riuḃlaċa irin críċ iaȯ, aзur
ráanзaȯar ȯo'n aonaċ áȯḃal-ṁór, aзur ȯo rinneaȯar luċt na
críċe an níȯ céaȯna rin .i. ro ṁarḃaȯar uile⁴ iaȯ. Aзur ir
iaȯ muinntir Ċloinne Ríз Innre h-Orc ir mó ȯo ṁarḃ iaȯ
mar an зcéaȯna. Aċt tá ní ċeana, ní ċáiniз neaċ ḃeó no
marḃ ȯíoḃ tar air. Iar mḃeiċ aiċiȯ imċian ȯo Ċoȯ aiṁlaiȯ
rin зan rзéala na críċe ȯ'fáзail, ir í cóṁairle air ar ċinnreat
an ċríoċ ȯ'ionnraiȯe⁵, aзur níor ṁair ȯe fluaз aca aċt céaȯ
timċeall зaċ fir ȯíoḃ, aзur ȯo ċonncaȯar ráċ árȯ aoiḃinn
uaċa, aзur ráanзaȯar mullaċ an ráċa rin, aзur ȯo tóзḃaȯar
trí puḃaill⁶ áilne éaзraṁla ar an ráċ rin, зur ḃa "Ráċ na

---

¹ A reads "buadhibhsi", and "buaine".   ² The last forty-nine words
are added from H.   ³ H reads "aontuigheas Cod sin".   ⁴ Thus
A 25. A reads "anoidhe iad", i.e. "a n-oiȯe".   ⁵ This is from

" It is best to send there [enough] people to force their news out
of them against their will, for fear they may not give their tidings
submissively, and let twenty hundred be despatched from you, and ten
hundred from us," said the Gruagach of the Branch, "for that
number will bring tidings with them, will they, nill they." Then
that thirty hundred launched themselves towards the assembly,
and the people of the country began to smite and quickly-slay
them.   And it was the people of the sons of the King of the Orkneys
who most slew the people of the son of the King of Norway, for
they were least on their guard against them; for it was through
guile and treacherous-deceit of the Great Macaomh that the children
of the King of the Orkneys had gone to meet and accost the children of
the King of Norway, to make amity and friendship with them in that
way.   However, nobody, either dead or alive, came back of the people
of the sons of the King of Norway.

Cod thought it long that he was without getting news of his
people.   It was then the Gruagach of the Branch spake, and what
he said was that it were right to send another band to seek tidings
of the country for them.

" How many shall go there ? " said Cod.

" We and all the hosts, except the people of the three ships in
which ye are, O sons of the King of Norway." Cod said that it were
well to do so, and when the fleet heard it they launched themselves
in active bands into the country, and they reached that terrible-great
assembly ; and the people of the country did the same thing again—
they slew them all.   And it was the people of the sons of the King
of the Orkneys who, in like manner [as before], most slew them.
Howsoever, no one of them came back, either dead or alive.   And after
Cod's being for a long time in this manner, without receiving news
of the country, the plan they resolved on was to approach the
land.   And none of their army remained living except a hundred
round each man of them ; and they beheld a high and beautiful rath
at a distance from them, and they reached the summit of that rath,
and they raised upon that rath three beautiful variegated tents, so

---

H, which usually reads " chinnseat " for " chinneadar ".   L reads " Do rangadar
na sgéala sin clann righ na h-Ioruaidhe agus tagaid i dtir go tinneasnach ".
⁶ A " pupaille ".   L " poible ".   A 25 " puibaill ".   H " puible ".

oċrí pobaill" ainm an ráċa rin, air ar ruiḋeaḋ iaḋ, ó ḟin a leiċ i zcríoċaiḃ na Sórċa.

Níor ċian ḃóiḃ annrin, an ċan ḃo ċonncaḃar an ċ-aon óżlaċ ḃ'á n-ionnraiḋe, ażur ir aṁlaiḋ ḃo ḃí an ċ-óżlaċ rin ażur pflearż pile fá n-a ċeann, ażur inneall ḃraoi rair, ażur ḃraċ cuana corcar-ċiúṁraċ uime[1], ażur pflearż ḟionn-airżiḋ 'na láiṁ. ḃeannaiżear an ċ-óżlaċ rin ḃe ḃriaċraiḃ blarċa ḃeól-ṁilir, ażur ḃo ḃeir rżéala ḃóiḃ aṁail ḃo pfeallaḃ fror a muinnċir, ażur ro innir ḃóiḃ żur ḃ' í rin críoċ na Sorċa ma oċárla iaḋ[2], ażur ḃ'iarr orra ḃul żo Críoċaiḃ na h-Ioruaiḋe ċar a n-air arír. Ir annrin ḃ'ḟiaffruiż Coḃ ḃ'á ḃráiċriḃ cféaḃ an ċóṁairle ḃo ḃéanfaḋaoir.

Aḃuḃraḃar-ran żur ḃ'í a żcóṁairle féin caċ ceann-árḃ conraoiḃeaċ[3] ḃo ċaḃairċ ḃóiḃ ar an uair reo ḃ'eażla naċ ḃfruiżríḋe ar aon láċair arír iaḋ. "Ir maiċ an ċóṁairle rin," ar Coḃ, "ażur luiżim-re i ḃfriaḃnaire m'arm ḃá oċużaḃ ríḃre a aċarraċ[4] rin ḃe ċóṁairle ḃam żur orraiḃ féin ḃ'ḟéaċrainn niṁ m'arm ar oċúr."[5]

Ir annrin ḃ'ḟiaffruiż Coḃ ḃe'n ḃraoi ca h-ainm ḃo ḃí fair. "Cufaire[6] Camċoraċ m'ainm-re," ar ré, "ażur ir ċruaż ḃoiliż liom-ra an níḋ ḃo ḃ'áil liḃ-re ḃo ḃéanaṁ, .i. an ḃiar ir annra[7] liom żur ab coṁ-ċuicim ḃóiḃ inḃiú." Ḋ'ḟiaffruiż Coḃ ḃe'n Ċufaire Camċoraċ "Cféaḃ é ḃo ċáirḃear linne, ó'r coṁ-olc leaċ rinn?" ażur ḃuḃairċ rir "rloinn ḃo ċáirḃear ḃúinn anoir." Ażur ḃo ḟreażair an Cufaire Camċoraċ é, ażur ir eaḋ aḃuḃairċ, "Sżelżan Aċir[8] Ḋeiḃ mic Ġlair an ċ-aċair ḃ'á rużaḃ mire," ar re, "ażur nuair ḃí mo ṁáċair ċorraċ orm-ra, ḃo żaḃ Ríż na Sorċa mar ḃalċa mé, ażur ċáim aiże ó ḟin ale: ḃo ċuiḃ-re ḃíom, .i. Ilżrearaċ ḃe ċríoċaiḃ na h-Ioruaiḋe mo ṁáċair. Ażur ḃo ċuil[9] an ċonn żráḃ ażur an-ḃáiḃ żráḃa fó mo ċroiḋe, ar ḃfaicrin ḃo

---

[1] Thus L. A reads "brat cumhan". A 25: "b. cumhan ceathar-bheannach, agus ionnal druadh agus deagh dhuine aladhna air, fleasg aluinn fileadh ina laimh, brat caomh corcair ciúmhsach uime aga imfholach". [2] The last twenty-six words are from H, which gives the sense best. A reads "do briathraibh alligheanta [i.e. ealadhanta]". [3] L 39 reads "céadfadhach". [4] Thus L; A reads "saoibhsi clachladh sin". [5] H "nach ngeubhainn uaibh". [6] F "curoire cam". H "conaire". [7] A reads "doilighe". [8] H omits;

that the name of that rath on which they were set up was the " rath of the three tents " ever since, in the lands of Sorcha.

They were not long there when they beheld the one youth coming towards them; and this is how that youth was—he had a poet's garland round his head, and the appearance of a druid, and had a fair purple-bordered mantle round him, and a wand of white silver in his hand. That youth salutes them with tasteful sweet-voiced words, and brings them tidings of how their people had been treacherously-deceived, and told them that this was the land of Sorcha upon which they had happened; and he asked them to go back again to the lands of Norway. Then Cod inquired of his brothers what plan should they adopt.

They answered that their own plan would be to give them high-headed furious battle in that hour, for fear lest they should not be all found in one and the same place again. "Good is that advice," said Cod, "and 1 swear in the presence of my weapons that if ye were to give me any other advice, it would have been upon yourselves I should have first tried the venom of my arms."

Then Cod inquired of the druid what was his name. "My name is Curairè [Kurr-ĭr-yă] Crook-foot,(¹) and I think it a sad pity, the thing which ye desire to do, namely, that the two I best love, are to fall together this day." Cod asked Curairè Crookfoot, "What is your friendship with us, since you think it equally bad our [falling]?" and he bade him "trace back now your friendship for us." Then the Curairè Crookfoot answered and said, "Sgelgan Atis Deib mic Ghlais was the father to whom I was born," said he, "and when my mother was pregnant with me, the king of Sorcha accepted me to be an attendant(²), and I am with him ever since: your share of me is this, Ilgreasach of the lands of Norway was my mother. And a wave of love and loving affection flooded through my heart on seeing your

---

L reads "aitios mac duilbh mic glais". A 25 "Sgála athais mhac deilbh mhic ghlais". ⁹ P reads "do tuil mo tonn báidhe triom". A reads "toil" for "tuil", and A 25 "an toil agus an taongrádh do ghabh me". L "do dháil an ton conailbhe fúm".

(¹) Literally "the Crooked-footed Curaire." "Curaire" has no meaning that I know of, though the definite article is, in almost all the mss., used before it.
(²) "dalta", a young attendant lad of good family, or a pupil.

ṁuinncipe-pe b'á mapḃaḋ. Aċt atá ní ċeana, ċuġap ġráḋ m'anma ḃaoiḃ-pe. Aġup ip ḃeapḃ liom piḃ ḃo ċuicim le pṫuaġ na cpíċe-peo, óip ní h-ionċaċa pluaġ ná pocpaiḃe an ḃoṁain piu, aġup a ġcóṁċpuimniuġaḋ i n-aon láċaip, pe líonṁaipeaċt a ġcupaḋ aġup a ġcaiċ-ṁiliḃc."[1]

Ruġaḃap ap an oiḋċe pin ġup ḟoillpiġ lá ġo na lán-ḟoillpe ap n-a ṁápaċ, ġup éipiġ an ġpian op a cpann-ḟoḃail ceinciḃe, op ḃpeaċ na caliṁan cpompóḃaiġ ġup ḟoillpiġ pí cnuic céiḃe aġup caḃáin aġup coillte ceann-ápḃa bapp-ġlapa cnuap-iomḃá ḃe ġaċ leaċ.[2] Ip ann pin aḋuḃaipt Coḃ pip an ġCupaipe Camċopaċ ḃul ḃ'ḟóġpaḋ caċa ap ṁac Ríġ na Sopċa ġona ṁópḟpluaġ. Aġup aḋuḃaipt an Cupaipe Camċopaċ le Coḃ, "ip pnáiṁ i n-aġaiḋ eapa, no ġaḃ um ġaineaṁ, no cuapġan ḃapaċ ḃe ḃopnaiḃ, no ḟaḃóġaḋ ceineaḋ ḟa[3] inḃeap, no ip ġlac um ġaċ ġpéine no ceap i ġceann piuċċa,[4] no ip léim 'na leabuiḋ ap leóṁan,[5] ḃul i ġceann ṁic Ríġ na Sopċa."

"Leiġ peaċaḋ an paoḃ-cóṁpáḋ aḃeip tu," ap Coḃ, aġup ip cuma ḃo ḃḟí ḃ'á páḃ.[6] Do ċuip Coḃ a láiṁ i ġcóṁppann[7] a pġéiċe, aġup ċuġ liaġ ḃpuimneaċ ḃeappġuiḃe[8] ḃe ḃeapġ-óp, aġup ċuġ ḃo'n ḃpaoi an c-óp. Aġup iap na ġlacaḋ ḃo'n Cupaipe Camċopaċ ḃo ċeilġ an liaġ luaċ-ṁóp ḟo ċalaṁ, aġup po ġaḃ ḃuḃa aġup ḃoṁeanmna é[9], aġup map ḃo ċonnaipc Coḃ pin ḃo pinneaḋ pó-nuaill copcpa ó ḃonn ġo báċap ḃé, aġup ḃ'ḟiappuiġ Coḃ ḃé "an a' coipmeapġ an óip ḃí pé?"

Duḃaipt an Cupaipe Camċopaċ náp ḃ'eaḋ, naċ copmap no cpom-ċeapaċt ḃí aiġe ap an caḃapcap ḟuaip,[10] aċt ġup cpuaġ ḃoiliġ leip an ḃiap ba h-annpa leip ġup ba ċoṁ-ċuicim ḃóiḃ apaon.

---

[1] The last thirty-three words are from L. A omits them; I read, however, "gcuradh" for "gcuraidhe". [2] The last twenty-eight words are also from L. [3] Thus ꝑ and L. A reads "um". A 25 "re". [4] II reads "fiuchte"; A 25 "fuachta". [5] Last seven words from H. ꝑ adds "no as buain meala do minbheacoiph agus as morghort formagh danacal gan fal ga iomchosnam daiphsi". [6] Last fifteen words from H. [7] Thus L. A 25 has "a ccuibhribh". A has apparently "ccobhran". ꝑ "ccobran". [8] The adjectives are from H. [9] Last seven words from H. [10] Last

people a-slaying. And in very truth I have given to you the love of my soul, but I am certain that ye shall fall by the hosts of this country, for neither the hosts nor armies of the world are fit-to-fight them, even though they were gathered together in one spot, through the abundance of their heroes and their battle-champions."

They bore away that night until the day shone with its full-light upon the morrow, until the sun arose over her fiery standing-tent above the face of the heavy-sodded earth, until she lighted up on every side hills and slopes and hollow-plains and heavy-headed green-topped many-fruited woods. It was then Cod said to the Curairè Crookfoot to go and proclaim battle against the son of the king of Sorcha and his great hosts. But the Curairè Crookfoot said to Cod, " It is a swimming against a waterfall or it is a gad([1]) round sand, or a beating of an oaktree with fists, or a kindling of a fire at a river's-mouth, or it is a closing-of-the-palm round a sun-beam, or it is heat against boiling, or it is a leap into a lion's bed to go to meet the son of the king of Sorcha."

" Lay aside that silly discourse you talk," said Cod, but it was no use for him to be speaking([2]). Then Cod put his hand into the hollow of his shield and he took out a ridgy polished lump([3]) of red-gold, and gave the gold to the druid. And when the Curairè Crookfoot took it, he cast the precious lump upon the ground, and melancholy and dispiritedness seized him. And when Cod saw that he became a "ronuaill"([4]) from head to foot, and he asked him "Was it refusing the gold he was?"

The Curairè Crookfoot said that it was neither refusing nor complaining he was of the present he got, but that it was a sad grief to him the two whom he loved best that they had to fall together.

---

twelve words from H. "tormas", which L also reads, is apparently the same as "toirmeasg"; there is an "a" before both in H, which I have omitted.

([1]) *I.e.* a withy-band.   ([2]) Literally "and it was indifferent", *i.e.* without effect, "he was saying it".   ([3]) Literally "flag".   ([4]) Zimmer has shown that this word was originally "rothanol", and meant the beam of a mill. It apparently means that his body all turned like a mill-wheel, with indignation.— See Zimmer's article on this word: Zeitschrift f. Celt. Phil., I. i., p. 85.

"Ná h-abaıp¹ pın," ap Coḃ, "níop ċuıp an talaṁ ap a muın pıaṁ neaċ mo ḃıonġḃála-pa ınḃıu."²

Ip annpın ḃo ċuaıḋ an Cupaıpe Camċopaċ ḃ'ıonnpaıḋe an ṁóp-ḟlóıġ pın ṁıc Ríġ na Sopċa ḃo peıc aıtıpıġ³ Cloınne Ríġ na h-lopuaıḋe. Aġup aḃuḃaıpt pıp map po : "Cé líonṁap ḃo ċaċa aġup cé mıleaḃta ḃo ċupaıḃ, aġup cé cpóḃa ḃup⁴ mıleaḋa, ba neaṁ-ċpóḃa ḃup ġcupaıḃ aġup ba h-eaṁ-neaptmhup ḃup ġcaċa aġup ba meaċta ḃup mılıḋe, aġup ba neıṁ-tpeópaċ ḃup ḃtpéınḟıp aġup ba tana ḃup ḃtpom-ḟlóıġ aġup ba pġaoılte ḃup mbuıḋne aġup ba neaṁ-ċpóḃa ḃup paop-ḟlóıġ aġup ba neaṁ-ċupata ḃup n-óġ-pıġċe ap ċeann Cloınne Ríġ na h-lopuaıḋe." Aġup ní ċuġ Ríġ na Sopċa ḃ'á uıḋe⁵ ná ḃ'á aıpe cpéaḃ ḃó ḃí an Cupaıpe Camċopaċ ḃ'á páḃ, ap ṁéaḃ a ḃeıċnıp⁶ aġ ınneall na ġcaċ n-ıomapcaċ pın tap ċeann Cloınne Ríġ na h-lopuaıḋe. Aġup ó naċ ḃtuġ, ḃ'ḟıll an Cupaıpe Camċopaċ ı ḃḟpıċınġ na conaıpe céaḋna, aġup níop panaḋ leıp ġo páınıġ an tulaċ a paḃaḋap Clann Ríġ na h-lopuaıḋe; aġup níop aıtın ıaḃ, óıp ḃo ċlaoclaıġ ḃaċ ḃealḃ aġup ḃéanaṁ na ḃḟeap ḃo ḃ'ḟeapp ḃeılḃ ınneall aġup éaġopġ ḃ'ḟeapaıḃ an ḃoṁaın ġo h-ıomlán, óıp ḃo ṁeap-lapaḋap a púıle 'na ġceannaıḃ, aġup ḃo ċóıṁ-éıpġeaḋap a ḃḟuılc 'na ġcolġḟeapaṁ, ıonnup ġo ḃḟanpaḋ mıon-úḃall nó móp-áıpne ap ḃápp ġaċ aon poınne ḃ'á ḃḟoltaıḃ cpaoḃ-pġaoılte. Aċt atá ní ċeana ḃo ċpeaċnaḋap⁷ a ġcuıpp 'na ġcaċ-éıḃıḃ⁸ aġup ḃo ċóıṁ-ḃeapġaḋap a nġpuaḋa ḃonn-ḃpeaca,⁹ aġup ḃ'ḟıappuıġ Coḃ pġéala na ġcaċ móp-áḋḃal pın ḃe'n Ċupaıpe Camċopaċ. "Ip áḋḃal pın pe ınnpın," ap an Cupaıpe Camċopaċ, "óıp níop cumaḋ coıllte ḃá ḃlúp pıaṁ naċ ḃlúıċe tıaġap a n-apm ġcopcap-ḃeapġ op a ġceannaıḃ,"¹⁰ ap an Cupaıpe

---

¹ H reads "na biodh an mheisneach sin agadsa asamsa, oir tuingimsi a ttuinghid mo thuatha nach bhfuil isin Sorcha fear mo dhiongbhála-sa a láthair catha no cruadh-chomhlainn a haithle na feille fiorghránna gráineamhail do rinneadh ar mo mhuinntir". ² P inserts here a long passage not very legible about the evil dreams which oppressed the host: "nir bo sámh siotchánta codladh no comhsanadh sluagha na Sorcha an aga sin or do biomdha an aislingthe aduathmar iongantacha, agus a bfasttine fiorgraneamoil an aga sin, agus do bhadar neóil neamhghlana an aieoir agus faidhe fuar fliocha na fiormaiminnte agus taighleora siotluatha", etc. ³ A 25 reads "do reic aisge C. R. na hI." L "do reic C. R. na hI." ⁴ A, as usual, reads "mur" for "bhur".

" Do not say that," said Cod, " for the earth never put upon its back a man who is my equal([1]) this day."

It was then the Curairè Crookfoot went to that great host of the son of the king of Sorcha, to tell the admonition of the children of the king of Norway, and he spake to him thus :— " Although plentiful are your battalions, and though warlike your champions, and though valorous your warriors, yet valorless shall be your champions, and weakly your battalions, and cowardly your warriors, and unguide-ful your strong ones, and thin your heavy hosts, and dispersed your bands, and un-valorous your well-born bands and champion-less your young kings, on account of the children of the king of Norway." But the King of Sorcha took neither heed nor notice of what the Curairè Crookfoot was saying, for all his haste in arranging those numerous battalions, preparing for the children of the king of Norway. And since he did not, the Curairè Crookfoot returned by the same way he came, and no halt was made by him until he reached the hill where were the children of the king of Norway. And he did not recognise them, for the colour, shape, and make of those men who were best of shape, figure, and appearance of the men of the entire world, had altered ; for their eyes quick-flamed in their heads, and their hair stood up together sword-straight, so that a small-apple or a big-sloe might rest upon the top of every bristle of their separated hair. And then too their bodies quivered in their battle-armour and their brown-spotted cheeks reddened together ; and Cod asked the Curairè Crookfoot for tidings of these terrific battalions. " Awful is that to tell," said the Curairè Crookfoot, " for never were created woods however close, that the covering of their purple-red weapons above their heads is not closer still," said

---

⁵ Thus Ᵽ and A. The others read " aghaidh ". ⁶ Thus L. Ᵽ has " ar roimhét anteinneanois do bhi air ". A has " athineannuis ". A 25 "a aithneis". ⁷ Ᵽ reads " chroithneadar ". H " chriothnuigh ". L " chroitheadar ". ⁸ Thus H. A reads " a meadhon nionna*thar* ". H adds " go gcuala sum bloisg bhearnach agus bag gearan croidhe gach laodhch curaidh diobh ina gcompar ag togar go tinneasnach do chum an chatha ". ⁹ Thus L. A has " gealdeirge tean ghealla ". Ᵽ has " tainbreaca tibirgeala taithneamhacha ". ¹⁰ H omits this passage. Ᵽ reads " or na coillte as dluithe ar an domhan as dluithe daingneinaid sin a gcroinn crann-ruadh ". A reads " nach dluithe atá os cceann deargar anairm crosorda anairde ".

([1]) Or, perhaps, " a man able to repel me "

Camċoraċ. Do b' iomöa ríр aiñra¹ aġur airlinġ ionġantaċ do ċonncaöar na ріóiġ an oiöċe rin, aġur do bí an ріrmamenc uile ar coñicarɡaö or a ɡcionñ, aġur do b' iomöa báöö béal-öearɡ luaċ-ċaiñteaċ aġur bran-eóin bonnluaċ ar eiċilleaö, aġur reiċiöe² ríor-ġránöa aɡ ríor-ṗairöine na mór-olc rin or ceann na рluaġ an oiöċe rin, aġur níor b'ionɡna döiö carranɡaire. Óir ir é rin crear ár na beaċaö .ı. Caċ ceaċaröa³ ar ṁáiġ na Cearáile aġur caċ maiġe cuir na üroṁoraċ aġur caċ maiġe na öcrí ürearc ı ɡCríoċaiö na Sorċa. Ir annrin do cóɡbaö cri rról-ṁeirɡe do Ċloinn Ríġ na h-Ioruaiöe, ɡo рánɡaöar ı ɡceann na mór-ṗluaġ rin.

Ir annrin do ċuɡ Coö borb-ruaċar ríoġ-laoiċ aġur rrïoṁ-ġairɡiġiö crïo na caċaiö rin, no ɡo рáiniɡ ṗá ċóṁair an ċaċa a raiö Ríġ na Sorċa, aġur níor ċonailbeaċ ná cáiróeaṁail ṗáilte na beire beaġ-laoċ rin b'á ċéile, aġur ċuɡaöar achuran⁴ ɡarb-ġéar an-iarṁarcaċ b'á rean-armaiö b'a ċéile,⁵ aġur ar mbrireaö a nɡorm-ċraoireaċ ı n-éiöiö aġur ı ɡcorraiö a ċéile, do ṗíneaöar na láṁa ɡo léaöṁaċ riċ-ġoineaċ leir na cloiöṁċiö clairleaċana cror-óröa caoṁ-ṗaoüraċa ɡo öcuɡaöar ráiġciöe roiġeaö-ġéara ríor-ġonca ṗó na ċéile, aċc cá ní ċeana öá öceanɡiñaö cáiröe coṁ-öírle ar ċóṁair a ċéile ní ċiüṗraiöír caoü re rear üíoü reoċ a ċéile, re luar a n-iombuailte aġur re méaö a ürola aġur a ürollraċta ṗá na n-áiġıö aġur ṗá na n-ċaöanaiö.⁶ Iomċura na coöa eile de ċloinn Ríġ na h-Ioruaiöe: ċuɡaöar a n-aiġċe mar a üracaöar clann Ríġ Inre h-Ore aġur níor b'ṗáilte caraö aġur níor ċuirm,⁷ ṗáilte na nöeaġlaoċ rin b'á ċéile. Aċc acá ní ċeana ní ṗéiöir ɡníoṁarċa ɡaċa ɡairɡiöíɡ ro leiċ aca d'innrin, aċc bloö⁸ beaɡ de ɡníoṁarċaiö an öeaġ-laoiċ rin, .ı. Coö mac Ríġ na

---

¹ P has misplaced this passage, and omits it here.   ² L "féithidhe"; A 25 "feitheadh".   ³ The last fifteen words are from L, which makes "beatha" feminine.   ⁴ Written also "catharga" and "cathardha". It is often referred to in Irish writing, and seems to have been the name for the battle of Pharsalia.   ⁵ A 25 reads "tugadar comhathchusan; L "achmusán".   ⁶ This passage, from "ar mbriseadh" to "éadanaibh" is from L, which gives the best text. A reads "cairde na coigeibh", and "re mead a bhfala agus

the Curairè Crookfoot. Many was the visionary-appearance and the wondrous dream-figures that the hosts saw that night; and the whole firmament was in one confusion above their heads; and many was the red-mouthed quick-talking raven, and foot-spreading vulture a-flying, and truly-disgusting creature ever-prognosticating those great evils above the hosts that night. And it was no wonder for them to prophesy, for that was the third slaughter of the world, namely, the *Cath Ceathardha*(¹) on the Plain of Thessaly, and the battle of Moytura of the Fomorians(²), and the battle of the Plain of the Three Graves in the lands of Sorcha. It was then the three satin standards were up-lifted by the children of the king of Norway until they reached those great hosts.

It was then Cod gave the furious rush of a king-hero and prime-warrior throughout those battalions, until he reached the battalion where was the king of Sorcha. And neither loving nor friendly was the welcome of those two good heroes for one another, and they gave a rough-sharp very-powerful ..... (?) of their tried(³) weapons to one another. And on the breaking of their blue javelins in one another's armour and bodies they stretched their hands powerfully, woundingly, with the broad-furrowed gold-hilted finely-edged swords [in them] till they gave arrow-sharp lacerating thrusts to one another. Howsoever if equally dear friends were to meet one another, they would not trust one man of them more than another, for the quickness of their mutual-striking, and for all the blood and gore in their visages and faces(⁴). As for the other sons of the king of Norway, they turned their faces where they beheld the children of the king of the Orkneys; and it was not the welcome of friends, and it was not a feast, the welcome of those good heroes for one another. However, it is impossible to tell the deeds of each hero separately, except a little fragment of the deeds of that good

---

a bhfolraite". ⁷ A 25 reads "níor bhfáilteach cuirm na ", etc.
⁸ A has "bleadh"; A 25 bladh; the others omit.

(¹) See above, p. 69. (²) Fought between the Tuatha De Danann and the Fomorians, known as the great battle of Moytura.—See my *Literary History of Ireland*, pp. 285-291. (³) Literally "old". (⁴) This seems to mean that if a friend of either chanced to come up while they were fighting, he would not know which was which.

h-Ιορuαιᴅe. Ιр αnnрιn ᴅо leιᵹeαᴅαр nα рlóιᵹ n-ιоmαрᴄαċ'¹ рó-ṁóр' рιn ᴄрí ᵹáрᴄα coṁ-ṁóрα le ᴄeιlᵹeαn α n-αрm nᴅιúḃрαιᴄᴄe ι n-áιрᴅe, αᵹuр ᴅeιріᴅ eólαιᴅe ᵹо nᴅeαᴄαιᴅ ᴄαoᵹαᴅ ғeαр n-αрmαċ рe ᵹαoιċ αᵹuр рe ᵹeαlᴄαιᵹeαċᴄ ó nα ᴄроm-ᵹáрᴄαιḃ рιn. Ɑᵹuр ғóр ιр ᴄoрᵹαрᴄα² ᴅо ḃαᴅαр nα рlóιᵹ ι n-αlᴄ nα h-uαιрe рιn, оιр ᴅо ḃαᴅαр ᴅрonᵹ αᴄα αᵹuр α ᵹᴄoрα ᴄeαрᵹᴄα ᴅíoḃ αᵹuр ιαᴅ αᵹ ᴄuαрᵹαn α n-eαрᴄαрαᴅ рe n-α láṁαιḃ, αᵹuр ᴅрonᵹ eιle ᴅíoḃ αᵹuр α láṁα ᴅ'α n-eαрḃαιᴅ, αᵹuр ιαᴅ αᵹ ᴄuαрᵹαn α n-eαрᴄαрαᴅ рe n-α ᵹᴄoрαιḃ αᵹuр рe n-α ḃрιαᴄlαιḃ, αᵹuр ᴅрonᵹ eιle ᴅíoḃ αᵹuр α n-αḃαċ αᵹuр α n-ιоnαċαр αрᴄα αᵹuр ιαᴅ ᴅ'á ḃрolαċ ιр nα h-eιᴄрιᵹιḃ oр nα lιnnᴄιḃ ғolα ғlαnnрuαᴅ ᴅо ғιleαᴅ αр ᴄoрραιḃ αᵹuр αр ᴄрéαċ-ᴄαιḃ nα lαoċ αᵹuр nα ᵹᴄuрαᴅ,³ αᵹuр ᴅрonᵹ eιle ᵹαn ᴄneαᴅ ᵹαn ᴄрéαċᴄ оррα, αᵹuр ιαᴅ αᵹ ᴄuр nα ᵹᴄoрр αр [α] muιn ᴄрαрnα ᴅ'á nᴅíon ғéιn αр ғuαιm nα h-úрluιᵹeαċᴄα рιn nα n-óᵹlαoċ.⁴ ᴄíoᴅᴄрáċᴄ ᴅо ḃ' ιоmᴅα рᵹιαċ ᴅ'á рᵹoιlᴄeαᴅ αᵹuр lúιċрeαċ ᴅ'á luαιċ-ċeαрᵹαᴅ, αᵹuр ᴄαċ-ḃáрр ᴅ'á ċрuαᴅ-ḃрúᵹαᴅ, αᵹuр ғóр ᴅо ḃ' ιоmᴅα ᴄloιᴅeαṁ рe ᴄnáṁ αᵹuр ғéιċe ғíoр-ᵹránᴅα⁵ αр ғúᴅ αn ċαċα ι n-αlᴄ nα h-uαιрe рιn. Ιоmᴄuрα ṁιᴄ Ríᵹ nα Sорċα αᵹuр ṁιᴄ Ríᵹ nα h-Ιорuαιᴅe ᴅо ḃ' ιоmᴅα ᴄneαᴅα ᴅoιṁne ᴅιαn-ḃáιр αᵹuр ᴄрéαċᴄα ᴅо-leιᵹιр αᵹ ріор-ᴅóрᴄαᴅ αᵹuр αᵹ ғιleαᴅ uαᴄα αр ᵹαċ leιċ.⁶ Ɑᴄá ní ċeαnα, ní ғéαᴅғαᴅ neαċ αр ᴅрuιm αn ᴅоṁαιn ᴅá ṁéαᴅ ᵹlιoᴄαр nо

---

¹ nιоmαрᴄαᴅ is sometimes used for iomarcach, the *n* comes, I think, from the article which precedes "iomarcaidh," as *tá an iomarcaidh agam.*

² Thus ꝃ. A has "ainmioch", L "truagh". ³ Last thirty-three words inserted from L. ⁴ Last ten words from L.

⁵ ꝃ has "fead cloidh[imh] re cn. agus feigeadha fíor-truadha. L reads nearly the same. ⁶ ꝃ inserts here nearly a page descriptive of the effects of the battle, which is found in none of the other MSS. It begins: " Do fhreagradar na dúile uachtaracha accomhdhúil an chatha sonn, ag aisneis na nolc agus na nimheadh bai ar na ndenamh san losoin, agus ba mearlupur an mhuir ag iomluadh na nes*ad*? agus na neasba sin, agus do togbadar na tonna tromgartha truadh tinneasnach agus iolguth adbul iongantach ag a caoineadh an oilein sin, agus do buireadair na biastta agus ad geisedar na garbhchnuic le gab*h*adh na greisi sin, agus ad criothnuigheadar na coillte da caion*e*adh, agus ag caion*e*adh na geuradh ar cheana, agus do gairedar na glaschlocha ag iomradh . . . . agus do guiladar na gaotha ag admhail na nardécht agus do criothnuigh an talamh tromfhódach ag tairngire an tromair sin, agus do gormbr*u*thaigh an grian re coigeadal an glasluagh, agus do niam dubhadar na neóil re hathaigh na huaire sin, agus do chomgaredar coin agus cuanarta badba agus braineoin agus geilte glinne agus arachtasa(?) aieóir

hero Cod, son of the king of Norway. It was then those excessive very-great hosts uttered their equal-great shouts, casting on high their missive weapons, and those-who-know say that fifty armed men went frenzied([1]) and lunatic from those loud shouts. And moreover it is overthrown the hosts were in that hour([2]), for there were some of them and their feet lopped off them, and they smiting their enemies with their hands, and more of them and their hands wanting, and they smiting their enemies with their feet, and [tearing] with their teeth, and more of them and their internals and entrails out of them, and they covering themselves in the ridges above the pools of crimson red blood, which was shed from the bodies and the wounds of heroes and champions, and there were more without any wound or hurt on them, but they putting the bodies on top of them- selves cross-wise to protect themselves from the sound of that conflict of the champions. However, many was the shield a-splitting and the breastplate quickly-lopped and the helmet hard-bruised, and many was the sword moreover hideous with bone and muscle throughout the battle in that hour. As for the son of the king of Sorcha and the son of the king of Norway, many were the deep wounds of stringent-death and the unhealable gashes ever pouring and spurting([3]) from them on every side. But indeed no one on the ridge of the earth, no matter how great the wisdom or the

---

ag mear caoineadh an mhórchatha sin, oc a De nimhe, do b' iomdha," etc.

([1]) Literally "went with wind", for the Irish believed that those who went mad could "walk upon the winds with lightness". ([2]) Literally "in the joint of that hour". ([3]) Literally "flowing". P, the oldest MS., inserts here a long but not very legible passage which is not in the others, and is worth reproducing. It begins: "The upper elements answered, in the presence of that battle, pro- claiming the ills and venoms that were being done upon that day, and quick- spoken(?) was the sea announcing those hurts(?) and losses, and the waves raised sorrowful rapid grief-shouts and various-voices, fearful, wonderful, lamenting that island; and the beasts roared, and the rough hills screamed with the danger of that fight(?), and the woods shook lamenting it, and lamenting too for the heroes, and the grey lochs shouted saying [here the MS. is illegible], and the winds wept in acknowledgment of those great deeds, and the heavy-sodded earth shook, prophesying that heavy slaughter, and the sun glowed-blue at the noise of the grey-hosts, and the clouds blackened at that hour, and the hounds and dog-packs, the ravens and scallcrows, and the mad ones of the glen, and the spectres of the air, were quickly keening for that mutual battle. Oh, God of heaven, many was the, &c.

eólap b'á mbeaḋ aigc, leaċ no cpian na móp-olc pin b'innpin.

Ip annpin ċáinig aipgenta[1] báip aġup beaġ-ṗaoġail bo Ríġ na Sopċa, aġup ap na ḃpaicpin pin bo ṁac Ríġ na h-Iopuaiḋe bo ċuṁṁiġ mac Ríġ na Sopċa, map bo puġ an Mánaċ ʒpe ḃpaoiḋeaċt uaiḋ é, aġup ċuġ aipe pó-ṁaiṫ aġup ʒo ppíoċnaiṁaċ. ba ġeapp [ap] a h-aiċle pin ʒo ḃpacabap aʒaċ aċ-uaċṁap ʒpánba cuca, aġup ó bípʒip beapʒ lomnoċʒa.

Ip annpin bo ċuṁṁiġ Coḋ ap an úḃall-ṁeall iapainn bo ḃí i ʒcuiḃpeaċ[2] a pʒéiċe aġup cuʒ láṁ na ċimċeall aġup ċuʒ poʒa an upċaip ap an aiċeaḋ, aġup bo ċápla an ʒ-upċap i láp a aiʒċe aġup a ḃuiḃ-ċabain[3] bó: imċupa an upċaip bo puʒ an ʒ-úḃall comċpom b'a inċeaṅ ʒap [a] ċúil-ċeann peaċʒap, aġup bo leiʒ an ʒ-aiċeaċ pʒpeab aċ-uaċṁap cpuaiḋniṁneaċ op áipb ap, aġup bo ṗill i ḃppiċinʒ na conaipe céabna aġup ʒé'p beaʒ neapʒ ṁic Ríġ na Sopċa poiṁe pin, ba lúʒa 'na ḃiaiḋ pin é, óip bo ḃí púil le caḃaip an Ṁánaiʒ aiʒe ʒonuiʒe pin.

Ip annpin ċuʒ Coḋ buille bo ṁac Ríġ na Sopċa, ʒup pʒoilʒ an caċbápp ópḃa bo ḃí pá n-a ċeann, aġup ċuʒ mac Ríġ na Sopċa buille eile bo Ċoḋ aġup bo pʒoilʒ a pʒiaʒ aġup bo ċuip ap a leaċ-ʒlúin ċlí é. Aġup ʒóʒḃap Coḋ a láṁ i n-aʒaiḋ buille ṁic Ríġ na Sopċa aġup ċuʒ pé an bapa buille ċuiʒe, aġup bo buain a ċeann aġup a láṁ ḃeap bé bc'n buille pin.

Ip annpin bo buain Coḋ a caċbápp b'á ċeann b'a ṗionn-ṗuapaḋ, aʒ iappaiḋ ʒaoiċe, aġup bo ḃí ceó bopċa op ceann an ċaċa, i n-alʒ na h-uaipe pin, aġup b'ṗéaċ Coḋ ap puḋ an ċaċa aġup bo b' ionʒna leip naċ ʒcualaiḋ pé puaim no poʒap[4] a ḃpáiċpe ann, óip ba ʒnáċ leó beiʒ aʒ púp an ċaċa ʒap éip a ċup. ba ṁaiċ an ʒ-áḋḃap meapʒʒa mí-laoiċ beiʒ aʒ peiʒioṁ an ċaċ' i n-alʒ[5] na h-uaipe pin, óip bo b' iomḋa eiʒiḋe[6] po ʒpánba ʒapḃ-ʒlópaċ op collaiḃ ceann-ċpoma, aġup linnʒe pola an peaḋ an ċaċa an ʒan pin, ionnup naċ leiʒpeaḋ blúp na ʒcopp piúḃal bo na cpó-linnʒiḃ pin.[7]

Ip annpin bo ċuaiḋ Coḋ b'iappaiḋ a ḃpáiċpeaċ ap puḋ an

---

[1] Thus A. L reads "áirgeana"; A 25 "airghointeach".   [2] Thus A. H reads "a gerannóig". L "a gcomhrainn".   [3] H reads "gur chuir inchinn amach tre shinistribh a chinn agus tre polluibh a shrón agus a chluas". [4] Thus ꝑ. A reads "foghar buillig".   [5] A often reads "alta" for "alt",

knowledge he had, could enumerate one-half or one-third of those great woes. It was then that symptoms of death and shortness of life came upon the king of Sorcha; and when the son of the king of Norway perceived them he remembered the son of the king of Sorcha, how the Mánach([1]) took him away from him by enchantment, and he gave heed very well and diligently. Short time they were after that, until they saw a horrible hideous giant coming towards them, and he fierce, red, stripped [he was the Mánach]. Then Cod remembered the apple-ball of iron that he had in the hollow of his shield, and he passed his hand round it, and gave a choice cast at the giant, and the shot chanced upon the middle of his face and black visage. As for the shot, the iron apple took its own size of the brain out through the back of his head behind, and the giant let from him on high a fearful venomous screech, and he returned the same way he came. And though small was the strength of the son of the king of Sorcha before that, it was less after it, for he had hoped for the Mánach's help up to that moment. It was then Cod dealt the son of the king of Sorcha a blow, so that he split the golden helmet that was upon his head, and the son of the king of Sorcha gave another blow to Cod, and he split his shield and put him on his left knee. And Cod raises his hand against the blow of the son of the king of Sorcha, and he gave him the second blow, and of that blow he took off his head and his right hand. It was then Cod took off the helmet from his head to refresh himself, seeking air([2]). And there was at that hour a dark fog above the battle; and Cod looked throughout the battle and he wondered that he did not hear the noise or shoutings of his brothers in it, for it was their custom to be ranging the battle after joining it. A good cause of confusion it were, to an unwarlike man, to observe the battle then in that hour, for many was the exceeding-ugly rough-voiced creature above the heavy-headed bodies, and pools of blood throughout the battle at that time, so that the closeness of the bodies would not allow the pools of gore to flow away([3]).

It was then Cod went to seek his brothers throughout the battle,

---

but not always.   ⁶ L reads ꝼeiꞇiꝺe. A eiꞇiꝺa.   ⁷ Ᵽ extends this passage at great length, but not very intelligibly.

([1]) See p. 75.   ([2]) Literally "wind".   ([3]) Literally "allow walking [movement] to the blood-pools".

ċaṫa aʒur ruair Ceaḋ marḃ ar lár an ċaṫa aʒur trí mic Ríġ
Innre h-Orc marḃ ar ʒaċ taoḃ ḋé, aʒur a ḃleaġ raoi; aʒur
ḋo ruʒ leir ar an tulaċ, ḋo ḃí or cionn an ċaṫa, é. Aʒur
ṫáiniʒ réin ḋ'iarraiḋ Ïliceaḋ ra'n ʒcaṫ aʒur ruair 'na ċrorair[1]
cró é, aʒur ḋo b' imṟníoṁaċ atuirreaċ aċṁéalaċ ḋo ḃí Coḃ
an uair rin, aʒur ḋo ṫoċail reart ḋomain raḋa rairrinʒ ḋóiḃ,
aʒur ḋo ċuir i ḃroċair a ċéile iaḋ inr an ḃreart, aʒur ḋo
rearaḋ [leir] a ʒcluiṫċe caointe, aʒur ḋo rʒríoḃ a n-anmanna
i n-óʒam, mar ba ʒnáṫ. Aʒur téiḋ ro'n ʒcaṫ arír ḋ'ḟior an
ḃruiʒċeaḋ aon nḋuine beó ḋ'á ṁuinntir, aʒur ba ḋíoṁaoin ḋó,
óir ni raiḃ rear rairneire rʒeul ḋíoḃ ʒan marḃaḋ aiċiḋ
imċian roiṁe rin, aʒur noċar ṫuit le n-a n-oireaḋ réin ariaṁ
ar tuit riú irin lá reaṁ-ráiḋte.[2] Ðo ruiḋ Coḃ ar ċloiċ ṫar
éir na h-oiḃre rin,[3] aʒur aḋuḃairt: "Ir linn réin ḋo ḋéanam
ár ʒcóṁairle rearta, óir níor ʒnáṫ linn beiṫ 'n ár n-aonar",
aʒur aḋuḃairt an laoi ann :

"Truaġ cuma na ʒcuraḋ-ra[4]
    Aniú naċ imriḋ arma[5],
    Ʒleo riu noċa(r) ḃ'ḟurara
    Ðo b' iaḋ an ḃuiḋean ċalma.

"Mé ar an tulaċ bárr-ʒloin-re[6]
    Ní h-ionʒnaḋ rinn i mbaoʒal,
    Ð'éir mo ḋeire ḋearḃráṫar,
    Noċa rluaġ neaċ 'na aonar.

"Níor ḋulta i nḋáil aon-ċaṫa[7]
    Ʒo bráṫ tar éir an ḟeill-re[8],
    Cia táim uirri ḋ'aoin-iarraiḋ[9]
    Mallaċt ar ċat na h-innre.[10]

"Ðoilʒe liom 'ná an turar-ra
    An tréan-ċlann ċalma Iorruaiḋ[11]
    Aʒ tuitim 'r na caṫaiḃ-re,
    Ðo ḃeir mo ċroiḋe ro ṫruaiġ."[12]

---

[1] Thus A 25, for the usual "cosair". A reads "easar cró".   [2] The
last forty-three words are from Π, but I have edited *arís* for *dorithis*, and *oiread*
for *iorad*.   [3] Thus L. A reads "don leat deas don obair".   [4] A "na
ccuiridh so", which I edit as above.   [5] Thus L. A reads "nach iomcharann
anois"; Π reads "nocha imrid anosa a n-arma".   [6] Ꝑ reads "misi fan
tul*ach* armgonach". Π reads "mise ger bham meardhána".   [7] Thus L ;
Ꝑ reads "i ndail tsaoirfiaga". A "fiadh*aigh*". Π has "nior dhiult ondáil saor-
fhidhaigh.   [8] Thus I edit Ꝑ's "an fhillsi". A has "na feil*e*".   [9] Thus

and he found Cead dead in the midst of the battle, and the three sons of the king of the Orkneys dead upon the other side of him, and his spear beneath him; and he bore him with him to the hill that was above the battle-field. And he himself came to seek Micead in the battle, and he found him a gory mass. And it was melancholy sad and sorrowful Cod was in that hour, and he dug them a deep, long, wide grave, and he placed them together in the grave, and their funeral games were performed by him, and he wrote their names in Ogam, as was customary. And he goes into the battle again to try if he might find any one of his people alive, but it was in vain for him, for there was never a man to tell tidings of them but was slain a long time before that; and there never fell by the same [small] number of men so many as fell by them in the aforesaid day. Cod sat himself upon a stone after that work, and said: "It is by ourselves we must make our plans in future, for we were never wont to be alone [before]"; and he spake the lay here:

> "Vain our heroes valiancy
> Their weapons work no longer,
> Death they gave their challenger
> Ah would we had been stronger.([1])

> "I on this clear-topped hillock,
> It is no wonder we to be in danger,
> After my two brothers,
> No man is a host by himself.

> "No man should go to the meeting and battle
> For ever after this treachery,
> Although I am engaged in one-search after her,
> A curse upon the cat of the island.

> "More sorrow to me than this journey,
> Are the strong valiant children of Norway
> Falling in these battles,
> It makes very sorrowful my heart."

I edit, doubtfully, from Ⱄ's "daoiniara"; and H's "dion iaramh"; and A's "do dein iarraidh. [10] All the copies read "na saor-innse", except H. [11] Ⱄ reads "an dias do gein Ioruaidh". [12] Ⱄ has "nocha liomsa nach lan truaig".

([1]) This verse is in the metre of the original, a cumasc or mixture of Cass-bhairdne and Little Rannaigheacht. Literally "alas the plight of these heroes, to-day, that they exercise not weapons, contending with them was not easy, it was they who were the valorous band".

H

A h-aiċle na laoiᵭe rin ᵭo ċoċail¹ ró crí reapca ar an máiᵹ rin .i. reapc Cloinne Ríᵹ na h-Iopuaiᵭe, reapc Cloinne Ríᵹ Innre h-Orc, aᵹur reapc iiic Ríᵹ na Sopċa, aᵹur ᵭo'n iiáiᵹ rin ᵹoirċeap "Máᵹ na ᵭerí bfeapc" i ᵹeríoċaiᵭ na Sopċa o írn a leiċ.

Aᵹur ᵭ'ráᵹaᵭap buiᵭne mópa an eaċ rin beó, ar ᵹaċ leiċ, aᵹur ní ċiúbpaiᵭír rém caoᵭaᵭ re ċċile re h-uaiiian aᵹur re h-imeaᵹla an iiióp-ᵹleo rin. Ir ann rin ᵭo ᵭí Coᵭ aᵹ aiiiare ar na ceiċre h-árᵭaiᵭ uaiᵭ ᵹaċa nᵭíreaċ, aᵹur ir ᵹeapp ᵭo ᵭí ré a h-aiċle [na] n-aiiiare rin ᵹo bfaca aon óᵹlaoċ ᵭ'á ionnpaiᵭe ra' máiᵹ ᵹo ᵭíreaċ, aᵹur ir é óᵹlaċ ᵭo ᵭí ann .i. an Curaire Camċopaċ .i. an ᵭraoi ó ċian, aᵹur ᵭo ċoirᵭir Coᵭ ceópa róᵹ ᵭó, aᵹur níor iiió a lúċᵹáir ᵭá bfeicreaᵭ a ᵭráiċre² ᵭo ċeaċc beó ar an uaiᵹ ċuiᵹe 'ná roiiii an Curaire Camċopaċ: aᵹur ᵭ'ríarruiᵹ an Curaire Camċopaċ rᵹéala an ċaċa ᵭe Coᵭ, aᵹur ċuᵹ Coᵭ rᵹéala ᵭó map ᵭo ᵭí aiᵹe, ionnur ᵹur ċuir [an] Curaire i ᵹcuiiiine aᵹur i ᵹ-cóiii-uaim feara aᵹur filiᵭeaċca iaᵭ, ᵭ' eaᵹla ᵹo raċaᵭ báċaᵭ no buan [éaᵹ] cimċioll orra ᵭá éir.³

Ir annrin ᵭo ċonncaᵭar eallca ᵭe ᵹéiriᵭ ᵭa n-ionnpaiᵹe ó'n ᵹcuan; aᵹur ᵭ'filleaᵭar ᵭo ċum an ċuaiii arír, aᵹur ᵭ'fill aon ᵹéir aiiiáin ᵭíoᵭ o'n ᵹcuan map raiᵭ Coᵭ aᵹur an Curaire Camċopaċ, aᵹur aᵭuᵭairc an ᵹéir map ro : "Ir cruaᵹ cuirreaċ ᵭoiliᵹ liom an rioċc rin i bfaicim ċu a iiic Ríᵹ na h-Iopuaiᵭe."

" An laᵭra ᵭaonᵭa rin iᵭ' ᵭeól a eóiii⁴?" ar Coᵭ.

"Ċuᵹ an fíor-ᵭia for-órᵭa rin ᵭam, ᵭ'aċċuinᵹe," ar an c-éan.

Aᵹur aᵭuᵭairc Coᵭ, " A ᵭia, ó ċárla urlaᵭraᵭ ᵭaonᵭa aᵹac, caᵭair rᵹéala ᵭúinn."

"ᵭo-ᵭéara ċeana," ar an ᵹéir, "ir mé ᵭo ċuir ċura 'r an rioċc a bfuil cu anoir."

---

¹ A, which loves strong sounds, reads here and in some other places, "do thochailt". ² Thus L, which gives the best reading of the last eight words. ³ The last twenty-three words are added from H which reads "feasa iad agus filidheacht," which I have transposed as above. ⁴ H reads "agus ro

After that lay he dug three graves upon that plain—the grave of the children of the king of Norway, the grave of the children of the king of the Orkneys, and the grave of the son of the king of Sorcha, —and that plain is the " Plain of the three graves" in the lands of Sorcha ever since.

And great bands-of-men had left that battle alive in every direction, and they themselves would not trust one another for the fear and terror [they took] of that great conflict. It was then Cod was looking straight from him round the four airts, and short time he was after such look till he beheld one young hero coming straight towards him through the plain : and this is the youth who was there, namely, the Curairè Crookfoot, the druid of a while back; and Cod bestowed on him three kisses, and not greater had been his joy had he seen his brethren coming alive out of the tomb to him, than his joy at [the coming of] the Curairè Crookfoot. And the Curairè asked Cod for tidings of the battle, and Cod gave him what tidings he had, so that the Curairè put them in remembrance, and in alliteration of knowledge and poetry, for fear lest a drowning [of oblivion] or everlasting death should go round upon them afterwards.

It was then they beheld a flock of swans coming towards them from the sea([1]), and they went back to the sea again, but one single swan of them returned from the sea to where Cod and the Curairè Crookfoot were, and the swan spake thus : " I think it a sad and a grievous pity the way in which I see thee, O son of the king of Norway."

" Is that human speech that is in thy mouth, O bird ?" said Cod.

" The all-golden true-God granted me that of a petition," said the bird.

And Cod said, "O God ! since thou hast chanced on human speech, give us tidings."

" I shall indeed," said the swan; " it was I who put thee in the condition in which thou art."

---

fhiafruigh (Cod) di cionnas ro fuair a h-aithghin urlabhra daonna do bheith aice amhlaidh sin."

([1]) Literally "harbour", but the word is often used in the sense of the open sea.

"Ḋá mba tráċ aċṁurḋín ḋúinn é," ar Coḃ, "ḋo ḃéar-
ṗamaoir, ḃuit é."

Ir annrin aḋuḃairt an ġéir, "Ġiḋ atá riḃre ir na
pioċtaiḃ rin, níor rġaoileaḃar mo ġeara-ra, aġur ní h-iaḋ
mo ġeara ṗéin ċaoinim, aċt ir truaġ aṁġar liom an pioċt
rin a ḃpuil riḃ-re; aġur ċuġar ḃrat Ríġ na h-Antuaiġe liom
ċuġaiḃ-re, aġur ciḃé corp ṗa ġcuirṫear é biaiḋ 'na pioċt
ṗéin, má raḃa no ġairiḋ, no ġo ḃráġṫar íocṗláinte ḋó, aġur
ir í mo ċóṁairle ḋuit-re a ċur um ċorraiḃ ḋo ḋearḃráṫar, ι
nḋóiġ ġo¹ mbeiṫ ι ġceineaṁain ḋuit íocṗláinte ḋ'ṗáġail uair
éiġin ḋo a n-aiċ-ḃeoḋuġaḋ," aġur ċuġ rí an ḃrat ionġantaċ
rin ḋó.

Ir annrin ḋ' éiriġ Coḃ aġur an Curaire Camċoraċ aġur
ḋo tóġaḋar béal na h-uaiġe, ḋo ċur an ḃrait ṗa na corraiḃ:
aġur ar n-a ṗaicrin rin ḋo'n Ċuraire Camċoraċ ḋo linġ ar
a muin aġur ṗuair ḃár ι ġcéaḋóir. Aġur ḋo éiriġ Coḃ aġur
ḋo ċuir an ḃrat umpa 'na ḋtriar, aġur ḋo leaġ béal na
h-uaiġe orra arír, aġur ní ḃfuair ḃár riaṁ aon ḋuine ba
ṁeara le Coḃ 'ná an Curaire Camċoraċ, óir níor ḃ' aonar
leir aġur a ḃeiṫ aiġe: aġur ceileaḃrar an eala ḋó aġur
ráiḋear na raiñ-re ria n-imċeaċt ḋí :

    " Truaġ na ġeara orrainn-ne²
    O ċárla tura iḋ' aonar,
    Sul ḋo ṗeallar orraiḃ-re
    Truaġ naċ ḋtáiniġ mo ṗaoġal.³

    " Iñé an eala ó'n ċaoṁ-innre
    Ir mé ḋoḃrán⁴ an eara,
    Ir mé cat na Saon-Innre
    ní mé ḋe ṁnáiḃ ba ṁeara.⁵

---

¹ The last twenty-six words are added from H.   ² I have edited this
poem from the readings of the various MSS. which are mostly corrupt. Thus A
reads "thárla ormsi". A 25 "oramsa". H "do ghuilsi". L omits this whole
verse. To give the extraordinarily various readings would lengthen these notes
most unduly, so I confine myself to noting only the more salient differences. L 27
alone reads the first line as I give it.   ³ Thus H : all the later copies read
saoghalsa, regarding *saoghal* as a monosyllable.   ⁴ Thus A and L, but

" If this were a time for us of reproach," said Cod, " we would give it thee."

It was then said the swan : "Although ye are in this condition, yet ye have not loosed my *geasa* from me ; still it is not my own *geasa* that I lament, but I think it a sad pity the state in which ye are ; and I have brought thee the mantle of the king of Antuaigh with me, and whatsoever body it be, round which it is placed, it will be in its own form, whether for long time or short, until a balm-of-healing be found for it ; and my advice to thee is to place it round the bodies of thy brothers, in hopes that it might be ordained for thee to obtain some time a healing-balm for their revival"; and therewith she gave him the wonderful mantle.

Then Cod and the Curairè Crookfoot rose up, and they lifted the cover of the grave, to put the mantle round the bodies. But on the Curairè Crookfoot's seeing that, he leaped down upon top of them and died forthwith. And Cod arose, and he placed the mantle round them all three ; and he laid the cover([1]) of the grave again upon them, and there never died anyone whose death grieved Cod more than that of the Curairè Crookfoot, for he did not think himself alone, and he to be with him. And the swan bade him farewell; and before going of her, she repeats these verses :

" Sore our *geasa*, every
   Misfortune on us lying,
  Ere I wrought thee treachery
   Would Death had left me dying([2]).

" I am the swan from the fair-island,
   I am the otter of the waterfall([3]),
  I am the cat of the Free Island,
   I am not the worst of women.

H reads "dobharchú".   [5] H reads "cidh bhinn idir mhnáibh deasa"; P changes the order of these two verses.

([1]) *Literally* "mouth ".   ([2]) Literally " Alas the geasa upon us, | since thou hast happened to be alone | Before I worked treachery upon you | alas that my [end of] life did not come ".   ([3]) See page 63.

" 'Ap ḋcoipʒ ʒo binn bómaine[1]
'S ann ḋo cuipeaḋ na ʒeapa,
Ḋ'inʒin Ríʒ na Ḋpeólainne
Níop ba leap-ṁáċaip leapa.[2]

" 'Ap nʒeapa ip ḋó-ḟuapʒailce
ní h-iompa ċáim ap buile,
Aċċ cuicim na ʒcupaiḋ-pe.
Ḋo-ḃeip mo ċpoiḋe po-cpuaʒ."[3]

[casċaR coḋ ḋo ḃeċuine.]

A h-aiċle na laoiḋe pin ḋo ċuaiḋ Coḋ pó'n ḃpíoḋ coille
ba ċoṁ-neapa ḋó, aʒup ċuʒ ʒual-eipe[4] móp leip ḋe ċpaoḃaċ
aʒup ḋe ḟlacaiḃ na coille, aʒup ḋ'ḟíoḃḃa paḋa bláċpéiḋe,[5]
aʒup ḋo ḋoiʒ cop móp cpéan ceineaḋ. Aʒup ḋo ċuic ḋopċaċc
na h-oiḋċe ap Coḋ, map pin. Aʒup ip ʒeapp ḋo ḃí pé ḋ'aiċle
na h-oiḋpe pin ʒo ḃpacaiḋ pé aon ċailleaċ ḋ'á ionnpaiḋe,
aʒup ip aṁlaiḋ ḋo ḃí an ċailleaċ pin aʒup aon ḟúil aṁáin i
ʒceapc-láp a ḋuiḃ-éaḋain ḃuaiṁpiʒ ḋpoċ-ḋaiċce, aʒup aon
ċop alcaċ inʒneaċ ʒeup[6] ḟúiċe, aʒup aon láṁ[7] map ċpann-
peóil coṁpaṁap loinʒe ap a h-uċc cnapaċ coppaċ, aʒup ḋo
ḟuiḋ an ċailleaċ ḋe'n caoḃ eile ḋe'n ceiniḋ, aʒup aḋuḃaipc
"1 ḋ' aonap[8] caoi a ṁic Ríʒ na h-Iopuaiḋe," ap an ċailleaċ.

"Ní h-eaḋ anoip," ap Coḋ, "óip acá cupa aʒam."

"Ní h-aʒaḋ acáim-pe," ap an ċailleaċ, "aċc cupa acá
aʒam-pa muna ḋcuʒaiḋ ċú mo ċíop ḋam."

"Cá cíop pin a ċailleaċ?" ap Coḋ.

"Coṁ-ḟaiḋ mo ċoipe ḋ'óp áluinn aiċ-leiʒċe," ap an ċailleaċ.

"Naċ ʒeaḃa ċú aipʒeaḋ uaim?" ap Coḋ.

"Ní ʒeaḃaḋ," ap an ċailleaċ.

"Ip ḋóiʒ liom naċ ḃpáʒann ċú aipʒeaḋ na óp uaim-pe,"

---

[1] Ḟ has "ambeinn boboinne"; H has "h-eas bobhuinne".　　[2] Thus H;
A has "ni dhi bu maith maise".　　　[3] All the мss. but L 27 read *truagh*, and
even in it the *i* has been eliminated by a later hand, but it seems necessary to
make a better rhyme. In H the verse reads "mo gheasa dam gidh doilghe |
ni hiompa atáim dom buaidhreadh | acht tuitim na deisi caomh-churadh | do bheir
mo croidhe go ro truagh".　　　　[4] A reads "gual eiradh". A 25 and
L; ʒualaipe; Ḟ "guaileire", from which I have edited as above.　　[5] H reads
"eire ro mhór do barrasgar craobh ndosach ndeigh dhíogan agus do gheug

" Our errand to Binn Bomaine(¹)
It was there the *geasa* were imposed,
To the daughter of the king of Dreolainn
It was not a stepmother of luck(²).

" Our *geasa* are hard-to-be-loosed,
It is not about them I am maddened,
But the falling of these heroes,
Which makes my heart very sad."

[Cod meets Bethuinè.]

After that lay, Cod went into the woody thicket that was nearest to him, and he took with him a great shoulder-load of the branches and rods of the thicket, and of long, fair, smooth wood, and he lighted a great strong tower of fire. And thus the darkness of the night fell upon Cod. And short time he was after that work until he beheld a single hag coming towards him, and this is how that hag was : She had only one eye in the very middle of her black, gloomy, ill-coloured countenance, and one jointed, talon-like, sharp foot under her, and one arm(³), like the thick mast a of ship, [coming] out of her knotty, crooked bosom ; and the hag sat upon the other side of the fire, and said, "Alone you are, son of the king of Norway," said the hag.

" Not so now," said Cod, " for I have you."

" It is not you who have me," said the hag, " but I who have you, unless you give me my tribute."

" What tribute is that, hag ?" asked Cod.

" The length of my foot of fair, refined gold," said the hag.

" Will you not take silver from me ?" said Cod.

" I will not," said she.

" I 'm sure that you get neither silver nor gold from me," said

lubach lan leabhar na coille céadna leis, ionnus gur fhodoigh morc mor teine ".
⁶ Thus H. A has " ciorclach ciordubh.   ⁷ H adds " ciordhalach cuislineach ".
⁸ Thus I edit from the " ataonar " of A.

(¹) See above, page 63.   (²) " Leasmhathair leasa " is a play upon words, the word " stepmother" in Irish bearing also the possible interpretation of "luckmother ".   (³) Literally " hand ".

ar Coḋ. "Aġur a ċailleaċ," ar ré, "créaḋ ḟá ḋeara ḋuit-re an cíor rin ḋo ḃeiṫ aġaiḃ amuiċ ar ġaċ aon?"[1]

Do ráiḋ an ċailleaċ: "An t-aṫair ḋ'á ruġaḋ mire ḋo ṫuit ar an tulaċ-ra, aġur ir é ir eiric ḋaṁ-ra,—cia ḃia ḋoġní teine ar an tulaċ ro an oireaḋ úḋ ḋ'ór ḋ'ḟáġail ḋaṁra, no ceann an ḟir rin ḟéin."

"Níor ċleaċtar cóṁrac cailliġe ḋo ḋéanaṁ riaṁ, aġur ġiḋeaḋ ḋo ġéan[2] anoir é má 'r éiġin ḋam."

Ir annrin aḋuḃairt an ċailleaċ, "An áil leat-ra teaċt ar ḟeir oiḋeaċta[3] liom ḟéin anoċt, a ṁic Ríġ na h-Ioruaiḋe?"

Aḋuḃairt Coḋ, "ḋá ḋtuġaḋ ḋuine ba ġráince[4] iná ṫura cuireaḋ na h-oiḋċe anoċt ḋam ir ḋearḃ ġo nġeaḃainn uaiḋ é, aġur ġeaḃaḋ uait-re é."

Ir annrin ḋ'éiriġ an ċailleaċ i ḋtorac na rliġe, aġur ḋo lean Coḋ í ġo ḋtárla ḋóiḃ bruiġean ċeann-árḋ cloġaraċ uaiṫne uċt-ḃláiṫ ḟuinneóġaċ,[5] aġur ḋo ċuaḋar irteaċ innti, aġur ḋo b' aoiḃinn an Rí-ḃruiġean rin, aġur ir í teine ḋo ḟuaraḋar ar urlár na cáṫraċ rin .i. teine ḋe ċloċaiḃ buaḋa, aġur ní[or] éiriġ ḋe no ḋeataċ ḋí, aġur ḋo ḃaḋar cáṫaoiriġ ḋ'ór áluinn i ḃroċair na teineaḋ rain, aġur peall rróil i nġlaic ġaċ caṫaoireaċ ḋíoḃ, aġur ḋo ḟuiḋ Coḋ i ġcáṫaoir ḋíoḃ aġur ḋo ḟuiḋ an ċailleaċ i ġcáṫaoir eile ḋíoḃ rin. Aġur ḋo rġaoil Coḋ a earra caṫa aġur cóṁraic ḋé, aġur ḋ'éiriġ an ċailleaċ aġur ṫuġ rí corn cloċ-ḃuaḋaċ cúṁḋaiġṫe i láṁaiḃ Cuiḋ, aġur iḃear Coḋ ḋeoċ ar an ġcorn rin, aġur a h-aiċle na ḋiġe ḋ'ól, ṫuġ an ċailleaċ biaḋa raora ro-ċaiṫte ċuiġe, aġur ḋo ċaiṫ Coḋ a leór-ḋóṫain ḋíoḃ, aġur ba ṁilir-ḃriaṫraċ ḋeaġ-ċóṁráiḋteaċ cailleaċ na bruiġne le Coḋ. Aġur ḋo b' ionġnaḋ leir ġan ḋo ḃeiṫ ḋe ḋaoiniḃ aici aċt í ḟéin aṁáin, aġur ḋo ḟiafraiḋ Coḋ ḋe'n ċailliġ, a[n] raiḃ irin ġcáṫair áluinn rin aċt í ḟéin aṁáin na h-aonar. "Ir ḋearḃ ġo ḃḟuil," ar an ċailleaċ, aġur ḋo ċruaḋ-ċroiṫ an ċailleaċ rlaḃraḋ ḋo ḃí i láiṁ léi,[6] aġur ḋo ċáinig caoġaḋ cailleaċ arteaċ, aġur ḟearar na mná ḟáilte ḟria Coḋ, aġur iaḋ

---

[1] The last nineteen words are from II : " annuich " is a common northern pronunciation of " amuigh ". [2] L reads " do ghéan ". A " do dhéana." A 25 " do dhéanad ". [3] Ḟ reads " ar fulachta agus ar aoghaidheacht ".

Cod; "and hag," said he, "what is the cause of your having that tribute abroad on everyone?"

Spake the hag: "The father to whom I was born fell upon this hill, and the eric [fine] I have is—whoever makes a fire upon this hill, that he must get me that much gold, or [I must get] the head of the man himself."

"I never practised combat with a hag, but yet I shall do so now if it be necessary for me."

It was then the hag said, "Would you like to come and enjoy hospitality with myself, to-night, O son of the king of Norway?"

Said Cod, "If a person [even] uglier than you were to give me an invitation for to-night, it is certain I would accept it from him, and I shall accept it from you."

Then up rose the hag and went before([1]), and Cod followed her, until they met a high-headed, belfry-like, green, bosom-smooth, window-studded mansion, and they went into it. And delightful was that royal mansion; and the fire which they found on the floor of that steading was a fire of precious stones, and neither vapour nor smoke arose from it, and there were chairs of fair gold in front of that fire, and a satin cushion in the seat([2]) of every chair of them. And Cod sat in one chair, and the hag in another chair. And Cod loosed from him his suit of battle and combat, and the hag arose and gave a goblet of precious stones into his hands, and he drank a drink out of that goblet, and after his taking the drink, the hag gave him excellent edible meats, and Cod ate his full enough of them; and it was sweet-spoken, and full of good converse, the hag of the mansion was with Cod. And he wondered at her having no people with her, but herself alone; and Cod asked her was there anyone but herself alone in that fair burg. "Surely is there," said the hag, and with that she vigorously-shook a chain which she had in her hand([3]), and there came in fifty hags. And the women welcomed Cod; and they

---

[4] Thus H. A reads "acht gead grainne tusa da", etc. Ᵽ also reads "gráince".
[5] H reads "álainn caomh-chúplach, agus í alainn eagsamhail, go gcaithireach orrdha aongantacha ar a hurlar, go tteineadh", etc.   [6] H reads simply "slabhra na bruighne".

([1]) Literally "in the beginning of the way".   ([2]) Literally "grasp".
([3]) Another MS. reads "the chain of the mansion": every house appears to have had its chain.

uile ı ʒcoṗaṁlaċc ṗıṗ¹ an ʒcéaḋ ċaıllıʒ. Iṗ annṗın ṗıaṗṗuıʒeaṗ Coḃ a ṗʒéala ṗéın ḃe'n ċaıllıʒ, aʒuṗ aḋuḃaıṗc maṗ ṗo :—

"Ríʒ ṗo ʒaḃ² ṗlaıċcaṗ aʒuṗ ṗoṗláṁaṗ ṗó ċṗíoċaıḃ na Soṗċa uaıṗ éıʒın³, ḃaṗ ba ċoṁaınm Roıʒne ṗoṗʒ-ʒlaıṗ mac Rıṗína ṗúḃlaıʒ, mıc Laoıṗıʒ lámṗaḋa⁴, aʒuṗ ní ṗaıḃ ḃe ċloınn aıʒe aċc aon ınʒean aıṁáın aʒuṗ ní ṗaıḃ mac Ríʒ ná ṗo-ṗlaıċ ná Cıʒeaṗna ṗo ċṗı ṗoʒaıl-ṗannaıḃ an ḃeaċa naċ ḃcuʒ ṗí éaṗaḋ coċmaṗc aʒuṗ caḃaṗcaıṗ aṗ ʒaċ aon ḃíoḃ ṗo leıċ. Aʒuṗ ḃo ʒaḃaḋ lá aonaıʒ aʒuṗ áṗḃ-oıṗeaċcaıṗ leıṗ an Ríʒ ṗın, aṗ ṗaıċċe an ḃúna ṗo a ḃṗuıl cuṗa anoċc, aʒuṗ čánʒaḋaṗ maıċe aʒuṗ móṗ-uaıṗle cṗíċe na Soṗċa ʒo h-ıomlán ċum an aonaıʒ ṗın, aʒuṗ ḃo ṗuıḃ a n-uaıṗle aʒuṗ a n-áṗḃ-ṁaıċe ı ḃcıṁċıoll an Ríʒ ʒo h-uaṗal onóṗaċ, aʒuṗ ċuʒ an Ríʒ ṗúıl 'na ċıṁċıoll ʒo ḃṗacaıḃ lonʒ luċcṁaṗ lán-aıḃḃṗeaċ ḃṗeac-ṗeólcaḋ aʒ cıʒeaċc ı ḃcíṗ ı ʒcuan na caċṗaċa-ṗa, aʒuṗ ní čáınıʒ ḃe ṗluaʒ no [ḃe ṗocaıḋe] aıṗḃí aċc aon óʒlaċ aıṁáın, aʒuṗ čáınıʒ aṗ an culaċ ṗo ċall, aʒuṗ ḃo ṗáıč a ṗʒıaċ ı ḃcaoḃ na culċa-ṗa, aʒuṗ ḃo čóʒaıḃ a ılċleaṗa oṗ a ċeann ʒo h-uaċḃáṗaċ. Aʒuṗ ní ṗaıḃ ḃe na ṗlóıʒcıḃ uıle neaċ ḃ'aṗ leıʒ an eaʒla ḃul ḃ'ıaṗṗaıḋ ṗʒéala ṗaṗ an ṗıḃıṗe óʒ ıonʒancaċ ṗın, ʒuṗ cuıṗeaḋ ḃṗaoı ṗáčaċ ṗocal-ʒéaṗ aʒ ıaṗṗaıḋ ṗʒéal aṗ an nʒaıṗʒıḃeaċ caċḃuaḋaċ ṗın. Aʒuṗ ċuʒ an ḃeaʒ-laoċ ṗın ṗʒéala ḃó ʒan ımṗeaṗán, aʒuṗ ḃo ṗáıḃ ʒuṗ ḃ' é ṗéın Ceann ʒan colaınn⁶ mac Ríʒ na ʒCaıṗleán, aʒuṗ ʒuṗ ḃ'ıaṗṗaıḋ ınʒıne Ríʒ na Soṗċa čáınıʒ ṗé, aʒuṗ aḋuḃaıṗc a cuṗ ċuıʒe, no céaḋ ṗeaṗ n-aṗm ḃo ċuṗ ḃo ċóṁṗac ṗıṗ, aʒuṗ nuaıṗ ḃo ċuıcṗıḃíṗ ṗın an oıṗeaḋ eıle ḃo ċuṗ ḃo ċóṁṗac aʒuṗ ḃo ċaċuʒaḋ ṗṗıṗ. Aʒuṗ čáınıʒ an ḃṗaoı leıṗ na ṗʒéalaıḃ ṗın ḃo ċum an Ríʒ, aʒuṗ ḃo ċuaḋaṗ maıċe aʒuṗ móṗ-uaıṗle cṗíċe na Soṗċa ı ʒcóṁaıṗle, aʒuṗ ıṗ í cóṁaıṗle ḃo cṗíoċnuıʒeaḋ leó, céaḋ ṗeaṗ n-aṗm ḃo ċuṗ ḃo ċóṁṗac ṗıṗ an nʒaıṗʒıḃeaċ; aʒuṗ ḃo cuıṗeaḋ. Ní ṗaḋa ḃo ṁaıṗ an céaḋ ṗın ḃó.⁶ Aʒuṗ ḃo cuıṗeaḋ céaḋ eıle ḃo ċóṁṗac ṗṗıṗ,

¹ H reads "ar aon deanamh le".   ² Thus H and Ṗ, but A has "gabhistar".   ³ Thus L, but A has "feacht nallain"(?). Ṗ omits. ⁴ H reads *mic* Seadna Suibhlaig *mic* Luighidh l. Ṗ reads "*mic* Seanda tsiobhlaigh mic Laoisig lamfada". L reads "arach", A "eira". H reads "tocmairce".

[were] all of the same appearance as the first hag.   It was then Cod asked her for her own story, and she spake thus :—

"A king [there was], who on a certain time, assumed sovereignty and authority over the lands of Sorcha, whose name was Roighne Grey-Eye, son of Risina the traveller, son of Laoiseach Long-hand, and he had no children except one only daughter, and there was never king's son, nor great chief, nor lord, in the three plunder-divisions of life but she gave every separate one of them a refusal of espousal and gifts.   And a day of gathering and a high assembly was appointed by that king on the lawn of this dún, in which you are to-night, and the great men and nobles of the land of Sorcha came in full numbers to that assembly, and their nobility and high chiefs sat round the king, nobly and honourably.   And the king cast an eye around him, when([1]) he beheld a laden, full-fair, speckle-sailed bark coming to land in the harbour of this city, and there came out of her neither host nor army, but only one single youth.   And he came upon yonder hillock, and thrust his spear into the side of the hillock and performed in fearful guise his various battle-feats on high([2]).   And there was not one of all the hosts whom fear allowed to go seek tidings of that wondrous young knight, until a knowing, sharp-worded druid was sent to ask tidings of the battle-victorious hero.   And that good hero gave the druid his tidings without dispute, and said that he himself was Head without body([6]), son of the king of the Castles, and that it was to seek the daughter of the king of Sorcha that he came; and he said to send her to him, or else to send a hundred armed men to fight with him, and when those should fall to send as many more, to fight and to battle with him.   And the druid came with those tidings to the king; and the chiefs and great nobles of the land of Sorcha went into counsel, and what was resolved on by them was to send a hundred armed men to fight with the hero ; and these were sent.   That hundred did not stand him long.   And another hundred were sent to fight with him,

---

[5] Thus H.   A has "gan colladh".   L "colann gan ceann ".   A 25 "ceann na colladh ".   [6] Thus A 25.   A and H read "rug do", and L "rug an céad sin as".

([1]) Literally " till ".   ([2]) Literally "raised his various feats above his head frightfully ".   ([6]) Another ms. reads "Body without head", and a third "Head of the body ".

·aġus ní faḋa ruġ an céaḋ rín ḋó[7]. Aċt tá ní ċeana, ḋo ċuiteaḋar urṁór[1] rluaiġ críċe na Sorċa leir, aġus an ríġ féin, rġéal ba ṁó, rul ḋo táinig an tráċnóna ċuiġe. Aġus a ṁic Ríġ na h-Ioruaiḋe ir mire féin an inġean ḋo ḃí aġ Ríġ na Sorċa fo 'n am rin, aġus an tan ḋo ċonnairc mire an t-ár mór ar na rlóiġtiḃ,[2] ḋo ċuirear cealtar[3] ḃaoiġeaċta i ḃtimċioll na caṫraċa ro, ionnur naċ ḃfacaiḋ aon ḋuine an ċáṫair-re ó roin a leiċ, aġus ḋo ġaiḃ an ġairġiḋeaċ rin neart aġus treire aġus ceannar na críċe reó ó roin anuar, aġus a flioċt 'na ḋiaiġ[4]. Aġus fór a ṁic Ríġ na h-Ioruaiḋe, ir ar flioċt an ġairġiḋiġ rin atá an fear úḋ ḋo ċuit leat-ra, amuiġ, aġus ir é rin mo ċáirḋear féin riot-ra[5] a ṁic Ríġ na h-Ioruaiḋe," ar an ċailleaċ.

"Beir buaiḋ aġus beannaċt"[6] ar Coḋ, "ir maiṫ na rġéala rin, aġus innir anoir ḋúinn créaḋ ḋo ḃeir ġan ċoraiḋ ġan láṁaiḃ riḃ, i ġcruṫ éaġraṁail mar rin?"

"Inneórad rin ḋaoiḃ, a ṁic Ríġ na h-Ioruaiḋe," ar an ċailleaċ, "i nḋóiġ ġur[7] móiḋe rġáṫ aġus im-eaġla cáiċ róṁainn, ár mbeiṫ mar ro, aġus ní[or] ġnáṫuiġeaḋar ár ḃtaiṫiġe tríḋ rin," ar rí, "aġus [ir] ġan fior ḋo luċt na críċe reó támaoiḋ ran mbruiġin reo ḋe ġréar, aġus a ṁná," ar rí, "téiḋmiḋ ann ár ġcruṫ féin ġo lá.[8]"

Do rinne na mná rin aġus níor ḃ' éaġraṁla[9] mná 'ran ḋoṁan no iaḋ, ar feaḃar a nḋeilḃe aġus ar ḃreáġṫaċt a rġéiṁe.[10] Ir ann rin ḋo cuireaḋ luiḃe íce, no balroim, i ġcneaḋaiḃ aġus i ġcréaċtaiḃ mic Ríġ na h-Ioruaiḋe. Ir ann rin ḋ'fiarruiġ Coḋ ḋe na mnáiḃ an raiḃ íce no balrom aġ Ríġ na Sorċa.

"Do ḃí ċeana," an an inġean, "aġus ḋo ḃí uaṫaḋ ban ra ġcáṫair, lá éiġin, aġus táinig aṫaċ úr-ġránḋa i ḃroċair ḋo'n ċaiṫriġ reo, aġus an íce atá tura ḋ'iarraiḋ, ḋo ruġ leir i ġcéaḋóir í, aġus ḋo ċuaḋar ar ḃárr na caṫraċ rin, aġus ḋo ċoṅairc mé an uillféirt aṫaiġ rin aġ ḋul i mbéal na h-uaiṁe tá re taoḃ na mara ro fíor."

---

[1] Thus L and A 25. A reads "forgla". [2] H adds "agus m'athair do thuitim as mo los". [3] A spells this "calter". L reads "briocht draoidheachta". A 25 "ceó doilbhe draoidheachta". [4] The last twenty-two words are from L. [5] H reads "uime sin do chuadhas ar bhur

and that hundred did not last him long. But, however, very many of the hosts of the country of Sorcha fell by him, and the king himself—a greater calamity(¹),—before the evening came on him. And, I myself, O son of the king of Norway, am the daughter that the king of Sorcha had at that time, and when I beheld the great slaughter of the hosts, I put an enchanted spell round this burg, so that no one saw it from that out. And that warrior assumed strength, and might, and authority over this country ever since, and his race after him. And, moreover, son of the king of Norway, yon man who fell by you outside there, was of the descendants of that warrior, and it is that [causes] my own friendship for you, son of the king of Norway," said the hag [for thus avenging me].

" Take a victory and a blessing," said Cod; " good are those tidings, and tell us now what makes you be without feet or hands in strange guise like that."

" That I shall tell you, son of the king of Norway," said the hag, "[it is] in hopes that the shyness and terror of everyone before us might be the greater for our being like this ; and on account of that," said she, " they never made a practice of frequenting us, and it is without knowledge of the people of this country that we are constantly in this mansion; and women," said she, " let us go into our own shape till day."

The women did that, and there were no women in the world more remarkable than they for the excellence of their shape, and the splendour of their beauty. It was then herbs of healing, or balsam, were placed in the wounds and hurts of the son of the king of Norway. It was then Cod asked the women, had the king of Sorcha any healing, or balsam.

" He had, in truth," said the lady; " and there were of a certain day [only] a few women in the mansion ; and there came a hideous ugly giant up to the mansion, and the balm you are asking for, he carried it off there and then. And I went to the top of yon *cathair*, and I beheld that monster of a giant going into the mouth of the cave which is at the side of this sea below."

---

gceann-sa ". ⁶ The last four words are from H. II⁷ reads " go madh ".
⁸ The last eleven words are from H, which gives the best reading. ⁹ H reads " nochar báilne ". ¹⁰ The last nine words are from L.

(⁷) Literally " story ".

Iar rin d'ḟiaḟruiġ Coḃ de'n ċailliġ cṙéaḃ ḟaḃ d' aimṙir ó ḟuair a h-aċaiṙ ḃáṙ, "no ca h-ainm atá orc ḟéin?"

"Beċuine iṙ ainm ḃaṁra," aṙ ṙí, "aġuṙ tá tṙí ċéaḃ bliaḋan¹ ó ḟuair m'aċaiṙ ḃáṙ."

"Cṙéaḃ do ḃeiṙ beó ṙiḃ an ḟaḃ ṙin?" aṙ Coḃ.

"An dtuġaiṙ ḟo ḃeaṙa an coṙn aṙ a dtuġaṙ an ḃeoċ ḃuic ó ċiainiḃ?"

"Do ċoñaiṙc mé," aṙ Coḃ.

"Maiṙeaḃ," aṙ ṙí, "ġiḃ bé neaċ ólḟaṙ ḃeoċ aṙ ġaċ lá, ní luiġeann aoiṙ no úṙ-ċṙáḃ² aiṙ, tṙe ḃiċ ṙíoṙ, aġuṙ táiḃ ṙeóiḃ eile aġainn aṙ a ḃḟuiliḃ iomaḃ ḃuaḃ maṙ ṙúḃ."

Iar ṙin do cóiṙiġeaḃ iomḃaiḃ aġuṙ áṙḃ-leaba do Ċoḃ, aġuṙ cuiṙeaḃ bṙuit uaiṙle onóṙaċa aṙ an leaba ṙin. Ċuġaḃaṙ³ aṙ an oiḃċe ṙin ġuṙ éiṙiġ an ġṙian iona cioṙcal teinciḃe oṙ ḃṙeaċ na taliṁan tṙomḟóḃaiġe aṙ n-a ṁáṙaċ. Iṙ ann ṙin do ġaḃ Coḃ [a] earraḃ aiṙtiṙ⁴ aġuṙ imċeaċta uime, aġuṙ do iaṙṙ aṙ ṁnaoi ḃe na mnáiḃ ḃul leiṙ do ḃéanaṁ eóluiṙ do ċum na h-uaiṁe, 'na nḃeaċaiḃ an t-aċaċ. Do ċuaiḃ beċuine le Coḃ do ḃéanaṁ eólaiṙ na h-uaiṁe ḃó, aġuṙ do ṙinne an laoi :

> "'S tuiṙṙeaċ ṙin a ċompánaiġ⁵
> A Ċoiḃ na mbṙiataṙ maoṙḃa
> Cuiḃ deḃ' eaċtṙa ġaḃlánaiġ⁶
> 1 mbéal uaiṁe iṙ tu iḃ' aonaṙ.

> "Do ṙluaġ ġion ġuṙ an-áiḃṙeaċ
> Saoilim naċ baoġal ḃuit-ṙe,
> Ġé taoi anoiṙ ġo tuiṙṙeaċ
> Moṙ tíṙ d'á dtuġaiṙ tuiṙṙe."

A h-aiċle na laoiḃe ṙin do ċuaiḃ Coḃ ṙan uaiṁ, aġuṙ ḟuaiṙ ḟoṙġailte í, aġuṙ ṙliġe ċaol ċúṁanġ ḃoṙċa ann, aġuṙ do lean Coḃ an tṙliġe ṙin ġo dtáṙla máġ⁷ ṁín áluinn ḃó iaṙ

---

¹ H reads "dá mhile bliadhan", ꝑ céad bliadhan go ttuilleadh".   ² Thus H, but A has "urchar". L "urchóid".   ³ L and A 25 read "rugadar".   ⁴ A reads "aistire".   ⁵ H omits this lay. ꝑ omitted it too, but a later hand tries to insert it in the margin; I read "'S" for "Is", to make the line scan.   ⁶ Thus L. A has "gabhlannach". ⁷ H reads "maighion (?) sgothach mor aluinn".

Thereafter Cod asked the hag what length of time was it since her father died, " or what is your own name ?"

" Bethuinè([1]), is my name," said she, " and it is three hundred([2]) years since my father died."

" What makes you to be alive so long ?" said Cod.

" Did you observe the goblet out of which I gave you the drink, a while back ?"

" I saw it," said Cod.

" Well then," said she, " whatever person shall drink a drink out of it, every day, neither age nor misery rest upon him through time eternal, and we have other jewels in which are, in like manner, many virtues."

Thereafter a couch and a high bed were arranged for Cod, and noble, honourable mantles were spread upon that bed. They bore away that night until, upon the morrow, the sun rose in its fiery circle above the face of the heavy-sodded earth. It was then Cod put round him his suit of travel and journey, and he asked a woman of the women to go with him to guide him to the cave into which the giant had gone. Bethuinè went with Cod to show him the way to the cave, and she made the lay :

" Comrade, art thou sorrowful,
   Cod of the words right pleasant,
In these caves all horrible
   With dangers ever present ?([3])

" Thy host although not very showy,
   I think that to thee there is no danger,
Although thou art now sorrowful,
   Many is the country to whom thou hast given sorrow."

After that lay, Cod went into the cave, and found it open, and a slender narrow path in it. And Cod followed that path, until after leaving the cave, he came upon a lovely smooth plain, and he

---

([1]) Pronounced Bĕh-in-a or Bĕh-in-ya.   ([2]) The oldest ms. reads " a hundred years and more ". The Trinity College ms. reads " two thousand years ". ([3]) This verse is a " cumasc " of Cass-bhairdne and Little Rannagheacht ; the seventh line, however, does not end, as it should, in a trisyllable. Literally " It is sorrowful, O companion | Cod of the courteous words, | part of thy difficult(?) adventures | in the mouth of a cave, and thou alone."

ḃfáġḃáil na h-uaiṁe ṙin, aġuṙ tápla oileán[1] beaġ ḋó, aġuṙ ḋo ġaḃ ṙé aġ min-iaṙṙaiḋ an oileáin no ġo ḋtápla tiġ[2] beaġ ṙo-áluinn ḋó, aġuṙ teine ġan ḃe ġan ḃeataiġ aṙ ṙaḃóġ ann, aġuṙ an tiġ ṙin aṙ na eaġaṙ aġuṙ aṙ na úṙ-luaċṙaḋ[3] ḃe ċaonnaċ[4] an tṙléiḃe, aġuṙ ḃe luiḃeanaiḃ na taliṁan, aġuṙ ḃe ḋuilleaḃaṙ na ġcṙann. Aġuṙ ṙo ṙuiḋ Coḃ ann, aġuṙ ṙo ḃuaim [a] aṙm aġuṙ [a] eaṙṙaḋ aiṙtiṙ[5] aġuṙ imċeaċta ḋé aġuṙ aḋuḃaiṙt ṙé, "Anṙaḋ ann ṙo anóċt aġuṙ má tá ataiġ inṙ an oileán ṙo iṙ annṙo ḃíḋ ḃe ġṙéaṙ," aġuṙ ḃo ḃí nóin aġuṙ ḃeiṙeaḋ an laé ann an uaiṙ ṙin.

Aġuṙ iaṙ ḃteaċt na h-oiḋċe[6] ċonnaiṙc Coḃ ataċ úṙ-ġṙánḃa aċ-uaċṁaṙ ḃ'á ionnṙaiḋe, aġuṙ ṙiaḋ ṙeólmaṙ aṙ a ḋá ḃinn leiṙ[7], aġuṙ ḃo ṫṙeaṙġaiṙ ġo láṙ aġuṙ ġo lán-taliṁain é aġuṙ ṙeannaṙ ġo h-aċlaiṁ é ḃá éiṙ[8], aġuṙ ḃo ċuiṙ aṙ ċeiṫṙe bioṙṙaiḃ ṙaḃa ṙionn-ċoill a ċeiṫṙe ceaṫṙaṁna, aġuṙ ṙaḃoiġeaṙ moṙc tṙeaċtan-ṁóṙ teine ṙiṙ[9], aġuṙ níoṙ laḃaiṙ aon ṙocal ṙe Coḃ ṙiṙ an ṙaé ṙin. Aġuṙ ḃ'ṙiaṙṙuiġ Coḃ ḃe'n ataċ ann ṙin : "Cá leiṫ ḃíoḃ ṙin mo leiṫ-ṙe?" Aḋuḃaiṙt an ṙeaṙ móṙ, "Ni ṙaoilim-ṙe ġuṙ leat ceaċtaṙ ḃíoḃ,"[10] aġuṙ an tan ṙá ḃeiṙḃċe[11] ullaṁ an ṙeóil ċuġ an t-ataċ láiṁ na timċeall, aġuṙ ṙuġ ḃ'á ċaoḃ ṙéin ḃe'n teine í. Iṙ ann ṙin ċuġ Coḃ ṙiċ ṙanntaċ ṙáṙ-lúṫṁaṙ[12] aṙ an ḃṙeaṙ móṙ, ġuṙ ċuiṙ a ċúiġ caoil i ġceann a ċéile, aġuṙ ḃ'áil leiṙ a ċeann ḃo ḃuaint ḃé.

"Ná maṙḃ mé," aṙ an t-ataċ, "aġuṙ biaiḋ mé úiṁall ḃuit aṙ ṙo ṙuaṙ."

"Tá connṙaḋ aṙ an nḃéanṙainn ṙin," aṙ Coḃ.

"Cá connṙaḋ ṙin?" aṙ an t-ataċ.

"An íce atá aġat ḃ'ṙáġail ḃaṁ-ṙa," aṙ Coḃ.

"Níl an íce aġam-ṙa ġo ḃeaṙḃta," aṙ an t-ataċ, "aġuṙ a ḃṙuil ḃ'á ṙġéalaiḃ aġam ḃo ḃéaṙ[ṙ]aḃ ḃuit-ṙe é." Aġuṙ ḃo ṙġaoil Coḃ i ġcéaḃóiṙ ḋé. Iṙ annṙin aḋuḃaiṙt an t-ataċ ṙá ṙáiḃtiḃ ġṙéine aġuṙ iaṙġa,[13] ġo nḃéanaṙaḋ ṙé ṙíṙinne ḃo Ċoḃ.

---

[1] No mention of the "oileán" in H.   [2] H reads "teaguis taithneamhach".
[3] Thus L, but A has " ar teaghar agus ar na teagha".   [4] Thus H. A has "caodhnach "; L " cúnach".   [5] A, as usual, reads "aistire".
[6] Last five words from H.   [7] Ṗ has "bheinn na lamh".   [8] Last seven words from H.   [9] Last nine words from H, but I have written *teine* for *tine*.   [10] Thus L. A has skipped this by mistake.   [11] Thus I edit

chanced upon a little island(¹), and he proceeded to closely-search the island, until he came upon a small, very-handsome house, and a fire without vapour or smoke kindled in it. And that house was arranged and freshly-strewn(²) with moss of the mountain, and with herbs of the ground, and with foliage of the trees. And Cod sat in it, and took off his arms and his habiliments of travel and journey, and said " I will stop here to-night, for if there are giants in this island, it is here they constantly be," and it was then the hour of nones and the end of the day.

And on the coming of night, Cod beheld a very-hideous, horrible giant coming towards him, and a fatted deer with him by his two horns. And he felled it to the floor and ground, and thereupon he flays it readily, and he sets its four quarters on four long spits of white hazel, and he kindles around it an enormous heap of fire, and during all that time he spake not one word to Cod. And then Cod asked the giant, " Which half of those is my half ?" The big man said, " I do not think that either of them is yours." And when the flesh was cooked(³) and ready, the giant put a hand round it and brought it to his own side of the fire. Then Cod gave an eager very-active leap towards the big man, so that he put his five smalls together(⁴), and he was minded to take off his head.

" Do not kill me," said the giant, " and I shall be submissive to you from this out."
" There is a condition on which I would do it," said Cod.
" What condition is that ?" said the giant.
" To get for me the salve which you have," said Cod.
" Indeed I have not the salve," said the giant, " but all that I know about it(⁵) I will tell you." And Cod loosed him at once. It was then the giant said, under invocation of sun and moon, that he

the " beirfa" of A; the others omit. some contraction beginning with " solam ". simply " fa na mionnaibh."   ¹² L reads " so lamaidh ". ꝑ has ¹³ Thus A 25. A has

(¹) Something must have here dropped out of the mss., for one cannot talk of an island in a plain.   (²) Literally " be-rushed " or " rush-strewn ". (³) Literally "boiled".   (⁴) See page 35, line 14.   (⁵) Literally " all of its stories that I have, I shall give them ".

I

Iṗ annṗin aḋuḃaiṗt an t-ataċ: "do ḃí an íoc-ḟláinte ṗin[1] aġ an ataiṗ d'á ṗuġaḋ miṗe, aġuṗ táinġaḋaṗ tṗiaṗ ataċ ċuġainn, aġuṗ ṗuġaḋaṗ an íce ṗin uainn; aġuṗ toṗaḋ mo ṗeaṫa do ṗuġ miṗe uaṫa. Aġuṗ do ċuaḋaṗ i mbéal uaiṁe tá ṗe taoḃ an oileáin ṗeó, aġuṗ ní'l a ḃeaġ no a ṁóṗ d'á ṗġéalaiḃ aġam ó ṗoin a leiṫ." Aġuṗ ṗuġaḋaṗ aṗ an oiḋċe ṗin, no ġuṗ ṗoillṗiġ an lá ġo n-a lán-tṗoillṗe aṗ n-a ṁáṗaċ oṗṗa. Iṗ annṗin do ċuaiḋ Coḃ i ġceann aiṗtiṗ aġuṗ imṫeaċta, aġuṗ do iaṗṗ ṗé aṗ an ḃṗeaṗ móṗ dul, do ḋéanaṁ eólaiṗ dó, aṗ an uaiṁ a nḋeaċaḋaṗ na h-ataiġ. Iṗ annṗin duḃaiṗt an ṗeaṗ móṗ náċ ġeaḃaḋ maiṫeaṗ na talṁan aġuṗ aon ṗúil aṁáin do ṫaḃaiṗt aṗ aon aiṫeaċ[2] díoḃ, aġuṗ dá dtuġtaoí maiṫeaṗ na cṗuinne óḋ ṗéin naċ ġeaḃaḋ é, aġuṗ dul aṗ a n-aṁaṗc aṗíṗ.

"Taṗṗ, a ṗiṗ ṁóiṗ," aṗ Coḃ, "aġuṗ ná bíoḋ uaṁan ná im-eaġla oṗt an ṗeaḋ ḃiaṗ tu [ann] mo ċuiḋeaċta-ṗa." Iaṗ ġcloṗ na mbṗiaṫaṗ ṗin do'n ṗeaṗ móṗ do ċuaiḋ ṗé leiṗ, ġo doṗuṗ béil[3] na h-uaiṁe.

[castar coḃ do ġrian ġnúis-ṡolais.]

Aġuṗ do ċuaiḋ Coḃ i dtoṗaċ na ṗliġe iṗteaċ inṗ an uaiṁ, aġuṗ ṗuaiṗ ṗliġe coṁ-doṗċa innti,[4] aġuṗ iomaṗcaiḋ de ionġantaṗaiḃ dó-áiṗṁiġte. Aġuṗ táṗla oileán beaġ dó aġuṗ ṗaiṗṗġe aṗ ġaċ taoḃ dé, aġuṗ cloiḋe[5] coṁṗanna tṗe láṗ an oileáin ṗin, aġuṗ tṗéaḋ de ċaoṗaċaiḃ aṗ ġaċ taoḃ dé ṗin, aġuṗ aon ṗeiċe coṗcaṗḋa eatoṗṗa, aġuṗ do ḃí a leaċ de na caoṗċaiḃ duḃ aġuṗ an leaċ eile ṗionn díoḃ, aġuṗ an tan tiġḋíṗ na caoiṗiġ duḃa do'n taoḃ a mbíoíṗ na caoiṗiġ ṗionna do ḃíoíṗ uile ġléġeal[6] aġuṗ an tan tiġḋíṗ na caoiṗiġ ṗionna do taoḃ na ġcaoṗaċ nduḃ de'n ċloiḋe, do ḃíoíṗ uile duḃ, aġuṗ iṗ é an ṗeiċe do ċuiṗeaḋ na caoiṗiġ amaċ 'ṗ aṗteaċ ṗo an cloiḋe,[7] aṗ an oṗḋuġaḋ ṗin. Aġuṗ do ḃí Coḃ d'á ḃṗéaċain ṗeal,[8] aġuṗ do ċuaiḋ do'n ċuiḋ eile de'n oileán, aġuṗ táṗla loċ

---

[1] Thus II. A has "ioce".   [2] H "fomhóir".   [3] A "béal"; the others omit.   [4] H has "dorcha dóieolais trithe".   [5] Thus H. A has "cladha".   P "cloighe".   [6] I have followed H here which gives the best reading. A reads "uilliog" for "uile", nearly as pronounced.   [7] A here

would deal truly with Cod. Then the giant spake, " The father to whom I was born had that healing-balm, and three giants came to us, and they brought that healing-balm from us, and it was the speed(¹) of my running which saved me from them; and they went into the mouth of a cave which is on the side of this island, and I have no more tidings of them, either great or small, from that out." And they bore away that night, until the sun with its full light shone upon them on the morrow. It was then Cod faced for voyage and travel; and he asked the big man to go and show him the way to the cave into which the giants had gone. But the big man said that he would not take all the goods of the earth and cast one eye on any giant of them—that if the riches of the world were to be given him he would not take them and come within sight of them again.

" Come, big man," said Cod, " and let you have neither fear nor horror, so long as you shall be in my company." And, after the big man heard those words, he went with him to the mouth of the door of the cave.

[Cod meets Bright-faced Sun.]

And Cod went forward on the way(²) into the cave, and he found in it a very-dark path, and multitudes of innumerable wonders. And he found a little island and a sea on each side of it, and a dividing ditch through the middle of that island, and a flock of sheep upon each side of it, and one scarlet ram amongst them, and one half of the sheep were black, and the other half were white. And when the black sheep would come to the side on which the white sheep used to be, they used to be bright-white, and when the white sheep would come to the black sheep's side of the ditch, they used to be all black, and it was the ram who used to drive the sheep out and in over the ditch, in that manner. And Cod was a while regarding them. And he went to the other side of the island and chanced upon a fair lake, and a beautiful flock of bright-white birds ever-

---

spells the word " claidh", which is the pronunciation of " Leath Choinn", " cly ", rhyming to " fly ".   ⁸ Last seven words are from A 25.

(¹) Literally " fruit ".   (²) Literally " went in the beginning of the way in ".

áluinn ḋó, aġur ciṫ[1] áluinn ḃ'ċanaiḃ[2] ġlé-ġeala, aġ ríp-ċirże
ruar ar láp an loċa rin, aġur ní ḟilleaḋ aon ċinín ríor arír[3]
ḋíoḃ aċc aġ ríp-éirże ruar ḋe ġnáċ. Aġur aḋuḃairc Coḋ ġur
maiċ leir ríor ḋo ḃeiċ aiġe cia ar a ḋciġeaḋ na h-éin ġléiġeala
rin, aġur ċuġ ḃrac uirże[4] ḃí aiġe amaċ, aġur ċuġ a uċc ar
an loċ, aġur céiḃ ḟaoi ġo ġreann aġur ġo ġrinnioll, aġur
ḟéaċar ar ġaċ caoḃ ḋé, aġur ḃo ċonnairc ḋún[5] ḋaċ-áluinn
ḋearġ-óir i ġcéaḃóir uaiḃ. Aġur ḃo ċuaiḋ ann, aġur céiḃ ré
arceaċ inr an ḃúnaḋ, aġur ċápla inġean ċruċaċ ċaoṁ-áluinn[6]
ḋó, aġur calla[7] ḃ'ór áluinn Airrice ḟo n-a ceann, ġo cloċaiḃ
buaḋa aġur ġo niaṁannaiḃ[8] ḟionn-ċorcra, aġur ġo ġeamaiḃ
ḟionn-airġiḋ aġ ḟolaċ a h-órṗoilc, aġur ḃrac ḋe'n ċorcar-
ḟróil[9] na cimċeall, aġur peall ḃe ḟróil uaiċne ḟúiċi ġo
n-éaḃuiġiḃ uairle onóraċa or ġaċ caoḃ ḋí. Aġur ir aṁlaiḋ
ḋo ḃí an inġean rin aġur rlac ġeal ina láiṁ, aġur rġian
ḃeaġ ran láiṁ eile, aġur ḃo ḃí rí aġ rnoiḋe na rlaice rin,[10]
aġur ġaċ rlior ḃ'á mbaineaḋ ḋe'n crlaic ḃ'éirżeaḋ 'na
n-éanaiḃ ġléġeala cre ḟuinneḋġaiḃ na caċraċ[11] amaċ.

Aġur ḃo ḃ' ionġnaḋ le Coḋ náḋúir na rlaice rin, aġur ḃo
ḃeannuiġ ḃo'n inġin aġur ḃo ḟreaġair an inġean é, aġur ir
eaḋ aḋuḃairc: "Cia hé aġainn naċ ionġnaḋ a ċéile; óir ir
ionġnaḋ leac-ra mire, aġur ir ionġnaḋ liom-ra cura!"
Ḃ'ḟiarruiġ an inġean a rġéala ḟéin ḋe Coḋ aġur ċuġ-ran
a rġéala ḟéin ḃí, ó ċúr ġo ḃeireaḋ. Ḃ'ḟiarruiġ Coḋ an
céaḋna ḃi-re aġur ḃo ḟreaġair an inġean é, aġur ir eaḋ
aḋuḃairc: "Mire Ġrian Ġnúir-ḟolair inġean Ríġ Ḟoraoire
na n-Ionġnaḋ aġur ir é rin an Ríġ ir mó cúṁaċca 'ran ḃoṁan
ḟe n-a linn, aġur a ṁic Ríġ na h-Ioruaiḋe ḃo ḃ' annaṁ ḟriċ[12]
eólar an ḃúna-ra ṗóṁaḋ riaṁ, aġur ġaḃ an crlac ro aġur
ḃéana ḃṗeir[13] ḃ'á rnoiḋe." Ḋo ṗuġ Coḋ ar an crlaic aġur ḃo

---

[1] H has "alt".   [2] A 25 "d'éanlaidhibh".   [3] H reads "gac én diobh ag fill*eadh* anuas do ridhis".   [4] H reads "tug a bheirt uisge cuige do baoi a ccobr*ann* a sgeithe, gur gabh uime i".   [5] H has "sonnach".   [6] H "caoin-déanmhach".   [7] L "ealla". A 25 "cáil". H, F, and A "calla".   [8] Thus L. A has "do neamuina".   [9] F adds "ar tonngail". L "ar tonngaile".   [10] H reads "ag buaint casna don chaomh shlait".   [11] H "fuineogaib agus shinistribh and dúnadh, agus do ghluaiscadh iomluaguil na hardghaoithe aiaerdha iad comluthmhar sin ionnas go

rising up out of the middle of that lake, and never a little bird of them used to return down again, but always [they were] continuously-rising up. And Cod thought([1]) that he would like to know out of what place those bright birds were coming, and he took out a water mantle([2]) that he had, and he laid his bosom on the lake, and he goes under it to the bed and gravel, and he looks about him on every side, and therewith beheld a beautifully-coloured mansion of red gold at a distance from him. And he went to it, and enters the mansion. And a shapely gentle-loving girl met him, and a covering of beautiful African gold upon her head, with precious stones, and with white-purple shimmerings, and with white-silver gems covering her golden hair, and a mantle of purple satin round her, and a cushion of green satin under her, with noble, honourable cloths above her on every side. And this is how that girl was: she had a white rod in her hand, and a little knife in the other hand, and she was slicing the rod, and every slice that she used to take off the rod, they used to rise up and out, as bright birds, through the windows of the mansion.

And Cod marvelled at the nature of that rod, and he saluted the girl, and the girl answered him, and said: "Which of us does not wonder at the other, for you wonder at me, and I wonder at you!" Then the girl asked Cod for his story, and he told her his own story from beginning to end. Cod asked her for the same, and the girl answered him, and this is what she said: "I am Grian Gnúis-sholais [Bright-faced Sun]([3]), daughter of the king of the Forest of Wonders, and that man is the most powerful king in the world while he lives([4]), and seldom it was, O son of the king of Norway, that the way to this palace was ever found [by anyone] before you, and take you this rod and whittle it for a little. And

---

siolf*adh* fear a bhfaicsiona gurab ein do bheith ann ". [12] Thus L. A reads "fior coluis ". [13] L reads " seal ". "dreis" is " dreas ", or more usually " greas " in Munster.

([1]) Literally " said ". ([2]) See page 29, where a glass-helmet takes the place of the *brat uisge*. In the "Children of Tuireann", the hero uses, to dive under the sea, his " water apparel and his glass helmet-of-light ". ([3]) Pronounced " Gree-an Gnoosh-hullish ", *i.e.* " Sun countenance-of-light ". ([4]) Literally " in his own time ".

ċaiṫ ṛeal ḋ'á ṛnoiḋc, aġuṛ níoṛ ċuiṛ olc na anḃṛainne ḋ'á
ḃṛuaiṛ ṛiaṁ ṛoiṁe ṛin ḟaiṛ.[1] Aġuṛ ḃ'ḟiaṛṛuiġ Coḃ ḃí an
ṛaiḃ a leiṫéiḋ ṛin ḋe ḟlaiṭ 'ṛan ḃoṁan aċṭ í ṛéin. "Ṭá
ġo ḋeaṛḃṫa," aṛ an inġean, "aġuṛ an ṭí aġ a ḃṗuil, ní
ḃéaṛ[ḟ]aḋ uaiḋ í ṭṛé ġṛáḋ no ṭṛe ḟuaṫ[2] no ṭṛe imeaġla,
aġuṛ iṛ é an ṛeaṛ ṛin m' aṭaiṛ ṛéin, .i. Ríġ Ṗoṛaoiṛe na
n-lonġnaḋ." Aġuṛ ċuġaḋaṛ aṛ an oiḋċe ṛin ġuṛ ḟoillṛiġ an
lá ġo n-a lánṭṛoillṛe aṛ na ṁáṛaċ.

Iṛ annṛin ḃ'ḟiaṛṛuiġ Coḃ ḋe'n inġin ṛġéala na n-aṭaċ
ḃo ṛuġ an ícc leó.[3] Ḋo laḃaiṛ Ġṛian Ġnúiṛ-ḟolaiṛ aġuṛ iṛ
eaḋ aḋuḃaiṛṭ: "Ní ṛaḋa uaiṭ Ṗoṛaoiṛ na n-lonġnaḋ, aġuṛ
ṭáiḋ na h-aṭaiġ ḋe'n ṭaoḃ eile ḋe'n loċ ṛo, aġuṛ an níḋ aṭá
ṭuṛa ḋ'iaṛṛaiḋ, .i. an íce, ḃ'a mbeaḋ ṛí aġainn ba leaṭ-ṛa í
ġan ḟuiṛeaċ, aġuṛ ṛaċaḋ ṛéin ṛeal leaṭ ḃo ḋéanaṁ eólaiṛ
ḋuiṭ."[4] Ḋo ṛuġ an inġean Coḃ léi i ṛliġe eile, ionnuṛ náṛ
ḟliuċaḋ aon ṛuainne ḋ'á éaḋaċ ina ṫimċioll. Iaṛ ḃṭeaċṭ i
ḃṭíṛ ḃóiḃ, ḃ'ḟiaṛṛuiġ Coḃ ḋe'n inġin an ṛaiḃ ṛeaṛ ḋionġṁála[5]
aici.

"Ḋo ḃí ṛin aġam," aṛ ṛí, "aġuṛ ni ḃṗuil anoiṛ, aġuṛ ni
ḃiaiḋ ġo bṛáṭ."

"Ḃa ṁaiṫ linne méaḋ éiġin ḋe ṛġéalaiḃ an ḟiṛ ṛin ḃo ḃeiṫ
aġainn," aṛ Coḃ.

"Ġeaḃaiṛ-ṛe ṛin ġan aiṁṛaṛ," aṛ an inġean, .i. "Ciaḃán
Ġlún-ġeal mac Ríġ na h-éanlaiṫe[6] ṭáiniġ ḃom' ṫaḃaiṛṭ-ṛi ḋe'n
ḋún-ṛo i ṛaḃaiṛ-ṛi aṛéiṛ, aġuṛ iṛ aṁlaiḋ ḃí an ṛeaṛ ṛin;
ṫuġ inġean Ríġ Ġṛéaġ ṛṛuṫ[7] ṛíoṛ-ḋóḃal ṛeiṛce ḋó, aġuṛ
ṭáiniġ ṛí leiṛ i ġṛṛuṫ a ċon ṛéin an oiḋċe ṛin. Aġuṛ ḃo
ṛuġ miṛe aġuṛ an cú leiṛ iṛin luinġ, aġuṛ ṫuġ ṭoṛaċ na
luinġe ḃo ṁuiṛ aġuṛ a ḋeiṛeaḋ ḃo ṫíṛ aġuṛ ṛeólaṛ ġaċa
nóiṛeaċ ġo ḃṭáiniġ ḋ'á ṫíṛ ṛéin,[8] aġuṛ iaṛ ḃṭeaċṭ i ḃṭíṛ ḃó,
aṛ na ṁáṛaċ ḃo ḃí an ḃṛaoiġeaċṭ uṛlaṁ léi, .i. cia bé an
ċéaḋ eiṫiḃe[9] ḃo ċeiṛġeóḃaḋ ḋóiḃ, ġo ġcuṛṛeaḋ ṛí Ciaḃán Ġlún-

---

[1] H reads "an mhéid do fuair dolc agus díomna —— do dhíochair snoidhe na
slaite uadh e". [2] Thus A 25; but A reads "tre uatha no tre imeagla
no iomad". [3] H adds "ó Righ na Sorcha". [4] Last nine
words from A 25. [5] H reads "fear a diongbhala". A 25 reads
"da mhalairt féin aice". [6] L has "h-Antuithe"; H "héanlaighthe".
[7] L " sruth rabharta ró-ghrádh". [8] The last thirty-one

Cod took hold of the rod and whittled at it for a while, and every evil and every feebleness that he had ever met before, ceased to affect him(¹). And Cod asked her was there [any other] such rod in the world but itself. " Truly, is there," said the maiden, " but he who has it will not give it up either for love, or hatred, or fear, and that man is my own father, the king of the Forest of Wonders." And they bore away that night, until the sun shone, with its full light, upon the morrow.

It was then Cod asked the girl for tidings of the giants who had brought the salve away with them. Bright-faced Sun spake, and said : " The Forest of Wonders is not far from you, and the giants are on the other side of this lake, and as for the thing you are looking for, the salve, if we had it, it would be thine without delay : and I myself shall go with you for a while to show you the way." The girl then brought Cod with her by another way [from that in which he had come], so that not a hair of his habiliments was wetted round him. And after they had landed, Cod asked the girl if she had a fitting husband.

" I had that," said she, " but I have not now, and shall not have for ever."

" We would like to know something of the story of that man," said Cod.

" You will get that, without doubt," said the girl : " Ciabhán [Kee-a-vaun] White-knee, son of the king of Éanlaith(²), came to bring me away [in marriage] from this palace, in which you were last night. And this is how that man was : the daughter of the king of Greece had given him a desperate stream of affection, and she came [unknown to him] that night in the shape of his own hound. And he took me and his hound with him aboard his bark, and gave its prow to the sea and its stern to land, and he sails straight away until he came to his own country. And, after his landing on the morrow, she had her enchantment ready, namely, whatever was the first living-creature that would meet us(³), that she would put Ciabhán White-knee in the form of that creature.

words are from H.   ⁹ H has " aithide " ; L " ni " ; A 25 " eitidhe ".

(¹) Literally " did not put upon him ".   (²) This seems to mean " of
the Birds ".   (³) Literally " them ".

ġeal ı ṗıoċt an eıċıḋe ṙın. Aġuṗ ıṗ í an ċéaḋ níḋ táṗla ḋóıḃ,
.ı. ṗeaḃac ṗúl-ġoṗm[1], aġuṗ nuaıṗ ċonncamaṗ an ṗeaḃac ḃo
éıṗıġ Cıaḃán ġlún-ġeal ı ṗıoċt ṗeaḃaıc eıle uaınn, ġuṗ éıṗıġ
aṗ áṗ ḃṗıaḋnuıṗe, ḃ'eıtıl aıeṗḃa, ı ġcuıḋeaċt an tṗeaḃaıc
eıle, ġo ḃṗuıl aıṁlaıḋ ṙın[2] ó ṙoın aleıċ; aġuṗ ċıġ ṗé ṗan
mbıle úḃ ċall ḃo-ċíḃ tuṗa, ġaċ aon lá, aġuṗ bím-ṗe aġuṗ é
ṗéın aġ ṗéaċaın a ċéıle. Aġuṗ éıṗġıḋ ṗé aṗíṗ uaım ı ġcoṁ-
luaḋaṗ na ṗeaḃac eıle ó ṁeóḃan laoı amaċ."[3]
Ṗıaṗṗuıġeaṗ Coḃ ḃí, an ṗaıḃ 'ṗan ḃoṁan aen níḋ ḃ'ṗóıṗṗeaḋ
aṗ Cıaḃán Ġlún-ġeal?
Aḋuḃaıṗt an ınġean naċ ṗaıḃ, "óıṗ na ġeaṗa ḃo cuıṗċeaṗ
ḃe ḃṗuım uıṗġe,[4] ní ċuıṗċeaṗ aṗ ġcúl ıaḃ ġo ḃṗáċ."
Iṗ tṗuaġ an ṗġeul ṗın," aṗ Coḃ, "aġuṗ luıġım-ṗe ṗo m'
aṗmaıḃ ġaıṗġıḋ ḃa mbeaḋ ṗġaoıleaḋ aṗ a ġeaṗaıḃ ṗo tṗí
ṗoġaıl-ṗannaıḃ an ḃoṁan ġo ḃtıúḃṗaınn-ṗe ċuġaıḃ é ḃ'aıṁ-
ḃeóın ṗeaṗ aġuṗ ban an ḃoṁaın uıle." Ḃo ċeıleaḃṗaḋaṗ Coḃ
aġuṗ Ġṗıan Ġnúıṗ-ṗolaıṗ ḃ'á ċéıle.

[ṖORAOIS NA N-IONĠNAḊ.]

Iṗ ann ṗın ċuġ Coḃ a aġaıḋ ġo Ṗoṗaoıṗ na n-ıonġnaḋ,
aġuṗ níoṗ ċıan ḃó an tan ḃo ċonnaıṗc tṗıaṗ aṫaċ ḃıaḃluıḃe
ḃuḃ-ġṗánna[5] ḃ'á ıonnṗaıḋe, aġuṗ beaṗt ḃe ċṗoıcnıḃ ṗıaḃ-maol
aġuṗ ṗeaṗbóġ umṗa, aġuṗ láṁa cıoṗclaċa cıaṗḃuḃa[6] aca.
Aġuṗ beannuıġeaṗ Coḃ ḃóıḃ ına ḃteanġa[7] ṗéın, aġuṗ ḃo b'
ıonġna leó ṗaıcṗın Cuıḃ, aġuṗ ċuġaḃaṗ ġṗáḃ ṗo ṁóṗ ḃó, aṗ
ṗeaḃaṗ a ḃealḃa,[8] aġuṗ ċuġaḃaṗ ṗġéala ḃó ġan ımṗeaṗán.
Iṗ annṗın ḃ'ṗıaṗṗuıġ Coḃ ṗġéala na h-íce ḃe na h-aṫaċaıḃ.
"Iṗ tṗuaġ ṗın,"[9] aṗ na n-aṫaıġ, "óıṗ ḃo bí íce aġaınn-ne
annṗo, aġuṗ ṗuġaḋ uaınn í ġo Ṗoṗaoıṗ[10] na n-Ionġnaḋ, aġuṗ ḃá

---

[1] L reads "súlghorm seitrioch".   [2] The last sixteen words are from H.
[3] The last twelve words are also from H.   [4] L has "do druim mara no inbhir";
H has "oir do bi an nuradsin daingidheacht agus daingcis aice do nar [fhag]
si dáil fuasgalta air".   [5] L reads "báḃḃa ball-ṗúıleaċa".   [6] H omits;
L reads "aon lámh chorcra chiordhubh as ucht gacha fir aco".   [7] H omits;
L reads "ionna theangain féin".   [8] H and L "deilbhe".   [9] Thus L;
A reads "truagh a nabair"; A 25 "a nabarthar".   [10] I observe a uniform ortho-

And the first thing that met us([1]) was a blue-eyed hawk. And as soon as we beheld the hawk, Ciabhán White-knee rose up away from us in the form of another hawk, until he rose out of our presence, of an aerial flight, in the company of the other hawk, so that he is in this plight ever since. And, he comes into yonder tree which you see there, every day, and he and I be looking at one another; and he rises up again away from me in the company of the other hawks, once the middle of the day comes ([2])."

Cod asked her, was there anything in the world that would succour Ciabhán White-knee?

The girl said that there was not, "for the *geasa* that are imposed on the top of water, they are never rescinded.([3])"

"That is a sad story," said Cod, "and I swear, by my arms of valour, if there were any loosening of his *geasa* in the three plunder-divisions of the world, that I would bring him to you in spite of the men and women of the entire world." Then Cod and Bright-faced Sun bade each other farewell.

[THE FOREST OF WONDERS.]

It was then Cod faced for the Forest of Wonders, and it was not long until he beheld three devilish, black-ugly giants coming towards him, and garments of the skins of wild deer and roe-buck round them, and circular jet-black hands they had. And Cod salutes them in their own language, and they wondered to see Cod. And they conceived for him a very great love for the excellence of his shape, and they told him their story without dispute. Then Cod asked the giants for tidings of the salve.

"Alas!" said the giants, "we had that salve here, and it was carried away from us to the Forest of Wonders, and if we

---

graphy of "foraois", but it is equally often spelt "forais", and even "foras".

([1]) Literally "them".   ([2]) Literally "from the middle of the day out".
([3]) Literally, "are never put back".   Observe that it was in the water that Féithlinn, who first put the *geasa* on the sons of the King of Norway, was herself enchanted: see above, page 63.   It was while they were bathing in the water that their step-mother changed the children of Lir into swans.

mbeaḋ rí aġainn ḋo ḃéarrfamaoir ḋuit-re í, ar ṁéaḋ an ġráḋ
ċuġamar ḋuit-re; aġur ná lean-ra ġo bráċ í," ar riaḋ, "óir
ir aiṅlaiḋ tá an Ḟoraoir rin aġur bile buaḋaċ 'na lár aġur
iollraḋ¹ ġaċa ḋaċa inr an ġcrann rin, aġur ní'l toraḋ ḋe
ċorċaiḃ an ḃeaċa naċ ḃfuil ar an ġcrann rin, aġur ir
ḋoiliġ ḋo aenneaċ ḋ'á ḃfaicfeaḋ é rġaraḋ rir, tre ḃiċ ríor,
ar ṁéaḋ a ionġantair, aġur ní ḋeaċaiḋ aon ḋuine arteaċ ran
ḃForaoir rin riaṁ ċáiniġ amaċ arír ġo bráċ, ar ṁéaḋ a
ḋraoiḋeaċta², aġur ná lean-ra an íce rin ġo bruinne an ḃráċa
no ġo foirċeann an ḃeaċa."

"Luiġim-re fá m' armaiḃ ġuil aġur ġairġiḋ," ar Coḃ, "ḋá
ḃfuiġinn-re an íce ann-ro naċ anfainn ann-ro ġan Ḟoraoir na
n-lonġnaḋ ḋ'ḟaicrin, ar ṁéaḋ a tearta³ aġaiḃ-re, aġur ḋéanaiḋ-
re eólar ḋaṁ-ra ċum na Ḟoraoire ionġantaiġe ġo luaċ," ar Coḃ.

Ḋo rinneaḋar na h-aċaiġ eólar na Ḟoraoire ḋo Coḃ, aġur
ní ḋ'á ġceaḋ no ḋ'á ġcómairle ċuaiḋ ré ann, ar uaṁan
luċt na Ḟoraoire. Ir annrin ḋo ċuaiḋ Coḃ ġo Ḟoraoir
na n-lonġnaḋ, aġur ċonnairc ré bile na mbuaḋ uaiḋ, aġur
ḋo ċonnairc ré iomaḋ ḋe ḋaċaiḃ éaġraṁla aġur ḋe ċorċaiḃ
ionġantacha fo ġeuġaiḃ trom-leaċana an bile bláiċ-ionġ-
antaiġ rin, aġur ro ḟeaċain é. Aġur ċárla trí fir ḋéaġ ḋó,
aġur a ḋtrí cinn ḋéaġ ḋ'earḃaiḋ orra, aġur Ríġ-ṁíleaḋ
ró-ċalma ar lár na ḋruinġe rin, aġur brat⁴ buaḋa ḋ'ór áluinn
Affaice uime, aġur folt faḋa f[e]amuineaċ⁵ fór-órḋa for
a ċeann, aġur mionn ḋ'ór áluinn fá n-a ċeann ġo nḋealḃaḋ
leóġan aġur liorarḋ aġur ġo ġríoḃ ionġantaċ aġur [ġo]
beiċiḋiġiḃ éaġraṁla ar n-a n-eaġraḋ ḋe láiṁ ruaḋ aġur raor-
ċearḋ ar an óir-ṁionn rin, aġur ní ḟacaiḋ Coḃ an oireaḋ rin
ḋe ḋaoiniḃ riaṁ ba éaġraṁla 'ná an ḃuiḋean ṁarḃ rin. Aġur
ḋo ċonnairc arr⁶ áluinn ġo ġcloċaiḃ mbuaḋa fá ċoir an Ríġ-
ṁíliḋ rin, aġur ḋo fín Coḃ a láiṁ ḋo buain na bróiġe ḋé, aġur
ḋo ċeilġ an ċor uaiḋ ar⁷ feaḋ naoi ġcéimeann ar a ċúl é.
Ir annrin ḋo laḃair ceann na colna, "ní ḟáróċaḋ aon ḋuine an
ċor rin fo'n am ro anḋé."

---

¹ H " go niollradh ". L " agus deallradh ". ² L " do bhithin na
draoidheachta sin ". ³ H has " a teiste agus a tuarasgbhála ".
⁴ Thus L. A has " beart ". ⁵ L " fáinneach ". ⁶ H " ass ordha

had it we would bestow it on thee, on account of all the love we have given thee, and never go thou after it," said they, "for the way of that Forest is this: there is a Tree of Virtue in its middle, and a variety of every colour in that tree, and there is no fruit of the fruits of life that is not in that tree, and it is difficult for anyone who may see it to part from it through time eternal, for all its marvellousness; and no man has gone into that Forest who ever came out of it again, for all its enchantment: and do not thou pursue that salve till the womb of judgment, or the end of life."

"I swear by my arms of bravery and valour, that if I were to get the salve here, I would not remain here without seeing the Forest of Wonders, after all your report of it, and do ye quickly show me the way to this wonderful forest," said Cod.

The giants then showed Cod the way to the Forest, and it was not of their will, nor of their advice, that he went there, for fear of the inhabitants of the Forest. It was then Cod proceeded to the Forest of Wonders, and he beheld at a distance from him the Tree of Virtues, and he saw many various colours and wondrous fruits beneath the heavy-broad branches of that flower-marvellous tree; and he shunned it. And there met him thirteen men, and they lacking their heads: and in the midst of that band a valorous king-warrior, and a precious mantle of fair gold of Africa around him, and long clustering(¹) very-golden hair upon him, and a diadem of fair gold round his head, with imagery of lions and leopards, and with a wonderful griffin, and with various beasts set in order by the hands of sages and free-workmen, on that gold diadem; and Cod never beheld the same number of people who were more remarkable than that dead band. And he saw a handsome sandal with precious stones on the foot of that kingly hero, and Cod stretched out his hand to take the shoe from off him, but the foot cast him from him nine paces backwards. Then the head of the body spoke: "This time yesterday, no man could have insulted that foot."

---

go clochaib buadha uime chois". A 25 "osann"; "L "bróg"; A "osanna".
⁷ Thus H. A reads "go feadh naoi ccéimeanuibh".

(¹) Literally "sea-weedy".

"Dar liom tá úrlaḃraḋ aġaḋ a ċinn," ar Coḃ.

"Atá," ar an ceann.

"Taḃair ḋo rġéala ḋúinn," ar Coḃ, "aġur rġéala na buiḋne-rċó eile."

"Tá connraḋ ar a ḃtiúḃrainn," ar an ceann.

"Cá connraḋ rin?" ar Coḃ.

"Peart ḋo ċlaiḋe[1] ḋam péin aġur ḋo na fearaiḃ eile reo," ar an ceann, "aġur ár n-áḋnacal fó ċéaḋóir[2]."

Aġur iar ráḋ na mḃriaṫar rin ḋó, ḋo ruġ Coḃ ar ṁanaoir muirne[3] ṁóir leaḃair ḋo ḃí aiġe i n-aice a rġéiċe, aġur ḋo ġaḃ aġ toċailt na h-uaiġe i ġcéaḋóir, ġur ba h-ollaṁ í.

"Dar liom atá an peart ollaṁ," ar an ceann.

"Ir ollaṁ anoir," ar Coḃ. Aġur ir ann rin aḋuḃairt an ceann an laoi :—

"Truaġ ḋeireaḋ na ġcuraḋ-ra.[4]
Ní maiṫ branḋuḃ[5] ġan fuirinn,
D'aon ṁac Ríġ na hAlmaine
Ní fóġnann leaḃa cúṁanġ.

"Drearal beóḋa ḃonb-ḃriaṫaċ
Deaġ-ṁac Ríġ Tíre-an-tSneaċta,
Fiaḋaḋ a'r Fionn forniata[6]
Ġur a nḃéanaḃaoir nná eaċtra.

"Conc a'r Cairḃre coṁġaireaċ[7]
An ḋiar ro fiar ar m'uilinn[8]
Uaiṫne a'r Artúr ollḃaḋaċ[9]
Naċ ḋtuġ ḋo laoċraiḃ urraim.

"Laiġne ḋearġ ir Tuireann[a]
Cuirtear rinne[10] re ċéile,
Ainm na ḋíre ḋeireannaiġ[11]
Feaċna fionn ir béinne.

---

[1] H "tochailt". [2] The last five words are from H. [3] H "ar an mhanaois a fuair a gcomligar dhó". L "an mainis mhúirnidhe do bhi aige anaice asgéithe". A 25, "ar an maonaois mhoir mhuirnglobhar". A 25, "nr an manaois mhúirnigh do bhi ar iomchar aige". A "muirigh", from all which I edit as above. [4] L reads "truagh deir an cómhrádh so". A 25 "is truagh deireadh an chomraidh si". A reads "na ccuiraighsi", from which I edit as above. [5] H reads this line "a laoich is fearr fulaing". A has "brananam". L "branadh". L 27, "brannamh", from which I edit as above. A 25 omits this line and makes complete hash of the poem. [6] Thus H. A has "folt

"Head, methinks thou hast human speech," said Cod.

"I have," said the head.

"Give us thy story," said Cod, "and the story of this other company."

"There is a condition upon which I would give it," said the head.

"What condition is that?" said Cod.

"[You] to dig a grave for myself and for those other men," said the head, "and to bury us out of hand."

And after his saying those words Cod grasped the great broad spear that he had near his shield, and began to dig the grave forthwith, until it was ready.

"Methinks the grave is ready," said the head.

"It is ready now," said Cod.   And thereupon the head spoke this lay :—

> "Alas! for these warriors
>   The chess-board now is chess-less;
> Son of King of Almainè,
>   Narrow thy couch and restless.(¹)

> "Breasal the lively, of the rough-words,
>   The good son of the King of the Land-of-Snow;
> Fiachadh and the furious Fionn,
>   To whom women used to come on adventures.

> "Corc, and Cairbrè the shouting,
>   Are these two west, at my elbow;
> Uaithne [*Oon-yă*] and the mighty Arthur,
>   Who gave not submission to heroes.

> "Laighne [*Lyna*] the Red, and Tuireann,
>   Let us be placed together;
> The names of the two last
>   Are Feachtna the White and Béinnè.

---

glan orarmach"; the next line has a foot too many.   ⁷ Thus H.
L "cosgarthach".   A "congaireach".   ⁸ L "fo thír ar muillinn".
⁹ Thus H.   A "orarmach".   ¹⁰ Thus H.   A has "cuirir
line".   I have added an "a" to "Tuireann" in the first line to make it scan.
¹¹ L "diongmhála".

(¹) This is the same metre as before.   Literally: "Alas! the end of these heroes | not good a chessboard without chessmen, | the son of the King of Almainè, | a narrow bed suits not.

"Cuirṫear rinn ran aḃaiḃ-ri¹
A ḟir an Grḟoilṫ ḟionnḟuair²
A ġil ḃeirġ óiġ³ aḃraḋuiḃ
Aḃuḃrar focal ró-ṫruaġ."

A h-aiṫle na laoiḋe rin ḃo ċuaiḃ an ceann i ġcionn ḃ'innrin ḃo Ċoḃ, aġur aḃuḃairṫ mar ro:⁴—"Iollán Ór-Armaċ mac Ríġ na h-Almáinne an ḟear ḃ'ar ceann mire, aġur Clann Ríġ Ṫíre-an-ṫSneaċta an ḃá ḟear ḃéaġ ro 'mo ṫimċeall, aġur ir ḃearḃ-ċómalṫaiḋe ḃaṁra iaḃ, aġur ṫuġar-ra ṫuile ṫrom-ġráḃ aġur rruṫ ríor-ḟeirce ḃ'inġin Ríġ ḟá ṫuinn," ar an ceann.⁵ Aġur ir aṁlaiḃ ḃo ḃí an ḃean rin: ḃo ḃí móiḃ uirri⁶ naċ beaḃ ḟear aici aċṫ an ḟear ḃo ḃéar[ḟ]aḃ bile na mbuaḃ ar Ḟoraoir na n-lonġnaḃ ċuici; aġur ḃo ḃí ḃe ṁéaḃ ġráḃ na mná rin aġamra, nár ḟéaḃar ġan ḃul ḃ'iarraiḃ bile na mbuaḃ, aġur ṫáiniġ mo ḃearḃ-ċómalṫaiġ liom, aġur ḃo h-imireaḃ ḃraoiḃeaċṫ orrainn ann ro, aġur ir é [an] ċéaḃ níḃ ḃo ċonncamar ċuġainn .i. ḟear beaġ aġur cruiṫ ċaoin-ṫéaḋaċ ċeol-ḃinn aiġe ina uċṫ leir, aġur ṫuġ an ḟear beaġ ḃorn ar an mbéal ḃo'n ḟear ḟá ċóiṁneara óḃ aġainn-ne, aġur ṫuġ an ḟear rin a cloiḃeaṁ amaċ ḃo ḃualaḃ ḟir na cruiṫe, ḃar leir ḟéin, aġur ní h-é ḃo ḃuail, aċṫ ḟear aġainn-ne, ionnur ġur rinn ḟéin ḃo ḃiṫċeannuiġ a ċéile⁷ ṫre ḃraoiḃeaċṫ ḟir na cruiṫe. Aġur cia h-ionġna rin? Ir iomḃa ionġanṫar ir mó 'ná é i ḃḞoraoir na n-lonġnaḃ má'r ríor, aġur ciḃ maiṫ linne ṫura ḃ'ar n-aḃlacaḃ, ir ḃoiliġ linn⁸ ċu ḃ'ḟanaṁain an faḃ rin, ḃ'eaġla ḃraoiḃeaċṫa na foraoire ionġanṫaiġ[e] reo."

Ir annrin ṫuġ Coḃ a láṁa ṫimċioll Iollain Ór-Armaiġ aġur ḃo ċuir i lár na ḟearṫa é, aġur ḃo ċuir reirear ar ġaċ ṫaoḃ ḃé, aġur ḃo rġríoḃ a n-anmanna i n-oġam⁹ or an ḃḟearṫ, mar ba ġnáṫ aca an uair rin.

A h-aiṫle na h-oiḃre rin ḃo ḃí Coḃ aġ min-iarraiḃ aġur aġ aṁarc na foraoire aġur ba ġearr a h-aiṫle an aṁairc¹⁰ rin

---

¹ A has " sa adbhaidh sin ". H " sa nuadhbhaidh si ". L "san uaidh sin " ; A 25 "san aobhaigh sin ". ² L has " fior chraobhaice ", and omits the last two lines, as does A 25. ³ H reads "a ghil dheirg óig". A " geildeirg ". ⁴ In H this story of the heads precedes the poem. ⁵ The last fourteen words are from H which best gives the sense. ⁶ H " mionna agus luighe ". L " geasa ". ⁷ H reads " acht ga ttáim ris ", ar

" Let us be placed in this dwelling,
    O man of the cool gold-locks ;
    O bright ruddy youth of the dark eyebrows,
    I have spoken a word very sorrowful.''

After that lay, the head fell to telling [its story] to Cod, and it
spake thus :—" Golden-armed Iollan, son of the King of Almain, is
the man whose head I am, and the children of the King of the Land-
of-Snow are these twelve men round me, and they are my foster-
brothers.   And I gave a flood of heavy love and a stream of constant
affection to the daughter of the King Under-Wave," said the head.
" And this is how that woman was.   She had an oath upon her that
she would have no man but the man who would bring to her the Tree
of Virtues out of the Forest of Wonders.   And it came, of all the love
I had for that woman, that I could not but go to seek the Tree of
Virtues, and my foster-brothers came with me.   And enchantment was
wrought upon us here ; for the first thing we saw coming towards us
was a little man and a gentle-stringed harp with him in his bosom, and
the little man struck a fist on the mouth of the man of us who was
nearest to him, and that man drew his sword to strike the man of the
harp, as he thought, but it was not he whom he struck, but a man of
us ; so that it was ourselves who beheaded one another, through the
enchantment of the man of the harp.   And what wonder is that?
There is many a marvel greater than that in the Forest of Wonders,
if it is true."

Then Cod put his hands around gold-armed Iollan, and placed him
in the middle of the grave, and he placed six on each side of him, and
he wrote their names in Ogam above the grave, as was the custom with
them at that time.

After that work Cod was closely examining and regarding the
forest, and short time it was after his regarding it, until he beheld the

---

an ceann, '' ro dithcheannad sin uile ''.   5 H reads '' is mor an
ceannach dúinn muill do chur ort oir is mor agus is adhbhal ár ndiol feirte
agus is imchian d'aoinfhear amhain ár nadnacal, agus ráidhios an laoi '', as above.

    9 Thus H, the others omit '' i n-ogham ''.
    10 Thus L, but A has ''na h-iarraidh'', making the verbal noun feminine, which
is unusual.

ʒo ḃpacaiḋ ḟeap na cpuice aʒup a ċpuic ḟá n-a uċc leip
ċuiʒe, aʒup táiniʒ ḋo láċaip Ċuḃ. Aʒup ċuʒ Coḃ ríċeaḋ[1] ap
ḟeap na cpuice, aʒup ḃuaileap an ċpuic ḟó an ʒcappaiʒ cloiċe
ḟá ċóṁncapa ḋó, aʒup ḃo ċuip blaḋ in ʒaċ áipḃ ḃe'n ḟopaoip
ḃí. Aʒup ciompuiʒeap an ḟeap beaʒ an ċpuic apíp i nḃiaiḋ a
ċéile, aʒup ḃap leac níop ḃain buille ná béim ḃí. Ḋo puʒ Coḃ
an ḃapa ḟeaċc ap an ḃḟeap beaʒ ʒup pʒap a ċeann pe n-a
ċolainn.[2] Ip annpin ḃ'éipiʒ an ḟeap beaʒ apíp aʒup ḃo imċiʒ,
aʒup a ċeann ina láiṁ, aʒup a ċpuic inp an láiṁ eile. Aʒup ḃo
b' ionʒna le Coḃ an cleap pin.

Níop cian, iap pin, a h-aiċle an ḟip ḃiʒ ḃ'imċeaċc, ʒo
ḃpacaiḋ pé ḃáiṁ ionʒancaċ[3] ċuiʒe, aʒup ḃá ḃinn óip ḟaip[4], aʒup
beañ-buaḋḃaill[5] 'na ḃéal, aʒup ḃo ḃuail buille ap an mbeañ-
buaḋḃaill pin, aʒup ní paiḃ cac no cailleaċ no aipeaċca
ʒpánḃa éiʒcéilliḋe i ʒcpeiʒ no i ʒcuaip no i ʒcappaiʒ no i ḃciʒ
no i ḃcalṁain no i piʒ-ḃpoʒ piċe[6] no i néallcaiḃ aċ-uaċṁapa
aéḃip, naċ ḃcáiniʒ, ḟá ḟoʒaip na biñe-buaḋḃaill pin.[7] Ip
annpin ċuʒ Coḃ láṁ ḟá'n manaoip[8] muipne ṁóip leaḃaip ḃo
ḃí i n-aice a pʒéiċe, aʒup ċuʒ upċap ḃí, ʒup ċuip ċpíḃ an ḃáṁ í.
Aʒup nuaip ċápla an cpleaʒ ḃó ni mo pʒpeaḃaiḋ beaċuiʒiʒ
eile 'ná pʒpéaċ na pleiʒe ḟéin,[9] aʒup ba h-ionʒna le Coḃ
náḃúip na pleiʒe pin. Aʒup ip aṁlaiḋ ḃo ḃaḃap na beaċaiḃiʒ
eiʒcéilliḋe[10] pin, aʒup ḃponʒ ḃíoḃ aʒ pʒpeaḃpiḃ[11] aʒup ḃponʒ
ḃíoḃ aʒ búippiḃ, ḃponʒ aʒ baṗʒapnaiʒ aʒup ḃponʒ eile aʒ
cuapʒan na calṁan ḃ'á ʒceannaiḃ aʒup ḃ'á ʒcopaiḃ, aʒup
ní ḟéiḃip a áipeaṁ no a ḟaipnéip a paiḃ ḃ'olc aʒup
ḃ'áiċṁilleaḋ ḃpaoiḃeaċca ip an ḃḟopaoip i n-alc[12] na h-uaipe
pin, aʒup ní paiḃ cloċ ná cpann innci naċ paiḃ ap aon ċpiċ,
aʒup ap aon cóippneaċ[13]. Ip annpin ḃo ċuʒ Coḃ an ċloċ[14]
niṁe ḃo ḃí i ʒcuiḃpiḃ[15] a pʒéiċe amaċ aʒup ḃo ciompuiʒ na
h-eiċiḃiʒe éiʒcéilliḋe no ʒup ċuip i mbéal uaṁa[16] ip an ḃḟopaoip

---

[1] Thus A 25. A reads "sithibh", the others "amus".   [2] Thus L and
II 25. A reads " re na cuell mcithe ".   [3] H reads " imdhisgir allata".
[4] A 25 reads " as gach leithcheann leis ".   [5] H " bcannbhlátheagair
buadhbhaill ".   [6] L " i sioth-bhroghaibh siansánachta ".
[7] Thus II. A has " fo guth an blath bine buadhbhuill ".   [8] H " manaois
moir leabhar do bhi aige ". L " mainis múirnigh do bhi a nglotuinn a sgéithe ;
A "manais muirn ". I edit as before.   [9] II " noch ar mhó sgreadghoire an

man of the harp coming towards him, and his harp with him in his bosom, and he came up to Cod. And Cod gave a leap at the man of the harp, and smites the harp upon the rock of stone nearest him, and he sent a fragment of it [flying] into every quarter of the forest. And the little man gathers up the harp again, piece after piece, and you would have thought that neither stroke nor blow had ever touched it. Cod seized the little man the second time, and separated his head from his body. Thereupon the little man rose up again and departed with his head in his hand, and his harp in the other hand. And Cod marvelled at that exploit.

It was not long after that, when the little man had departed, until he beheld coming towards him a wondrous ox, and two gold horns on him, and a horn-trumpet in his mouth, and he smote a blow upon that horn-trumpet, and there was never cat, nor hag, nor hideous senseless spectre, in crag nor in hollow, nor in rock, nor in house, nor on land, nor in fairy-palace of faerie, nor in the dreadful clouds of the air, but came at the roar of that horn. It was then Cod passed a hand round his great broad spear that was beside his shield, and gave a cast of it, so that he sent it through the ox. And when the spear reached it, not greater was the screaming of any other beast than the screaming of the spear itself, and Cod marvelled at the nature of that spear. And this is how those senseless creatures were, some of them screaming and some of them bellowing, and some of them moaning, and some of them stamping the ground with their heads and with their feet; and it is impossible to enumerate or rehearse all the evil and the confusion of enchantment in the forest in the joint of that hour, for there was neither stone nor tree in it but was in one shaking and in one thunder. It was then Cod took out the venomous stone that was in the hollow of his shield, and he collected the senseless creatures, until he drove them into the mouth of a cave in the forest; and it had been a good

daimh no na sleagha ba dhéin ".   10 H " eathuidigh égcéilleigh na foraoisi ".
11 L has " ag sgréachaidh", " ag osnadhach", " ag snagaireacht", and " ag buirthigh ". L 27 has " snagarnach " and " buirfeadhach ". A 25 has " aige bascarnaigh". My own MS. has " screadaigh", " buirfighe", and " basgarnaidh". 12 I read " alt " all through, but A often makes it " alta". H reads " san moimeint sin ".·   13 Thus L, but A has " toirnigh ". A 25 has " aon toran amháin ".
14 L " an chloch-cholg ".   15 Thus A 25. A has " do bhi ccaobhrach", my own MS. " cobhrach ".   16 A reads " uaimche ". L reads " aithidighe " for " eithididhe ".

K

iaḋ; aġur ba ṁaiċ[an] c-áḋḃar mearġċa mi-laoiċ i ḃḞoraoir na n-lonġnaḋ an can rin ḃeiċ aġ éirceaċc le h-uallġáire aġur re rġréaċaiḋ aġur re criċ-ḃuirṫiḋ¹ na n-arraċc n-iolċruċaċ rin.

Aċc cá ní ċeana, ċáiniġ Coḋ car éir na h-oiḃre rin ar ḟeaḋ na ḟoraoire, aġur ba ċuirreaċ im-ḟníoṁaċ aiċṁéalaċ é, aġur ba ḃeaġ nár ḃ' aiċreaċ leir ceaċc ḋo'[n] ḃḞoraoir rin, aġur ḋo ḃ' iomḋa ḟaolċú niṁneaċ riúḃlaċ ar ḟo-luaimneaċ,² aġ éirġe ar ġaċ caoḃ ḋé, aġur ní ḃeireaḋ orra, aċc iaḋ aġ imċeaċc uaiḋ in ġaċ aon áirḋ ina ró-ḃuinneaḋaiḃ rói-reaċa.³

Ir annrin ḋo ċonnairc Coḋ bancraċc ró-áluinn ban ċuiġe, aġur Ríoġan ċeannárḋ ċéaḋraċaċ i ḋcoraċ na buiḋne rin, aġur eiliocram⁴ órḋa, ar ceaċrar, roimpi amaċ, aġur ċáiniġ an inġean rin ḋo láċair Ċuiḋ ṗá'n ġcumaḋ rin, aġur aḋuḃairc, "A ṁic ionġancaiġ," ar rí, "ḋo ḃ' anaṁ oiḋe⁵ róṁaḋ riaṁ i ḃḞoraoir na n-lonġnaḋ, aġur an méaḋ ḃur áil leac ḋe ḟeóḋaiḋ uairle na ḟoraoire beir leac é, aġur an ḟoraoir ḋ'ḟáġḃáil anoċc."

"Ḋar an luiġe ġniḋim⁶ le Ḋia," ar Coḋ, "ní ġeaḃainn ór na cruinne⁷ aġur ġan ḟanaṁain i ḃḞoraoir na n-lonġnaḋ ḋ'aiṁḋeoin a ḃḟuil innci."

"A ṁic Ríġ na h-Ioruaiḋe," ar an inġean, " aġ rúḋ aġac an báṁ ḋo ġonair ó ċiainiḃ aġainn-ne ran eiliocrom."⁸ Mar ḋo ċualaiḋ Coḋ rin ċuġ a ċloiḋeaṁ amaċ, aġur ḋo ġaḃ aġ cóṁ-ċuarġain ar an eiliocrom no ġo nḋearnaiḋ ré bloġa beaġa béal-rġaoilce ḋé, aġur ḋ'imċiġeaḋar na mná uaiḋ. Iar rin ḋo leiġeaḋar aon ġáir ór árḋ arca, aġur cuiḋ ḋe'n eiliocrom i n-uċc ġaċa mná ḋíoḃ; aġur ir aċ-uaċṁar ḋo ḃí Ḟoraoir na n-lonġnaḋ i n-alc na h-uaire rin ó rinġala [na] n-oillḟiarc n-allṁurḋa rin. Aġur aḋuḃairc Coḋ ḋe ġuċ árḋ mór ḟollur-ġlan le luċc na Ḟoraoire, "ni ḟearr liom cearcall ceoḋlaca, ḋá mbiaḋ aġam anoċc," ar ré, "ná oillḟiarca na ḟoraoire reo." Ir annrin ḋo ċuaiḋ Coḋ ġo bile

---

¹ The last eleven words are from L. A has " o sgreadail" and " o sgiamhghal" and " o shiorbhuaidhreadh na ", etc. My MS. has " o sgeadaoil " and " o sgiamhghail " and " o shiorbhuaidhreadh ".

² Thus I edit the " fuath luaimneach " of A.

³ Thus L. A has " ina ruadh bhunaibh ro reatha ".

⁴ Thus L. H has " eletrom ". A " iollaitruim " : readers of Fiona Macleod will remember the use she has made of this uncommon word.

cause of confusion to a bad hero in the Forest of Wonders at that time to be listening to the wailing, and the screeching, and the tremulous bellowing of those many-shaped spectres.

Howsoever, Cod came back through the forest after that work, and it was tired and anxious and sorrowful he was, and it was little but he repented his coming [at all] to that forest. And many was the venomous, wandering, wolf nimbly-going, rising up on every side of him; and he used not to overtake them, but they going away from him in every quarter, in quick running throngs.

It was then Cod beheld a very fair bevy of women coming towards him, and a high-headed, sensible queen at the head of that band, and a golden bier [borne] by four, out before her. And that lady came up to Cod in this guise, and said: "Wondrous youth,"(¹) said she, "it was seldom that there was ever a guest before thee in the Forest of Wonders, and all that thou desirest of the noble jewels of the forest do thou bear away with thee; only leave the forest to-night."

"By the oath which I make to God," said Cod, "I would not accept all the gold of the universe and not remain in the Forest of Wonders, in spite of all that are in it."

"Son of the King of Norway," said the lady, "there is the ox for thee which thou woundedst a little time back, which we have in the bier." When Cod heard that, he drew his sword and fell to smiting the bier, until he made small shattered fragments of it; and the women departed from him. After that, they let from them one shout on high, and part of the bier in the bosom of every woman of them. And it was appalling the Forest of Wonders was at that hour, from the noises of those strange monsters. And Cod called with a loud great clear voice to the inhabitants of the forest: "Not better would I like a sleeping couch, if I had it to-night," said he, "than to be fighting with the monsters of this forest." It was then Cod went to the Tree of

---

⁵ Thus I edit the "annamh aoidhe" of A. L reads "oidhche comhnuightheach".

⁶ Thus I write the "niom" of A. L has "dar luighe mo thuatha do mhionnaibh". H "tuingim fam' armaibh".

⁷ H has "forgla maithios".

⁸ The last three words are from H. I changed the orthography of "eiliotram" to keep it uniform.

(¹) Literally, "son."

na mbuaḋ aġur ċuġ ġual-eipe¹ móp leip ḋe ġéaġaiḃ an ḃile ḃláiċ-ḃuaiḋiġ ionġanċaiġ pin ġo nḋeapna ḃoċ aġup béal-pġalan ḋé ap láp na popaoipe. Aġup ni ap ċoimipce luċċ na popaoipe ḋo ċuaiḋ Coḋ an oiḋċe pin, aċc ap ċoimipce a láiṁe aġup a lainne péin.

Aġup ḋo ṗaḋaiġ ceine cṙéan² móp an uaip pin, aġup ní paiḃ paḋ oplaiġ ḋe'n ṗopaoip pin ġan eiċiḋe píop-ġpánḋa ḋo ḃeiċ innci, aġup ḋo leiġiḋíp ġápċa ġṙáineaṁla ina ċimċioll, ionnup ġo ḋciġiḋíp na piapca pin pá'n ceiniḋ, ḃ'ionnṙaiḋe Ċuiḋ.

Aċc cá ní ċeana, ba ṗaṁailce le puiċne puaḋ-ġaoiċe no pe puaim pṗíoṁ-ċuinne pe h-eap aċ̇ġaṗḃ, nualaiṁ³ coḋa⁴ ḋíoḃ, aġup ba ṗaṁailce pe puaim móp-ġaoiċe pe ġapḃ-ċnocaiḃ cuiḋ ḋíoḃ; ba ṗaṁailce le péalcannaiḃ loinneapḋa a púile 'na ġceannaiḃ. Aġup ḋo ḃí an ċappaiġ pin .i. Coḋ mac Ṙíġ na h-lopuaiḋe ġan ċlaoċlaḋ cpoċa no céille no ḃeilḃe, ġan copuġaḋ meanmna no meapuġaḋ bpiaċap, aġ éipceaċc pip na móp-olcaiḃ pin.

Ip annpin ḋ'éipiġ Coḋ, an⁵ ḋapa peaċc, aġup ċuġ láṁ 'na ḋcimċioll aṁail aoḋaipe aġ ciompuġaḋ cṙéaḋa, aġup ḋo ċiompuiġ ġo béal uaṁa⁶, ġup ċuip i mbéal na h-uaṁa céaḋna apíp iaḋ⁷. Aġup ḋo lean ipceaċ iaḋ, aġup an c-appaċc aip a mbeipeaḋ ḋo ḃuaileaḋ ap an ḋapa h-appaċc é, ġup ċuip ḋiċ pó-ṁóp ḋó-áipṁiġċe oppa, aġup ḋo lean ḋóiḃ ġo ġpinneall na h-uaṁa, aġup ní ṗeaḋap cá leiċ a' nḋeaċaḋap uaiḋ pá'n am pin.

Aġup ċáiniġ Coḋ amaċ, iap pin, aġup ní ḃpuaip ap muip no ap cíp piaṁ an oipeaḋ pin ḋ'aimpip ba ṁeapa leip, 'ná an peaḋ ḋo ḃí pé⁸ apciġ inp an uaiṁ. Aġup níop lúġaiḋe aiċ-ṁilleaḋ na popaoipe, ḋap leip péin, ġaċ a nḋeapna pé ḋe ḋíoġḃáil ḋóiḃ. Aġup ḋo ċáiniġ ċum na ceine aġup ní ḃpuaip aon ċpiċíp⁹ beó ḃí: aġup ip aṁlaiḋ puaip an boiċ ḋo ḃí aiġe, ina ḋoipe ḋlúiċ ḋe ċaol-ċpannaiḃ péiḋe pópaḋa, aġup ġaoċa ġéapa ġpoḋ-neiṁneaċa ḋ'á lúbaḋ¹⁰ aġup pneaċca pliuċ lán-cpom aġ lúbaḋ na ġcpann pin, aġup linnce puapa píop-

---

¹ H has "gual eire".   ² H reads "torc treathan mhór teine".
³ L has "anál agus uanfach".   ⁴ A reads "cuideach" instead of "coda".
⁵ A reads "ar an dara feacht."   ⁶ A generally makes the gen. of *uaim*
⁷ Last nine words are from H, but   "uaimhe" and "uaimha"), or even
I read "arís" for the "do risi" of H.   "uaimche".

Virtues, and he bore off with him a great shoulder-load of the branches of that blossom-virtued wondrous tree, so that he made of it a hut and a booth in the middle of the forest. And it was not under the protection of the inhabitants of the forest that Cod went that night, but under the protection of his own hand and his own blade.

And thereupon he kindled a great strong fire ; and there was not the length of an inch of that forest without some utterly hideous creature in it, and they used to utter fearsome cries round about him, so that those monsters (¹) used to come round the fire up to Cod.

And indeed it was like the rushing of red wind or the sound of a huge wave down a jagged waterfall, the wailings of some of them, and the noise of some of them was like the sound of a great wind against rough-hills, and their eyes in their heads were like to gleaming stars. But that rock, Cod, son of the King of Norway, was unchanged in shape or sense or form, his courage unmoved, his speech unwandering, listening to these great evils.

It was then Cod arose the second time, and he gave a hand round about them, like a shepherd gathering a flock, and he collected them to the mouth of a cave, so that he drove them into the mouth of the same cave again. And he followed them in, and the monstrous-thing on which he would lay hands he used to strike him on the second monster, so that he inflicted a very great innumerable loss upon them, and he followed them up to the bed of the cave, and there is no knowledge of what direction they went from him at that time.

And Cod came forth, after that, and he never experienced by sea or by land the same length of time during which he suffered more (²) than whilst he was inside in the cave. And it seemed to him that none the less for all the loss he wrought them, was the malignity of the forest. And he came again to the fire, but he did not find one spark of it alive, and this is how he found the booth that he had, namely [changed into] a close oak-wood of thin trees, smooth and very high, and bitter quick venomous winds, and wet, full-heavy snow bending those trees, and

---

⁸ Thus L which gives the best reading.   ⁹ Thus H, but A has "critre".
¹⁰ Thus H : last thirteen words. A reads "doire do caoileach " and "i na crannaibh reidhe gaoithfhuaire ". L " na doire do chaol chrannaibh coimhreidhe".

(¹) Literally "worms."   (²) Literally "which was worse with him."

uirſe aſ rnoiḋc aſur aſ ríor-ċiberrin ioir na crannaiḃ ceann-péiḋe[1]. Aſur ir dóḃal ſe n'innrin tuararſḃáil Ḟoraoire na n-lonſnaḋ mun am rin, aſur níor ḃ' in-ċreiḋte ó ḃraoiċiḃ dá ḃſearaiſe ná ó úſḋar dá ſlice, a raiḃ d' aiċṁilleaḋ draoiḋeaċta ar ſeaḋ Ḟoraoire na n-lonſnaḋ an tan rin. Ir annrin ċárla aċaċ ríor-ſránda do Ċoḃ ſe taoiḃ na Ḟoraoire, aſur bearc de ċroicniḃ fiaḋ maol aſur fearḃóſ uime, aſur dá ḃinn coṁ-ſlara ſaḃair fair ċre na cloiſinn[2], aſur láṁ ciorcla ciarḃuḃ aiſe, aſur aon ċor mar ċrann-reól loinſe lán-ṁóire faoi, aſur loirſſearraḋ impeaṁar d'iarann aċleaſſta ina láiṁ, aſur laoſ[3] im-ḃírſir allata[4] ran láiṁ eile ar éill aiſe. Aſur iar dteaċc do láċair óḋ d'ſiarruiſ Coḃ rſéala óé, aſur d'ſiarruiſ ſór créaḋ é dóḃar a ḃráiſḋeanair ar an ḃfiaḋ-maol. Aduḃairc an t-aċaċ naċ raiḃ ſonn [air] rſéala d'innrin, aſur "naċ mó do ḋéanſaḋ ar maiċe[5] ſe neaċ eile é, aſur ní ċiuḃra[ḋ] níor mó de mo rſéalaiḃ duit-ſe no do ḋaoiniḃ eile, aċt aṁáin ſur mearuſaḋ oiḋċe do ċuſ ir an ḃforaoir mé."[6]

Annrin mar do ċualaiḋ Coḃ ſlór neaṁ-ċláċ an aċaiſ, níor ſéaḋ a ſulanſ, aſur ċuſ buille cloiḋiṁ ċre ċeann an ſir ṁóir, aſur ba ſaṁailte ſe fuaim rrſíoṁ-darac, foſar aſur torann an aċaiſ, aſ roċcain ſo lár aſur ſo lán-talṁain óó. Ir annrin ċuſ an t-aċaċ clireaḋ colna[7] ſo dtárla 'na ſearaṁ ar aon ċoir arír, aſur an cloiḋeaṁ ċrarna ċre n-a ċeann. Ir aṁlaiḋ do ḃí Coḃ an uair rin ar ſualainn an ſir ṁóir, aſur a óá ḋorn i nḃornċlaḋ[8] a cloiḋiṁ ſéin, aſur níor ſéaḋ a leiſean amaċ, aſur do ruſ an t-aċaċ ar a luirſ i láiṁ leir, aſur ar an crlabraḋ do ḃí ar an ḃfiaḋ-maol ran láiṁ eile, aſur do ionnruiſ an t-aċaċ doſur-ḃeól na huaṁa ḃí ran ḃforaoir, ſó an ſcuma rin. Ba nár ſe Coḃ an clear rin, aſur ba beaſ nár ḃ'ſearr leir bloḋ mór d'á ſaoſal do ċeaċc 'ná an ſoraoir d'ſáſḃáil an oiḋċe rin. Aſur iar roċcain ſo dorur na h-uaṁa óóiḃ, do ċruaḋ-ſáirſ[9] Coḃ dorn-ċlaḋ an cloiḋiṁ ſo

[1] L, last six words from H.

[2] Last nine words are from H. L has "da. b. comfhada gharbh-ghlasa gabhair ar a lámha chiar-chlamhach cíordubh aige".

[3] H "dá laogh". L "damhlaogh".   [4] Thus H. A has "eallaigh".

[5] Thus L. A has "re maith re", etc.   [6] Last ten words from H.

cold linns of spring water flowing and constantly-welling between the smooth-headed trees. And it were awful to tell, the account of the Forest of Wonders at that time, and it were not to-be-believed from druids however knowledgeable, or from author however wise, all the destruction of enchantment that was then throughout the Forest of Wonders. It was after that a hideous giant met Cod beside the forest, and a garment of the skins of hornless deer and roebuck about him, and two goats' horns of equal grayness on him, [growing] through his skull, and a circular jet-black hand he had, and one leg like the mast of a full-great ship under him, and a thick club-staff of refined iron in his hand, a wild un-tamed calf in his other hand by a thong. And after coming up to him Cod asked him his news, and asked him, moreover, what was the reason of the captivity of the wild-deer [calf]. The giant answered that he had no mind to tell tidings, " and that he would do it none the more to please another, and I will give to you no more of my tidings than to other people, except this only, that it was going-astray of night that brought me into the forest."

Then, when Cod heard the unsubmissive voice of the giant, he could not endure it, and he gave a stroke of his sword through the big man's head ; and like the noise of a prime-oak [falling] was the crash and sound of the giant as he came to the earth and to the ground. It was then the giant gave a twist to his body until he came standing again on one leg, and the sword through his head. And this is how Cod was then, namely, on the shoulder of the big man, and his two hands in the handle of his own sword, and he was unable to let it out, and the giant grasped the club in one hand, and the chain that was on the hornless deer in the other hand, and he made for the door-mouth of the cave that was in the forest, in that guise. And Cod was ashamed of that feat, for little but he had preferred a great piece of his life to be lost (¹) than leave the forest that night. And after their reaching the door of the cave Cod tightly-grasped the handle of

---

⁷ Thus H. A has "cliosad cola ". A 25 "cleasa colla". L "cliseadh colla ".·
⁸ H i "ndornchuire" ; L "anorchloinn ". A 25 "andornchalad ". A " dorn cla ", which I edit as above.
⁹ L " chruadh-nasg ".

(¹) Literally " to come."

ġlac láiḋip, ġo nḃeápnaiḋ bloḋa beaġa¹ ḋe, ionnup ġup ċuit péin ḋe ġualainn an aitiġ ġo talṁain.

Aġup iap poċtain² ċum na talṁan ḋo Ċoḋ, tuġ púil ċaipip, aġup ip eaḋ ḋo ċonnaipc an caipte coṁ-ṁóp cloiċe ap nḋéanaṁ ḋe'n aiteaċ aġup an cloiḋeaṁ tpíḋ, ó'n taoḃ ġo³ ċéile.

Aġup níop péaḋ Coḋ an cloiḋeaṁ ḋo ċappainġ ap an ġcappaiġ [act] ḋo ċuġ piċe ppap ap an luipġ poṁopḋa ḋo ḃí aġ an ataċ, aġup ip eaḋ aḋuḃaipt, "ip paḋa ġo ḋtápla mo ḋíol⁴ ḋ'apm ḃam ġo ḋtí anoċt." Ip annpin ḋo pill Coḋ ap puḋ na popaoipe aġup ip aṁlaiḋ ḋo puaip í, eiḋip ċpannaiḃ aġup cloċaiḃ, 'na h-aon leic ṗuaip oiġpeaċta⁵ an uaip pin, aġup níop ṁait aḃḃa⁶ cóṁnuiġte an uaip pin í, aġup aḋuḃaipt Coḋ, "ip maipġ ḋuine coṁṫeaċ⁷ táiniġ i ḃpaḋ ġo Popaoip na n-lonġnaḋ, aġup ní ba peapp ḋóiḃ-pean má ba beó mipe amápaċ."

Aġup ní paiḃ piop cpéaḋ ḋo ḋéanpaḋ, an t-am pin, óip ba ṁóp uipġe na popaoipe aġup ba iomḋa eiċiḃe píop-ġpánḋa aġup ġealta ġlinne, aġup ḋeaṁain aéḋip aġ pġpeaḋpaiḋ aġup aġ béicpiḋ ṗá'n aimpip pin i ḃPopaoip na n-lonġnaḋ; aġup ḋa ḋteanġṁaḋ a ċapaiḋ ġaoil i ġcóṁpoġup ḋo neaċ, ní ċluinpeaḋ iaḋ ó ċaint aġup ó ġápċaiḃ na n-appaċta pin.

Aġup ḋo pnuain Coḋ náp ḃaoġal ḋó iaḋ, óip níop luċt tpoḋa ná teanġṁala iaḋ.⁸ Ip annpin ḋo ċonnaipc Coḋ lóċpann lonnapḋa lán-álainn ap lapaṁ ḋ'á ionnpaiḋe, aġup inġean óġ iol-ċpotaċ ċeann-ápḋ ċéaḋpaḃaċ aġ iomċup an lóċpainn pin, aġup tuġ Coḋ aiċne uippi, .i. ġup b'í Ġpian Ġnúip-ṗolaip inġean Ríġ Popaoipe na n-lonġnaḋ ḋo ḃí ann, aġup táiniġ ḋo láċaip Ċuiḋ, aġup ḋ'ṗeap páilte ġo ppíoċnaṁaċ pia Coḋ ina ainm aġup ina ṗloinneaḋ, aġup aḋuḃaipt an inġean, "A ṁic Ríġ na h-lopuaiḋe, ḋap liom péin ip olc puaip tu Popaoip na n-lonġnaḋ ó táiniġ tu innti, aġup tap liom-pa ḋo mo ḃpuiġin péin, má olc maiċ⁹ pe [a] ḃpuil innti." Ba ṁait le Coḋ an cuipeaḋ pin ḋ'ṗáġail, aġup¹⁰ ḋ'imċiġeaḋap pómpa leiċ ap leiċ, aġup tápla ḃpuiġean ċeannápḋ ċloġapaċ aoiḃinn

---

¹ L and H " mírcanna mion-bhruighte ".   ² Last thirteen words from H.
³ H " guroile ".   A 25 " na chéile ".   ⁴ Thus H. L " mo dhiongmhala " ;
A " mo tsáith ".   ⁵ The last fifteen words are from H, which gives the
best reading. L reads " oigheartha ". A " oigriata ".   ⁶ Thus H. A has

the sword with a firm grip, till he made little fragments of it, so that he fell himself off the shoulder of the giant to the ground.

And after Cod's reaching the ground, he threw an eye back, and this was what he saw: a great pillar of stone made of the giant, and the sword through him from one side to the other.

And Cod was not able to draw the sword out of the rock, but he gave a quick leap at the Fomorian club that the giant had, and he said, "It is long since I met a weapon meet for me till to-night." It was then Cod returned throughout the forest, and this is how he found it; both trees and stones in one flag of ice at that time, and it was not a good dwelling-place at that hour. And Cod said, "Alas, for a stranger who has come from far to the Forest of Wonders, and they shall not be the better for this if I am alive to-morrow."

And he did not know what he would do at that time, for great was the water of the forest, and many was the disgusting creature and *geilt* of the valley, and demon of the air screaming and bellowing, at that time in the Forest of Wonders; and if one's kindred friend were to come close up to a man he would not hear him from the talk and shoutings of those spectres.

But Cod considered that they were not a danger to him, for they were not things of fight or conflict. It was then Cod beheld a shining beautiful lamp, lit-up, and coming towards them, and a young well-shaped high-headed sensible maiden bearing that lamp. And Cod recognized her, that it was Bright-faced Sun, daughter of the King of the Forest of Wonders, who was there; and she came up to Cod, and she earnestly bade Cod welcome in his name and surname, and the girl said, "Son of the King of Norway, methinks it is evil thou hast found the Forest of Wonders, since thou hast come into it, and come with me to my own palace, whether those who are in it like it or dislike it." Glad was Cod to get that invitation; and they went forwards, side by side, and they came to a high-headed belfry-like delightful flower-

---

"aidhbhe". L "ait". ⁷ Thus L. A "daoidhid". ⁸ Last seven words from L. H omits the preceding sentence. ⁹ This is a common idiom of the present day. The English reader would expect the conjunctive "no", which the Scotch insert: cf. the well-known Gaelic song, " Triallamaoid an rathad mór, olc *no* maith le cach é ". ¹⁰ The last nine words are from L.

ḃláiṫ-ionġantaċ ḋóiḃ, aġur ba h-ilġréaraċ iolċroṫaċ an
ḃruiġean rin, óir bo ḃaḋar móráin aoiḃnear innci, aġur bo
ḃí reaċt nḋoirre uirri, aġur céaḋ fear n-arm¹ ar ġaċ aon
ḋorar ḋíoḃ, aġur níor ċumaḋar láiṁa ruaḋ na raor-ċearḋ
o bo cruċaiġeaḋ an ċruinne² baraṁail³ bo'n ċaċraiġ rin, ar a
h-ilġréaraiḃ, óir bo ḃaḋar móráin be ċloċaiḃ uairle aġur be
liaġaiḃ loġṁara ina ṫaoḃaiḃ, aġur ir í caṫair bo b'ḟearr
ḋealḃ aġur ḋéanaṁ ran boṁan í, ó Ċaṫair na h-Irbirne amaċ.
Aġur fuaraḋar ar a ġceann innci Ríġ forarḋa flaiṫeaṁail
i ġcaṫaoir áluinn órḋa, aġur crí caoġaḋ ríoḃre ġo mbearcaiḃ
óir ór-loirġṫe ar ġaċ taoḃ bé, aġur bantraċt i mbraṫaiḃ
rróil i n-árḋ-ġrianánaiḃ an ḋúna ḋeaġ-ṁairġ rin.

Aġur b'éiriġ an Ríġ rin aġur bo rug ar láiṁ ar Ċoḃ, aġur
bo ċuir na fuiḋe ó i n-ionaḋ Ríġ inr an Ríoġ-ḃruiġin rin, aġur
ċánġaḋar maiṫe na cáṫraċ, iḃir fear aġur mnaoi, b'á
ionnraiḋe aġur bo ċuireaḋar fáilte rria Coḃ, ġiḋ naċ raiḃ
b'á eólur aca aċt [a] ḟaicrin i ḃroċair na h-inġine, aġur
méaḋ na honóra bo ḃí aġ an ríoġain bó.⁴ Ir annrin
b'ḟiarfruiġ an Ríġ⁵ be'n inġin, "Cia h-é an Rioḃre óġ aṁulcaċ⁶
iol-ċroṫaċ ċuġ rí léiṫe bo'n ceaġlaċ?"

Aḋuḃairt an inġean, "Coḃ mac Ríġ na h-Ioruaiḋe an fear
úḋ," ar rí, "aġur cuġaiḋ-re bó ġaċ níḋ iarrfar orraiḃ, aġur
muna bcuġaiḋ riḃ be ḃur nḋeoin é ir éiḋir leir a ḃuain ḋíḃ be
ḃur n-aiṁḋeoin, aġur ġiḋ ġur líonṁar ḃur rlóiġ ir ró ḃeaġ iḃir
láṁaiḃ an ḟir úḋ iaḋ,⁷ óir ir leir an ḃfear úḋ bo rraonaḋ caṫ
ar Ríġ na Sorċa, aġur bo ċuit an Ríġ féin leir, aġur iomaḋ
rlóiġ mar aon frir. Aġur ní h-é rin aṁáin, aċt ir iomḋa
fuaṫ aġur arraċta coṁaiġṫeach eile bo ċuit leir, aġur ir
fearr baoiḃ-re ġaċ níḋ iarrfar orraiḃ bo ċaḃairt bó 'ná
impearán bo ḃeit eaḋraiḃ aġur é. "An ḃfeaḋair-re," ar an
ríġ, "cá níḋ iarrfar orrainn?" "Ní ḟeaḋar," ar an inġean,
"aċt ġur bóiġ liom ġo ḃfuil lorġaireaċt aiġe ar an íce atá
aġaiḃ-re." Fiarraiġear an flaiṫriġ féin créaḋ be ṁaiṫear na
roraoire le raiḃ a ḟúil.⁸ Ir annrin aḋuḃairt Coḃ, "Ir í ḃreiṫ

---

¹ H reads "fromhtha fior arrachtach".
² Thus H. A reads "ó cathair na hIsbirne".
³ H reads "a commaith darus". A 25 has "maca hamhla na cathracha sin".

wondrous steading; and of divers decorations variously-formed was
that steading, for there were many delights in it, and there were in it
seven doors, and a hundred armed men on each door of them, and the
hands of sages and free-artificers never wrought since the universe
was created the like of that *cathair* for its various decorations, for there
were many noble stones and precious gems in its sides, and it is the
cathair of best appearance and best make in the world, from the *cathair*
of Isbirne, down. And they found awaiting them in it a sedate princely
king on a beautiful golden throne, and thrice fifty knights with dresses
of gold, gold-embroidered, on each side of him, and a company of
ladies in mantles of satin upon the high grianáns or sunny-houses of
that well-favoured dún.

And the king rose up, and he grasped Cod by the hand and put
him sitting in the king's place in that royal mansion, and the nobles
of the city came, both men and women, to Cod, and bade him welcome,
although they had no knowledge of him, except only to see him along
with the maiden, and all the honour that the queen paid him. It
was then the king inquired of the girl, "Who was that young,
beardless, well-shaped knight whom she had brought with her to
the household?"

The girl spake, "Cod, son of the King of Norway, is that man,"
said she, "and do ye give him everything he shall ask of you, and
unless ye give it to him of your own good will he is able to take it
from you against your will; and although numerous are your hosts,
they are very little in the hands of that man, for it was by that
man a battle was broken on the King of Sorcha, and the king himself fell by him and many hosts along with him; and it is not that
alone, but many is the horror and other strange spectre that fell by
him, and it is better for you to give him everything he shall ask of
you than for there to be a quarrel between you and him." "Do you
know," said the king, "what thing he will ask of us?" "I do not,"
said the girl, "but I am sure that he is on the track of the salve
which you have." The monarch himself then asks Cod, which of the
good things of the forest was he expecting. Then said Cod, "The

---

⁴ The last twenty-three words are added from **H**.
⁵ **H** "an flaithruire".   ⁶ This word is added from **H**.
⁷ Last eleven words are from A 25.   ⁸ The last forty words are added from **H**.

ꝺo ḃéaρρainn-ρe oρρaiḃ .i. ḃρeiċ ḃealuiġċe ıoıρ ḃuρ ġceann aġuρ ḃuρ ġcolainn aġuρ maiċeaρ na cáċρaċa aġuρ na ꝉoρaoıρe ꝺo ḃeiċ aġam ꝉéın, muna mbeaḋ an ınġean ꝉo ꝺo ḃuρ ꝺceaρaρġan¹ oρm," aρ Coꝺ.

Iaρ ġcloρ na mḃρıaċaρ ρın ꝺo luċċ na cáċρaċ uıle, ꝺo leıġeaꝺaρ aρ a nġlúınıḃ ıaꝺ, aġuρ ċuġaꝺaρ a láṁa ı láıṁ Cuıꝺ aġuρ ġaḃaꝺaρ leıρ maρ ċρıaċ aġuρ maρ ċıġeaρna, ıoıρ ꝼρıoll aġuρ uaρal, aġuρ ċuġaꝺaρ ġρıan aġuρ ġealaċ ꝺo ḃeiċ ꝺꝼleaρ uρρamaċ ꝺó aρ ꝼeaḋ a ꝉaé.² Aġuρ ċuġ Ġρıan Ġnúıρꝼolaıρ cóṁaıρle ꝺo Ċoꝺ ρın ꝺo ġaḃáıl uaċa aġuρ aꝺuḃaıρc, "Iρ cóρaıꝺe ḃuıc an ṁuınncıρ úꝺ ꝺo ġaḃáıl ċuġaꝺ naċ ρuġaꝺ a mbuaıꝺ ρıaṁ ρóṁaꝺ, ρe h-uaċaꝺ no ρe h-ıomaꝺ." Aġuρ a h-aıċle na mḃρıaċaρ ρın ꝺo ꝼuıꝺ an ınġean ı ġcáċaoıρ áluınn aġuρ ꝺo ċuaıꝺ luċċ na caċρaċ uıle ꝉó ċíoρ ꝺo Ċoꝺ, o ρın ρuaρ, aġuρ ꝺo ġaḃ Coꝺ ρın uaċa.

Iρ annρın ꝺo cóġḃaḋ ḃuıρꝺ ꝼlím-leaċna na Caċρaċ aġuρ ꝺo ꝉolċaıġeaḋ ıaꝺ ꝺ'éaꝺaıġıḃ uaıρle ıonġanċaċa, aġuρ ꝺo ꝼuıꝺ an móρ-ċeaġlaċ ρın, aġuρ ċuġaꝺ bıaꝺa ρaoρa ρo-ċaıċṁe ꝺ'á n-ıonnρaıꝺe, aġuρ ꝺeoċa ρóı-ṁeaρġċa ıl-ċıneálaċa,⁴ aġuρ ꝺo ġaḃaꝺaρ aġ ól aġuρ aġ aoıḃneaρ ġo mba ρúḃaċ ρóı-ṁeanmnaċ [ıaꝺ.] Ꝺ'éıρġeaꝺaρ luċċ cıúıl aġuρ oıρꝼıꝺe aġuρ aoıρ ealaꝺna ꝺo ġaḃáıl a nꝺánca aġuρ a nꝺρéaċca aġuρ a ġcρaoḃa coıṁneaρa aġuρ a [n]ġéaġa ġınealaċa ꝺo ċáċ ġo coıċċeann.⁵ Iρ annρın ċuġ Coꝺ a láṁ ı ġcoḃρainn a ρġéıċe, aġuρ ċuġ cumaoın a ealaꝺna ꝉéın ꝺo ġaċ aon ꝺꝼoḃ, aġuρ aꝺuḃaıρc Coꝺ, "Iρ maiċ ꝺo'n ḃρuıġın ρeo naċ ꝺcuġamaρ eólaρ ı ꝺcoρaċ na hoıḃċe uıρρı." Aġuρ maρ ꝺo ċualaꝺaρ muınncıρ na ꝉoρaoıρe ρın ó Ċoꝺ, ꝺo ġaḃ eaġla aġuρ uaṁan móρ ıaꝺ, aċc cá [nı] ċeana ꝉóρ, ba ḃınn ρe mnáıḃ aġuρ ba ꝼeaρḃ ρe ꝼeaρaıḃ aρ ċan ρé.⁶

Aċc cá ní ċeana, ċuġaꝺaρ aρ an oıꝺċe ρın no ġuρ ꝼoıllρıġ an lá ġo n-a lán-ꝼoıllρe aρ n-a ṁáρaċ. Iρ annρın ċuġ Coꝺ láṁ aρ ımċeaċc, aġuρ ċuġaꝺ an cρlaċ ıonġanċaċ ρın ꝺó, aġuρ a ċloıḃeaṁ⁷ ꝉéın, aġuρ aꝺuḃaıρc Ġρıan Ġnúıρ-ꝼolaıρ, "A ṁıc

---

¹ L reads "do ghaibh bhur tteasragan". ² Last fourteen words added from L.
³ Last fourteen words added from L. ⁴ The last eleven words are from H.
⁵ H omits all this description of the feast and of what Cod said.

judgment that I would pass upon you would be a judgment of parting between your heads and your bodies, and for myself to have the good things of the *cathair* and of the Forest, if it were not for this maiden rescuing you from me," said Cod.

And when all the people of the *cathair* heard these words they went down on their knees and gave their hands into Cod's hand, and accepted him as chieftain and lord, both high and low, and they swore by the sun and by the moon to be faithful and obedient to him throughout their life. And Bright-faced Sun counselled Cod to accept that from them; and she said, "It is the more due for you to accept [the offer of] those men over whom a victory was never gained before you, either by few or by many." And after those words, the maiden sat upon a beautiful throne, and those people of the city all became tributary to Cod from that out, and Cod accepted that from them.

It was then the thin broad tables of the burg were raised, and they were covered with noble wondrous cloths, and that great household sat down, and fine edible meats were brought to them, and drinks well(¹) mixed of various kinds, and they began to drink and make merry until they were hearty, and in good spirit. Up rose the musicians and minstrels and men of science to sing their poems and lays, and their branches of kinship, and their trees of genealogy, to all in general. It was then Cod put his hand into the hollow of his shield, and he gave to each one of them the award of his own science; and Cod said, "It is well for this palace that we did not make its acquaintance at the beginning of this night." And when the people of the forest heard that from Cod, fear and great terror seized them: one thing now, women thought it sweet, and men thought it bitter, all that he spake.

Howsoever they bore away that night until the sun shone with its full light upon the morrow. It was then Cod took in hand his departure, and that wondrous rod was given to him, and his own sword ; and Bright-faced Sun said : "Son of the King of Norway, the cat of

---

⁶ L reads "ba bhinn leis an inghin ar chan Cod agus ba doibhinn leis an dteaghlach uile é". ⁷ "claoidheamh" in A 25 and L. "claidheamh" in A.

(¹) Literally "easily-mixed."

Ríġ na h-Iopuaiḋe ḋo puġ Cat na Saop-ınnpe an íce atá tupa ḋ'ıappaıḋ léıte, aġup tá pí péın aġup ḋo ḃṗáıtpe-pe ı ḃtıġ ḃetúıne[1], ınġıne Ríġ na Sopċa, ap ḋo ċcann." ḃa ḃınn le Coḃ na pġéala pın, aġup tánġaḋap an ṁuınntıp pın aġup Ġpıan Ġnúıp-ḟolaıp leıp, ġo loċ na h-lonġnaḋ ap aıp apíp, aġup ḋ'ḟáġ Coḃ beaċa aġup pláınte aca.

Aġup ní h-aıtpıpteap pġéala ımċeaċta aıp, ġo páınıġ Caċaıp ḃeúıne ı ġCpíoċaıḃ na Sopċa, aġup puaıp pé Ceaḃ aġup Míceaḃ aġup an Cupaıpe Camċopaċ aġup cat na Saop-lnnpe ınntı, maılle pıa, aġup ḋ'ḟeapaḋap páılte poıṁ Coḃ aġup ḋo ṗóġaḋap ġo ḃíl aġup ġo ḋıacpaċ é,[2] aġup ḋo ġaḃaḋap aġ taḃaıpt a pġéala péın ḋóıḃ o túp ġo ḋeıpeaḋ, map ḋo h-aıtḃeóḋaıġeaḋ tpe ḃuaḋaıḃ na h-íce ḃo puġ Cat na Saop-lnnpe ċuca, ıaḋ.[3] Aġup ḋo ınnıp Péıtleann Ïlonġṗúıleaċ map ḋo puġ an íce léıte ḃo'n taoḃ eıle. Act tá ní ċeana ḋo pġaoıleaḋ a ġeapa ḃe ċat na Saop-lnnpe, an oıḋċe pın, aġup ap na ṁápaċ níop ḃ'éaġpaṁla[4] bean pan ḋoṁan 'ná í.

Aġup ḃo ġaḃaḋap láṁ ap ımċeaċt, aġup ḃo tánġaḋap ġo h-aċláṁ ḃ'ıonnpaıḋe [a] luınġe péın, aġup ḃo ċuaıḃ Ceaḃ aġup Míceaḃ aġup Péıtleann Ïlonġṗúıleaċ aġup an Cupaıpe Camċopaċ ınntı. Ip annpın aḃuḃaıpt Coḃ naċ paċaḃ beó no maıḃ péın ġo Cpíoċaıḃ na h-lopuaıḋe, aġup lollán óp-apmaċ mac Ríġ na h-Almáınne ḃ'ḟáġḃáıl 'na ḋıaıḋ maıḃ ı ḃḞopaoıp na n-lonġnaḋ. Ceıleaḃpaıḃ ḃ'á ċéıle annpın, aġup tóġaḋap clann eıle Ríġ na h-lopuaıḋe peólta na ḟean[ġ]-luınġe tap ḃpom-ċlaḋ ġaċ ḃoṁan-ḟaıppġe, aġup ní h-ınnıpteap [a] pġéal-uıḋeaċt no ġo páıġaḋap Cpíoċa na h-lopuaıḋe. Aġup puıcpeam annpın ıaḃ ġan eapḃaıḃ, aġup tpáċtam ap ġaċ nıḃ ḃap éıpġıḃ ḃo Coḃ a ḃḞopaoıp na n-lonġnaḋ.

Pılleap Coḃ poıṁe an oıḋċe pın[5] ġo Cáċaıp ḃeúıne, ġo Cpíoċaıḃ na Sopċa, aġup ḃo ḟan 'na ṗappaḃ an oıḋċe pın, ġo moċa na maıḃne ap n-a ṁápaċ. Aġup ḃo ġaḃ Coḃ ap pın ġo h-uaıṁ na n-lonġnaḋ ap na ṁápaċ, aġup ḃo ġaḃ map paıḃ Ġpıan Ġnúıp-ḟolaıp ınġean Ríġ Ḟopaoıpe na n-lonġnaḋ, aġup ḃo ınnıp ḃí ġupaḃ ḃ'ḟéaċaın a' ḃḞeaḃpaḋ aıtḃeóḋuġaḋ ḃo ḋéanaṁ

---

[1] L "beothuinne". A 25 "beithuinne".

the Free Island has brought away with her the salve that you are looking for, and she herself, and your brothers [whom she has made alive
again] are before you in the house of Bethuinè, daughter of the King
of Sorcha. Sweet were those tidings to Cod; and those people and
Bright-faced Sun came with him back again to the Lake of Wonders,
and Cod left with them life and health [i.e. bade them farewell].

And no tidings of his going are told until he reached the burg of
Bethuinè in the lands of Sorcha, and he found Cead and Micead, and
the Curairè Crookfoot, and the cat of the Free Island there, along with
her, and they welcomed Cod and kissed him lovingly and fervently,
and they commenced to tell him their own tidings from first to last,
how they were brought to life, through the virtue of the salve which
the cat of the Free Island had brought them. And Bright-eyed
Féithleann told them how she had taken the salve with her, on the
other side. Howsoever, her *geasa* were loosened from the cat of the
Free Island, on that night. And on the morrow there was no woman
in the world more beautiful than she.

And they took in hand their departure, and they came to their own
ship with speed, and Cead and Micead, and Bright-eyed Féithleann,
and the Curairè Crookfoot embarked in it. It was then Cod said that
he would not go, alive or dead, to the lands of Norway, and leave
Golden-armed Iollan, son of the King of Almain behind him, dead, in
the Forest of Wonders. They bade farewell to one another then ; and
the other sons of the King of Norway raised the sails of the slender
vessel over the back-ridges of each deep sea, and their tidings are not
told until they reached the lands of Norway. And let us leave them
there without a want, and let us speak of everything that fell out to
Cod in the Forest of Wonders.

Cod returns that night to the burg of Bethuinè to the lands of
Sorcha, and he remained with her that night, until early morning on
the morrow. And on the morrow Cod departed thence to the Cave of
Wonders, and betook himself to where Bright-faced Sun, daughter of
the king of the Forest of Wonders, was; and he told her that he was

---

² Last fourteen words added from L.   ³ Last fourteen words are added from H.
⁴ H "ailne".   ⁵ Last twenty-six words are added from H.

ar Iollán Óṙ-armaċ ċáiniġ ṙé, ḋo ḃí marḃ i ḃḟoraoir na n-lonġnaḋ, ó ḋo ḃí an íce aiġe ḋo aiċḃeóḋaiġ a ḋearḃṙáiċṙe ṙéin,[1] aġur aḋuḃairt Ġrian Ġnúir-ḟoluir ġur cóir an toirc rin. Aġur ċánġaḋar araon ḋ'ionnraiḋe na ṙearta ina raiḃ Iollan óṙ-armaċ aġur a ṁuinntir, aġur ḋ'ḟorġail Coḋ an ṙeart oṙṙa, aġur ċuġ íce i mbéal ġat ṙir ḋíoḃ ṙo ṙeaċ, aġur ḋ'óirġeaḋar rlán uile an uair rin.

Ir annrin ḋ'ḟiarṙuiġ Coḋ ḋe'n inġin an raiḃ ar óruim an ḋoṁain níḋ ḋ'ṙóirṙeaḋ ḋo Ċiaḃán Ġlúinġeal ó n-a ġearaiḃ. Aḋuḃairt an inġean ġan contaḃairt naċ raiḃ.

"Ar ġráḋ h-oiniġ[2] ná ceil orm-ra má tá ṙior aġat."

"Ir olc ḋo rinnir rin ḋ'iarraiḋ orm-ra," ar an inġean, "óir ir eaġal liom ġur triḋ ḋo ċiucṙar ḋo ḃár, má ċuirir ṙóṁaḋ ṙurtaċt ḋ'ḟáġail ḋó."[3] Aġur aḋuḃairt mar ro, "Danuite, inġean Ríġ Ġréaġ, ḋo ċuir na ġeara úḋ ṙair, aġur ḋá mbeaḋ an ḃean rin aġainn-ne ḃa ḋearḃ ḋo Ċiaḃán Ġlúinġeal a ġeara ḋo leiġear."

Aḋuḃairt Coḋ, "Ir ṙaḋa ġur innir tura rin ḋaṁ-ra."

"Eaġla ḋo ċuitim ann, ḋo ḃí orm-ra," ar an inġean, "óir ní h-urura ḋul ḋo'n Ġréiġ, óir ir iaḋ ir lia ḋe ḋaoiniḃ ir an ḋoṁan ġo h-iomlán."

"Ba beaġ an tairḃe rin ḋóiḃ," ar Coḋ "ḋá nḋeaċainn-ṙe[4] ḋo'n Ġréiġ." Ir annrin ċáiniġ Ríġ Foraoire na n-lonġnaḋ amaċ ar ċeann Cuiḋ aġur Iollán Óṙ-armaiġ, ḋ'a mbṙeiċ ḋo'n ċáṫraiġ, aġur ḋo ċuaḋar leir, aġur ba ḋearḃ naċ ḃḟuaraḋar riaṁ oiḋċe ir ṙearr ṙuaraḋar 'ná an oiḋċe rin.

eaċtra ċuiḋ aġus iolláin 'san nġréiġ.

Aġur ar n-a ṁárac ḋo ċṙiallaḋar, aġur cuireaḋ bile na mbuaḋ le muinntir Iollán Óṙ-armaiġ ġo hinġin Ríġ Tíre ṙó Ċuinn, aġur ḋo ḃearuiġeaḋ lonġ luċtṁar ḋeaġ-ḋíonṁar ḋó ṙéin aġur ḋ'Iollán Óṙ-armaċ, aġur ní ruġaḋar ḋe ḟluaġ ná ḋo ṙoċaiḋe leó aċt iaḋ ṙéin araon,[5] aġur ċuġaḋar aġaiḋ

---

[1] The last thirteen words are added from H.   [2] H "hinidh"; A "heineidh".
[3] Last sixteen words added from H.   [4] Thus L, but A reads "da ndeachaidh mise".

come to try if he would be able to bring to life again Golden-armed
Iollan, who lay dead in the Forest of Wonders, since he had the salve
which had brought to life his own brothers. And Bright-faced Sun
said that it were right to attempt it. And they came together to the
grave in which lay Gold-armed Iollan and his people; and Cod opened
the grave over them,(¹) and put the salve in the mouth of each man
of them separately, and thereupon they all rose up whole.

It was then Cod asked the girl, was there on the ridge of the earth
anything that would relieve Ciabhan White-knee of his *geasa*.   The
girl answered without doubt that there was not.

"For the love of thy generosity conceal it not from me, if thou
knowest of it."

" Ill hast thou done to ask me that," said the maiden, " for I fear
me lest though that may come thy death, if thou undertakest to find
him succour," and she spake thus: " Danuitè, daughter of the King
of Greece, it was, who imposed those *geasa* on him, and if we had
that woman [prisoner], a healing of his *geasa* were certain for Ciabhan
Whiteknee."

Said Cod: "Long it was till thou didst tell me that."

" It was fear of thy falling in the matter, that was on me," said
the maiden, "for it is not easy to go to Greece, for it is they who are
the most numerous of people in the entire world."

"That shall be small advantage to them," said Cod, "if I go to
Greece." It was then the King of the Forest of Wonders came out to
meet Cod and Gold-Armed Iollan, to bring them to the mansion, and
they went with him; and it is certain that they never passed a
pleasanter(²) night than they passed that night.

THE ADVENTURES OF COD AND IOLLAN IN GREECE.

And on the morrow they departed, and the Tree of Virtues was
sent with Gold-Armed Iollan's people to the daughter of the King of
the Land Under-Wave (³); and a laden well-protected bark was prepared for himself and Gold-Armed Iollan, and they took with them

---

⁵ Thus L and A 25. A reads " do mbáin ".

(¹) Literally " on them."   (²) Literally " found a better."
(⁵) See above, pp. 23 and 127.

L

aр an nᵹрéiᵹ an uaiр рin: aᵹuр ꝺo ḃí Iollán aᵹ múnaꝺ cólaiр
ᵹaċa ḃoṁan-ḟaiрᵹe ꝺo Ċoꝺ, aᵹuр рeal eile aᵹ ḟéaċain
ionᵹantaр na ḃⱦonn, no ᵹo ꝼánᵹaꝺaр ꝺo'n ᵹréiᵹ. aᵹuр
ꝺo ċuaꝺaр i ꝺⱦíр, aᵹuр ꝺo ċoncaꝺaр caⱦaiр áluinn óрꝺa
uaċa, aᵹuр aonaċ aḃḃal-ṁóр ina ⱦimċioll. ꝼiaррuiᵹeaр Coꝺ
ꝺ' Iollán cia h-é an ċaⱦaiр, no cia h-é an ⱦ-aonaċ aḃḃal-ṁóр ꝺo
ḃí ina ⱦimċioll, óiр ba h-eólaċ ꝼan nᵹréiᵹ é.[1] ꝺo inniр Iollán
рin ꝺo Ċoꝺ aᵹuр aꝺuḃaiрⱦ an laoi ann, maр рo рíoр :

"" Inniр ainm na caⱦраċ-рa
A Iollám na n-aрm ḃрaoḃраċ,
ꝼoillрiᵹ ꝺúinn ᵹo meaрꝺána[2]
Na рluaᵹa aḃ óiú 'рan aonaċ.""[3]

"" ꝼilleaꝺ uaiⱦi ní aḃрaim-рe[4]
Cia ꝺeacaiр ꝺul ꝺ'á ꝺⱦaoḃaꝺ,
Caⱦaiр na h-Aiⱦne an ċaⱦaiр-рe
Um Ríᵹ ᵹréaᵹ ⱦá an ⱦ-aonaċ.

"" Sluaᵹ ꝺocраċ na caⱦраċ-рa
'S maiрᵹ le a ḃꝼuil a ḃꝼuaċa,
A ṁic Ríᵹ na h-Iорuaiꝺe
Ní ꝼaoilim áр ꝺⱦeaċⱦ uaⱦa.""[5]

"" Ná h-abaiр an coṁráꝺ-рin
A Iollain na n-aрm n-Óрꝺa,
ba beaᵹ ꝺe na рlóiᵹⱦiḃ-рe
ṁaiрꝼeaр,[6] aᵹainn, ⱦрáⱦ-nóna.

"" Inᵹean Ríᵹ an ꝺúna-рa
ṁaꝺ ole рe luchⱦ an éiꝺiᵹh[7]
ᵹo ᵹрian[8] ᵹaрꝺa ᵹnúiр-ꝼolaiр
béaрꝼaꝺ aр aiр no aр éiᵹin.

"" Ní ḃꝼuil a n-eaᵹla oррuiñ-ne
ᵹiꝺ óiрꝺeiрc iaꝺ 'рᵹaċ inniр[9],
Ainm na caⱦраċ ceann-áiрꝺe
Ⱦaрр a Iollain a'р inniр.""

---

[1] The last six words are added from H.   [2] Thus H. The others
have "abair linn go ballach", or "go ro bhailleach", or "go balach".
[3] Thus H. The others have " ainm na cathrach-sa an aonaigh ".
[4] Thus H. The others read " ni mholain ".
[5] Thus L and H. A has " mollaim filladh uathe ".   [6] L "'na mbeathaidh ".
[7] Thus A 25. H has " a heagnadh ". L " a heide ". A " re lucht eidigh ".
[8] H reads " go gréin ".   [9] Thus H. A has " oiric iad an gach innis ";
A 25 " ce adhbheil iad re faxin ". L " a aigheadh óirdhearc sin an innse ".

neither host nor army, but only themselves both, and then they faced for Greece.   And Iollan was [one time] showing Cod the way over each deep sea, and again beholding the wonders of the waves, until they reached Greece.   And they landed, and beheld at a distance from them a fair golden city, and a huge assembly round about it. Cod asked Iollan what was the city or what was the very-great assembly that was round about it, for Iollan knew Greece.   And Iollan told him that, and [they] spake the lay, as it is down here:—

COD.   " Tell us of those battlements,
             What is the city yonder.
          Tell us, friend of gallantry,
             What hosts around it wander."(¹)

IOLLAN.   " To return from it I do not advise,(²)
                Although it is difficult to go trust them.(³)
             The city of Athens(⁴) is this city,
                Round the King of Greece is the assembly.

          " The difficult hosts of this city,
             Alas for who incurs their enmity.
          O son of the King of Norway,
             I do not think we shall escape from them."

COD.   " Say not that discourse,
             O Iollan of the Golden Arms,
          There shall be few of these hosts
             Whom we shall have living by evening.

          " The daughter of the king of this fortress,
             Though it be displeasing to the people of the armour,
          [Her] to the brave Bright-faced Sun(⁵)
             I shall bring of good will or forcibly.

          " Their fear is not upon us,
             Although renowned they are in every isle.
          The name of the high-headed city,
             Come, O Iollan and tell.(⁶)"

(¹) The metre is the same as before.   Literally : "Tell the name of this city, |
O Iollan of the edged weapons, | reveal to us now, quickly-bold, | the hosts whom
I see in the assembly."   (²) Literally "say."
    (³) Or perhaps "to go meet them."   (⁴) The Irish for Athens, by an undesigned
    (⁵) See above, p. 119.   coincidence, means also "knowledge."
    (⁶) The lay thus ends with the same word which began it, which is a very
usual habit in Irish poems.

α h-aiċle na laoiḃe ṗin ċáṅᵹaḃaṗ ᵹo ṗaiċċe caċṗaċ na h-αiċne, aᵹuṗ ḃo ċóᵹaḃaṗ poḃal áluinn éaᵹṗaṁail ionᵹanċaċ aṗ leaċ-ċaoḃ na ṗaiċċe ṗéaṗ-uaiċne ṗin, aᵹuṗ ba ḃeacaiṗ an poḃal ṗin ḃ'ṗéaċain an ċan ṗin, óiṗ ḃo ṗᵹaoileaḃaṗ cleaṗa ᵹṗáineaṁla ina n-ṁiṗ-ċiṁċioll, aᵹuṗ ní ḃṗiċ ḃe ṗluaᵹ na caċṗaċ neaċ ḃo ṗaċaḃ ḃ'iaṗṗaiḃ ṗᵹéal oṗṗa, aᵹuṗ ó náṗ ḃṗiċ, ċuaḃaṗ ḃo'n ċaċaiṗ aᵹuṗ ḃo ḃúnaḃaṗ na ḃoiṗṗe oṗṗa ṗéin.¹

Ioṁċuṗa ḃuinne ḃoṗb-ċṗéan mic Ríᵹ na h-αṗṗaice, iṗ í ṗin uaiṗ aᵹuṗ aiṁṗiṗ ċáiniᵹ ṗé ḃo ċaḃaiṗc Ḃanuice,² inᵹin[e] Ríᵹ Ḋṗéaᵹ, aᵹuṗ ṗáiniᵹ ᵹo ḃoṗuṗ an ḃúna ṗo'n am ṗin, aᵹuṗ ḃo iaṗṗ oṗᵹlaḃ ᵹo h-úṗṁaiṗ[n]eaċ.³ Ċáiniᵹ an ḃoiṗṗeóiṗ ḃ'á inṗin ṗin ḃo'n Ríᵹ, aᵹuṗ ba luaċᵹáiṗeaċ luċc an ḃúna ḃe'n ṗᵹéal ṗin, óiṗ b'é ṗin aon ṗeaṗ ba ṁó ċeiṗc ᵹaiṗᵹe ṗan ᵹcuiḃ ṗin ḃe'n ċṗuinne ina aiṁṗiṗ ṗéin, aᵹuṗ ba ṁaiċ leó a ċeaċċ ċuca le linn na n-aoiḃeaḃ ṗin eile, aᵹuṗ ḃo leiᵹeaḃ aṗceaċ é aᵹuṗ ḃo ṗinneaḃ úṁla aᵹuṗ ṗoṗaḃ ḃó.⁴ Iṗ annṗin ḃ'ṗiaṗṗaiḃ ḃuinne ḃoṗb-ċṗéan, " Cia h-é an poḃal éaᵹṗaṁail, ḃo ċonnaṗc ḃo leaċ-ċaoḃ na ṗaiċċe ?" αḃuḃṗaḃaṗ cáċ naċ ṗaiḃ a ḃeaᵹ no a ṁóṗ ḃ'á ṗᵹéalaiḃ ṗin aca ṗéin : leiᵹiḃ an cóṁṗáḃ ṗin ṗeaċa.⁵ Iṗ annṗin ḃ'óiṗᵹeaḃaṗ luċc ṗṗeaṗḃail aᵹuṗ ṗṗiċeola an ciᵹe, aᵹuṗ ḃo ċóᵹaḃaṗ ḃuiṗḃ ċoṗ-ṗaṁṗa ċaoiḃ-leaċana na caċṗaċ, aᵹuṗ ḃ'ṗoluiᵹeaḃaṗ iaḃ ḃ'éaḃaiᵹiḃ uaiṗle onóṗaċa, aᵹuṗ ḃo ḃáileaḃ ḃeoċa ᵹaṗᵹa ᵹaḃailceaċa oṗṗa, nuaḃ biḃ aᵹuṗ ṗean ḃiᵹe⁶, ᵹuṗ ab ṗuḃaċ ṗo-ṁeanmnaċ iaḃ, ionnuṗ náṗ ṁeaċċa meanmna na míleaḃ ná na ᵹcuṗaḃ ṗo'n am ṗin ḃóiḃ,⁷

Ioṁċuṗa na ḃeiṗe Ríoiṗe ḃo ḃí ṗan bṗoḃal inniṗċeaṗ ṗeal eile. αḃuḃaiṗc Iollan Óṗ-aṗmaċ ᵹo ṗaċaḃ aṗ cuaiṗc maṗ a ṗaiḃ Ríᵹ Ḋṗéaᵹ, aᵹuṗ ḃo ṗuᵹ a ḃeaṗc caċa leiṗ, aᵹuṗ ċáiniᵹ ḃo'n ḃúnaḃ aᵹuṗ ḃo iaṗṗ ṗoṗᵹlaḃ, aᵹuṗ ḃo ṗuᵹ an ḃoiṗṗeóiṗ an ṗᵹéal ṗin ċum an ceaᵹlaiᵹ, aᵹuṗ ḃo inniṗ ᵹuṗ b'é an ḃaṗa ṗeaṗ ḃo ḃí ṗan ṗoḃal é. αᵹuṗ aḃuḃṗaḃaṗ a leiᵹean aṗceaċ, aᵹuṗ náṗ ċóiṗ ḃiúlċaḃ ṗoiṁ aon nḃuine aṁáin ċoiḃċe; aᵹuṗ ḃo leiᵹeaḃ [é] aṗceaċ ḃo'n

---

¹ The last fourteen words are added from L.   ² L reads " Dathnuaidhe ".
³ L "go húirmhisneach". H "go hormaisneach".   ⁴ The last twelve words are added from L.   ⁵ The last five words are added from H.
⁶ The last five words are from H.

After that lay they came to the lawn round the city of Athens, and they raised a beautiful, variegated, wondrous tent on one side of that grass-green lawn, and it was difficult([1]) to then behold that tent, for they practised([2]) terrific feats of arms round about them; and there was not found a man of the host of the city who would go to ask tidings of them, and since there was not, [the people] went into the city and closed the doors upon themselves.

Now about Buinnè [Bwin-yă] Rough-strong son of the King of Africa : that was the very hour and the time that he came to carry off Danuitè, daughter of the King of Greece.   And he reached at that time the door of the *dún* and boldly asked for admittance.   The porter came to tell that to the king, and the people of the *dún* were rejoiced at the news, for this was the one man of most fame for valour in that part of the world in his own time ;   and they were glad of his coming to them at the same time with these other [unknown] guests;   and he was let in, and obeissance was paid him and preparations made for his remaining([3]).   It was then that Buinnè Rough-strong inquired, "What is that handsome tent I beheld on one side of the lawn?"   They all answered that they had no tidings of it themselves, either great or small : and they put the conversation by.   It was then the attendants and ministers of the house rose up, and they raised the thick-footed broad-sided tables of the *cathair*, and they covered them with noble, honourable cloths, and rough, fermented drinks were presented to them, the new of food and the old of drink, so that they were merry and hearty, so that the courage of the warriors and of the champions at that time was not timid for them.

As for the two knights who were in the tent, that is told another time.   Gold-armed Iollan said that he would go pay a visit to where the King of Greece was, and he took with him his habiliments of battle, and came to the fortress and demanded admission([4]).   And the gatekeeper brought those tidings to the household, and told them that he was the second man who was in the tent.   And they said, to let him in, that it was not right to ever refuse a person [who came]

---

[7] H " co nar bhionfh*eadh*ma cuiridh no cathmil*eadh* diobh a nalt na huaire sin ".

([1]) *I.e.* " it would frighten one to behold it."   ([2]) Literally " loosed."
([3]) Literally "and there was submissiveness and a resting made for him."
([4]) Literally " asked opening."

ċaṫraiġ, aġur ṫáinig ar láp na caṫraċ aġur polmuiġċear[t] ionaḋ puiḋe ḋó aġur iarrar an ríġ air puiḋe ir an ionaḋrin. Aḋuḃairt Iollan naċ puiḋreaḋ[2], aġur go raiḃ amuiġ rġéal ba ṁó 'ná é réin.

"Sloinn an ṗear rin ḋúinn," ar Ríġ Ġréaġ.

"Coḋ mac Ríġ na h-Iopuaiḋe atá ann," ar Iollan, " aġur aon uaiṫne ġairġe an ḃeaṫa ir ainm ḋílear ḋó."

"Cṗéaḋ ġluairear do'n ċaṫraiġ reo riḃ ?" ar Ríġ Ġréaġ.

"Ar ċeann t' inġine ṫánġamar," ar Iollan, " aġur ir éiġin a taḃairt ḋúinn má olc maiṫ liḃ é."

"Níor ḃ' olc linn rin," ar an ríġ, " muna mbeaḋ ṗear níor ṗearr 'ná é aici ṗéin."

"Cia an ṗear rin ?" ar Iollan.

"bunne ḃoṗb-ṫṗéan mac Ríġ na hAṗṗaice an ṗear úḋ," ar an ríġ.

An tan do ċualaiḋ Iollan rin do ṗinneaḋ roċnúaill[3] corcra ó ḃonn go baṫar ḋé, aġur ṫuġ buille ḋe'n trleiġ do ḃí 'na láiṁ i ġcláp uċta aġur úṗ-ḃṗuinne, ar an Ríġ, ġur ċuir ṗaḋ láiṁe laoiċ ḋe ċrann cṗuaiḋ-raṁar na craoiriġe tṗe na ḋṗuim amaċ, aġur leiġear ṗéin do ċum an ḋoṗair é, ġan ṗuiliuġaḋ ġan ṗóiṗḋeaṗġaḋ do ḋéanaṁ air. Aġur do luiġ. tṗom-ċuiṗre ar luċt na caṫraċ uime rin, aġur annrin aḋuḃairt bunne ḃoṗb-ṫṗéan leo, aġur ir é aḋuḃairt go raċaḋ do ḋiċċeannaḋ na ḃṗear úḋ do ḃí ran bpobal ṗo ċéaḋóir, muna mbeaḋ go mb' ṗearr leir a nḋiċċeannaḋ[4] lá ar n-a ṁáraċ, i ḃṗiaḋnaire na nĠṗéaġ[aċ] 'ná anoċt.

Iomṫura Iollain Óṗ-aṗmaiġ, ṗáiniġ go a ṗobal ṗéin ġan ṗuiṗeaċ, aġur do ṗuiḋ ina ionaḋ ṗéin. Ṗéaċar Coḋ ar Iollan Óṗ-aṗmaċ aġur do ċíḋ ruċaḋ[5] na ṗeiṗġe ina ġnúiṗ aġur ina aġaiḋ, aġur ir eaḋ aḋuḃairt, "Tuiġim go nḋeaṗnair éaċt éiġin ó ṗoin." "Do ṗinnear[6] ċeana," ar Iollan. "Máiṗeaḋ[7] ir éaċt uaṗal," ar Coḋ. "Má'r éaċt uaṗal an Ríġ, do

<hr/>

[1] Thus H. A has "leigthear".   [2] H has "atá muich [this is a common pronunciation of amuigh in "Leath Chuin"] duine is fearr ina mé ar bheagán comhluadair agus ni shuidhfead-sa no go rachad go tti é ".
[3] A "ro nuaill". A 25, "ro néall". L "rothnuaill".
[4] H reads "aonach a bhfeóil chasgartha do bheith ag na sluagha ar na mhárach".
[5] H has "ruamna agus ruidheadh". L "ruamanna". A 25 "ruchadh ".

single. And he was admitted into the *cathair*, and he came into the midst of it, and a place to sit in was vacated for him, and the king asks him to seat himself in that place. Iollan said that he would not, for that there was outside someone([1]) greater than himself.

" Tell us the name of that man," said the King of Greece.

"It is Cod, son of the King of Norway, who is in it," said Iollan, " but the one pillar of the valour of life is his proper name."

" What brings you both to this city ? " said the King of Greece.

" For your daughter we have come," said Iollan; " and she must be given to us whether you like or dislike it."

" We would not dislike it," said the king, " if she herself had not a better man than he."

" Who is that ? " said Iollan.

" Buinnè Rough-strong, son of the King of Africa, is that man," said the king.

When Iollan heard that he became a purple *rothnuail*([2]) from sole to crown, and dealt a blow of the spear that he had in his hand on the broad breast and bosom of the king, so that he drove the length of a hero's hand of the hard, thick shaft of the javelin out through his back, and he launches himself to the door, unreddened by his own blood([3]). And, on that, heavy dispiritedness seized the people of the city ; but Buinnè Rough-strong spake to them and said that he would go to behead those men that were in the tent at once, if it were not that he proposed to behead them on the morrow in the presence of the Greeks rather than that night([4]).

As for Gold-armed Iollan he reached without any delay his own tent, and sat in his own place. Cod looks at him, and he sees the flush of anger in his countenance and visage ; and he said : "I understand that you have performed some feat since [you went out]." " Ay, did I," said Iollan. " Why, then, it was a noble feat," said Cod. " If [to slay] the king is a noble feat," said Iollan, " I slew

---

⁶ A adds " do bear an", which seems nonsense.   ⁷ L " adamair (?) is eacht", etc.

([1]) Literally " a story."   ([2]) See above, p. 87, note 4.   ([3]) Literally " without blooding, without reddening, being done on him."   ([4]) The Trinity College MS. reads, " preferred the hosts to have on the morrow the fair [assemblage] of their flesh-butchery."

ṁarḃar é," ar Iollan. "beir buaiḋ aġur beannaċt," ar Coḃ,
"ir óirḃearc an ċéaḋ ġníoṁ rin ḃo rinnir inr an ċaṫraiġ, aġur
ni ḃṗuil ḃ'á iṁṗníoṁ orrainn aċt naċ i ġceart-láṗ caċa na
nġṗéaġaċ ḃo marḃaḋ leat é—a lor caċa amárač."[1]

Ir annrin ḃ'éiriġ ḃrearal béilḋearġ mac Ríġ Ġréaġ aġur
ré céaḋ curaḋ caċ-ċalma ar an ḃraiċċe amaċ, ḃo ḃíoġailt
a aċar ar an muinntir ḃo ṁarḃ é. Aġur ḃo ċíḋ Coḃ iaḋ aġ
teaċt aġur ċáiniġ ḃeallraḋ ġléiġeal ḃ'éaḃaiġiḃ na ġcuraḋ
rin, aġur ḃearcar Coḃ ar an ḃraiċċe, amaċ ar an bprobal,
aġur ḃo ċíḋ an taiċnioṁ ionġantaċ ċáiniġ ḃ'éaḃaiġiḃ na
ġcuraḋ, aġur ċáiniġ i ḃtoraċ na ḃronġḃuiḋne rin, aġur ċuġ
aon tuarġain orra ġur ab lia a mairḃ 'ná a mbeó.[2] Aċt tá
ní ċeana, ní ḃeaċaiḋ fear innrin rġéal ar ḃioḃ aċt ḃrearal
béilḋearġ aṁáin, ḃo ċuaiḋ ġo ḃorar an ḃúna ḃe ċoraḋ reaċa.[3]

A haiċle na hoiḃre rin ċáiniġ Coḃ ḃ'á fobal, aġur ḃo fuiḋ ina
ionaḋ féin, aġur ḃo fiarraiḋ Iollan rġéala ḋé, aġur aḃuḃairc
Coḃ, "Ċárla ḃronġ éiġin ḃe na Ġréaġaċaiḃ ḃam, aġur táiḋ
'na ġcorar cró ar feaḋ na raiċċe, aġur ní eaḃar-ra an uairle
no an-uairle iaḃ." "Ir mairġ naċ ḃtuġair neaċ beó ḃioḃ
leat," ar Iollan. "Créaḋ é an t-áḃḃar ċuġ ort rin ḃo
ráḋ?" ar Coḃ. "Ríḃire óġ árraċtaċ ḃo ċonnarc," ar Iollan,
"aġur muna mbeaḋ luar[4] ḃo ṗáġḃar an ḃruiġean, ar nġoin
Ríġ Ġréaġ ḃam, ḃo íocfainn é uaiḋ[5] an ġníoṁ ḃo rinnear."

Ḋo ruġaḋar ar an oiḋċe rin ġur éiriġ an ġrian ġo n-a
lán-folar ar n-a ṁáraċ orra. Ir annrin ḃo ruġ Coḃ ar a
ḃeart caċa, aġur ċáiniġ amaċ ar an ḃraiċċe, aġur ḃo ḃuail
béim barċrainn ar a rġéiċ ġo lonn loirġneaċ, ionnur[6] naċ
raiḃ cloċ ná crann ḃe'n ċaṫraiġ naċ raiḃ ar aon ċriċ ó'n
torann-ċlear rin, aġur ḃo ċuaḃar mná aġur mionḃaoine na
caṫraċ i ḃtairiḃ aġur i ḃtáiṁ-néalaiḃ báir ó'n trom-torann
rin. Ir annrin aḃuḃairc buinne borḃ-ċréan mac Ríġ na
h-Arraice, "Níor ṗáġḃar," ar ré, "cúl no crfoċ, iaċ, innre, nó
oileán[7], ar muir no ar tír, fo ċri ṗoġal-rannaiḃ na cruinne,[8]

---

[1] The last twenty-one words are added from H.   [2] The last forty-eight
words are from L. A reads simply "tainig do druim airm agus eidigh". A 25 the
same.   [3] H has "do toradh a reath agus a roinn luais".   [4] L "a luaithe".
[5] L reads "d'iocfainn ris é". A 25 and the other omit. H omits all this
conversation.   [6] H reads "ionnus go ndeachadar almha agus innle cruith agus

him." "Take a victory and a blessing," said Cod, "that first deed that you have done in the city was an illustrious one, and the only thing we regret is that it was not in the midst of the Greeks' battle he was slain by you through fight to-morrow."

It was then uprose Breasal Redmouth, son of the King of Greece, and six hundred battle-valiant heroes on the lawn outside to avenge his father on the people who slew him. And Cod sees them approaching, and there came a bright gleam from the armour of those heroes; and Cod looks out on the lawn from his tent, and beholds the wondrous glistening that came from the heroes' armour, and he came to the front of that band and gave them one smashing so that their dead were more numerous than their living. Howsoever, not a man of them escaped to tell tidings, but Breasal Redmouth alone, who got to the door of the *dún* through the speed(¹) of his running.

After that work Cod came to his tent and sat in his own place; and Iollan asked tidings of him, and Cod said : " I met some band of the Greeks, and they are [left] a slaughtered heap through the lawn, and I know not whether they be noble or ignoble [those I slew]." "It was a pity that you did not bring one of them alive with you," said Iollan. "What reason makes you say that?" said Cod. "A young powerful knight I saw," said Iollan, "and were it not for the speed with which I left the palace after my stabbing the King of Greece, I should have paid at his hands for the deed I did."

They bore away that night until the sun shone upon them with its full light on the morrow. It was then Cod grasped his implements of battle, and came out upon the lawn, and smote a stroke of a handstick on his shield fiercely, furiously, so that there was neither a stone nor a tree of the city but was in one quivering from that noise-feat; and the women and minor people of the *cathair* went into weaknesses and trances of death from that great sound. It was then Buinnè Rough-strong, son of the King of Africa, said : "I never left," said he, "corner nor country, territory nor islet nor island, on sea or on land, in the three plunder-divisions of the world but I have visited,

ceathra an cheanntair asgéin agus asgaol fa dhiamruibh agus fa dhroibealaib na críche a cceadoir ris an bhfothram sin".   ⁷ Last four words from L. H has " cearn árd no árceann.   ⁸ Last eleven words are from H ".

(¹) Literally " fruit."

nár ċuartuiġċear, aġur ní ċualar ar muir ná ar tír baraṁail ḋo'n béim-rġéiċe rin, óir atá an ċaṫair uile ar aon-ċriṫ."

Ir annrin ḋo ċuir buinne ḃorb-ṫréan a carra caṫa uime aġur ṫáinig ḃrearal béilḋearġ aġur urṁór na nĠreaġa[ċ], aġur teaġlaċ na caṫraċ amaċ. Ir annrin ṫuġ Coḃ aġur buinne ḃorb-ṫréan a n-aiġṫe ṫar a ċéile. Ir annrin ṫánġaḃar na Ġréaġaiġ ar an ḃraitċe amaċ, aġur ir ḋó-ḟairneire an líon ṫánġaḃar ann, óir táiḃ reaċt ḋteaġlaiġ ḃéaġ ran nĠréiġ, aġur oċt ḋtuaṫa ḃéaġ in ġaċ teaġlaċ ḋíoḃ, aġur ní raiḃ rear ioṁċuir crainn ġaṫa aca naċ ḋtáinig ġo caṫair na h-Aiṫne[1] an lá rin ró táre an ríġ, ḋ'á ḋíoġailt ar an ḋruing ḋo ṁarḃ é. Mar ḋo ċonnairc Iollan bárr ḋaoine aġ breiṫ ar Coḃ, ṫáinig ré féin ro ṫoraċ na nĠréaġaċ, aġur ḋo riġne[2] buiḋne ḃrirte béal-rġaoilte ḋíoḃ, ó'n ġcaṫraiġ, aġur ní réiḃir fairnéir no innrin ar ṫuit le h-Iollan i n-alt na huaire rin ḋe fluaġ na nĠréaġaċ. Ir annrin ṫuġ Coḃ aġur buinne ḃorb-ṫréan a n-aiġṫe ar a ċéile[3]. ba ṁaiṫ an t-áḋḃar meirġe mílaoiċ[4] beiṫ aġ féaċain an ċóṁlainn rin, aġur ḋo ḃrireaḋar a[5] n-airm ar a ċéile, aġur níor fuiliġ ceaċtar ḋíoḃ ar a ċéile, re reaḃar na hiomḃeaġla ḋo ronrat, aġur ḋo ḃaḋar mar rin ġo ḋeireaḋ an ċaoṁ-laoi ġan earba meanm[n]a no aiġeanta ar ċeaċtar ḋíoḃ, aġur ḋo ronrat ċoṁforaḋ córṁraic re ċéile an oiḋċe rin.

Iar rin téiḋ Coḃ ḋ'á ḟobal féin, aġur ḋo ċuaiḋ buinne ḃorb-ṫréan ċum na caṫraċ, aġur maiṫe na nĠréaġaċ mar aon frir. Aġur ṫuġ Coḃ an trlat ṫuġ Ríġ Ḟoraoire na n-Ionġnaḋ ḋó, amaċ ar coiḃreaċ[6] a rġéiṫe, aġur ḋo ḃí ḋ'á rnoiḋe aiṫiġ, aġur ṫuġ ḋ'Iollan í, ġo nḋearna an ġcéaḃna ria,[7] aġur níor ċuir coġaḋ no cruaḋ-ċóṁlann ḋ'á ḃ'ruair riaḃ riaṁ orra a h-aiṫle na huaire rin. Ir annrin aḋuḃairt Coḃ, "Ḋo ċuaiḋ tura aréir ar cuairt ġo caṫair na h-Aiṫne, aġur raċaiḋ mire anoċt innti." Ḋo ċuir Coḃ a earra caṫa uime, aġur ḋo ċuaiḋ ġo ḋorar an ḋúna aġur ḃ'iarr a orġlaḋ. Aġur téiḋ an ḋoirreóir ḋo'n ḋún ḋ'á innrin ġo raiḃ Coḃ ran ḋorar, aġur ní ċualaiḋ muinntir an ḋúna no luċt na caṫraċ beaġán coṁuiġṫeaċ[8]

---

[1] This word is generally spelt "athaine" in A.

[2] H reads "agus imrios fhíoch agus fheargluinne forra".

[3] The last ten words are from H, but I read "ar a chéile" for the "for oile" of H, to make the language uniform.   [4] L reads "teannta deaghlaoch".

yet I never heard, on sea or on land, the like of that shield-blow, for the whole city is in one quivering."

It was then Buinnè Rough-strong put his battle armour on him, and Breasal Redmouth and a great number of the Greeks and the household of the *cathair* came out. It was then Cod and Buinnè Rough-strong faced one another. And then the Greeks came out upon the lawn, and it is untellable the number who came, for there are seventeen tribes([1]) in Greece, and eighteen sub-districts in each tribe of them, and there was not a man of them who bore spear-shaft but came to the city of Athens that day, at the news of the king [being slain] to avenge him on the people who slew him. When Iollan saw excess of numbers bearing down on Cod, he himself came to the forefront of the Greeks, and made broken scattered bands of them from the city; and it is impossible to tell or enumerate all that fell by Iollan of the host of the Greeks in the joint of that hour. It was then Cod and Buinnè Rough-strong faced one another, and it had been a good cause of intoxication to an unwarlike man to be observing that conflict; and they shattered their weapons on one another, and neither of them drew the other's blood, through the excellency of the defence they made, and they were thus till the end of the gentle day, without lack of valour or courage on either of them, and they made a truce from fighting with one another that night.

After that Cod goes to his own tent, and Buinnè Rough-strong returned to the city, and the nobles of the Greeks along with him. And Cod took out the rod that the King of the Forest of Wonders had given him from the hollow of his shield, and he was whittling it for a while, and he gave it to Iollan till he did the same with it, and no war nor hard-conflict of all they ever experienced, afflicted them after that hour. It was then Cod said: "You went to visit the city of Athens last night, and I shall go into it to-night." Cod put his battle armour round him, and he went to the door of the *dún* and demanded admission. And the porter goes to the *dún* to tell them that Cod was at the door; and the people of the *dún* and the men of the city had

---

[5] L reads "gó'r dhiubhraiceadar".   [6] H "a gcobhra*nn*".   A 25, "gcuibhribh".
[7] The last fifteen words are from H.   [8] L reads "beag choinmhe".

([1]) Literally "households". The ʒ is sometimes aspirated and sometimes not in the MSS.

ṁarḃ ba lúġa orra 'ná é', aġur ir í ḟreaġra ċuġaḋar air, náp ċóir cáċair na h-aiċne ḃ'ḟorġlaḋ ġo héirġe ġréine ar na ṁárac. Aġur mar ḋo ċualaiḋ Coḃ an ḟreaġraḋ rin, ċuġ ġuala ḟrir an ġcómlaḋ aġur ḋo rinne bloḋa beaġa buanréabċa ḋí, aġur ḟá ṁairġ ḋo'n ceaġlaċ cuma ċáiniġ Coḃ ḟá'n ḃḟeirġ rin, aġur ar nḋul arceaċ ḋó ċuġ aon cuarġain cóṁ-ċalma ar ċáċ ġo coicċeann. Ir aṁlaiḋ ḋo ḃí ḃuinne ḃorḃ-ċréan ḟá'n am rin ina ḟeompra coḋalca, aġur ċáiniġ ḟá'n copann-ċlear ḋóḃall-ṁór rin, aġur ċuġ ré ḟéin aġur Coḃ a n-aiġċe ar a ċéile, aġur ḋo ċuireaḋar an ċaċair ar aon ḃriċ. Ḟá'n am rin ḋo ċuala Iollan Óp-armaċ an mórċorann rin, aġur ċáiniġ ḋo'n ċaċraiġ i ġcéaḋóir. Iar na ḟaicrin ċuca ḋo ṁaiċiḃ an ceaġlaiġ ro ḃruiḋ riaḋ na ċoinne aġur 'na ċoṁaircuir aġur ro ġuiḋ riaḋ é um ceanracc éiġin ḋo ḋéanaṁ ar Coḃ, aġur ġo nḋéanraḋaoir ḟéin an ġcéaḋna ar ḃuinne ḃorḃ-ċréan, ḃ'ḟior an ḃḟuiġċiġ uaċa caraḋraḋ no compánċur ḋo ċeanġail re aroile. Ḋo níḋ aṁlaiḋ, aġur beiḟear Iollan ar Coḃ aġur beiḟear uairle aġur árḃ-ṁaiċe an ḋúna ar ḃuinne ḃorḃ-ċréan, ionnur ġur cuireaḋ ó ċéile iaḋ, aġur ġur ċuirnreac a ḃḟíoċ aġur a ḃḟearġ-luinne, i ġcéaḋóir, aġur ġur ġeallrac luċc na caċraċ ḟanaṁain ar ḃreiċ Iollain ḟéin, ġiḃé cúir uma raiḋ an laoċ-ṁíle Coḃ ḋóiḃ. Aoncuiġear ḃuinne ḃorḃ-ċréan aġur Coḃ um ḟuireaċ ar an ḃreiċeaṁnar rin, aġur ceanġalcar riċ aġur ríoċċáin eacorpa ar ġaċ caoḃ ar an ġcoinġioll ċéaḋna.²

Iomċura an ceaġlaiġ, ḋo ċóġaḋar ḃuirḋ aġur beinnriḋe an ciġe, aġur ḋo ḟuiḋ Coḃ aġur Iollan Óp-armaċ ar ġualainn a ċéile, aġur ḋo ḟuiḋ ḃuinne ḃorḃ-ċréan ar an nġualainn eile ḋe Coḃ, aġur ḋo ḟuiḋ Ḋanuice inġean Ríġ Ġréaġ ar an caoḃ eile ḋe ḃuinne ḃorḃ-ċréan, aġur ḋo ġaḃaḋar aġ ól 'r aġ aoiḃnear.

Ir annrin ḋo ċuaiḋ Iollan Óp-armaċ i ġceann rġéal ḃ'innrin, aġur ḋo innir a ċoirġ ó ċúr ġo ḃeireaḋ .i. ġur ḋo léiġear Ċiaḃáin Ġlún-ġeal mic Ríġ na h-Éanlaice ḋo ċánġaḋar, aġur

---

never heard of a handful of strangers that was more unpleasant to them than he([1]). And the answer they gave was, that it was not law to open the city of Athens until the rising of the sun on the morrow. And when Cod heard that answer, he placed his shoulder to the side of the gate and made small shattered pieces of it; and it was woe to the household the guise in which Cod came in that anger: and on his entering in he gave one valorous overthrow([2]) to every one in common. And this is how Buinnè Rough-strong was at that time, namely, in his sleeping-couch, but he came at that terrific-great noise-feat, and he and Cod faced one another, and they set the city in one quivering. At that time Gold-armed Iollan heard that great noise, and came at once to the city. And when the chiefs of the household saw him coming, they approached and accosted him, and they prayed him to quiet Cod in some sort, and that they would do the same by Buinnè Rough-strong, to try could they make them join [in] friendship and amity with one another. They do this; and Iollan takes hold of Cod, and the nobles and high chiefs of the *dún* take hold of Buinnè Rough-strong, so that they were separated from one another, so that their anger and furious rage abated thereupon, in such wise that the people of the city promised to abide by the judgment of Iollan himself, [in settlement] of whatever cause [for wrath] the battle-hero Cod had against them([3]). Buinnè Rough-strong and Cod consented to abide by that judgment; and peace and quiet are brought about([4]) between them on each side, on those same conditions.

As for the household, they raised the tables and the benches of the house; and Cod and Gold-armed Iollan sat, one beside the other, and Buinnè Rough-strong sat at the other side([5]) of Cod, and Danuitè, daughter of the king of Greece, at the other side of Buinnè Rough-strong, and they commenced to drink and be merry.

It was then Gold-armed Iollan proceeded to tell [their] tidings, and told their errand from first to last, how it was to heal Ciabhán White-knee, son of the King of Éanlaithe, they were come, and to

---

([1]) Literally " who was less on them than he." I have heard this idiom used, even at the present day, in the county Galway. ([2]) Literally " smashing," " pounding." ([3]) A curious idiom. I think the above is the correct translation of it. ([4]) Literally " joined." ([5]) Literally " shoulder."

oo bpeiċ Danuite, inġean Ríġ Ġréaġ, leó, óip ip f oo ċuip na ġeapa pin paip, poiṁe pin. Do ġab lollan páða éapġa[1] aġup ġpéine oppa pá paniṁuin map aoéapaò pé péin, aġup ċuġaoappan pin oó ġo neaiṁ-pallpa. Aġup ip f bpeiċ[2] oo ċuġ lollan: "Inġean Ríġ Ġréaġ aġup buinne bopb-ċpéan oul pe Coò ġo Loċ na n-lonġnaò aġup buinne bopb-ċpéan ueiċ 'na óġlaċ aġ Coò ó pin puap, aġup iaò oo òul i n-éinpeaċc ġo Popaoip na h-lonġnaò i bpoptuaċaiò lppinn, oo leiġeap Ċiaoáin Ġlúinġil," aġup aouoaipc cáċ ġo coicċeann ġup cóip an cpiall pin oo òéanaiṁ, aġup ġup ṁaiċ an bpeiċ oo ċuġ lollan.

Aġup ap n-a ṁápaċ oo ġoipeaò Ríġ Ġréaġ oo buinne bopb-ċpéan[3], aġup oo ġab pe Coò map ċiġeapna. Ip annpin oo pġapaoap o'a n-ól[4], aġup oo ċuaoap o'a n-iomòaiòiò. Aġup po éipġeaoap ap na ṁápaċ, aġup oo ċpiallaoap na maċa pin, .i. Coò, lollan Óp-apmaċ, buinne bopb-ċpéan, aġup Danuite inġean Ríġ Ġréaġ, aġup ní h-aiċpipceap pġéalaiòeaċc oppa no ġo pánġaoap Loċ na n-lonġnaò, aġup oo ċuaiò Ríġ Popaoipe na n-lonġnaò leó an oiòċe pin, aġup ċuġ Ġpian Ġnúip-polaip pleaò uapal onópaċ òóiò, aġup cuipeaò Ciaoán Ġlúinġeal 'na pioċc péin ap na ṁápaċ, aġup oo ġab pé pe Coò map ċiġeapna.

Sġapaiò pe ċéile annpin aġup pillear buinne bopb-ċpéan aġup Danuite oo'n Ġréiġ. Iap ġceileaòpaò òóiò-pean céiò Ciaoán aġup Ġpian Ġnúip-polaip o'á n-acapòa péin.

Ioméupa Cuiò, ġluaipear poiṁe ġo[5] h-uaiṁ na n-lonġnaò, aġup níop ċian oó an can oo ċualaiò ġpeapaċc na mbolġ o'á luaiċ-péioeaò, aġup puaim na n-ópo o'a luaċ-bualaò, aġup oo ċuaiò Coò ċum na ceapòċan ġan puipeaċ, aġup oo ċuaiò apceaċ innci, aġup ċápla oá péap òéaġ òó innci, oe ġaiòniò cpoicneach[a][5] ciapòuba, aġup o'ſeapaoap páilce ſpia Coò ġo ſpíoċnaṁaċ 'na ainm aġup 'na ſloinneaò, aġup o'ſiappaiò Coò pġéala òíoò. Do labaip ſeap aca, "A ṁic Ríġ na h-lopuaiòe, i bpoptuaċaiò lppinn acá cu anoip, aġup Suapṁaol ip ainm oo'n ġaòa òáp ceapòċa í peó. Aġup an ċéaò uaip ċáiniġ cupa annpo oo ċionnpġain ſé an cloiòeaṁ

---

[1] A reads "éisge". [2] A reads "breath". [3] H says that Breasal Béildearg was made king. [4] Thus I edit "dá ndul" of A; the others omit.

bring Danuitè, daughter of the king of Greece, with them, for it was she who had imposed those *geasa* upon Ciabhán before that. Then Iollan made them swear by moon and sun, to abide by what he should say, and they gave him that promise promptly. And the award Iollan gave was, "that the daughter of the King of Greece and Buinnè Rough-strong should go with Cod to the Lake of Wonders, and that Buinnè Rough-strong should be Cod's man from that out, and that they should go together to the Forest of Wonders in the Outskirts of Hell, to heal Ciabhán White-knee," and all in general said that it were right to make that journey, and that good was the award that Iollan had given.

And on the morrow Buinnè Rough-strong was appointed([1]) King of Greece, and he accepted Cod as over-lord. It was then they ceased drinking, and went to their couches. And those chiefs arose in the morning and departed, namely, Cod, Gold-armed Iollan, Buinnè Rough-strong, and Danuitè, daughter of the King of Greece, and no tidings are told of them until they reached the Lake of Wonders; and the King of the Forest of Wonders went with them that night, and Bright-faced Sun gave them a noble, honourable banquet, and Ciabhán White-knee was restored to his own shape on the morrow, and accepted Cod as over-lord. They part from one another then, and Buinnè Rough-strong and Danuitè return to Greece. After bidding them farewell, Ciabhán and Bright-faced Sun depart to their own patrimony.

As for Cod, he proceeds to the Cave of Wonders; and it was not long until he heard the puffing[?] of the bellows quick-blowing, and the noise of the sledge-hammers quick-striking, and Cod went to the forge without delay, and entered into it; and twelve men, skinny, dark-black smiths, met him, and bade Cod welcome heartily in his name and surname. And Cod asked tidings of them; and a man of them spake, "Son of the King of Norway, in the Outskirts of Hell you are now, and Suasmhaol is the name of the smith whose forge this is. And the first time you came here he began to make this

---

[5] The last twenty-eight words are from H. [6] Thus I edit the " croichneach " of A. L has " criochnacha ". A 25 " ciorclacha ". H omits.

([1]) Literally "called." According to H, Breasal Red-mouth was made king.

ḃo ḃċanaṁ ḃuic, aᵹur cá ré ullaṁ anoir." Ir annrin ċuᵹ Suaiṁaol an cloiḃcaṁ i láṁ Cuiḃ, aᵹur aḃuḃairc naċ uḃcárnaḃ ioip orḃ aᵹur inncóin a coṁ-maiċ rin ḃo cloiḃcaṁ piaṁ poiṁe rin; aᵹur ḃuḃraḃai ᵹo ḃfuaraḃai mórán ḃ'á rᵹċalaiḃ poiṁe rin, "aᵹur ir uiṁe rin ḃo rinncamai an cloiḃcaṁ rin ḃuic, aᵹur ċuᵹamai aċairaċ anma orc .i. Ᵹiuaᵹaċ na Ciorᵹala¹." Aᵹur ḃo lean an poraiṁ rin ḃo Coḃ ó ṁin ruar.

Ᵹluaireai Coḃ leir, ar a h-aiċle, aᵹur ní ḃċarnaiḃ cóṁnaiḃe ᵹo ráinᵹ ᵹo Cáċair na beċuine i ᵹcrioċaiḃ na Sopċa an oiḃċe rin, aᵹur roillriᵹear ḃí mar ḃ'éiriᵹ ḃó, aᵹur ḃo ḃí cáċ aᵹ innrin rᵹéala a n-eaċcra aᵹur a n-imċeaċca féin ḃ'á ċéile.

Níor ċian ḃóiḃ mar rin, an can ḃo ċualaḃar óᵹlaċ [aᵹ] ḃorar an ḃúna, aᵹur ir é óᵹlaċ ḃo ḃí ann .i. an Cupaire Caṁċoraċ, aᵹur ḃo leiᵹeaḃ arceaċ é, aᵹur ba ṁór-lúċᵹáireaċ iaḃ roiṁe, aᵹur ḃo fearcalaḃ aᵹur ḃo frioċólaḃ ᵹo huaral onóraċ é. Aᵹur a h-aiċle rin ḃ'ṁiarruiᵹ Coḃ rᵹéala ḃé: "Cá rᵹéala maiċe aᵹam pe n-innrin ḃuic," ar an Cupaire Caṁċoraċ; " ḃo ᵹaḃaḃar ḃo ḃráiċre an crear rann ḃe'n ḃoṁan .i. rann na hAria Móire ᵹo Caċair an cSroċa Ḃeirᵹ. Aᵹur ir aṁlaiḃ cá an ċaċair rin, cá crí prioṁ-froċa na cimċeall, aᵹur cáiḃ cre ḃoiᵹir ḃonn-ruaiḃ ḃearᵹ-larraiᵹ, aᵹur ní láṁċai a caoḃaḃ² pe ró-ṁéaḃ a ḃceara aᵹur a ḃceanḃála, aᵹur ᵹiḃbé ċeaᵹḃai inncí aon oiḃċè aṁáin, ní ḃiaiḃ 'na fláince ó rin amaċ, ó ṁéaḃ an ḃeallruiᵹċe aᵹur an ceara³. Aᵹur ní'l ḃ'fearaiḃ inncí aċc aon ċéaḃ aṁáin⁴, aᵹur cá crí ṁíle ḃe ṁnáiḃ⁵ inncí, aᵹur ir bean ir bainríoᵹan orra .i. Eiceall inᵹean Ríᵹ na h-Aria Móire, aᵹur ir aca ṁeaḃruiᵹċear por-ṁór ᵹairᵹe an ḃeaċa. Aᵹur níor ṁaiċ pe ḃo ḃráiċriḃ-re pilleaḃ ó'n ᵹcaċraiᵹ rin ᵹan úṁluᵹaḃ ḃo bainc ḃí, aᵹur ir aṁlaiḃ ḃo ċuaiḃ rin ḃíoḃ,⁶ aᵹur cáiḃ ceanᵹailce cruaḃ-ċuiḃriᵹċe inncí, aᵹur ba ṁaiċ ᵹaċ olc ḃ'á ḃfuaraḃar piaṁ aᵹ féaċain uilc na caċraċ rin⁷. Aᵹur ċánᵹar-ra ar an eaċcra rin ar peaḃ na beaċa ḃo ḃur n-iarraiḃ-re, ḃ'á innrin

---

¹ H "ha hiorguile". A 25 "na Ciorgaile". L "na Ciorainne". ² H reads "a taghall". ³ L adds " do bheidhdís a-nairm ina ndoirnib mion brúighte,

sword for you, and it is ready now." Then Suasmhaol gave the
sword into Cod's hand, and said that there was never made between
hammer and anvil so good a sword before. And they said that they
had heard many stories about him before that, "and that was why
we made you this sword, and we have given you another name, the
Wizard of the Battle-feats"; and that nickname remained with Cod
ever after.

Thereafter, Cod goes on his way, and he made no stop until he
reached the *cathair* of Bethuinè, in the lands of Sorcha, that night,
and he makes known to her how he had succeeded, and each was
telling the other the tales of their adventures and of their
wanderings.

They were not long in this manner, until they heard a youth at
the door of the *dún*, and the youth that was there was the Curairè
Crookfoot, and he was let in, and very-joyous were they at his
coming, and he was entertained and attended-to, nobly and
honourably. And after that Cod asked him for news. "I have good
news to tell you," said the Curairè Crookfoot; "your brethren have
taken the third division of the world, namely, the division of Greater
Asia, up to the City of the Red Stream. And this is how that city is:
there are three chief streams round about it, and they are in a brown-
red, crimson-lit flame, and for the excess of their heat and fires, none
venture to approach them, for whoever chances on them, for only a
single night, will never have his health from that out, from all the
flaming and the heat. And there are no men in it, except a hundred
only, but there are three thousand women in it, and a woman is
queen over them, namely, Eiteall [Ett-yǎl], daughter of the King of
Greater Asia, and it is by them that a great portion of the valour of
life is remembered. And your brothers did not like to return from
that city without reducing it to subjection; howsoever, that failed
them, and they are bound and tightly fettered in it, and every evil
they ever met was good in comparison with the ills of that city.
And I came through the world on these adventures to seek for you

---

agus a n-earradh agus a n-eadach na smól agus na luaith ".   ⁴ Thus H and
L, but A has "aon laoch mháin ".   ⁵ Thus H. A and L read " bean ".
⁶ H has "is am. do ch. sin dóibh, go bhfuil", etc.   ⁷ A 25 has "ag féachain
mar atáid anois".

rin ḋuit-re, aġur ir mór eaġla ḋuit féin rómpa rúḋ," ar an Curaire Camċoraċ.

Aċt tá ní ċeana, ċuġaḋar ar an oiḋċe rin ġo maiḋin ar na máraċ, ġur foillriġ lá ġo n-a lán-foillre. Éirġear Coḋ annrin, aġur cuirear an file ar ċeann ḃuinne ḃorḃ-ċréan ḋo'n ġréiġ, aġur ḋo ċuġ an Curaire Camċoraċ rġéala ḋó, aġur táiniġ ar rin ḃ'Almáin, aġur ċuġ Iollan Ór-armaċ leir, aġur táiniġ ar rin ġo Ciaḃán Ġlúinġeal mac Ríġ ar h-Éanlaiċe aġur ċuġ leir é, aġur ní h-aiċririrtear rġéalaiḋeaċt orra no ġo ránġaḋar Caċair na ḃeċuine i ġcríoċaiḃ na Sorċa i n-éinfeaċt. Ċoirḃreaḋar teóra póġ ḃ'á ċéile annrin, ionnur ġo mba[1] fuḃaċ ró-ṁeanmnaċ iaḋ, aġur ḋo ḃaḋar ann rin an oiḋċe rin.

[imċeaċt ċuiḋ ġo caṫair an tsroṫa ḋeirġ.]

Aġur lá ar na máraċ ċuġaḋar láṁ ar imċeaċt, aġur ir í long ruġaḋar leó .i. long ḃuinne ḃorḃ-ċréan, aġur ḃ'fuiġill na hairce féin í, aġur ir inr an Airc ḋo ḃí Naoi feaḋ ḃí an ḋíle ḃ'á cur, aġur tar éir na ḋíleann ḋo fáġaḋ 'ran Airric 'na cranngaill[2] í, aġur táiniġ rí i n-oiġreaċt a fean aġur a finnrear ċum ḃuinne ḃorḃ-ċréan, aġur ḋo rinne Ríġ na h-Affraice long luċtṁar lán-aiḋḃreaċ ḋe'n ċranngaill rin, aġur atá teóra buaḋ aice .i. buaiḋ ġaoiċe, buaiḋ eólair, aġur buaiḋ airḋir[4], aġur ḋo ċuaḋar an ḃuiḋean curaḋ rin innti .i. Coḋ mac Ríġ na h-Ioruaiḋe, ḃuinne ḃorḃ-ċréan mac Ríġ na hAffraice, Iollan Ór-armaċ mac Ríġ na hAlmáinne, aġur Ciaḃán Ġlúinġeal mac Ríġ na h-Éanlaiċe, aġur an Curaire Camċoraċ. [ir ann] rin ċuġaḋar toraċ ḋo ṁuir aġur ḋeireaḋ ḋo ċír, aġur ḋo ḃaḋar aġ tairḃeal na ḋtonn ḋtiuġ-ruaḋ [rin] na fairrġe fíor-ḋoiṁne cúḃar-ḃáine, aġur real eile aġ ḋéanaṁ fíor-eólair na fairrġe, aġur real eile aġ ceanġal a ġcáirḃear re ċéile[3], ġo ránġaḋar Críoċa na h-Iopuaiḋe; aġur ḋo ċuaḋar ġo Cáċair na ġCeann .i. dún Ríġ na h-Iopuaiḋe, aġur ḃ'éirġeaḋar luċt na caṫraċ rin 'na

---

[1] A often reads "gur ba" for "go mba" as here.
[2] A reads "crannghill" and "crannait".

and tell you; and great is the fear, even for you yourself, from them," said the Curairè Crookfoot.

Howsoever, they bore away that night until the morning of the morrow—until the day shone with its full light. Cod rises then, and he despatches the poet [the Curairè] to Greece for Buinnè Rough-strong, and the Curairè Crookfoot gave him tidings [of Cod's brothers], and out of that he passed into Almain, and brought Gold-armed Iollan with him, and he came from thence to Ciabhán White-knee, son of the King of Éanlaithe, and took him with him; and no tidings are told of them until they reached the *cathair* of Bethuinè, in the lands of Sorcha, all together. There they bestowed three kisses on each other, so that they were merry and hearty, and they passed the night there.

[COD GOES TO THE CITY OF THE RED STREAM.]

And, on the morrow, they took in hand their departure, and the ship which they took with them was the ship of Buinnè Rough-strong, and it is of the remnant of the ark itself; and it was in the ark that Noah was, whilst the flood was in progress, and after the flood it was left in Africa a heap-of-wood [?], and it passed in the inheritance of his elders and ancestors to Buinnè Rough-strong: and the King of Africa made a laden full-fair bark of that wood-heap, and it has three virtues, virtue of wind, virtue of knowledge, and virtue of journey; and that band of heroes entered it, namely, Cod, son of the King of Norway, Buinnè Rough-strong, son of the King of Africa, Gold-armed Iollan, son of the King of Almain, and Ciabhán White-knee, son of the King of Éanlaithe, and the Curairè Crookfoot. It was then they gave its prow to sea and its stern to shore, and they were voyaging those thick-red waves of the very-deep, white-foamed sea, and at another time taking the accurate bearings of the sea, and at another time cementing their friendships with one another, until they reached the lands of Norway. And they went to the City of the Heads, the *dún* of the King of Norway, and the people of that city rose up before them, and the

---

³ A 25 adds "agus buadh nach bhféadann muir a bathadh no re gaoith a hingreim".   ⁴ The last nine words are from L.

ȝcoιnne, aȝυρ an Ríȝ ρéιn, aȝυρ ðo ȝαbαðαρ ð'α bρóȝαð ȝο ðíl aȝυρ ȝο ðιαcραċ, aȝυρ ċuȝαðαρ a n-αιmρıρ ı ðτíρ ı bρoċαıρ an Ríȝ aȝ mυıρn aȝυρ aȝ mαcnαρ, aȝ ól aȝυρ aȝ aoıbnεαρ. Aȝυρ aρ ȝcαıċcαın na h-αιmρıρε ρın ðóıb ðo ȝαbαðαρ láṁ aρ¹ ımċεαċτ, aȝυρ níoρ lεıȝcεαðαρ ðe ρlóıȝcıb no ðe ρocαıðıb lεó aċτ ıαð ρéın αṁáın .ı. an cεαċραρ αðυbραmαρ, aȝυρ an Cuραıρε Camċοραċ, aȝυρ ðo ċuαðαρ ð'á luınȝ, aȝυρ ba bρónαċ ðραoıċε aȝυρ ðεαȝ-ðαoıne εαlαðnα aȝυρ mıon-ðαoıne na cρíċε ı nðıαıð na ȝcuραð ρın, aȝυρ ðo ρáıð an Cuραıρε Camċοραċ an lαoıð :—

"Cεαċραρ ċánȝαðαρ a n-oıρ
O ınnρıb ıαρċαıρ² an ðoṁαın
Níoρ ċαıρðεαl cαlaṁ no cοnn
Cεαċραρ ba ċρóðα ı ȝcómlαnn.

"Cá aρ cúρ an cεαċραρ cαoıṁ
Ȝıolla óȝ ı n-εαραıðh ρınn-ȝıll,
Coð mαc Ιορυαıð na n-αρm ρεαn,
Áððαρ áıρðρıȝ an ðoṁαın.

"buınne ðoρb-ċρéαn mαıρȝ ρá mbεαnραð³
An ðαρα ρεαρ ðe'n ċεαċραρ
Sȝıαċ ȝο nðoıρρıb óıρ na h-αıce⁴
Ðεαȝ-ṁαc Ríȝ na hAρραıce.

"Ιollαn Óρ-αρmαċ na ðcρεαρ⁵
An cρεαρ cuραð ρá ċoıṁðεαρ;
ρεαρ bεıρċε⁶ buαıð' ȝαċα báıρε
Oıȝρε Ríȝ na hAlmáınne.

"ρεαρ ρollṁuıȝċε⁷ ȝαċ ραıċċε
Ðεαȝ-ṁαc Ríȝ na hἐαnlαıċε,
Ðαρ ba hαınm Cıαðán Ȝlúṁȝεαl
An cεαċραṁαð⁸ ρεαρ ðe'n ċεαċραρ."

A hαıċle na lαoıðe ρın ðo ċonncαðαρ cáċαıρ ċεαnn-áρð ıορċαṁαıl εοċαıρ-bláıċ ıοnȝαncαċ, aȝυρ ðúnca ðεαȝ-ȝεαlα uαċα, aȝυρ ð'ρıαρραıȝ Coð ðe'n Cuραıρε Camċοραċ aρ⁹

---

¹ A reads "tar imtheacht". ² H omits this lay. L and A 25 read "dion iarthair". There is a syllable too much in this line, the *an* before *domhain* is probably a late accretion. ³ L reads "mar so" (or "fo") a *mbeanann* ". L 27 "mairg fo a mbean ". The line is utterly corrupt. ⁴ Thus A 25. A reads "Sgiath go hiorsaibh ". L " Sgaith irse óir na hairce ". L 27 " Sgiath irse óir na haice". ⁵ L "na geleas ". ⁶ L " bearrtha": the word spoils the scansion; the line may have been originally "fear buaidhe gacha báire". ⁷ L "le bhfollamuigthear gach baire ".

King himself, and they fell to kissing them lovingly and fondly. And they passed their time on land with the King in cheerfulness and sport, drinking and making merry. And after spending that time, they took in hand their departure, and they allowed no hosts nor bands with them but themselves alone, the four whom we have named, and the Curairè Crookfoot, and they proceeded to their ship: and sorrowful were druids, and good men of science, and the minor people of the land, after those heroes; and the Curairè Crookfoot spake the lay:—

> "Four men sailing, from the West,
> From the sea-isles the furthest.
> Ne'er were seen on land or sea
> Four other men so mighty.(¹)

> "There are first the gentle four,
> The young lad in white-bright armour,
> Cod, son of Ioruaidh, of the tried(²) weapons,
> The makings of a High-king of the World.

> "Buinnè Rough-strong, alas for whom he touches!
> The second man of the four.
> A shield with golden doors(³) beside him,
> The good son of the King of Africa.

> "Gold-armed Iollan of the conflicts,
> Is the third hero, who was equally-fine,
> A man who carries off the victory of every goal,
> The heir of the King of Almain.

> "A man who empties every lawn,
> The good son of the King of Éanlaithe,
> Whose name is Ciabhán White-knee,
> The fourth man of the four."

After that lay, they beheld a high-headed, inhabited [?], flower-bordered, wondrous city, and fine white mansions at a distance from them. And Cod asked the Curairè Crookfoot did he know that fair-

---

⁸ A reads "ceathradh", which makes the line scan. It was originally written, I think, without the *an* before it.   ⁹ Thus H. A has "nar".

(¹) Literally: "Four have come East from the isles of the West of the world. There never voyaged land or wave, a four who were more valiant in combat." "Anoir" literally means "from the east", but this appears to make nonsense.— Metre, *Deibhidh*.   (²) Literally "old".   (³) There is, evidently, some corruption here.

b'aitne ḋó an ċríoċ ċaoiṁ-áluinn rin. "Atá aitne aġam uirri," ar an Curaire Camċoraċ: "Tír na bFear bFionn an tír úo, aġur Cátair na ḋTri ġCeann[1] ainm na caṫraċ úo," ar ré, "aġur ir innti atá ḋo ċliaḃain-re .i. Ríġ na bFear bFionn, aġur, ó tárla ḋúinn iaḋ, ir cóir cuairt aġur céiliḋe ḋéanaṁ aiġe." Aġur ḋo ċuireaḋar a lonġ i ḋtír, i ġcuan na caṫraċ, aġur ḋo ċuaḋar ar an ḃraitċe i ġcéaḋóir, aġur ċuġaḋar cách ḋo[2] ḃaraṁail ġur b' iaḋ féin ḋo ḃí ann, óir ní raiḃ beaġán buiḋne irin ḋoṁan ba óirḋeirce no iaḋ, aġur ḋo ḟáiltiġ Ríġ na bFear bFionn rompa, aġur ḋo ḟanaḋar trí lá aġur teóra oiḋċe i ḃfoċair an Ríġ, aġur ba ċonailḃeaċ[3] cáirḋeaṁail cóṁairle an Ríġ ḋóiḃ, aġur ḋo innir an Curaire Camċoraċ ḋo Ríġ na bFear bFionn mar ḋo ḃí Clann Ríġ na h-Ioruaiḋe i ġcaṫraiġ an tSroṫa Ḋeirġ i láiṁ, ceanġailte cruaḋ-ċuiḃriġċe, aġur ḋo innir ḋó ḋiaḃlaiġeaċt aġur ḋraoiḋeaċt na caṫraċ rin, aġur a raiḃ ḋe ḋeacraiġeaċt innti, aġur ġurab ḋ'ḟior an ḃféaḋraḋ na curaiḋ calma céaḋra[ḋa]ċa rin ḟurtaċt no ḟóiriġin ḋo ċaḃairt ḋóiḃ, ċánġaḋar ḋe'n toirġ rin ar an Ioruaiḋ aġur ar na h-áiteacaiḃ imċiana a raḃaḋar.[4]

Aḋuḃairt Ríġ na bFear bFionn: "Ḋo ḃéarfaḋ-ra conġnaṁ ḋaoiḃ ḋo ġaḃáil na caṫraċ rin," ar ré, ".i. brat ionġantaċ iol-ḃuaiḋeaċ atá aġam-ra," ar ré, "aġur ir cuiḋ ḋ'á ḃuaiḋiḃ naċ féiḋir ḋraoiḋeaċt na ḋiaḃlaiġeaċt ḋ'imirt, ar an té fá 'mbiaiḋ. Tá iolraḋ ġaċa ḋaṫa ann, aġur atá buaiḋ ar leiṫ ar ġaċ ḋaṫ ḋíoḃ aġur beiriḋ ré neaċ leir le toil a ṁeanma aġur a aiġeanta féin,[5] in ġaċ ionaḋ i n-ar mian leir féin," aġur ċuġ an Ríġ an brat rin ḋo Ḃuinne Ḋorb-ċréan. "Ní ḋaṁ-ra ir cóir an brat," ar Buinne Ḋorb-ċréan, "aċt ḋo'n Ċuraire Camċoraċ." Ḋo ċuir an Curaire Camċoraċ an brat uime. Ir annrin ḋ'ḟiarruiġ an Curaire Camċoraċ ḋe'n Ríġ cionnur fuair ré an brat.

"Inneóraḋ rin ḋuit," ar an Ríġ. "Lá éiġin ḋ'á raiḃ mire ar faitċe na caṫraċ ro aġur ċuġar rúil 'mo ċimċeall ar na ceitre h-árḋaiḃ, aġur ir eaḋ ḋo ċonnarcar lonġ luċtṁar

---

[1] Thus H. A has "na diorchonn". A 25 has "C. an droighin". L omits.
[2] L omits "do".   [3] L has "ba chonnill". A 25 "coinghioltach".

fine land. "I know it," said the Curairè Crookfoot, "that land is the Land of the White Men, and the City of the Three Heads is the name of that city," said he; "and it is in it your cousin is, the King of the White Men; and since we have chanced upon them it were well to pay them a visit and a call." And they thrust their ship in to land, into the harbour of the city, and went up at once upon the lawn [of the palace]; and everyone surmised that it was they who were in it, for there was no small band of men in the world more illustrious than they. And the King of the White Men bade them welcome, and they remained three days and three nights along with the King; and loving and friendly was the King's advice, to them. And the Curairè Crookfoot told the King of the White Men, how the sons of the king of Norway were in this city of the Red Stream, prisoners, bound, and tightly manacled; and he told him of the devilishness and enchantment of that city, and all the difficulty of it; and how it was to try if those valiant accomplished champions could bring them help or succour, they had come on that occasion out of Norway and the [other] far-away places in which they were.

The King of the White Men said, "I shall give you help to take that city," said he, "namely, a wondrous many-virtued mantle that I have," said he, "and part of its virtue is, that it is impossible to work enchantment or demonry against him who shall have it on him. There is in it a variety of every colour, and there is a particular virtue in each colour of them, and it brings a person with it, according to the will of his own mind and inclination, to whatsoever place he himself desires," and the King gave that mantle to Buinnè Rough-strong. "It is not to me it is right [to give] the mantle," said Buinnè Rough-strong, "but to the Curairè Crookfoot." Then the Curairè Crookfoot put the mantle around him, and he asked the King how did he come by the mantle.

"I shall tell you that," said the King: "Of a certain day that I was on the lawn of the city, and cast an eye round me to the four

---

4 The last thirty words are from H, only I have edited "curaidh" for "cuiridhe" and "de'n" for "don".

5 L adds "abhrithibh na bhfirmameint agus aneithibh na gaoithe".

lán-aiḃḃreaċ aġ leaġaḋ a reól ríor mar ċoṁarṫa rioċċána, aġur ċáiniġ rí i ġcuan na caṫraċ ro, aġur ḋo ċuaiḋ mire ḋ'á lionnraiḋe aṁail mar ba ġnáṫ liom ḋe ġréar, ġo nḋeaċar arcċaċ innci ġan ḟuireaċ, aġur ní ḃruairear neaċ beó no marḃ innci aċt aṁáin ġo ḃruairear criuċ ċeóil-ḃinn ċaoinċéaḋaċ aġ reinm uaite ḟéin, aġur eóin áilne ḋ'éin-ċineál aġ cóiṁ-linġe ciúil¹ na huaral-ċruice rin. Aġur ḋo ċuarcuiġear an lonġ ġo ḋcárla orm iomḋaiġ ar n-a rolaċ ḋe ḟról lán-ṁaireaċ, aġur ċáiniġ ró-ṁian ruain aġur ríor-ċoḋalta orm an can rin, aġur cuicim 'mo ċoirċim ruain aġur ríor-ċoḋalta, aġur iar múrġlaḋ ḋam, ir aṁlaiḋ ḟuairear an lonġ, ceanġailte ḋo ċor coṁ-reaṁar cairleáin, ar lár na ḟairrġe ríor-ḃoiṁne, ġan innir ġan ḟáċ ġan oileán i ġcoṁḟoġar ḋam. Éiriġim mo ḟearaṁ annrin. Aġur ḋo ċonncar ḋorar an cuir ar m' aġaiḋ ḟorġailte, aġur ḋo ċuaḋar arceaċ i ġcéaḋóir, aġur ránġar bárr an cuir, aġur ċárla orm annrin inġean ċroċaċ iol-ḃuaiḋeaċ ċaoṁ-áluinn, aġur calla ḋ'ór áluinn ró cloċaiḃ iol-ḃuaiḋeaċa ro n-a ceann, aġur na buaḋ-ċloċa rin ar na ġceanġal ḋ'or-narġ ríor-áluinn aġur ḃrat ḋe'n crról roine-aṁail uimpi. Aġur an can ḋo ċonnairc an inġean rin mire ḋo éiriġ 'na colaṁain coṁ-ḋíreaċ ina cearc-ḟearaṁ, aġur aġ éirġe ḋi ḋo ruġ mire ar an mḃrac ḋ'á ḟarḃoġ. Ḟáġḃar an ḃrat aġam-ra aġur imċiġear ḟéin uaim.² Ḋo ċuiġear annrin ġo raiḃ buaḋa iomḋa aiġe, aġur ḋo iarrar air mo ḃreiċ ḋom' ċaṫraiġ,³ aġur ḋo ṫóġ⁴ an ḃrat ionġantaċ iol-ḃuaiḋeaċ rin mire leir i ḃṟriċiḃ na ṟirmaminte, no ġo ránġar an ċaṫair reo; aġur ḋá ḋceaġṁóċaḋ beiṫiḋiġ éiġcéilliḋe an ḋoṁain ḋam, aġur an ḃrat rin umam, ní ḋéanṟaḋaoir olc no urċóiḋ ḋam, aġur ní loirġeann ceine aġur ní ḃáċann uirġe aġur ní ċoirmirġ[eann] arm an cí ṟa mḃiaiḋ an ḃrat rin uime ḋe ġréar, aġur aġ rin aġac imċeaċta an ḃraic iol-ḃuaiḋiġ rin." Aċt ċeana ṟá buiḋeaċ Coḃ ḋe'n caḃarcar⁵.

Ar n-a ṁáraċ ḋo ġluaireaḋar [aġ] imċeaċt, aġur ní mo cuirre [mic] Ríġ na h-Ioruaiḋe inḋiaiḋ na ḃṟear rin na cuirre Ríġ Ċire na ḃṟear ḃṟionn an lá rin, aġur ṟáġaiḋ

---

¹ Thus L. A has " a gcumadh agus cuibhling tiagar ".   H " ag coraireacht agus ag comhfhoghramh léithe ".

² The last ten words are from H, which also adds "ba maith an maisi disi sin".

airts(¹), 'twas what I beheld, a laden full-fair bark lowering its sail as a sign of peace, and it came into the harbour of this city; and I went over as far as it, as was always my custom, until I went into it without delay. And I found no one in it, alive or dead; but I found a harp of sweet music and gentle strings, playing of itself, and beautiful birds of one kind accompanying the music of that noble harp. And I searched the ship until I met with a couch covered with full-fair satin; and a great desire to drowse and sleep came over me then, and I fell in a numbness of slumber and deep sleep. And after I awoke, this is how I found the ship—bound to the thick tower of a castle in the midst of the very deep sea, without islet, or rath, or island near me. I rise then, and stand up. And I saw the door of the tower open over against me, and I immediately went into it, and I reached the top of the tower, and came there upon a shapely, attractive, gentle-fair girl, and a hood of fine gold with various precious stones about her head, and those precious stones bound with a very handsome gold tying, and a mantle of beautiful satin round her. And when that maiden beheld me, she rose up straight, standing as a column; and as she rose I grasped the mantle to arrest her. She leaves the mantle with me, and departs herself. I understood then, that the mantle had many virtues, and I asked it to bring me to my own city: and that wonderful many-virtued mantle took me with it through the expanse[?] of the firmament, until I reached this city. And, if all the furious(²) beasts of the world were to meet me, and that mantle round me, they would do me neither hurt nor harm; and fire does not burn, and water does not drown, and weapon does not stop him around whom this mantle shall always be;—and there is for you the adventure of that many-virtued mantle." And, indeed, Cod was thankful for that present.

On the morrow, they proceeded to depart, and not greater was the heaviness of the son of the King of Norway after those men, than the heaviness of the King of the Land of the White Men on

---

³ H reads " mfagbail san ionad a ttuigeórainn féin mo bhreith ".
⁴ A 25 reads" thogaibh".   ⁵ The last seven words are from L.

(¹) *I.e.* "quarters of the compass".   (²) Literally "senseless" .

iomapca beaṫaḋ aġup pláinte aġ an piġ, aġup ġluaipiḋ
pompa,[1] aġup ní h-aiṫpipτcap pġéalaiḋeaċτ oppa no ġo
páinġaḋap Caṫaip an τSpoṫa Ḋeipġ. Aġup ḋo ṫóġaḋap poḃal
áluinn ċaġpaṁail ionġantaċ leó op cóṁaip an loċa lán-ḋeipġ
pin, aġup ba ġpáincaṁail inneall a n-apm, óip ba ṗaṁailτe
le bpuiġin popġailτe [a] lapaṁlaċτ op a ġccann, aġup ní
ṗéaḋpaḋ ḋuine ap biṫ a ḃṗéaċain pe ġpáineaṁlaċτ [a]
n-inneall [aġup] a n-apm, aġup iomaḋ a ḃτopann-ċleap. Ip
annpin ḋo ṫánġaḋap op múpaiḃ na caṫpaċ amaċ, aġup ip
aṁlaiḋ ṫáiniġ Eiτeall [an ḃanṗlaiṫ] amaċ aġup léine áluinn
uimpi, aġup mionn cúṁḋuiġτe ġo n-óp-ġeamaiḃ[2] copcpa ṗá
n-a ceann, aġup polτ paḋa pop-ópḋa p[e]amuineaċ[3] pionn-
ḃuiḋe pop a ġeal-ġualainn, aġup ḋá ṗleaġ τeinτiḋe τoineaḋ
ina láiṁ, aġup ḋo ċeilġeaḋ i n-áipḋe iaḋ, aġup ḋo ġaḃaḋ ina
láiṁ apíp iaḋ, aġ poċτain ċum na τalṁan ḋóiḃ.[4] Ḋo ḃí ḋponġ
eile ḋe na mnáiḃ pin aġup plaḃpaḋ iapainn ġo po-ḋealġaiḃ
niṁe oppa i n-a láṁaiḃ leó, aġup ḋponġ ḋíoḃ aġ cleapaiḋeaċτ
leó ġo héaġpaṁail.

Ip annpin ḋ'iapp an Cupaipe Camċopaċ ap ḃuaiḋ an ḃpaiτ
a ḃpeiṫ ġo Caṫaip an τSpoṫa Ḋeipġ, aġup éipġear uaṫa i
ġcóiṁḋeaċτ na ġlan-ġaoiṫe ġéap-luaiṫe, ġup ġaḃ leaṫaḋ a
ḋá ḃonn ḋ'upláp an oiléin pin. Aġup ḋo ṗeapaḋap na mná
páilτe ġo ppíoċnaṁaċ poiṁe, óip ḃo ḃí aiṫne aca paip, aġup
iap ḃpaicpin an ṗobail ḋo na mnáiḃ ḋo ġaḃ eaġla ṁóp iaḋ.
Ip annpin ḋ'ṗiappuiġ na mná ḋe'n Ċupaipe Camċopaċ, " Cia
h-iaḋ luċτ an ṗobail ġpáineaṁail úḋ?"

Ḋo páiḋ an Cupaipe Camċopaċ : " Coḋ mac Rí̇ na
hIopuaiḋe, Iollan Óp-apmaċ mac Rí̇ na hAlmáinne, ḃuinne
ḃopḃ-ċpéan mac Rí̇ na hAppaice, aġup Ciaḃán Ġlúinġeal
mac Rí̇ na héanlaiṫe, an ceaṫpap aτá pan bpobal úḋ, aġup
níop ċuip an τalaṁ τpomṗóiḋeaċ ap a muin piaṁ ceaṫpap
ḋ'á macpaṁla púḋ, óip ip iaḋ ip τpeipe ḋe na τpéin-ṗeapaiḃ,
aġup ip uaiple ḋe na huaiplib, aġup ip cpóḋa ḋe na cupaiḋiḃ,
aġup ip meapḋa ḋe na míliḋiḃ, aġup ip pioċealτa bpiaṫpa ḋe
na ḋaoiniḃ, aġup ip ḋeaġ-aiṫne ḋe'n ḋponiġ ḋaonḋa."

---

[1] The last twelve words are from A 25.
[2] Thus L. A has " go nor gceiminigh ". A 25 " go nor geanamhla ".
[3] Thus A 25. A has "fat muineach".   [4] H omits the last several lines.

that day; and they leave the King with many farewells and blessings (¹), and go upon their way; and no tidings are told of them until they reach the City of the Red Stream. And they raised a handsome, variegated, wondrous tent in front of that full-red lake, and horrid was the guise of their weapons, for their blaze above their heads was like [the lights of] an open mansion, and no one could at all behold them through the horror of their mien and their weapons, and the abundance of their noise-feats. It was then they came out over the walls of the city, and this is how Eitcall [Ett-yäl] the chieftainess came. She had a fair *léine* around her, and a chased diadem, purple, with gold gems round her head, and she had long, gold, clustering,(²) light-yellow hair [falling] over her white shoulder, and two flaming spears of fire in her hand, and she used to cast them on high and to catch them again in her hand, as they reached the ground. There were others of the women with iron chains in their hands with venomous spikelets on them, and more of them were performing feats with them in various guise.

It was then the Curairè Crookfoot asked of the virtue of the mantle to bring him to the city of the Red Stream. And he rises up away from them in the company of the sharp-swift clear wind, until he gained the breadth of his two soles of the ground of that island. And the women eagerly bade him welcome, for they knew him [before], and when they saw the tent great fear seized them. It was then the women inquired of the Curairè Crookfoot, "Who are the people of yonder frightful tent?"

Spake the Curairè Crookfoot: "Cod, son of the King of Norway, Gold-armed Iollan, son of the King of Almain, Buinnè Rough-strong, son of the King of Africa, and Ciabhán White-knee, son of the King of Éanlaithe, are the four who are in that tent, and the heavy-sodded earth never put upon its back four the like of them, for they are the most powerful of the strong men, and the noblest of the noble, and the most valiant of champions, and the most active of heroes, and the most admirably-worded of men, and the men of best knowledge of the human race."

(¹) Literally "and they leave very-much of life and health to the king".
(²) Literally "sea-weedy".

Iſ annſin aḋuḃairc Ciccall, "Ní móiḋc ár mear-na oppa-
ran." "Ná h-aḃair na ſaoḃ-ḃriaṫra beaġ-ċaiṗḃeaċa ſin a
inġean," aſ an ḃſaoi¹, "aġuſ muna mbeaḋ ceaſ aġuſ cincaṁ-
laċc an cSpoċa Ḋeirġ ḃeaḋ ſioſ na ḃcſéanḟeaſ úḃ aġac-ſa,
óiſ iſ annſúḃ acá miſ cróḋa na cróḋaċca, aġuſ méaſ-ṁeaḋan
na míleaḋ, aġuſ uſſa caċa na ġcſíoc², aġuſ baſanca coſanca
cáiċ, aġuſ ſíġ-ḃile na cróiḃeaċca, aiġne ġan iomróġaḋ .i. Coḃ
mac Ríġ na hIoruaiḋe." Coinniġeaſ an ḃanṗlaiṫ an ſile na
ſoċaiſ ſéin an oiḋċe ſin³.

Aċc ċeana ċuġaḋaſ aſ an oiḋċe ſin, ġuſ éiſiġ an ġſian
ġo n-a lán-ḟoillſe aſ n-a ṁáſaċ, aġuſ ċáiniġ an Cuſaiſe
Camċoſaċ ſe buaḋaiḃ an ḃſuic a ócíſ, aġuſ ċáiniġ ḋo'n ſobal
a ſaḃaḋaſ na maiċe ſin, aġuſ ċuġ ſġéala na mban ionġancaċ
ſin ḋo Ċoḃ. Iſ annſin aḋuḃairc buinne ḋoſb-ċſéan, "Ḋo
ſaċainn leac a lollain Óſ-aſmaiġ," aſ ſé, "ḋ'ſéaċain an ḃſuil
ceaſ an cSpoċa Ḋeirġ maſ acá a ſiuċaḋ," aġuſ ċánġaḋaſ ġo
húiſ an loċa láin-ḋeirġ ſin, aġuſ níoſ ſéaḋaḋaſ ḋul ſaḋ
láiṁe laoiċ ḋe'n loċ ḋeaſġ ſin aſ ainṁeaſaſḃaċc an ceaſa,⁴
aġuſ annſin aḋuḃairc Coḃ ſiſ an Ḃſile, "Caḃaiſ-ſe iaſaċc
an Ḃſaic ſin ḃaṁ-ſa ġo ḃſéaċainn cionnuſ cá Caċaiſ an
cSpoċa Ḋeirġ ḋe'n caoiḃ aſciġ."

"Ní ſaċaiſ," aſ buinne ḋoſb-ċſéan, "óiſ ní ḃeiſeann an
ḃſac leiſ aċc aon ḃuine aṁáin, aġuſ aſ ġſáḋ c'oiniġ, ná
coiſmiſġ an cuſuſ umam ſéin," aſ ſé. Ċuġ Coḃ an ceaḋ ſin
ḋó⁵, ġo haiṁleiſġ. Iſ annſin ḋo ċuiſ buinne ḋoſb-ċſéan a
ḃſac caċa uime, aġuſ ḋo ġaiḃ an ḃſac aſ uaċcaſ a ġeal-aſm,
aġuſ céiḃ i ġcumaſ⁶ na ġaoiċe ġéaſ-ṡúḃlaiġe, aġuſ ḋo ġaḃ
leaċaḋ a ḋá ḃonn aſ láſ an oileáin. Iſ annſin ċuġaḋaſ luċc
an oileáin ſſaſa ḋiana ḋ'á n-aſmaiḃ ḋiúḃſaice ſaiſ, aġuſ
cſomaſ buinne ḋoſb-ċſéan a ċeann, aġuſ leiġeaſ ċaiſiſ na
ſſaſa ſin, ġo ḋcuġ aġaiḋ ſá'n ġcaċaiſ ġo neiṁ-ṁeiſḃċe⁷, aġuſ
ḋo ġaḃ aġ cuaſġain cáiċ ġo coicċeann, ġuſ ċuiſ a ſaiḃ amuiġ
aſceaċ ḋ'a n-aiṁ-ḋeóin; aġuſ an uaiſ ḋo ſuġ iomaḋ na láṁ
ſaiſ, aġuſ ciuġaḋ na ḃcſoṁﬂuaġ, ċuġ ḃiċ ḃo-áiſṁiġċe oſſa,

---

¹ The last ten words are from H.   ² Thus A 25. A adds "bair aigh
na ccuiraidh".   ³ The last eleven words are from H, but I edit
"an oidche" for "andoiche", and "coinnigheas" for "coinghios"; both
"congbhaigh" and "coinnigh" are still in common use.   ⁴ The last four

Then said Eiteall, "No greater for that is the heed we pay them." "Do not speak those foolish unprofitable words, maiden," said the druid, "for were it not for the heat and fieriness of the Red Stream you would [soon] know those strong men, for it is there is the valiant portion of valour, and the middle-finger of heroes, and the battle-prop of countries, and the sustaining warrant of all, and the King-tree of heroism, the mind without turning—Cod, son of the King of Nor-way." The chieftainess keeps the poet along with herself that night.

Howsoever, they bore away that night until the sun rose with its full light upon the morrow, and the Curairè Crookfoot landed through the virtues of the mantle, and came to the tent where these chiefs were, and brought to Cod tidings of those wonderful women. It was then Buinnè Rough-strong spake, "I would go with you, Gold-armed Iollan," said he, "to see is the heat of the Red Stream [as great] as its boiling is." And they came to the brink of that full-red lake, and they were not able to pass over even the length of a hero's hand of that red lake through the immoderateness of the heat. Then said Cod to the poet, "Give me the loan of that mantle until I try how is the city of the Red Stream on the inside."

"You shall not go," said Buinnè Rough-strong, "for the mantle brings with it only one person, and for the love of your generosity do not prevent me making the journey," said he. Cod gave him, reluctantly, leave to do that. Then Buinnè Rough-strong did on his battle garment, and took the mantle over his bright-weapons, and goes in the power of the sharp-travelling wind, and gained the breadth of his two soles of the middle of the island. Then the people of the island despatched impetuous showers of missile weapons at him; but Buinnè Rough-strong stoops his head and lets those showers pass him, till he turned his face for the city unflinchingly, and began to strike down all in common, so that in spite of themselves he drove to the inside all who were on the outside. And when the multitude of [hostile] hands reached him, and the bulk(1) of the great hosts, he inflicted on

---

words are from H. 5 H reads "Aontuigheas Cod sin dó, gér dhoiligh leis é". 6 Thus A 25. A has "a ccoimas". L "a gcumasg". 7 Thus L. A has "go neamheirbhfa", the combination "mhth" is sounded like "f".

(1) Literally "thickening."

aġur nuair ċáinig iomaḋ na ġcaċ ar ḃuinne ḃorb-érċan ḋ'imċiġ ré ṁ i muinġin a ḃruit r' ġcéaḋóir, aġur ḋo ċuaiḋ ḋo'n ṗobal 'na raḃaḋar na ġairġiḋiġ rin eile. Aġur ḋo ṗear ġaċ aon ḃíoḃ ro leiċ ráilte roiṁe, aġur ḋo ḃí reircan aġ taḃairt rġéala aġur tuararġḃáil luċt na caċraċ aġur teara aġur timneála an tSroċa Ḋeirġ.

Aġur ġiḋ mór a nḋraoiḋeaċt ḋo ḃáḋar lán ḋ'eaġla Ċuiḋ, aġur [a] ḃcaġ-ṁuinntire. Ir annrin ḋo ċuir Eiteall reara aġur teaċta ġo riġċiḃ an ḃoṁain uaiḋi; ar ḋtúr ġo Ríġ na hArra Móire ḋ'innrin na trom-ḋáiṁe rin ḋó. Ir annrin ḋo ċuir Ríġ na hArraice rġéala, aġur reara uaiḋ ġur na riġċiḃ eile. Ċáinig annrin ġo haċġcarr Tuireann tréan-ḃuilleaċ Ríġ na hArraice, aġur Ḋaire Ḋéaḋṗolair Ríġ na hAntuaiċe, aġur Raiġne Rorġ-leaċan Ríġ na hEiġirte, aġur Ioruaḋ mac Ḋealḃaiġ Ríġ na hIoruaiḋe, aġur ḃrotair ḃéal-ṗairrinġ Ríġ na ḃeaġ-innre, aġur Porraċ² Píoċṁar Ríġ Alḃann, aġur Paċtna³ Páċaċ Ríġ Éireann, aġur ḃrearal ḃéal-ḋearġ Ríġ Ġréaġ, aġur Lamporc Láṁ-ṗaḋa Ríġ Loċlann, aġur Siċear⁴ Súil-ġeal Ríġ Sacran, aġur Toireann Paoḃar-ḋearġ Ríġ Pranc, aġur Sinnrear Sálṗaḋa Ríġ na ġCaoileaċ, aġur an Ḋonn Ḋuḃ-ċorcra Ríġ na ġConċeann, aġur Amon Ġantaċ Ríġ na ġCoitre,⁵ aġur Miċéal Ríġ na ḃPear ḃPionn, aġur Riḋire an Ġleanna, aġur Ríġ Ċire an Óir, aġur mórán [ḋe] riġċiḃ eile naċ n-airṁiġtear ann ro.

Aġur ar ḋteaċt ḋe'n trom-ṗocraiḋe annrin, ḋo ċuir Ríġ an ḃoṁain teaċta uaiḋ ġo Ríġ na h-Ioruaiḋe, aġur ġo Ríġ na h-Arraice, aġur ġo Ríġ na h-Almáinne, aġur ġo Ríġ na h-Ċanlaiċe, aġur ċánġaḋar na ḃeaġ-riġċe i ḋtimċioll an Áirḋ-Ríġ. Aġur ḋ'ṗiarruiġ an t-Áirḋ-Ríġ ḋíoḃ, "créaḋ ċuġ an táir no an tarcuirne aġ a ġcloinn air réin, ċar urṁór ríoġ-ṁaicne an ḃoṁain, aġur maiċe ríoġra an ḃoṁain im ṗarraḋ-ra ann ro?"

"Ná bíoḋ ionġnaḋ ná iomċnúċ aġaḃ-ra uime rin," ar Ríġ na h-Ioruaiḋe, "óir ḋo ġaḃaḋar reaċt ríġ ḃéaġ ó'n Ioruaiḋ

---

[1] Thus L. A has "a bhrataigh". "bruit" and "brait" seem to be used equally often in this text as the gen. of "brat".   [2] "Fagarthach", in L.

[3] Thus H and L, but A has "Fiachadh".   [4] L has "Sitiol Súlmhar".

[5] L has "Rí na gCatceann".

them innumerable loss; but when the multitude of the battalions came upon him, he himself straightway departed, trusting in his mantle, and went over to the tent where the other heroes were. And each one of them separately bade him welcome, and he was giving them tidings, and an account of the people of the city, and of the heat and fires of the Red Stream.

And although great was their [power of] enchantment, they were full of fear of Cod and of his good band. It was then Eiteall sent from her, messengers([1]) and envoys to the Kings of the world, and first to the king of Great Asia, to tell him of that heavy band. It was then the king of Africa sent from him word and messages to the other Kings. There then came in short time Tuireann of the Strong-blows, King of Africa, and Dairè Bright-tooth, King of Antuaith, and Raighne Broad-eye, King of Egypt, and Ioruadh son of Dealbhach, King of Norway, and Brotair Wide-mouth, King of the Small Island, and Fotrach the furious, King of Alba, and Fachtna Fáthach, King of Erin, and Breasal Red-mouth, King of Greece, and Lamport Long-hand, King of Lochlann, and Sitear Bright-eye, King of England, and Toireann Red-blade, King of France, and Sinnsear Long-heel, King of the Kyles, and the Dark-purple Dun, King of the Houndheads, and Amon Gantach, King of the Coitre,([2]) and Michael, King of the White Men, and the Knight of the Glen, and the King of the Land of Gold,([3]) and many other Kings who are not mentioned here.

And on that numerous multitude's coming there, the King of the World despatched messengers to the King of Norway and to the King of Africa, and to the King of Almain, and to the King of Éanlaith, ([4]) and those good Kings gathered round about the High-king. And the High-king asked them : "What was it made their sons treat him with scorn and contempt, beyond the multitude of the world's princes and the kingly chiefs of the world who are in my presence here?"

"Neither wonder at it nor be jealous about it," said the King of Norway, "for seventeen Kings from Norway have gained the

---

([1]) Rather "tidings."   "Cior fios air" means "send for him."   ([2]) *Aliter* "of the Cat-heads."   ([3]) I do not know what is to be understood by the Land of Gold.   One of the poems ascribed to Ossian mentions it, "Sweet is the voice of man in the Land of Gold."   ([4]) These were the fathers of Cod, and the men who were with him besieging the city. This episode is very Irish.

Ríoġaċt an Doṁain, aġup ni mó 'ná cpi píġ ḃe ḃ' cinc-pe ḃo ġaḃ í."

"Cuiġim anoip," ap Ríġ an Doṁain, "ʒo ḃpuil an mac meanmnaċ móp-aiʒeantaċ atá aʒaḃ-pa aʒ ḃúil a nóiaiʒ na pipe¹ aʒup na paipḃine ḃo pinncaḃ óḃ i mḃpoinn a ṁáċap .i. ʒo nʒeaḃaḃ an ḃoṁan móp ʒo h-iomlán."

"Cá oċt mic óċaʒ ḃe cloinn aʒaḃ-pa, aʒup ní'l aċt cpiúp aʒam-pa, aʒup ni ḟaoilim ʒup mó cuiḃ na n-oċt mac óċaʒ pin aʒaḃ, 'ná cuiḃ mo ċpiúip mac-pa."

Ḃo ċoipʒeaḃap ḃ'á n-iomapḃáḃ annpin, aʒup ċuaḃap ap ḟaiċċe eaċpaċ an tSpoċa Ḋeipʒ, ap an ḃtaoḃ eile ḃe'n loċ, aʒup ḃo ċóʒḃaḃap poiḃle ḃéal-ḟaipppinʒe aʒup ḃoċa ḃíona ḃpuimneaċa pe taoḃ an loċa pin. Ip annpin ḃo ċuaiḃ píʒ an Doṁain aʒup Ríʒ na h-Antuaiċe ʒo h-úip an loċa lán-ḃeipʒ, aʒ ḃéanaṁ ionʒantuip ḃe'n tSpoċ Ḋeapʒ, aʒup ḃ'ḟiappuiʒ Ríʒ na h-Antuaiċe ḃe Ríʒ an Doṁain, "cpéaḃ ḃo ḃeip an cear ionʒantaċ po 'pan cppuċ² úḃ peoċ ʒaċ ppuċ eile?"

Ḃuḃaipt an píʒ, "peaċt ʒcloċa tá 'pan cppuċ² úḃ liom-pa," ap pé, "aʒup ip cuiḃ ḃ'á mḃuaiḃ ʒiḃé ppuċ no innḃeap 'na ʒcuipċeap iaḃ ip ʒnáċaċ leip ḃeiċ 'na ḃoiʒip ḃonn-puaḃ ḃeapʒ-laippaċ an peaḃ ḃiaḃ na cloċa pin ann."

"Aʒup an ḃpuil aon niḃ ḃo ċoipʒpeaḃ cear no cineall an tSpoċa Ḋeipʒ peo?" ap pé.

"Cá," ap Ríʒ an Doṁain, "aʒup ip caipipe liom-pa ḟiop a ḃeiċ aʒaḃ-pa, óip tá cloċ ḃuaḃaċ aʒam-pa peoċ ʒaċ cloċ eile, aʒup an uaip cuipċeap pan cppuċ² í, cpáʒann i ʒcéaḃóip, aʒup ḃo ʒeaḃċap na cloċa eile pe n-a ʒcnuapaċ,³ ap an ḃtpáċt. Aʒup póp, i ʒCaċaip na [ḃtpi] mḃeann 'pan Aipia ṁóip tá an cloċ pin ḃo ʒniḃ an ppuċ ḃo ċpáʒaḃ, aʒup tá i ḃpiop aʒup i ḃpaipḃine ḃúinn aon piḃipe ḃo ċeaċt ʒo Cúp na ḃtpi mḃeann aʒup an cloċ pin ḃo ḃpeiċ uainn ʒo h-aiṁ-ḃeónaċ, aʒup ʒo ḃpáʒainn-pe báp obann an oiḃċe pin. Aʒup tá cpi ċéaḃ piḃipe n-apmaċ ion-ċoṁlann aʒ coiṁéaḃ an cuip pin aʒup na ʒcloċ atá ann. Aʒup ni móp ḃe ḃaoiniḃ piaṁ [ḃ'á] ḃtuʒap piop an pʒéil pin."

Aċt ċeana, ċápla pá 'n am pin ʒiolla ʒpáḃa ḃe ṁuinntip

---

¹ MS. "piepe".   ² (3) MS. "ppuiċ", "cppuiċ".   ³ MS. "ʒcnópaċ".

Kingship of the World, and not more than three Kings of your race
have gained it."

"I understand now," said the King of the World, "that the
proud high-minded son which you have, is hankering after the vision,
and the prophecy which was made him in his mother's womb, namely,
that he would gain the Great World entirely."

"You have eighteen children, sons, and I have only three, yet I
do not think that the share of those eighteen sons of yours is greater
than the share of my three sons."

They ceased their disputing then, and went out upon the lawn
of the City of the Red Stream, on the other side of the lake, and
they raised wide-mouthed tents, and ridgy shelter-booths, by the
side of that lake. It was then the King of Antuaith and the
King of the World went to the edge of the full-red lake, marvelling
at the Red Stream. And the King of Antuaith asked the King of
the World, "What brings the wonderful heat into this flood beyond
every other flood?"

The King answered: "Seven stones that I have in that stream,"
said he; "and it is part of their virtue that whatever stream or river-
mouth in which they are placed, always turns to be a dun-red blaze
of crimson flame so long as the stones shall be in it."

"And is there anything that would prevent the heat or blaze of
this Red Stream?" said he.

"There is," said the King of the World, "and I think it friendly (?)
to let you know it, for I have a stone of virtues beyond every other
stone, and when it is put into the stream it dries up at once, and the
other stones may be gathered up([1]) on the bottom. And, moreover, it
is in the City of the Three Bens in Greater Asia, that that stone is
which dries up the stream, and it is in knowledge and prophecy for
us that one knight shall come to the City of the Three Bens and bring
from us that stone in our despite, and that I shall die a sudden death
upon that night. And there are three hundred armed knights fit for
conflict guarding that tower and the stones that are in it. And it is
not many people I have ever let know of that fact."

Howsoever, there happened to be at that time a favourite servant

([1]) Literally "are found to gather them on the shore."

Ríǵ na bḞeap bḞionn aǵ éiṛceaċṫ ṛe cóṁṛáḋ an ṛíǵ aǵ mnṛin an ṛǵéil ṛin ḋo Ríǵ na h-Ċnṫuaiṫe, aǵuṛ Ṫṛeaḃaṛ Ṫṛéan-luaṫ ainm an Ǵiolla.¹ Ċǵuṛ ṫáiniǵ annṛin ǵo Ríǵ na bḞeaṛ bḞionn, aǵuṛ ċuǵ na ṛǵéala ṛin ḋó ǵan ḟuiṛeaċ. Iṛ annṛin ḋo ċuiṛ Ríǵ na bḞeaṛ bḞionn an ḟeaṛ céaḋna ǵo Coḋ mac Ríǵ na hIoṛuaiḋe ḋ'innṛin an ṛǵéil ṛin ḋó, aǵuṛ ḋ'á ṛáḋ ṛiṛ ḟeiḋm ḟeaṛ an ḋoṁain ḋo ḟeaċnaḋ aṛ ḟeaḋ na huaiṛe ṛin.

Iomċuṛa Ċuiḋ aǵuṛ a ḋeaǵ-ṁuinnṫiṛe ḋo ċeanǵlaḋaṛ cóṁaiṛle cṛéaḋ ḋo ḋéanṛaḋaoiṛ, "Ḋo ḃéaṛa ḟéin cóṁaiṛle ṁaiṫ ḋaoib," aṛ buinne boṛb-ċṛéan, "iṛ cóiṛ ḋéanaṁ."

"Cá cóṁaiṛle ṛin?" aṛ Coḋ.

"Ṁiṛe ḋul aṛ ċeann [na] cloiċe ṫá i ḋṫoṛ na ḋṫṛí mbean[n] iṛ an Ċṛia Ṁóiṛ, aǵuṛ cuiṛiḋ-ṛe ceallṫaṛ ḋṛaoiḋeaċṫa in' buṛ ḋṫimċeall ǵo ṫeaċṫ ḋaṁ-ṛa ċuǵaib, aǵuṛ na ḋéanaiḋ aċṫ ḋímbṛíǵ ḋe ǵaċ níḋ ḟeaṛṫa, óiṛ iṛ ḋeaṛḃ báṛ Ríǵ an Ḋoṁain ḋo ṫeaċṫ iaṛ mbṛeiṫ na cloiċe úḋ uaiḋ. Ḋo cinneaḋ aṛ an ǵcóṁaiṛle ṛin, aǵuṛ ḋ'ḟáǵ buinne boṛb-ċṛéan iomaṛca beaṫaḋ aǵuṛ ṛláinṫe aca, aǵuṛ ḋo leiǵ i ǵceann aiṛċiṛ aǵuṛ imċeaċṫa é. Aǵuṛ i ǵceann aimṛiṛe na ḋiaiḋ ṛin, iaṛ n-imċeaċṫ ḋó, ċáṛla ḋṛoiċeaḋ móṛ aṛ aḃainn ṁaṛa ḋo ḃí iṛiṛ ḋá oileán, aǵuṛ móṛán ḋe ċolnaib aǵuṛ ḋe ċoṛṛaib ǵo ǵcṛéaċṫaib iomḋa oṛṛa aṛ ǵaċ ṫaoḃ ḋe'n ḋṛoiċeaḋ ṛin, aǵuṛ móṛán ḋe ċeannaib cuṛaḋ aṛ ǵaḃlaib aǵuṛ aṛ ḃeaṛaib² aṛ ǵaċ ṫaoḃ ḋé, oṛ úiṛ an ḋṛoiċiḋ ṛin. Aǵuṛ ċáṛla míleaḋ móṛ calma ḋó ann, aǵuṛ [a] uċṫ ṛe caṛṛaiǵ ṁóiṛ ċloiċe aǵuṛ é cṛéaċṫaċ cṛóilinnṫeaċ aṛ ḋṫṛéiǵean a ċuiḋ ḟola.

Ḋo ḃeannuiǵ buinne boṛb-ċṛéan ḋó aǵuṛ ḋ'ḟṛeaǵaiṛ an míleaḋ calma ṛin: aǵuṛ ḋ'ḟiaṛṛuiǵ ṛǵéala na móṛ-éaċṫ ṛin, aǵuṛ an áiṛ ṁóiṛ ṛin ḋé, aǵuṛ ḋ'ḟṛeaǵaiṛ an ḟeaṛ ǵonṫa maṛ ṛo é.

"Ċn Ḋṛeólainn an ṫíṛ 'a bḟuil ṫu, aǵuṛ miṛe ḟéin ba Ríǵ ḋí³, aǵuṛ ċáiniǵ ban-aṫaċ caillíǵe ḋ'áṛ n-ionnṛaiḋe, aǵuṛ ċuǵ ṛí áṛ cuṛaḋ aǵuṛ caṫ-ṁíleaḋ oṛṛainn, aǵuṛ ṫá ṛí anoiṛ

---

¹ The last forty-seven lines of text are from L alone; the others, curiously, omit, thus rendering rather obscure what follows, and showing what vicissitudes the story must have gone through. ² Last six words from H.
³ "bu ri oirre" in H.

of the King of the White Men([1]) listening to the King's discourse when he was telling that story to the King of Antuaith, and Treabhar Strong-swift was the fellow's name. And he came then to the King of the White Men and gave him those tidings without delay. Thereupon the King of the White Men sent the same man to Cod, son of the King of Norway, to tell him that story, and to bid him avoid the strength of the men of the world for that time.([2])

As for Cod and his good men, they took counsel as to what they should do. "I shall myself give you good counsel," said Buinnè Rough-strong, "which it were right to follow."

"What counsel is that ?" asked Cod.

"That I should go for the stone that is in the tower of the Three Bens in Greater Asia, and do ye put an enchanted covering round about you until I come to you, and make light of everything henceforth, for it is certain the death of the King of the World will come to pass after carrying away that stone from him." That council was decided on, and Buinnè Rough-strong left them blessings and farewell([3]), and launched himself on his journey and wanderings. And in the course of a while, thereafter, on his departure, he chanced upon a great bridge over a sea river, that was between two islands, and many bodies and corpses with many wounds upon them on each side of that bridge, and many heads of heroes on forks and on spits on each side of it, above the margin of that bridge. And he came then upon a great valiant champion with his breast against a great rock of stone, and he full of wounds and gashes and his blood leaving him.

Buinnè Rough-strong saluted him, and that valorous hero answered. And he asked him the history of those great deeds and of that great slaughter, and the wounded man answered him thus:

"Dreólainn ([4]) is the country in which you are, and I myself was King of it, and there came against us a giant hag, and she wrought for us a slaughter of heroes and champions. And she is now asleep

---

([1]) Whose daughter Cod had rescued. See pp. 63 ff.   ([2]) Literally "throughout that hour."   ([3]) Literally "much of life and health."
([4]) I have met this name in other Irish stories.

'na coυlaò aρ láρ an òροιċιò úò, ażuρ móρán òe ċoρρaιb na mιon-óιρneaċ bρúιżτe¹ aρ żaċ τaob òι."

Ażuρ a haιċle na mbριaċaρ ριn ρuaιρ Ríż na Òρeólaιnne báρ, ażuρ òo ċuaιò buιnne boρb-ċρéan ċum an òροιċιò ażuρ òo ċonnaιρc an ban-aċaċ caιllιże ριn 'na τοιρcιm ρuaιn ażuρ ρíoρ-ċòòlaτa. Ażuρ òo ċuιρ a hanál ażuρ a ρuanρaòaċ² ι bρaò ó'n òροιċeaò amaċ é. Iρ annριn òo ċuaιò buιnne boρb-ċρéan oρ cιonn na caιllιże ριn, ażuρ òo ράιò maρ ρo. "Q Ċaιlleaċ, ò'ρéaòρaιnn òul ċaρτ òá mba áιl lιom ρéιn, ażuρ múρżólaò aρ òo ċòòlaò ċu," ażuρ òo ċóżaιb cloċ oρ cιonn an òροιċιò ażuρ òo buaιl an ċaιlleaċ aρ láρ a huċτa ażuρ òo ċuιρ τonn òubρola τaρ a béal amaċ. Ażuρ až³ éιρże òí òo ċuιρ cloċ 'na ριnn ραċa⁴ ι mbρuιnn na caιllιże, ażuρ ċuż an ċaιlleaċ móρ-ρuaρżlaò aρ a bρáżaιò òo ċuιρ na cloιċe aιρτι. Ċuż buιnne boρb-ċρéan béιm cloιòιṁ òí żuρ ρżaρ a ceann ażuρ a colann ρéιċeaṁaιl ó ċéιle. Ażuρ τéιò buιnne boρb-ċρéan τaρ an òροιċeaò anonn an uaιρ ριn.

Ιomċuρa Ríż an Òoṁaιn ażuρ a ṁuιnτιρe, òo ċóιριżeaòaρ a bρobla ażuρ òo h-aċ-nuaòaò a òτeιnτe ażuρ a òτιneala leó, ażuρ òo ċaιċeaòaρ a mbιaòa neaṁ-áρρaòa ażuρ a nòeoċa mιlρe meιρżeaṁla, ażuρ 'na òιaιò ριn ċużaòaρ ċuca a żcρuιτeóραιò ceóιl-bιnne caoιn-τéaòaċ[a] ażuρ òo ċanaòaρ ceól ρíρ-bιnn ρíċeaṁaιl òóιb ρó'n am ριn. Ιomċuρa Ċuιò ażuρ a òeaż-ṁuιnτιρe: aρ n-ιmċeaċτ mιc Ríż na hQρραιce an oιòċe ριn uaċa òo ċaιċeaòaρ a mbιaòa ρaoρa ρó-ċaιċṁe ażuρ a nòeoċa żaρża żaбálτa míne meιρżeaṁla, ażuρ ιaρ ριn òo ρnaoιòeaòaρ ρlaτ na n-ιonżnaò. Iρ annριn aòuбaιρτ Coò ρe n-a òeaż-ṁuιnnτιρ. "Qn áιl lιb òul żo Ríż an Òoṁaιn aρ cuaιρτ ò'a ρéaċaιn cρéaò é an ρóżⁱ aτá aιże?" Aòuбρaòaρ ραn żuρ cóιρ ριn òo òéanaṁ. Iρ annριn ċużaòaρ an buιòean ċalma ċuρaòτa ċρóòa ριn a n-aιρm ċuca ażuρ ba ρaṁaιlτe⁶ ρe ρuιċne ρíoż-bρuιżne òeallρaò a n-aρm ażuρ a n-éιòιż aż τeaċτ ò'ιonnρaιòe ρeaρ an òoṁaιn an τan ριn.

Ażuρ ċáιnιż ριòιρe an uaιρ ριn ρeaċ uaιρ eιle, òe ċeażlaċ

---

¹ L "na noirnibh mionbhruighte". ² L "a huanfach", A 25 "a srannfach". ³ A "ar". ⁴ "na colg ratha rion luaithe" in L and A 25. ⁵ A "so", L "sogha", A 25 "soighe", from which I edit as above. ⁶ A generally uses this form; A 25 has simply "samhail"; L is intermediate, "sambuilt".

in the midst of yonder bridge, and many on each side of her in bruised fragments (¹)."

And after those words the King of Dreólainn died. And Buinnè Rough-strong went to the bridge and he saw that hag of a giantess in a fit of sleep and deep slumber. And her breath and her snoring drove him out far from the bridge. It was then Buinnè Rough-strong came above that hag and spoke thus : " Hag," said he, " I could pass by thee if I wished it myself, but I shall wake thee out of thy sleep," and he raised a stone over the bridge, and smote the hag in the middle of her breast, and she sent out of her mouth a wave of black blood. And as she rose he sent a stone flying into the hag's chest (²), and the hag gave a wide opening to her throat to put the stone out of it. Buinnè Rough-strong dealt her a sword stroke, so that he parted her head and her sinewy body from one another, and thereupon he passes over to the other side of the bridge.

As for the King of the World and his people, they set in order their tents, and their fires and lights were renewed by them, and they partook of their fresh meats and their sweet intoxicating drinks, and after that they brought to them their music-sweet, gentle-stringed harpers, and they sang ever-melodious, fairy-like music to them at that time. As for Cod and his good people, on the departure of the son of the King of Africa from them, they partook of their free easily-eaten meats and their drinks, rough, fermented, mild, intoxicating ; and after that they whittled at the rod of wonders (³). It was then Cod spake to his good people : " Would ye like to go visit the King of the World to try what cheer he has ? " They answered that it were right to do so. It was then that vigorous, valorous, valiant band took to them their weapons, and it was like the lights of a royal palace the gleam of their arms and armour as they came towards the men of the world at that time.

And at that time, of all times (⁴), there came a knight of the house-

---

(¹) Literally " in pieces small-bruised."
(²) This appears to mean " down her throat."   (³) See above, pp. 117-119.
(⁴) Literally "beyond another time."

Rí₰ an Ḋoṁain, amaċ aṗ pobal an Rí₰ ṗéin, a₰uṗ ḃo-éí na
cṗí coṁnle poṗ₰-₰oṗma ṗın amuı₰ ḃ'á ıonnṗaıḃe, a₰uṗ céıḃ
ı ḃcaıṗıḃ a₰uṗ ı ḃcṗoınnéalaıḃ báıṗ, a₰uṗ ḃo ḃí maṗ ṗın a₰a
ṗaḃa, a₰uṗ ıaṗ n-éıṗ₰c ḃó ḃo ınıṗ ḃo'n Rí₰ ₰o ṗaḃaḃaṗ cṗı
ṗléıḃce ḃonn-ṗnaḃa ḃeaṗ₰-laṗṗaċa[1] a₰ ccaċc ḃ'á ıonnṗaıḃe.
Ḋála Ċıṫḃ, ḃo ṗoınn ṗé a ṁuınncıṗ a₰uṗ ıṗ é ṗoınn ċu₰ ṗé
oṗṗa, ṗeaṗ ḃo ċuṗ ın ₰aċ áıṗḃ ḃe'n cṗlua₰ ḃíoḃ, a₰uṗ maṗ
ḃo ḃí ₰aċ a₰aıḃ aṗ Ċoḃ[2] ṗeaċ ₰aċ ḃuıne eıle ıṗ é áıṗḃ a
ḃcáṗla é, ınṗ an áıṗḃ a ṗaḃaḃaṗ cṗí Rı₰ċe ḃo ḃí 'na ₰cáıṗṃıḃ
ḃıle a₰ Rí₰ an Ḋoṁaın .ı. Rí₰ na Soṗċa, Rí₰ Inṗe hOıṗe, a₰uṗ
Rí₰ na hAncuaıċe, a₰uṗ ḃo ṗınneaḃaṗ caoṗ meaṗ₰ċa a₰uṗ
buaıḃcaṗċa[3] ḃe na ṗlua₰aıḃ ı n-alc[4] na huaıṗe ṗın, a₰uṗ ní
héıḃıṗ a n-áıṗeaṁ aṗ ċuıc le Coḃ ı n-alc na huaıṗe ṗın.
Ą₰uṗ ċáını₰ Iollan Óṗ-aṗmaċ ċum na coḃa eıle ḃíoḃ, maṗ
ṗaıḃ Rí₰ Ṗṗaıne, Rí₰ na Sıoṗaıle[5], a₰uṗ Rí₰ na hEaṗṗáınne,
a₰uṗ ba ḃó-áıṗṁı₰ċe ḃ'ṗíoṗ-eólaċ aṗ ċuıc ṗe hIollan ıaṗ ṗın,
a₰uṗ ċáını₰ Cıaḃán Ꙗlúın₰eal ḃo'n caoḃ eıle ḃíoḃ, a₰uṗ
ċáṗla Rí₰ Sacṗan a₰uṗ Rí₰ eıle aṗ ıaṗċaṗ an ḃoṁaın ḃó,
a₰uṗ ní héıḃıṗ áıṗeaṁ no ınṗın aṗ ċuıc le Cıaḃán Ꙗlúın₰eal
ḃe'n ṗuaċaṗ ṗın. Iṗ annṗın ḃ'ıonnṗuı₰eaḃaṗ na caċa céaḃ-
ṗaḃaċa ṗın a ċéıle. Aċc cá ní ċeana : ḃá ḃceaₗıṅaḃ ḃo ṁac
no ḃo ḃṗáċaıṗ aṗ ₰ualaınn ṗıṗ aca ḃo ṗaoılṗıḃ ₰uṗ bé
náṁaıḃ no eaṗcaṗaḃ ḃo ḃeaḃ ann, a₰uṗ níoṗ ḃ' ıon-áıṗṁı₰ċe
aṗ ċuıc le Coḃ[6], le hIollan, a₰uṗ le Cıaḃán Ꙗlúın₰eal, ḃíoḃ ;
a₰uṗ ba ċuma ṗın ı ḃṗaṗṗaḃ[7] aṗ ċuıc ḃe na ṗlua₰aıḃ ṗéın
ṗe ċéıle. Aċc cá ní ċeana, ċáṗla Rí₰ na hIoṗuaıḃe, Rí₰
Inṗe hOıṗe, a₰uṗ Rí₰ na Soṗċa[8] ṗe ċéıle, a₰uṗ ḃo ċuṁıṅ[ı₰]eaḃaṗ
a ḃṗíoċ a₰uṗ a ḃṗolcanaṗ ḃ'á ṗoıle, ₰uṗ ba ċoṁċuıcım ḃóıḃ
na ḃcṗıaṗ aṗ an máı₰ ṗın.

---

[1] Thus L, but A has "sluagh don ruadh dearg lasrach", H "tri croinn
donnruadha deargcorcra". [2] This is not very plain. The others omit.
[3] A "buadhartha", L "buadhearga", from which I edit as above. [4] A, as
usual, reads "[a] nalte na huaire sin". [5] L reads "Fraince" and
"Teasúile". [6] H reads this passage as follows : "Cuireas Cod Iollan fo árd
dona sluaghaibh agus Ciabhan fo ard eile, agus ionnsuigheas féin iad ina n-eidir
mheodhan. Ciodhtrácht do ronsat na curradha calma céadfadhacha sin caorrthann
cumuisge cumbuartha dona slóghaibh fo chéadoir, ionnus gur theitsiod ochtar dá
righthibh riú gan airiogh ar ar mharbhsat duaisle agus d'ardmaithe, d'ógaibh agus
d'anradhaibh agus go leór eile o sin amach. Agus airistear orra nach mór gur mó

hold of the King of the World out of the tent of the King himself,
and he beholds those three blue-eyed candles [of valour] outside,
coming towards him, and he falls into trances and swoons of death,
and he was thus for a long time. And after his rising again he told
the King that there were three brown-red mountains of crimson flame
coming towards him. As for Cod, he divided his people, and this
was the division he made of them,—to put a man in each quarter of
the compass [facing] the host. And as every face was turned towards
Cod beyond everybody else, the quarter in which he chanced was the
quarter in which were three kings who were dear friends of the King
of the World, namely, the King of Sorcha, the King of the Orkneys,
and the King of Antuaith. And they made a mingled, troubled ball
of the hosts in the joint of that hour, and it is impossible to enumerate
all that fell by Cod in the joint of that hour. And Gold-armed Iollan
came to the other portion of them, where were the King of France,
the King of Sicily, and the King of Spain, and it were incalculable
by a man of true knowledge all who fell by Iollan after that. And
Ciabhán White-knee came to the other side of them, and the King of
England and another king from the west of the world met him, and
it is impossible to enumerate or tell all who fell by Ciabhán White-
knee in that rush. It was then the sensible battalions attacked one
another. Howsoever, if a son or a brother chanced to be at the
shoulder of any man of them it would have been thought that it was
an enemy or foe who was in it, and it was not to be reckoned all who
fell of them by Cod, by Iollan, and by Ciabhán White-knee ; but that
was nothing compared with all of the hosts themselves who fell by
one another. Howsoever, the King of Norway (¹), the King of the
Orkneys (¹), and the King of Sorcha (²) met one another, and they
minded them of their [former] fury and enmity against one another,
so that the whole three of them fell together [mutually slain] on that
plain.

marbhsiod diob no do marbhadar féin dar oile tre mire agus mi-chéill an tréan
ndúsgadh tugadh orra fo chéadóir. Filleas Cod agus a dhias deagh-laoch da
phuible as a h-aithle. Ro caithsiod a mbi rompa don oidhche sin go subhach
soimheanmnach.
⁷ Thus I edit the " bhfara " of A. The others omit.
⁸ L reads, corruptly and carelessly, " Ri Sacsan, agus Ri Hior, agus Ri Franc ".

(¹) See p. 73.   (²) See pp. 73 and 83.

A haiċle na móp-olc pin ċáiinġ Coḃ aġup a ḃeaġ-iñuinċip ḃ'á bpobal péin aġup ġe'p móp eapḃa peap an ḃoiñain ó'n cpom-ċopann pin ba iñó eapḃa Ċuiḃ aġup a ḃeaġ-iñuinċipe pá ḃuinne boṗb-ċpéan. Iomcupa ḃuinne boṗb-ċpéan, mnipceap ponn peal eile. Ap bpáġbáil an ḃpoiċiḃ ḃó, ni eian ḃo ċuaiḃ an can ċápla Ríġ-eaċaip po-iñóp ḃó, aġup céiḃ apceaċ innci ġan puipeaċ¹, aġup ba hil-ġpéapaċ ionġancaċ áiḃ álinin ḃeaġḃéanca an ḃún pin, aġup ní bpuaip ḃe ḃaoinḃ innci aċc aon pḃipe aiñáin, iap ġcaiċeaiñ upiñóip a aoipe, aġup macaoiñ óġ aiñ-ulcaċ² neaiñ-áppaiḃ, aġup cailleaċ ċpíona ċpom liaċ ċapaċcaċ³ ḃe'n leiċ ḃe'n bpuiġin, aġup caop ḃ'iapann aiċ-leaġċa¹ i n-imeall na ceineaḋ aca. Aġup aġ puiḃe ḃo ḃuinne boṗb-ċpéan ḃo ḃeapġ an ċaop i ġcéaḃoip, aġup ap na ṗaicpin pin ḃo'n iñuinncip ḃo ḃí apciġ, ḃo éipġeaḃap uile aġup ḃo ċuġaḃap ceópa póġa ḃó, aġup ḃob' ionġna le ḃuinne boṗb-ċpéan, aġup ḃ'ṗiappuiḃ pġéala ḃe'n ḃeaġ-ḃuiḃin pin. Aġup ḃo ṗpeaġaip an peap ba ṗine aca é, aġup ip eaḃ aḃuḃaipc:—

"An Ipbéipne⁶ an ċpíoċ po 'na ḃṗuil cu, a iñic Ríġ na hAppaice. Ḃo ċáiinġ piapc ċuġainn, aġup ḃo ċoġain áp móp-ċpéaḃ, aġup ḃo iñapḃ áp nḃaoine uile na ḃiaiḃ, aġup ċuġ pí áp pluaġ aġup áp poċaiḃe oppainn, iḃip óġ aġup áppaiḃ, ionnup naċ maipeann aġuinn ḃ'áp plóġ aġup ḃ'áp poċaiḃe aċc a ḃṗuil ann po. Aġup ḃ'ṗáġaḃap áp pinpipiḃ i ḃṗíop⁸ aġup i ḃṗaipcine aġainn an cpáċ ḃo Iappaḃ an ċaop 'pan ceiniḃ ġo ḃciocpaḃ ḃuinne boṗb-ċpéan mac Ríġ na hAppaice ċuġainn aġup ġo bpóippeaḃ pé oppainn ó'n éiġean pin 'na ḃṗuilmíḋ, aġup ġo muippeaḃ an ṗiapc ionġancaċ úḃ."

Aġup ḃo ṗpeapḃalaḃ aġup ḃo ṗpiċealaḃ ġo huapal onópaċ é an oiḋċe pin, aġup ḃ'éipiġ ġo moċ ap n-a iñápaċ. Ip annpin aḃuḃaipc an peap aopḃa: "A iñic Ríġ na hAppaice; ip ionann aċaip ḃaiñ-pa aġup ḃo'n iñacaoiñ óġ úḃ ḃo-cí cupa, aġup ip í an cailleaċ úḃ áp máċaip apaon, aġup ḃ'aon coipċeap aġup ḃ'aon

---

¹ II "gan uirisiomh". ² Thus H. L and A 25 have "naoidheanda", A "iolcrothach". ³ L has "casaightheach". ⁴ A "at leathghtha", L "aithleighteach", from which I edit as above. ⁵ Thus L. A has "aniobire",

After those great deeds of evil, Cod and his good men came to their own tent, and though great was the loss of the men of the world from that heavy inrush (¹), greater was the want of Cod and his good men after Buinnè Rough-strong. As for Buinnè Rough-strong, that is here told for another while. After his leaving the bridge it was not far he went when he chanced on a very great royal *cathair*, and he goes into it without delay, and variegated, wondrous, high, handsome and well-made was that *dún*, and he found no people in it except one knight only, who had spent much of his span-of-life, and a young, beardless, youthful lad, and an ancient, bent, grey, coughing hag on the other side of the mansion, and they had a ball of refined iron on the brink of the fire. And on Buinnè Rough-strong's sitting down, the ball instantly reddened, and when the people who were inside saw that, they all rose up and they gave him three kisses; and Buinnè Rough-strong marvelled and asked tidings of that small band. And the eldest man of them answered him, and 'twas what he said :—

" Isbéirnè is this country in which thou art, O son of the King of Africa. There came to us a worm and it swallowed(²) our heavy flocks, and it slew all our people after them, and it wrought a slaughter of our hosts and people, both young and old, so that none of our hosts or people are alive except all who are here. And our ancients left it in presage and prophecy to us, that when the ball in the fire would light-up, Buinnè Rough-strong, son of the King of Africa, would come to us and relieve us from that distress in which we are, and would slay that wonderful worm."

And he was attended and served, nobly and honourably, that night, and he rose early on the morrow. Then said the aged man : " Son of the King of Africa, I and yonder young lad whom thou seest have the same father, and yonder old-woman is the mother of both of us, and of one conception and one birth are we both. But not the

---

A 25 "Iosbuirne".　　　　　⁶ II "i bfaisdine agus i bfíortarngaire", A reads "bhfíodhar", perhaps for "fíoghair", "figure".

(¹) Literally " noise."　　　　　(²) Literally " chewed."

coiṗḃeaṗc ṗinn aṗaon. Aᵹuṗ ní hionann ḃeaċa aṗ aṗ hoileaŏ ṗinn .ı. nnıi¹ an ĉĉaŏ-ḃeaċa ŏo cııᵹaŏ ŏo'n ṁacaoiṁ óᵹ úŏ, aᵹuṗ ᵹıŏ ḃĉ oilceaṗ² aṗ nnıi aṗ ŏcúṗ, ní ĉuṗeann aoıṗ ná uṗĉóıŏ² aṗ, cṗe ḃıĉ ḟíoṗ : aᵹuṗ aṗ ḃeaċa na nŏaoıne eıle ŏo hoıleaŏ ṁıṗe, aᵹuṗ uıṁe ṗın cáın áṗṗaıŏ maṗ ṗo." Iṗ anuṗın aŏuḃaıṗc ḃuınne ḃoṗb-ĉṗĉan : "Ŏĉancaṗ eólaṗ na Rí-ṗıaṗca ṗın ŏam." Ċĉıŏ an ṁacaoıṁ óᵹ aᵹuṗ ḃuınne ḃoṗb-ĉṗĉan maṗ a ṗaıḃ an ṗıaṗc, aᵹuṗ ıṗ anuṗın ḟuaṗaŏaṗ an ṗıaṗc, aᵹ ḟĉaĉaın aᵹuṗ aᵹ cıṁĉeallaŏ na caċṗaĉ, ŏ'á ḟĉaĉaın an ḃĉeaŏṗaŏ ŏul aṗceaĉ. Aᵹuṗ ó naṗ ḟĉaŏ, ŏo lúıḃ í ḟĉın cıṁĉeall na caċṗaĉ amuıᵹ, aᵹuṗ ĉuᵹ ḃuınne ḃoṗb-ĉṗĉan uṗĉaṗ ŏe'n ṗíᵹ-ĉṗaoıṗıᵹ ḃí 'na láıṁ aṗ an ḃṗĉıṗc ᵹuṗ ĉuıṗ an cṗleaᵹ cṗíĉe ŏo'n caoḃ eıle, aᵹuṗ anuṗın ĉuᵹ ḃĉıṁ ŏe'n lann leaĉanᵹlaıṗ ŏo ḃí 'na láıṁ aṗ an ḃṗĉıṗc ᵹuṗ ḃuaın a ceann ŏí. Ro ᵹaḃ, cṗaĉ, lúĉᵹáıṗe áoḃal an ṗıoıṗe um an ᵹníoıṁ ṗın⁴, aᵹuṗ ĉánᵹaŏaṗ an ḃunŏean ŏo ḃí ṗo ᵹlaṗ amaĉ le luĉᵹáıṗ ṁóıṗ. Iṗ anuṗın ĉuᵹ an ĉaılleaĉ ŏo ḃí ṗan ᵹcaĉṗaıᵹ Ḟıĉĉıoll⁵ óıṗ aṗ a ṗaḃaŏaṗ ıomaŏ ḃuaŏ aıṗ, ŏo ḃuınne ḃoṗb-ĉṗĉan, aᵹuṗ ıṗ uaıĉe ᵹoıṗĉeaṗ Ḟıĉĉıoll Ríᵹ na hAṗṗaıce ó ḟoın a leıĉ, aᵹuṗ ŏe ḟeóŏaıḃ maıĉe an ŏoṁaın é.

Aᵹuṗ ŏ'ḟáᵹ an ŏeaᵹ-laoĉ an ĉaĉaıṗ ṗın, aᵹuṗ nı h-aıĉṗıṗceaṗ a ıṁĉeaĉc ᵹo ṗáınıᵹ ŏo'n Áṗıa ṁóıṗ, aᵹuṗ ıaṗ nŏul ınṗ an ḃṗaıĉĉe ŏó, ŏo ĉóᵹ ṗoḃal ḟíoṗ-áluınn ᵹo ᵹcleaṗaıŏ ᵹṗáıneaṁla. Aᵹuṗ an can ŏo ĉonncaŏaṗ móṗ-ĉeaᵹlaĉ na caĉṗaĉ an ṗoḃal ṗın ĉánᵹaŏaṗ ŏo ŏĉanaıṁ ıonᵹancaıṗ na cıṁĉıoll, óıṗ ba h-ıonᵹna leó ĉaᵹṗaṁlaĉc an ṗoḃaıl. Aᵹuṗ nuaıṗ ḟuaıṗ ḃuınne ḃoṗb-ĉṗĉan ṗoṗᵹla luĉc na caĉṗaĉ amuıᵹ ó'n ᵹcáĉaıṗ, ĉĉıŏ cṗíoĉa no ᵹo ṗáınıᵹ ŏoṗaṗ an ŏúna, aᵹuṗ ĉĉıŏ aṗceaĉ. Aᵹuṗ ıaŏaṗ an ŏoṗaṗ 'na ŏıaıŏ⁶, aᵹuṗ cuᵹ báṗ oḃann aĉᵹeaṗṗ ŏ'á ḃṗuaıṗ aṗcıᵹ ŏe'n ceaᵹlaĉ, aᵹuṗ ĉuᵹ cuaıṗc con ó n-a cuaınne⁷ aᵹ mın-ıaṗṗaıŏ na caĉṗaĉ no ᵹo ŏcáṗla an ĉloĉ ŏo ḃí ŏ'[á] ıaṗṗaıŏ ŏó.

---

¹ H omits this passage.
² A reads "do hoiltir", L "gidh be hoiltear", from which I edit as above.
³ Thus L. A has "urchar". ⁴ The last eleven words are from H.
⁵ Thus L alone. A reads "Sithal", A 25 "Siteall", H "siothal", L 27 "sitheal", an uncommon word meaning "bowl."

same was the food upon which we were reared ; for poison was the first food that was given to that young lad; and whosoever is reared upon poison at the first, neither age nor harm affect him through time eternal : and it was on food [the same as that] of other people that I was reared, and therefore am I aged like this." It was then Buinnè Rough-strong said : "Let me be shown the way to that mighty worm." The young lad and Buinnè Rough-strong go to where the worm was, and it was then they found the worm looking-about and going-round the city trying if she could get in. And since she was not able to get in, she coiled herself round about the *cathair* on the outside ; and Buinnè Rough-strong gave a cast of the royal javelin that was in his hand at the worm, so that he sent the spear through it to the other side, and then he dealt a stroke of the broad-green blade upon the worm, so that he smote the head off her. Thereupon great joy of that deed seized the knight, and the company who were under lock came out with great rejoicing. It was then the old woman who was in the *cathair* gave a golden chess-board, in which were many virtues, to Buinnè Rough-strong, and it is from it the name of the "King of Africa's Chess-board" has been given ever since, and it is [one] of the precious jewels of the world.

And the good hero left that *cathair*, and his journeyings are not told until he reached Great Asia ; and, after his going into the green [of the city], he raised a truly-beauteous tent with [performance of] terrific feats. And when the great household of the city beheld that tent, they came round about it to wonder at it ; for they marvelled at the strangeness (¹) of the tent. And when Buinnè Rough-strong got a number of the people of the city outside, away from the city, he goes through them until he reached the door of the *dún*, and he enters it. And he closes the door behind him, and deals quick and sudden death to all of the household whom he found inside, and he gave the "visit of a hound from its whelps," closely-searching the *cathair*, until he met the stone that he was seeking.

---

⁶ H adds "ni is doiche no do riocht aon neach don teaghlach é ".
⁷ Thus L and A 25. A is corrupt and illegible.

(¹) Literally "variety " ; but the word appears to be sometimes used in this tale in the sense of " beauty."

Αʒυρ όo ρυʒ ιηρρι, αʒυρ όo έιηρ ι ʒειιόρεαέ[1] α ρʒόιέε í, αʒυρ έάιηʒ ʒo όoραρ αη όύηα, αʒυρ όo όí ρlυαʒ ηα εαέραέ αʒ coέαιlc ηα cρoιη-έαhιαη ʒo ηιαcα ηεαρc-έαlηα α όcιηέιoll αη cιιρ,[2] αʒυρ όo lυαέ-ρυαρʒαιl όυιηηε όoρό-έρέαη αη όoραρ αʒυρ έάιηʒ αηιαέ αρ αη όoραρ έιιη ηα ραιέέο, αʒυρ έυʒαόαρ ρlόιʒ ηα εαέραέ ρραρα όιαηα ό'ά η-αρηαιό όo-ρυlαηʒ όό, ηíoρ ό'ιoηlαιό[3] ʒαη íoc ριη, όιρ όo έυʒ όυιηηε όoρό-έρέαη ηαlαιρc ʒoηcα όo ʒαέ αoη όíoό ρά ρεαέ, αʒυρ ράʒόαρ coρ ηα όcρí ηόεαηη ιαρριη; αʒυρ ηí h-αιέριρcεαρ ρʒέαlαιόεαέc αιρ, ηo ʒo ράιηιʒ ʒo Cαέαιρ ηα ʒCloέ ηόεαρʒ 'ραη Όιʒιρc.

Αʒυρ ράιηιʒ όoραρ αη όύηα, αʒυρ ό'ιαρρ α ρoρʒlαό, αʒυρ cόιό αη όoιρρεόιρ ό'ά ιηηριη όo'η Ríʒ .ι. ηαc Ríʒ ηα hΑρραιcε όειέ 'ραη όoραρ. Αʒυρ αόυόαιρc αη Ríʒ α leιʒεαη αρcεαέ, αʒυρ όo ριηηεαό ριη ι ʒcέαόόιρ leιρ αʒυρ ράιlcιʒεαρ ηα h-υαιρle ι ʒcoιcέιηηε ρoιηέ[4], αʒυρ όo ρρεαρcαlαό ʒo hυαραl oηόραέ έ. Ιρ ʒεαρρ ʒo όcάιηιʒ αη όoιρρεόιρ αη όαρα ρεαέc αρcεαέ αʒυρ ό' ιηηιρ όόιό αoη όʒlαoέ όειέ 'ραη όoραρ αʒυρ όεαρc ʒεαl υιηε, αʒυρ αόυόαιρc αη Ríʒ α leιʒεαη αρcεαέ αʒυρ όo ριηηεαό αηιlαιό, αʒυρ έάιηʒ αρ lάρ αη όύηα. Ιρ αηηριη ό'ριαρρυιʒ αη Ríʒ ρʒέαlα όέ, αʒυρ αόυόαιρc αη ʒαιρʒιόεαέ ʒυρ ό'έ ρέιη Ιollαη Αριη-όεαρʒ ηαc Ríʒ αη Όoηαιη, αʒυρ ʒυρ αʒ cόρυιʒεαέc όυιηηε όoρό-έρέαη ηιc Ríʒ ηα hΑρραιcε έάιηιʒ ρέ, όo ράρυιʒ α όαιle αέαρόα, .ι. όαιle Ríʒ αη Όoηαιη, αʒυρ όo ηαρό ηόράη ό'ά ηιυιηηcιρ αʒυρ όo ρυʒ cloέ ηα ηόυαό υαιό.

Ιρ αηηριη αόυόαιρc Ríʒ ηα hΌιʒιρcε, "cά όυιηηε όoρό-έρέαη ι ηʒεαl ρε η-α έιoηηcαιό ρέιη,[5] αρ άρ ʒcυηαρ." Όo ό'ρíoρ όό, αρ αη άόόαρ ʒυρ αό αʒ Ríʒ ηα h-Όιʒιρcε όo h-oιleαό Ríʒ αη Όoηαιη.[6] Ιρ αηηριη όo loιηηεαό[7] αʒυρ όo lυαέ-ρεαρʒαό ρά όυιηηε όoρό-έρέαη ηαρ όo έυαlαιό αη cόηράό ριη Ríʒ ηα hΌιʒιρcε, αʒυρ όo έιριʒ 'ηα έolαηιαιη cόιη-όíρεαέ 'ηα έεαρc-ρεαραη, αʒυρ όo έυαιό αηιαέ αρ αη όραιέέε, αʒυρ όo leαη Ιollαη Αριη-όεαρʒ αηιαέ έ, αʒυρ ηíoρ ό'ράιlcε cαραό υιη έυιρη, ράιlcε ηα όειρε όεαʒ-lαoέ ριη ό'ά έέιle. Ιρ αηηριη αόυόαιρc

---

[1] Ρ "accomhroidh". [2] The last eight words are from H. [3] L has "nior bhairliogan gan íoc sin". A 25 "nior bairleagan". A has "fioch" for "íoc". [4] The last six words are from H. [5] Thus L. Ρ reads "angioll risin". A has "geal le na chior féin". H "angioll re na chiontaibh

And he seized it and placed it in the hollow of his shield ; and he came to the door of the fortress, and the host of the city were digging the heavy earth furiously and powerfully round the tower; and Buinnè Roughstrong suddenly opened the door, and came out upon the green, and the hosts of the city cast at him impetuous showers of their insupportable weapons; and that was not an exchange without repayment, for Buinnè Roughstrong gave each separate one of them a wound in return ; and he leaves the tower of the Three Bens after that, and no tidings are told of him until he reached the city of the Red Stones in Egypt.

And he reached the door of the *dún* and demanded admittance ;([1]) and the porter goes to tell the king that the son of the King of Africa is at the door.   And the king bade let him in, and that was at once done.   And the nobles welcome him generally, and he was treated nobly and honourably.   Brief time it was until the porter came in a second time and told them that there was a single young hero at the door, and white garments on him ; and the king bade let him in, and it was so done, and he came into the middle of the *dún*.   Then the king asked tidings of him, and he said that he himself was Red-armed Iollan, son of the King of the World, and that it was in pursuit of Buinnè Roughstrong, son of the King of Africa, he came, who had ravaged his paternal town, the town of the King of the World, and who killed many of his people, and who brought away from him the Stone of Virtues.

It was then the King of Egypt said, "Buinnè Roughstrong is, in pledge of his own crimes, in our power."   That was true for him, for this cause, that it was with the King of Egypt the King of the World had been reared.   It was then Buinnè Roughstrong flamed up, and was seized with sudden anger, when he heard that talk of the King of Egypt ; and he arose, a straight column, standing upright, and he went out upon the green, and Red-armed Iollan followed him out, and it was not the welcome of a friend to a feast, the welcome of those two good heroes to one another.   It was then Red-armed Iollan said,

ar ár gcumas do'n chor-so ".   [6] The last sixteen words are from A 25.   Ṗ says he was "na oide ag r. an domhain ".   [7] L has "lonnadh " and omits "fa". Ṗ has "londoigheadh uime ".

([1]) Literally " asked opening."

Iollan Airm-ḋearg, "Corġaiḋ teaġlaċ an Ríġ," ar ré, "ġo
ḃféaċaim féin aġur mac Ríġ na hAppaice¹ cómrac re céile."

Ir annrin ḋo ionnruiḋeaḋar an ḋiar ḋeaġlaoċ re céile,
aġur ḋo ronrat cómrac féiġ ḟuilteaċ ḟorḃarta ror[r]niata
ḃonn-mall ḃar-luaċ béim-láiḋir, aġur no ġo n-áirmiġtear
ġaimin mara no ḋuilliḋe ḟeaḋa no ḋrúċt ḟor ḟéar² no
ḟéar ḟor ḟaiċċe, no réalteanna aoir, ní háirmiġtear a
ḋtuġaḋar-ran ḋe cneaḋaiḃ aġur ḋe ċréaċtaiḃ ḋó-léiġir ar a
céile, aġur ḋob' é críoċ an cómraic rin ġo ḋtuġ ḃuinne
ḃorb-ċréan ḃraon ḃáir aġur ḃeaġ-ḟaoġail ḋo Iollan Airm-
ḋearg, aġur iar n-a ḟaicrin rin ḋo Ríġ na hÉiġipte aġur ḋ'á
ṫeaġlaċ ḋo ċuaḋar timċeall mic Ríġ an Ḋomain, aġur ruġaḋar
leó ġo Caṫair na ġCloċ nḊearg é, aġur ní mór ġo ḋtáinig
leir teaċt arteaċ, an tan ḋo ḟuair ḃár oḃann aṫġearr,
aġur ḋ'ḟáġaḋar ḃuinne ḃorb-ċréan 'na aonar ar an ḃraiċċe
amuiġ.

Aġur ḋo ċuit ḋorċaċt na hoiḋċe³ ar ḃuinne ḃorb-
ċréan annrin, aġur ḋo ċóġ roḃal 'na ḟearaṁ ar an ḃraiċċe,
aġur ḋ'ḟaḋuiġ tor tréan-ṁór teineaḋ⁴ ḟá an am rin. Ḃa
h-aiṁġaraċ⁵ ḋo ḃí ḃuinne ḃorb-ċréan ó cnéaḋaiḃ aġur ó
ċréaċtaiḃ an uair rin: aġur ḋo ḃí inġean ḟroċaċ ċaoṁ-áluinn
aġ Ríġ na hÉiġipte⁶, aġur ḋo ḃí rí aġ ḟéaċaim ḃuinne ḃorb-
ċréan inr an tcat-iorġail rin, aġur tuġ rí ḟearc a hanma ḋó,
aġur táinig ar cuairt ġo ḃuinne ḃorb-ċréan an tan rin, aġur
ḋo ḃeannuiġ ḋó ġo ġcaoinear⁷ comráiḋ aġur ġo milir-
ḃriaṫaraiḃ, aġur ḋ'ḟreaġair ḃuinne ḃorb-ċréan an ḃeannċaḋ.
Ir annrin tuġ an inġean cloċ ḃuaḋa ḋo ḃí aici amaċ aġur ḋo
ċumail [í] ḋo ċnéaḋaiḃ aġur ḋo ċréaċtaiḃ Ḃuinne ḃorb-ċréan,
ionnur nár ḟáġ cneaḋ no créaċt ġan leiġear ḋ'á raiḃ air, re
ḃuaiḋ na cloiċe rin. Aġur ḋo ġeall an inġean rit Ríġ na
hÉiġipte ḋo ḋéanaṁ ḋó.

Aḋuḃairt ḃuinne ḃorb-ċréan nar ḃ'ḟearr ḋó rit 'ná coġaḋ
aiġe. Aċt tá ní ċeana, tuġ an inġean ḃiaḋa raora ro-ċaiṫṁe
ḋó, aġur ḋeoċa réiṁe roimeaṁla, aġur ḋo ċaiṫ ḃuinne ḃorb-
ċréan a leór-ḋóṫain⁸ ḋíoḃ. Iar rin téiḋ an inġean ḋ'á

---

¹ F spells this "na hathfroige", and reads "eibhgite" for "Egipte".
² F, which becomes much more condensed towards the close of the story, omits
all this verbiage. ³ H reads "tig ciobar dorchadh na h-oidhche cuige".

" Keep back the household of the king," said he, "till I myself and the King of Africa try battle with one another."

It was then those two good heroes attacked each other, and they made a sharp, bloody, fierce, furious, slow-footed, quick-handed, strong-smiting conflict, and until the sands of the sea, or the leaves of the wood, or the dew upon the grass, or the grass upon the green, or the stars of the air be enumerated, all the wounds and unhealable gashes which they gave each other are not [to be] enumerated; and it was the end of that fight that Buinnè Roughstrong gave to Red-armed Iollan a drop of death and shortness of life. And when the King of Egypt and his household saw that, they came round the son of the King of the World, and they bore him with them to the City of the Red Stones, and he had but barely succeeded in entering, when he died shortly and suddenly; and they left Buinnè Roughstrong alone upon the green outside.

And the darkness of the night fell there upon Buinnè Roughstrong, and he raised a standing tent upon the green, and kindled thereafter a great strong tower of fire. And it was wretched that Buinnè Rough-strong was from wounds and gashes in that hour. And the King of Egypt had a shapely gentle-fair daughter, and she had been observing Buinnè Roughstrong in that battle-conflict, and she gave him the love of her soul, and she came to visit Buinnè Roughstrong then, and she saluted him with gentleness of discourse and with sweet words, and Buinnè Roughstrong answered her salutation. It was then the girl took out a stone of virtues which she had, and rubbed it to the wounds and gashes of Buinnè Roughstrong, so that she left neither wound nor gash of all that were on him, without healing, through the virtue of that stone, and the girl promised to make peace for him with the King of Egypt.

Buinnè Roughstrong said that he did not care more for peace with him than for war. Howsoever the girl brought him noble edible foods, and mild excellent drinks, and Buinnè Roughstrong ate his full of them. After that the girl returns to her sunny-chamber to sleep.

⁴ H reads " adhnas torc tine treatan ruaidh ".   ⁵ A has " hamhgear ".   ⁶ Ᵽ adds " angrionan os cionn na faichthe ar iomdhoidh uasail iongantoigh ".   ⁷ H "go bithbanda ". L " go carthannach "   ⁸ H " a lór dhaothchain ". A " deochain ".

Ɡpiandn do ċodlað. Iomċúpa Ríǧ na hĊiꞬipċe, ċap ċip báip mic Ríǧ an Doṁain, do bí Ɡo dubaċ dobpónaċ an oiðċe pin. Iomċupa buinne bopb-ċpéan, iap poillpiuꞬað do'n lá ap n-a ṁápaċ, do ċeanꞬail a ċopp ina ċaċ-éiniꞬ eaċa aꞬup epuadċóṁlann, aꞬup ċáiniꞬ amaċ ap an bpaiċċc, aꞬup do buail a pꞬiaċ Ɡo calma cupaċa, aꞬup do cualað an béicið pin i bppiċið na pipmamenċ. AꞬup nuaip do cualaið Ríǧ na hĊiꞬipċe an cpom-ċopann pin, ċáiniꞬ amaċ ap an bpaiċċc, aꞬup do ċóṁpaic pé péin aꞬup Ríǧ na hĊiꞬipċe pe ċéile, aꞬup ċuꞬadap il-iomad de ċneaðaið doiṁne dó-léiꞬip d'á ċéile. Aċc ċá ní ċeana, do ċuic an Ríǧ le buinne bopb-ċpéan.

AꞬup d'ḟáꞬaið buinne bopb-ċpéan epíoċa na hĊiꞬipċe, aꞬup ní h-aiċpipċeap pꞬéaluiðeaċċ aip, no Ɡo páiniꞬ Ɡo Caċaip an cSpoċa ÐeipꞬ map a paið a ṁuinnċip péin. Iomċupa Ríǧ an Doṁain, an oiðċe puꞬað an cloċ uaið do ċuic pluim¹ cpom ciuꞬ Ɡalaip aip, aꞬup bpiċ mapb ina iomdaið péin é ap n-a ṁápaċ. AꞬup iap dceaċc do buinne bopb-ċpéan map a paið a ṁuinnċip péin, do Ɡabadap d'á póꞬad Ɡo díocpaċ aꞬup piappuiꞬið pꞬéala dé, aꞬup ann pin do páið buinne bopb-ċpéan an laoið :—

SꞬéala² leac a Ðuinne Ðuipb
Ċabaip do pꞬéala Ɡan ḟeinꞬ³
Ipé pꞬéala pin leaċ buipð⁴
InꞬeilċ⁵ do ċuilꞬ⁶ ón cSpuċ ÐeapꞬ.

buinne.

Ċápla pan Dpólainn dúinn⁷
Món-buiðne 'p dpoiċead pe caob
Ap ndópċað pola Ɡo h-úp⁸
Ɡiolla púil-Ɡopm péibċe⁹ paop.

Aċá pa'n dpoiċead, ċpuaꞬ liom,
Cuipp ḟeanꞬa i n-eapbaið a Ɡceann,
Na plóiꞬ uile bonn ap bonn
Re húip na dconn ċoip a'p ċall.¹⁰

---

¹ H slaodan troim ghalair. Ꝓ omits.   ² H omits this lay.   ³ L and A 25 "osard".   Ꝓ "aosaird".   ⁴ L and A 25 have "is aon sgeal sin a shlat bhuird". Ꝓ "as slatburd".   ⁵ Thus L and A 25.   A has "ionneall".   ⁶ A 25 "chluig".   Ꝓ omits the last half of the fourth line, and introduces the lay in the following curious words : "agus tucsan na scela soin doibh go deadh [?] amhoil mar docualabhoir gottrasda gurab uime sin do rindeadar na draoithise .i. cur. c. c.

As for the King of Egypt, after the death of the son of the King of the World, he was sad and sorrowful that night. As for Buinnè Roughstrong, when the day brightened on the morrow he enclosed(¹) his body in his armour of battle and hard conflict, and came out upon the green and smote his shield valiantly and vigorously, and the roar of it was heard in the expanse of the firmament. And when the King of Egypt heard that heavy sound, he came out upon the green, and he [God] and the King of Egypt fought with one another, and they gave very many deep incurable wounds to one another. But, however, the king fell by Buinnè Roughstrong.

And Buinnè Roughstrong left the lands of Egypt, and no tidings are told of him until he reached the city of the Red Stream, where his own people were. As for the King of the World, the night the stone was taken from him, there fell upon him a heavy severe fit of disease, and on the morrow he was found dead in his bed. And on Buinnè Roughstrong's coming to where his own people were, they fell to kissing him affectionately, and they ask tidings of him. And it was then Buinnè Roughstrong spake the lay:—

> Buinnè Roughstrong tell thy tale
>   Of the land that thou hast sought,
> Fatted with the blood it poured
>   Thou thy sword from far hast brought. (²)

> BUINNE.

> There met us in Dreólainn
>   Great bands, and a bridge beside them,
> [And] pouring forth blood freshly
>   A blue-eyed youth, exhausted, noble.

> There are, round the bridge, I think it a pity,
>   Slender corpses, wanting their heads,
> All the hosts, foot to foot,
>   Beside the waves on this side and that.

agus dolbh daithgeal draei an laeisi". ⁷ L reads "thúrla sin dúinne a dhuine". ⁸ L "ar androichead follamh go hur"· ⁹ Thus I edit the "seada" of H; in L "seata". A 25 "seat". Ᵽ abbreviates here more than usual "g. a. s. g. s. s". ¹⁰ "is teann trall" in A.

(¹) Literally "bound." (²) This is in the metre of the original. Literally : Tidings with thee, O Rough Buinnè, give thy tidings without anger. Those tidings are . . . (?) the pasturing of thy sword from the Red Stream. *Metre :* Rannaigheacht Mór, without observance of alliteration.

Sípǝm[1] aŋ ŕéinniƃ na n-aŕm
ă ƃca5-aŋm ƃo ƃcaŋaiň ƃúiŋn.[2]
ŕá ŕ5éal ŕiŋ ŋc n5aƃcaŋ 5ŋáin
S5éal an uaŋ ŋin ŕá mƃiaƃ ƃúŋ.[3]

" A5 ŕo an ŕ5éal ƃ'ŕiaŕŋui5iŕ ƃíom
ă ŕiŋ 5lic[4] na mƃŋiaċaŋ mín,
ăn ƃŋeolainne[5] an cíŋ ŕeo ŕéin,
'Siŕ miŕe ané ŕá Rí5 ƃí.

" ƃao5al ƃuic-ŕe ƃul ŋe caoƃ
ăn ƃŋoióƃ aŋ éaol[6] an éuain,
ăcá 'na lui5e aŋ a láŋ
ăn ŕiaŋc ƃo éuiŋ áŋ na ŋlua5."

ƃ'ŕéaċaŋ ŕaoƃaŋ m'aŋm 5éaŋ
Ṁaiŋŕiƃ an ŕ5éal ŕo caŋ m'éiŕ,
ǐ n-éiŋic aŋ Ṁaŋƃ ƃc'n cŋlua5
ƃeancaŋ liom[7] a ceann ƃe'n ŕéiŋc.

Čáŋla ŋan Ioŋƃiŋne ƃúinn
ŕeaŋ aoŋṀaŋ a'ŋ macaom ó5,
Cailleaé óŋíon i 5caéŋai5 úiŋ
Ču5aƃaŋ ƃúinn ceóŋa ŕó5.

'San 5cácŋai5 acá ŕo'n 5leann
Ru5aŋ a ceann ƃe'n ŕéiŋc ŋuaiƃ[8],
ŕuaiŋeaŋ[9] ó'n 5caillí5 náŋ ƃ'ó5
ŕiċóioll[10] óiŋ 5o n-iomaƃ ƃuaiƃ.

ƃo éuic liom cea5laé an Rio5
Ni 5níoḿ ŋin ŕá ƃéanca ŋún,
Iaŋ mƃŋiŋeaƃ cuiŋ na ƃcŋí mƃeann
Ču5aŋ liom an éloé aŋ 5cúl.

Ṁac Rio5 an ƃoṀain, ŕ5éal ba Ṁó,
'Na éoŋaŋ óŋó éạƃ aŋceaé,
'S Rí5 na h-'Ci5iŋce éuic liom
Iŋ lollan ŕionn na n-aŋm n5eal.

---

[1] L and A 25 both omit this rann.   [2] Thus L 27, but A has " nainm sa shloineadh dinsin duin ".   [3] L 27 reads better, " sgeala an áir anba [ŕ anaboigh] úir ".   [4] L " a ghiolla ghlic ". ŕ " a ghil óg ". A " a fhir aobhtha ", from which I edit as above.   [5] A & L read " dúthchos dúinne an tir so féin ". [6] A reads " an droichead re taobh an chuain."   [7] A and ŕ read " uaim ". [8] A reads "ditceanis an piast ruadh".   [9] A " foris ".   [10] Thus L, which here spells it " fichioll ". A has, as before, " sitiol ". A 25 " siohal ". L 27 " síothal ". ŕ " sitheal ".

I ask the warrior of the weapons
    To make known to us his good name,
That was a tale at which horror is conceived,
    A tale in that hour from which shall come hardships. (?)

" Here are the tidings you have asked of me,
    O prudent man of the smooth words,
This country itself is Dréolainn ;
    It is I who was yesterday king of it.

" It is a danger to thee to pass beside
    The bridge beside the harbour :
There are, lying in its midst,
    The serpent who wrought the slaughter of the hosts."

I tried the venom of my keen arms
    (This story shall live after me)
In eric for all of the hosts whom she slew ;
    Her head is taken by me off the serpent.

There met us in Isbirnè
    An aged man and a youthful lad,
A withered hag in a fresh *cathair*,
    They gave to us three kisses.

In the *cathair* that is beneath the valley
    I took her head off the red serpent ;
I received from the hag who was not young,
    A golden chessboard with many virtues.

The household of the king fell by me :
    That is not a deed of which a secret should be made.
After breaking the tower of the Three Bens
    I brought back with me the stone.

The son of the King of the World, a greater deed, (¹)
    In a gory mass he comes in ;(²)
And the King of Egypt fell by me
    And Iollan the Fair(³) of the bright arms.

(¹) Literally " story."   (²) See p. 191.   He just came into the city when
he fell dead.   (³) There is no mention of a Fair Iollan of bright arms in the
prose, only of Iollan of the Red Arms, and he was son of the King of the World.
It would seem from the verse that Buinnè slew three different people, but only two
of them are mentioned in the prose narrative. This is very important, as showing
that the verse must have been the earliest of the two, and that the prose narrative
was founded upon it. Þ adds, if I remember right, that it was Buinnè's druid
Dolbh who made the lay to commemorate his great deeds.

Ní ḃḟuiarear ar muir ná ar tír
Troiḋ mar lollan na narm ngéar,
I ġCaeṗaiġ na Móṗ-ċloċ nDearġ,
Aġ rin aġaiḋ ḃearḃ mo ṟġéal.

A haiċle na laoiḋe rin ḃo cuireaḋ an ċloċ 'ran tSṗuċ
Ḃearġ aġur ḃo ḟuaraḋ aġur ḃo ciormaḋ an rruċ i ġcéaḃóiṗ,[1]
aġur ḃo ċuaiḋ Coḃ aġur a ṁuinnċir ġo Caċair an tSroċa
Ḃeiṗġ, aġur ċuġaḋar a ḃḟuaraḋar ḃ'óṗ aġur ḃ'ioṅṁar innci
leó, aġur ċuġaḋar ġearṗuġaḋ raoġail ḃ'a ḃḟuaraḋar innci
o ṗin ainaċ, aċc Eiċeall aṁáin.

Iomċura ḟear nDoṁain, ċuġaḋar a n-aiġċe ar Ċlainn Ríġ
na hloṗuaiḃe, aġur ḃo rinneaḃar úṁla óóiḃ.[2] Aġur ḃo ġoireaḋ
Ríġ an Ḋoṁain ḃo Ċoḃ mac Ríġ na hloṗuaiḃe, aġur an méaḃ ḃo
marḃaḋ ḃe na riġċiḃ rin ran ġcaċṗaiġ, ḃo ġoireaḋ riġċe eile
'na n-áiċ, ḃ'á n-oiġriḃ ḟéin; aġur ḃo ġoireaḋ Ríġ na hloṗuaiḃe
ḃo Ċeaḃ mac Ríġ na hloṗuaiḃe, aġur ċuġaḋ Eiċeall mar ṁnaoi
ḃó, aġur ċuġaḋ rann ḃe ċṗí rannaiḃ an Ḋoṁain ḃo ḃuinne
ḃorḃ-ċṗéan, aġur an méaḃ [ḃo ṁaiṗ] ḃe riġċiḃ an Ḋoṁain ar
an láċair rin ċánġaḋar ḃ'ionnraiḃe an áiṗḃ-ríġ rin, ḃo
ċeanġal a ġcuiṗ aġur a ġcáiṗḃiṗ ḟṗiṗ, aġur ḃ' ṗáġail cuillioṁ
aġur cuaṗaṗḃail uaiḃ, aġur cíora aġur cána ċaḃairc ḃó-ran ó
ṗin ruar. Ir annrin ḃo ġoireaḋ Ríġ na hAṗia Móiṗe ḃo
lilíceaḃ, aġur ċánġaḋar Clanna Ríġċeaḃ aġur ciġearnaiḃ
ḃúiċċe aġur barúin aġur biaḃċaiġ aġur caoiṗiġ ḃ'á ionnraiḃe
ḃo ġaḃail ḟorḃa[3] aġur ḟearaṁn uaiḃ, aġur ḃo ċaḃairc úṁla
aġur uṗṗama ḃó. Iomċura Ríġ an Ḋoṁain, .i. Coḃ mac Ríġ na
hloṗuaiḃe, ba ċrom conaiġe [ba] ḃinn-ḃéaṗlaċ na ḟileaḃa, ba
ṗoilḃiṗ roineaṁail na ṗóċaiḃe, aġur na cineaḃaċa, ba húṁal

---

[1] P reads as follows:—

Ceanġlaḃ a ġcuiṗṗ ina ġcaċ-ḃeirċiḃ caċa aġur ir í cóṁaiṗle aiṗ
aṗ cinnṗeac an cloċ ċaoṁ-ḃuaḋaċ ċuġ buinne ḃorḃ-ċṗéan ċuca ḃo
ċuṗ ṗon tSṗuċ nḃearġ ḃo ḃíoḃaḋ a ṫeaṗa aġur a ṫeanḃála. Ḃo
niġiḃ aiṁla ionnur ġuṗ coiṗneaḋ aġur ġuṗ ċṗéan-ṁúcaḃ ḃṗaoiḃeaċc
aġur ċṗéan laṗṗaċa an ċṗroċa ḃo ḃuaḃaiḃ na cloiċe a ccéaḃoiṗ.
Iaṗ rin ċéiḃ Coḃ cona muinciṗ ḟán ġcaċṗaiġ ġo ḟraoċa ḟoṗniaca
aġur ġo raċċṁar moṗ-aiġ́ionċaċ aġur noċ aṗ ḟanṗac no ġuṗ ġaḃṗac
eiciol inġean Ríġ na h-Aṗia Móiṗe banḟlaiċ na caċṗaċ aġur ġuṗ
rġaoil riaḃ ġaċ ḃoċaṗ ceanġail ḃá ṗoiḃ aṗ ċloinn Ríġ na h-loṗuaiḃe.
Ḃo cóṁ-aiṗġṗeac an ċaċaiṗ iaṗ rin, aġur ḃeiṗeḃ ṗoġaḃ a ṗéaḃ aġur

I never experienced on sea or on land
A fight like [that with] Iollan of the sharp weapons,
In the City of the Great Red Stones,
There is for you the truth of my tidings.

After that lay, the stone was placed in the Red Stream, and the stream was at once made cold and dried up. And Cod and his people crossed over to the City of the Red Stream, and they brought away with them all the gold and treasure they found in it ; and they gave shortness of life to all they found in it from that moment, except to Eiteall alone.

As for the men of the World, they turned towards the children of the King of Norway and made submission to them. And Cod, son of the King of Norway, was named King of the World ; and as many of those kings as were slain round the city, other kings from their own heirs were appointed kings in their places ; and Cead, son of the King of Norway, was called King of Norway, and Eiteall was given him to wife ; and a division of the three divisions of the World was given to Buinne Roughstrong, and all of the Kings of the World who were on the spot came to that High King to knit their sureties and friendships with him, and to receive pay and stipend from him, and to give him from that forward rent and tribute. It was then Micead was appointed(¹) King of Great Asia, and the sons of kings, and the lords of territory, and barons and hospitallers and chiefs, came to him to receive from him land and territory, and to pay him homage and submission. As for the King of the World, namely, Cod, son of the King of Norway, heavy were fortunes, sweet-spoken were the poets, courteous and fortunate were the peoples and the races, submissive

bioᵹnaiṗ ᵹaca haiṗm ba ḃṗuaiṗṗeac mnce aiṗce, iaṗ mḃṗeiċ buaḃa aṗ a laoċaiḃ aᵹuṗ aṗ [a] ḃeaᵹ-cuṗaḃaiḃ.

lomcuṗa muincipe Ríᵹ an Doṁain ciaᵹaiḃ a ᵹcoṁaiṗle ḃṗioṗ cia ḃá nᵹoiṗṗibiṗ aiṗḃ-ṗíᵹ aᵹuṗ aṗ í coṁaiṗle aiṗ aṗ ċinnṗeac ceannuṗ aᵹuṗ caoṁ ḟlaiċioṗ bo ċaḃaiṗc bo Coḃ bo ḃṗiᵹ ᵹuṗ aiċniᵹeaḃaṗ ᵹo ṗaiḃ cumaṗ a caiċme aᵹuṗ a coṗnaṁa aiᵹc . . .

This last line is of great interest, as it shows the Irish form of the proverb, "spend me and defend me," i.e. "caith agus cosain mé".

² Ꝑ says that it was the king of the white men, whose daughter, Féithlin, had been rescued by the children of Norway, and the king of Antuaigh, or Antuaith, her grandfather, who persuaded the kings to make Cod King of the World.   ³ Thus A and H 25, and L has "fóirbhe".

(¹) Literally " called."

aıżıoncaċ na hoıż[e], ażuṗ ḃa ḃınn-ṗoclaċ ḃeannemṗe le lınn an cṗém-ṗíż ṗın, no żo ḃṗuaıṗ ḃáṗ.[1]

---

[1] A has the following colophon :—

Ażuṗ buıḋeaċaṗ ḋo Ḋıa Uılc-ċúṁaċcaıż żo ḋcáınıż lıom a ċṗíoċnużaḋ anoıṗ, ażuṗ beannaċc Ḋía ḋo żaċ Cṗíoṗcuıḋc léıżṗeaṗ żuıḋc le hanam an cí ṗżṗíoḃ maṗ ṗo ṗém í. Vale lecto[r].

Ƒınıṗ.

aoḋ ṁc ḋoṁnaıll,
ḋo ṗżṗíoḃ an beażán ṗo.

Aż ṗo leaḃaṗ Ċomáıṗ Uí luınıż aṗ na ċṗíoċnaḋ ṗeaċcuaḃh la ƒıcec ḋo ṁíḋh luh an Ḃlıażaın ḋ'aoıṗ an cıżeaṗna .ı. míle ażuṗ ṗeaċc ccéaḃ ażuṗ ceaċṗa blıażna ḃéaż 1714, 7c. &c.

Ƒ ends thus :

"Gura bi eachtra chloinne riogh na h-Ioruaidhe an scel sin anuas, agus fos goirid fireolaigh ciorgaile na sceuloidheachta don eachtrasa, agus dolbh daithgheal draoi agus Curaire Camchosach do scriobh an eachtrasa a ffleascoiph fileadh agus anamhlorgoiph druagh, agus gurabi so an ceathramhadh teanga in artarraingeadh hi; agus do scaoileadh righte an domhain da cciriochaibh fpein oshin amach. Finid. Amen. Ailim trocoire ar an trionoid."

L ends :
"Le Seaghán O Domhnaill. Sirim guidhe an leaghthóra mar aon le n-a lucht éisteachta. October the 1st, 1778."

A 25 ends :
"Ag sin eachtra chloinne R. na h-Ioruaidhe ar na cur i gceart críoch le Seamus mac Ciarnáin 's an mbhliadhain d'aois úr dTighearna 1770. Guidh ar anamnaibh mharbh Purgeadair. Na dearmuid an sgríobhnóir Seámus Mac Ciarnáin, agus guidh ar anam Mbriartigh Mac an Bháird. Finit."

[but] spirited([1]) were the virgins, and sweet-worded were ladies during the time of that strong king, until he died.([2])

([1]) Or perhaps, if *umhall-aigiontach* be taken as one word, "humble-spirited."

([2]) A, the northern MS. which I have taken as the basis of the text has the following colophon:

"And thanks be to Almighty God that I have succeeded in finishing it now, and the blessing of God to every Christian who shall read [it], and pray for the soul of him who wrote it, this way, itself. [*i.e.* even so moderately well as this.] Vale lector.
"Finis.

"HUGH MAC DONNELL,
" Who wrote this trifle.

"This is the book of Thomas O'Luinigh, finished the 27th day of the month of July the year of the age of the Lord one thousand and seven hundred and fourteen years, etc."

P, the oldest MS., ends thus:

"So that story down [to this] is the Adventures of the Children of the King of Norway; and men of true knowledge call these adventures the battle-feats(?) of story-telling, and it was Dolbh Bright-hue the druid and the Curaire Crookfoot who wrote these adventures in poet's wands and in druid's tablet-staves, and this too is the fourth language into which it was translated. And the kings of the world were despatched to their own countries from that out. Finid. Amen. I beseech the Trinity for mercy."

The Munster MS. L ends thus:

"By John O'Donnell. I beseech the prayer of the reader together with those of his hearers. October the 1st, 1778."

A 25 ends:

"These are the adventures of the children of the King of Norway, rightly ended by James Mac Kernan in the year of the age of our Lord 1770. Pray for the souls of the dead in Purgatory. Do not forget the writer Séamas Mac Ciarnain [Kernan] and pray for the soul of Mriartach Mac an Bhaird [Murty Ward]. Finit."

GLOSSARY.

[This Glossary contains chiefly the words that are not found in O'Reilly's Dictionary, or which are given there with different meanings from those found in the text. For the explanation of several words in "The Lad of the Ferule" I am indebted to my friend the Rev. P. O'Leary, of Castlelyons, whose knowledge of the southern language is unique. The figures refer to the pages.]

Aċuṗan, 90, *also* coṁaṫċuṗan. Ṫu-
ɡaḃaṗ aċuṗanḃ'áṗcan-aṗmaiḃ
ḃ'á ċéile.

Aḃṗuaṗ, 38, very cold.

Aṁṁleiṗɡ, 172, ɡo haiṁleiṗɡ, reluctantly.

Aiṗeaṁ, 6, fame, *literally* 'count':
cf. English 'account.'

Aiṗeaċta, *or* aṗṗaċṫ, 128, monster,
spectre.

Aiṫeaċ, 114, *often used for* aṫaċ,
i.e. ṗaṫaċ, giant.

Aiṫiḃ, 82, *more usually* aṫaiɡ, *as*
aiṫeaċ *for* aṫaċ, time, length of
time.

Aiṫiṗiɡ, 88, *perhaps meant for gen. of*
aiṫeaṗɡ, advice, warning.

Alpaḃ, 26, voracious-swallowing.
"Aɡ alpaḃ na ṗeola," *song of*
an Sioṫa 'ṗ a ṁáṫaiṗ.

Aiṁɡaṗ, 100, *used as an adj.*, afflicted,
pitiable.

Aiṁṗa, 90, ṗiṗ aiṁṗa, a dream-vision.

Amuiċ, 104, *a common form of* amuiɡ
in Ulster and Connacht, outside,
abroad.

Amaṗ, 24, *literally* an attack, a hitting.
Ṙinne mé amaṗ aiṗ, I made at
him to hit him. Ḟuaiṗ mé amaṗ
aiṗ, I got a chance to hit him.

An, 112, *i.e.* ṗan, remain, stay.

Anaiṗṫe, *n.*, 34, broth, soup. Thus
pronounced in Central Connacht
also, but more usually written
anḃṗuiṫ.

Anṫuaiɡ, *n.*, 158, ṗíɡ na h-An-
ṫuaiɡe, the king of Antuaigh, the
Irish name for Antioch. *In Leabhar Breac*, Anṫuaiḃ.

Aṗḃnóṗ, *n.*, 50, high fame; *see*
uṗṗaḃnóṗ.

Aṗɡnaṁ *or* aṗɡnaḃ, *v.*, 60, 70, sailing,
voyaging. Aɡ aṗɡnaḃ an aiɡéin,
aɡ aṗɡnaṁ na ṗṗuṫ-ḟaiṗṗɡe.

Aṫaiḃe, *n.*, *see* ṗeiṫiḃe.

Aṫaloiṗɡ, *n.*, 8, *apparently the same
meaning as the modern* ṗloiɡiṗɡ,
a rabble (of children, cats, dogs,
etc.).

Aṫaṗḃa, *n.*, 158, patrimony, paternal
abode; *also used as an adj.*, 188.

baclainn, 12, *dat. of* bacla, the
hollow of the bent arm. Níoṗ
ḃṗaḃa ɡo ḃṗacaiḃ mé ɡunn'
aṗ mo ḃacalainn. *Munster
Song.*

ball, 42, aṗ an mball, *or* aṗ ball,
presently, on the spot.

bancuiṗe, 58, ladies, a troop of
women.

baṗaṁail, an equivalent, a likeness. Oiṗeaḃaḃḟeacaḃaṗ ṅeḃaoiniḃ ṗiaṁ ḃo ḃí baṗaṁail ḃóiḃ ṗan aonaċ ṗin, 80, *i.e.* as many as that. baṗaṁail ḃo'n ċáċṗaiʒ ṗin, the like of that city. *Also* an opinion, a surmise. Ċuʒaḃaṗ cáċ ḃo ḃaṗaṁail, 166, every one surmised.
[In modern Connacht, ʒo baṗaṁail means 'middling', like ʒo ṗeuṗúnca. Ʒo ḃe maṗ cá cu? Ʒo baṗaṁail.]

báṗṗ, 154, báṗṗ ḃaoine, excess of numbers.

baṗʒaṗnaiʒ, 128, lamenting. [*O'R.* *has* baṗcaṗnaċ.]

beaʒ. 36. Iṗ ʒeaṗṗ anoiṗ, beaʒ, ó ʒaḃ ṗé, it is almost no time since he went. beaʒ naċ, almost. Iṗ anoiṗ beaʒ-naċ ḃo ʒaḃ ṗé, it was only just now he went, 37, *n.* 9.

béal-ṗʒalan, 132, a booth, a shelter. ḃoc aʒuṗ beal-ṗʒalan.

beann, 36, 42, *perhaps* horn. Na ʒ-cúiʒ ceann na ʒcúiʒ mbeann aʒuṗ na ʒcúiʒ muinéall, of the five heads, the five horns, and the five necks. *I have met this description of a giant in a Kerry folk-tale.* Caċaiṗ na ḃcṗi mbeann, 176, the city of the three horns (or bens, hills?).

beann-ḃuaḋmuin and beann ḃuaḋmainn, 10, a horn for blowing.

beann-ḃuaḋḃaill, 128, *id.*

beaṗaċ, 32, sharp-pointed, prick-eared(?). Cluaṗ beaṗaċ, a pointed ear [*of a fox*]. Cilce beaṗaċa baṗṗa-ċluaṗaċa, 16. [*O'R. has* beaṗaċ, prattling, talkative.]

béiciḃ, 192, outcry, roar [*of a shield struck*].

beiṗḃiuʒaḃ, 16, boiling [*in Munster*].

beiṗiʒċe, 24, boiled. [*In Connacht* bṗuicce, cf. *the remark of the Mayo man when he first heard*

Munster Irish, "beiċ' na ṗacaiḃ aʒainn-ne baince niʒce bṗuicce 'ṗ icce nuaiṗ beiċ' Iluiṁneaċ aʒ ṗáḃ p-ṗ-ḋ-c-a-i-ḃ b-e-i-ṗ-i-ʒ-ċ-e!]

biaḃna, 6, *plur.* of biaḃ, food: *but* biaḃa, 40. [*Compare* ṗiaḃna, *plur. of* ṗiaḃ, p. 16.]

blaḃ, 128, = bloḃ, a fragment, piece.

bloiṗʒ-béiṁeanna, 42, resounding blows. bloiṗʒ, noise.

bṗoiċiniṗʒ, *also* bṗoċḃanuṗ, 10, *n.* 7, a place where badgers are.

buaḃ-buaḃmuin, *see* beann-buaḃ-ṁuin.

búiṗṗiḃ, 128, aʒ búiṗṗiḃ, bellowing.

buinne, *see* ṗo-buinne.

Caṗṗán (?), 34.

Céaḃna, 154, 156, *used as a noun under the form* an ʒcéaḃna, the same thing.

Cealltaṗ, 178; cealtaṗ, 108. Common in the phrase which often occurs of cealltaṗ ḃṗaoiḃcaċta, an enchanted covering, a spell of invisibility. Coḃaṗ atá ṗá ṁuiṗ aʒuṗ cealltaṗ ḃṗaoiʒeaċta uime.

Ceann, head; joy. Illo ċeann, Hail! Illo ċeann ṗá buṗ mbeiċ annṗin, 72, my joy that ʒe are there. I ʒceann, added to: ceaṗ i ʒceann ṗiuċḃa, 86. I ʒceann, to meet: ḃul i ʒceann Ríʒ na Soṗċa, 86. Ráiniʒ i ʒceann na ṗluaʒ, 90, he reached and met the hosts.

Ceiṗc, 54, troubling, questioning. Ná bíoḃ na ʒeaṗa ṗin ḃe ċeiṗc oṗṗaiḃ, let not those tabus trouble you.

Cliṗeaḃ colna, 134, a summersault: [*O'R. has* clioṗʒaḃ, start, bounce].

Coiḃṗuiḃ, 78, calm, settled. ḃa ṗé-ċiḋin coiḃṗuiḃ na cuanca.

Coiṁiʒċeaċ, 156, a stranger; *see* coṁaiʒċeaċ.

Coṁlinᵹe, 168. Aᵹ coṁlinᵹe ciúil, accompanying music (?).

Coipmoᵹall, 60, carbuncle.

Cóṁall, 10. Rinne mé mo cóṁall, I have executed my commission. Cóṁall, fulfilment.

Coṁaipcuip, 156. 'Na ċoinne aᵹup 'na ċoṁaipcuip, to meet and accost or approach him.

Coṁaiᵹteaċ, 138, strange, a stranger; see coiṁiᵹteaċ.

Cóṁᵹaḃailceap, 10, cuipim i ᵹcoṁ-ᵹaḃáilceap aᵹup i ḃpiaḃnuipe.

Cóṁᵹap, 44, approach, nearness, joining. I ᵹcóṁᵹap cinn aᵹup muiníl, at the joining of head and neck. A ᵹcóṁpac a ċinn aᵹup a ṁuinéil, 68, id. I ᵹcoṁᵹap 'Cipeann aᵹup Albann, 32, on the boundary of Ireland and Scotland.

Coṁᵹaipeaċ, 124, shouting (?).

Com-meapaċal, 48, confusion (?), as if meapḃal (?).

Cóṁpac, 68; see cóṁᵹap.

Coṁpann, in the expression, i ᵹcoṁ-pann (or ᵹcoḃpainn, 140) a pᵹéiṫe, in the hollow of his shield; see cuiḃpiḃ.

Coṁtpom, 94, a like weight or size. Coṁtpom ḃ'á inċeañ, its own size of his brain.

Coṁ-uainn, 98, alliteration in Irish verse.

Conaiᵹe, perhaps fortunes, from Conaċ, wealth. Aᵹ milleaḃ biacaċ líṁḃe um a móp-ċonaċ. MS. of Cat Cnuca.

Conaiᵹeaċ, 50, wealthy (?) [O'R. gives conaiḃ, soft, gentle, affable].

Conpaoiḃeaċ, 84, furious. Cat ceann-ápḃ conpaoiḃeaċ ḃo ċaḃaipc ḃóiḃ. "Ro ᵹaḃ conpa caca é," battle fury seized him. MS of Iollan Apm-ḃeapᵹ.

Cop copaiᵹ, 58, the prow (of a ship).

Cpannᵹaill, 162, a heap of wood (?).

Cpíoċnuiᵹ, 106, literally finish, used with cóṁaiple, to settle, to arrange.

Cpopaip cpó, 96, for copap cpó, a gory mass trampled down.

Cúb, 12, bend. Ċúb pé a ᵹlún.

Cuiḃpiḃ, 128, and cuiḃpeaċ, 188, and coiḃpeaċ, 154, used in the expression i ᵹcuiḃpiḃ a pᵹéiṫe, in the binding or hollow of his shield: see coṁpann. I find i ᵹcóṁ-pac a pᵹéiṫe, used in the same sense in a MS. of Iollan Apm-ḃeapᵹ, and i ᵹcpannóiᵹ is also used: see 94, n. 2.

Cuip ap, 154, 186, to oppress, affect, injure.

Cúipín, 44, cushion.

Ḃeacpaiᵹcaċc, 166, difficulty.

Ḃéan ap, 18, to make for. Aᵹ ḃéanaṁ ap an ceaċ, drawing towards the house. Ḃéanaiḃ oppa, 26, they make for or at them. Ḃo pinneap uippi, 26, I made at her. Ḃo pinn ap an loċ, 28, it made for the lake.

Ḃéancúp, 12. Ḃéancúp maiṫeapa, makings of goodness, i.e. peculiar excellence (?). [O'R. has ḃéan-cap, activity.]

Ḃípᵹiᵹce, 36, exterminated, emptied of. Cá an coḃap i nḃípᵹ, the well is without water (in Munster).

Ḃípᵹiuᵹaḃ, extermination.

Ḃiacpaċ, in the expression ᵹo ḃil ḃiacpaċ, lovingly and fondly. [O'R. has ḃiocpaċ, diligent, zealous.]

Ḃimbpiᵹ, 178. Ḃeun ḃimbpiᵹ ḃe, make nothing of it, despise it.

Ḃo. Ip é áḃḃap pá paiḃ pé ḃóiḃ, 72, the reason he "went for them" was.

Ḃoḃap-ċeó, 74, a water-fog. [I find in a MS. of Cat Cnuċa the phrase ḃoiᵹip-ċeó ḃluc-lcaċan ḃpaoiḃeaċca.]

Ꝺoilḃ, 14, *literally* gloomy, *but here apparently equivalent to* ꝺoiliᵹ, difficult. [*O'R. has* ꝺoipḃ, hard, peevish, difficult.]

Ꝺoilḃꞇe, 74, enchantment (?) ; *or the comparative of* ꝺoilḃ, gloomy.

Ꝺpeip, 116, *also written* ꝺpeap, ᵹpeip, *and sometimes* ᵹpeap, a while, a time, a spell [of work]. Ꝺéan ꝺpcip ḃ'á pnoiḃe, take a spell at whittling it. Ꝺpeap map-cuiᵹeaċꞇa, a spell of riding.

Ꝺpuiꝺ le, 28, approach. Ꝺpuiꝺ leip an ꞇeine, come near the fire. Ꝺpuiꝺ pé léi, he approached her.

Ꝺpuimneaċ, 86, ridgy (?). Liaᵹ ꝺpuimneaċ ꝺe ḃeapᵹ-óp. *In a MS. of* Caꞇ Ⅿuiᵹe Ⅿoċpuime *and elsewhere, I find the expression* pleaᵹ ꝺpuimneaċ. ḃoꞇ ꝺpuimneaċ, 186, a booth with a ridgy back (?).

Ꝺuaiḃpeaċ, 74, gloomy, dark. *Of a fog,* ceó ꝺuaiḃpeaċ, 74; *of a face,* ꝺuḃ-éaḃann ꝺuaiḃpeaċ, 102. I nᵹleanncaiḃ ꝺuaiḃpeaċa, *Love Songs of Connacht,* p. 78. *In a MS. of* Caꞇ Cnuċa *I find,* ᵹlacaꝺap calaꝺḃopꞇ aᵹ innḃeap ꝺuaiḃpeaċ Ꝺuiḃlinne.

Ꝺulꞇa, desirable to go.

'Caᵹpaṁail, 108, 122, strange. I ᵹcpuꞇ éaᵹpaṁail, in strange shape. Ꝑoḃal éaᵹpaṁail, 148, a remarkable tent, *also* beautiful. Níop ḃ' éaᵹpaṁla mná pan ꝺoṁan no iaꝺ ap ḟeaḃap a nꝺeilḃe, 108. Níop ḃ'éaᵹpaṁla bean pan ꝺoṁan 'ná í, 142, there was no woman in the world more beautiful than she.

'Eiḃip, 22, cloċa éiḃip, some sort of granite-like stones, called by the peasants in English, "fairy stones".

Ciꞇiḃe, 94, 118, creatures, living things; *see* ꝑeiꞇiḃe.

Coċaip-ḃláiꞇ, 164, flower-bordered (?).

Cóin, 168, *plur. of* éan, a bird.

Cólċa, 56, expertness.

Cólᵹaipeaċ, 8, knowing, knowledgeable.

Cólup, guiding, pointing out the way. Ꝺéan eólup ꝺam, show me the way. Ⅿúin an ꞇ-eólup ꝺam, 18, teach me the way. Ꞃinneaꝺap eólup na popaoipe ꝺó, 122, they showed him the way to the forest.

Ꝑá, 16. Ꝑá map ip ꞇupa an máiᵹipꞇip, since you are the master.

Ꝑaoiḃeaċ, 36. Aᵹ ᵹul ᵹo paoiḃeaċ, weeping bitterly. [*Common in Munster poems.*]

Ꝑé, 32, *dialectic form of* paoi, under him.

Ꝑéaċaim, 190, I try.

Ꝑeamuinneaċ, 122, clustering (of hair) ; *literally* seaweed-like.

Ꝑeapᵹaiᵹ, 12, to become angry.

Ꝑéiḋm, 178, service, power. Ꝑéiḋm peap an ꝺoṁain ꝺo ḟeaċnaꝺ.

Ꝑeip, 38. An ꝑeip láiṁe na leapꞇan (?).

Ꝑéiꞇeaṁail, sinewy.

Ꝑiaꝺaċ, 10, *n.*, 6, a resort of deer.

Ꝑiaꝺᵹuiḃeaċꞇ, 10, deer-hunting.

Ꝑiaꝺ maol, 64, some sort of hornless deer (?).

Ꝑiannuiᵹeaċꞇ, 40, story-telling about the Fenians.

Ꝑiꝺ *or* pìꝺe, 4, = iꝺ, a chain, ring. [iꝺ means at present the extreme ring or link in the chain].

Ꝑinneaċap, 4, tribe-ship, nationhood. [*O'R. has* pineaċap, inheritance].

Ꝑinniḃeaᵹ, 6. Ꝺo pinniḃeaᵹ ap na bopꝺaiḃ, there was whitely-laiddown on the tables (?).

Ꝑinneaṁail, 8, *perhaps the same as* pineálꞇa, 'fine,' *or cognate with* pionn, white.

Ríonnabean, 38, *a Munsterism for* ríonn-bean, fair woman. ' Cn ḟinnebean ṗabaċṗoḃ áluinn ó5.' *Song by David Fitzgerald.*

Piteiḃe, 66, *or* peitiḃe, *also* peitiḃe *and* peiteaḃ = eitiḃe *or* ataiḃe, a living thing, a creature, [*often* an uncanny thing. *Keating has* ataiḃe oiḃċe, things, or spirits, of the night].

Piúᵹ, 20, *m.* and *f., see* 21, *n.* ⁹, the ferule of a stick ; *perhaps cognate with* ioḃ *or* iḃ ; *see* ṗiḃ.

Poċaiṗ-ḃláiṫ, 62, *perhaps for* eoċaiṗ-ḃláiṫ, flower-bordered.

Poiḃṗeaċ, 42, of sods, soddy (?).

Po-ḃealᵹ, 66, 170, a spikelet.

Poiṗ, 20, = oiṗ, fit, suit.

Poiṗniaṫa, 90, furious, powerful ; *also in a MS. of* Caṫ Ṁuiᵹe Ṁoċṗuime, *and elsewhere.* Comṗaṫ ṗéiᵹ ṗuilṫeaċ ṗoṗḃaṗṫa ṗoiṗniaṫa.

Poiṗḃineaċ, 34. ḃṗiaṫṗa ṗoiṗḃineaċa ṗáiᵹeaṁla. This is a common expression, but the exact sense is doubtful. [*O'R. has* ṗoiṗḃineaċ, serious, *and* ṗoiṗṫeanaċ, arranged in good order.]

Polċaiᵹ, 140, cover (?). Polaiᵹ, conceal.

Polmuiᵹ, 150, *perhaps the same as* polṁaiᵹ *or* polaṁaiᵹ, to empty. *Here it appears to mean* to vacate (a chair). Peaṗ pollṁuiᵹte, 164, an emptier.

Pollṗaċṫ, 90, gore. Puil aᵹuṗ pollṗaċṫ.

Polṫanuṗ, 182, enmity. Sᵹeul méaḃaiᵹṫe polṫanaiṗ | Níoṗ ċṗeiḃṫe aṗ a ċéile. *MS. Book of the O'Byrnes : also* palṫanuṗ.

Poṗ-ṗáilṫeaċ, 66, welcome-giving.

Poṗ-óṗḃa, 68, 98, 170, all-golden.

Poṗᵹla, 186, a great number. Ṫá ṗoṗᵹla ṗluaiᵹ an ḃoṁain aṗ ṫí ḃo ḃáṗuiᵹṫe : *MS. of the*

bṗuiᵹean Caoṗṫann. [I have heard the word ṗoṗaᵹan used in this sense.]

Poṗṗᵹaoilṫe, 52, diffusive. Poṗṗᵹaoilṫe ṗe innṗin.

Poṗaiᵹiṗ, 6, = ṗoṗaoiṗ, forest.

Poṗṗuiṗ, 10, = ṗoṗaoiṗ, forest.

Poṗḃaṗṫa, 90, furious ; *see* ṗoiṗniaṫa.

Poṗṫuaṫa, 158, regions (?). [O'Donovan gives, in his supplement, "ṗoṗṫuaṫa, strange tribes in a territory"; but here it seems to mean the territory itself, not 'outskirts' as I have translated it].

Poṗaḃ, 148, a resting. Rinneaḃ ṗoṗaḃ óó, *apparently*, preparations were made for his stay.

Pṗiṫealaiṅ, 24, *usually* ṗṗiṫeólaḃ, ministering.

Pṗaoċ-ċuṫaċ, 42, mad with fury.

Pṗiṫiḃ *or* ṗṗíoṫaiḃ, *in the phrase* I ḃṗṗiṫiḃ na ṗiṗmamenṫe, 74, 76, 192, etc., in the expanse (?) of the firmament.

Pṗiṫinᵹ, *in the phrase* I ḃṗṗiṫinᵹ na conaiṗe céaḃna, back over the same road.

Ᵹaḃálṫa, 180, fermented.

Ᵹaḃála, 38, *also* ᵹaḃálṫaċ, fermented. Mistranslated ' distilled ' in text, as though from ᵹaḃáil, to receive, as if ' receiving the liquor as it came from the still.' But the poteen-makers of Connacht call their ' barm ' that ferments their 'pot-ale', ᵹó-áil. Now, ᵹaḃail, ' to sing ', ' to go ', ' to take ', is pronounced the same way. Hence, ᵹaḃála, ᵹaḃalṫaċ, ᵹaḃalṫa, and ᵹaḃailṫeaċ, must mean ' fermented with barm.'

Ᵹaḃáilṫeaċ, 148, *see last word.*

Ᵹaḃáil, 166, to take. Ḃo ᵹaḃáil na caṫṗaċ, to take the city.

Ʒabáil, 42. Aʒ cur ʒabáil na mbuillıдeaд аn Ⅲurċaд *seems to mean* getting the better of Murough in blows (?).

Ʒablánaċ, 110 (?).

Ʒaıreaċtaċ, 52, laughing. Rorʒ ʒorm ʒaıreaċtaċ.

Ʒap-ḟaıllrıʒ, 10, *see* ʒnaıдlrı.

Ʒéan, дo ḟean, I will do.

Ʒlaıc, 104. 1 nʒlaıc cataoıreaċ, in the seat of a chair (?).

Ʒloṁan ʒáıpe, 66, a yell of a laugh (?). ʒloṁan *also means* a muzzle for young calves. [*O'R.*]

Ʒnáınce, 104, = ʒnánna, ugly.

Ʒnaıдlrı, 6 (*also* ʒarḟaıllrıʒ), rıaд-ʒuıдeaċta, thickets for deer-hunting (?).

Ʒrear, 36, a spell of time or of work; *see* дrear *and* дreır.

Ʒrearaċt, 158. Ʒrearaċt na mbolʒ, the urging or puffing of the bellows.

Ʒroд-neıṁneaċ, 132, swift and venomous (of winds).

Ʒualeıne, *also* ʒualaıne, 102, a shoulder-burden.

Iarʒa, 112, = éarʒa, the moon.

Im, *an intensitive prefix, not noted in O'Donovan's Grammar, nor in O'Reilly's Dictionary*. Im-ċıan, 82, very far; ım-éarʒaıд, 54, very quick; ım-reaṁap, 66, very thick; ım-rıʒın, 72, very tough.

Imbeaʒaıl, 154, defence (in fighting), *misspelt in* le reaдar na h-ıom-дeaʒla, 154.

Imrıʒeaдar, 42, *3rd pers. plur., past tense of* ımır, play, practise.

Iomдeaʒla, 154, *see* ımbeaʒaıl.

Ionall, 38, appearance, guise; *properly* ınneall.

Ionluaıдte, 64, worth mentioning.

Iornaıд, 52, *apparently* 'an eagle' (?).

Iortaıṁaıl, 164, inhabited, *or* full of houses (?).

Iorдaıʒte, 50, housed, entertained (?).

'Irleán, 42, a hollow, a low place.

Láṁ, *used with* taдaır *and* ʒaд. Tuʒaдan láṁ ar ımteaċt, 162.

Ḟaдaдan l. a. ı., 164, they took in hand their departure.

Leaċ-ıomapca, 22, *literally*, half too much, appears to mean 'unfair measure.'

Leıʒ (*used with the acc. of the pers. pron.*), to rush. Дo leıʒ na raon ро-реaċa é, 64, he went with a rushing race. Дo leıʒeaдan na ruaċar ро-реaċa ıaд, 80. Дo leıʒeaдan na дeıċ ʒċéaд rın ıaд д'ıonnraıдe an aonaıʒ, 82.

Léırıʒ, 16, to arrange in deßnite order. Léırıʒ is a Munster form.

Líon, 82, number. Cá líon? how many?

Loınncaд, 188. Дo loınneaд raoı, he flamed up; *also* дo lonдaıʒeaд uıme, *see* p. 189, *n.* 7. [*O'R. has* lonaıд, he coloured, grew red.]

Loırʒneaċ, 152, burningly, *i.e.* fiercely. Ʒo lonn loırʒneaċ.

Lúʒa, 156. Реar ba lúʒa orra 'ná é, a person they hated, disliked, more than he. [I have, I think, heard this idiom in Galway.]

Luıne, 60, amusement.

Ⅲaıte, 134, kindness. An maıte ре neaċ eıle, for the sake of another. An maıte leır féın дo ʒnıд an cat crónán, it's to please itself the cat purs (*a common proverb*).

Ⅲaıдın le, 6, *apparently a Munster form of* maılle le, along with. [*In Connacht* maıдın le *is the modern equivalent of* ıomtura *or* дála, as to, with regard to.]

Ⅲám, 34, a handful.

Ⅲanaoır muırne, 124, a kind of spear. [*O'R. gives* muıreann, *gen.* muırne, a dart.]

206   GLOSSARY.

Maċa, 158, chiefs, *more commonly* maiċe.

Maplaċaċ, 31, abusive (?).

Meabnac, 40, *used with* ʀᵹcinne, *apparently* a dagger.

Meanaᵹánca, 32, *Munster for* meanᵹánca, brisk, lively.

Meanᵹ, 42, neck (?), *or for* monᵹ, hair.

Meaḃap-ᵹlónaċ, 38, cheerful-voiced.

Méin, 36, buċ méin liom, I would like to.

"Caob le ʀeanaiḃ úpcpoiḃeaċ buċ méin liom ʀcaḃ le dúil ᵹpinn."

Song of the Crúisgín lán.

Meinᵹ = meanᵹ, treachery.

Meiʀᵹeaṁail, 180, intoxicating.

Mí-líoċaċ, 18, of bad complexion, wan, ill-visaged.

Miocaipe, 52, = mioċaip, courteous, loving.

Min-ṁeaḃpaḃ, 50, = min-ṁeaḃpuᵹaḃ, closely studying.

Mion-oipneaċ, small fragments.

Moċa, 142, earliness, early hour. [*More properly* moiċe, *I should think.*]

Monᵹ-ṗúileaċ, 62, bright-eyed (?). [*This word also occurs in a MS. of* Caċ Cnuċa, "inᵹion monᵹṗúileaċ."]

Mopc, 112, *used with* ceineaḃ, a great fire. *See* cop.

Muipʀeaḃ, 184, would kill.

Muipne ; *see* manaoip.

Neiṁ-ṁeipḃce, 172, strongly, unflinchingly.

Niaṁannaiḃ, 116, *dat. plur.* of niaṁ, brightnesses, shimmerings.

Nomenc, 20, moment.

Nualainn, 132, wailing.

Oiᵹneaċa, 64, icy.

Oiᵹneaċca, 136, for oiᵹneaċa, iced, frozen.

Oipiʀcaiṁ, 64, halt, stay.

Oiʀ = ʀoiʀ, 22, *n.* ¹, to fit.

Ollaiṁnaiᵹ, 24, prepare, make ready.

Opḃán, a fragment, piece. [Cf. the Shaksperian *ort*, a fragment: "Tho fractions of her faith, orts of her love."—*Troilus and Cressida.*]

'Oploipᵹce, 44, golden, gilt.

Papcuinᵹ, 52, some red or crimson plant (?) ; a very common word in these stories, but not identified.

Plaicín ᵹlúine, 12, the knee-cap.

Ppap, 136, quick, sudden. [*O'R. has* ppaḃ.]

Ppoiṁinpil, 8, Provincial, head of an order.

Ppoinn-ceaċ, 22, refectory. [Cf. O'Coilleáin's poem on Timoleague Abbey, acá ḃo ṗpoinn-ceaċ ᵹan biaḃ 'ʀ ḃo ṗuan-liop ᵹan leabaiḃ ḃláiċ.]

Popc, 30. Do cuᵹ ap popc é, he brought it ashore.

Raiᵹpeaṁail *or* péiᵹpeaṁail, 6, abundant. [A common word, I believe, in Munster.]

Rannᵹaċ, 32, bounding, swinging. Siúḃal pannᵹaċ, a bounding or swinging gait.

Raċa, *probably for* peaċa ; *gen. of* piċ, a run.

Reic, 88, tell. Do peic aiċipiᵹ.

Réiḃ, 40, *used of ale*, ready to drink (?).

Réiḃ-ceaᵹlaċ, 10, standing household (?). [Réiḃ, 'ready,' seems to imply a household always ready for service. I have heard the word in a Kerry folk-tale.]

Réiᵹpeaṁail, 8, *see* paiᵹpeaṁail.

Réimeaṁail, 28. ᵹo péimeaṁail, with pride, power.

Riaᵹapcálca, 20, *appears to mean* arranged ; see *n.* [The affix álca appears to indicate a foreign word.]

Rinn, 180. Do ċuin cloċ 'na rinn peaċa (?).

Ro-ḃuinne, 130, a great stream or throng.

Roċnuaill, *see p.* 87, *n.* 4.

Ruċaḃ, 150. Ruċaḃ na ḟeinġe, a flush of anger. [*O'R. has* ruiċean, red-hot, blazing.]

Ruiċne, 132, flame. Ruiċne ruaḃġaoiċe, a rush of red [*i.e.* blighting] wind. [*O'R. has* ruiċneaḃ, flame].

Ruċaġ, 28, a rush, the run of a person who takes a leap.

Saḟraiġ, 20, 21, *n.* 7, = raṁaċ, *more properly* ráṁċaċ, *pronounced* ráraċ, a staff or big stick like the handle of a spade.

Saṁailce, 170, 180, = raṁail, like.

Seallaḃ, 50, a glance, a sight, = Siolla, *id.* 64.

Seannaṁail, 6, *perhaps for* raineaṁail, particular, exquisite.

Seiḃce, 192, exhausted, blown.

Sġabal, 10, a shoulder-piece [*in modern language* a scapular.]

Sġéal, a story, *used idiomatically for* niḃ, a thing, 108; *for* ḃuine, a person, 150.

Sġeinn, 26, fly-off, jump.

Sġioḃ, 36, snatch or sweep away.

Sġoċaċ, 32, bushy-haired.

Síl, 50, = raoil, think. [The northern pronunciation and that of Connacht is *sheel*, not *seel*, hence this verb has of late been often spelt ríl.]

Sileaḃ, 4. Ḟlearġ aġ rileaḃ *aliter* rilleaḃ an a ḟolc.

Sinġala, 130, roaring, noise [English *sing*?].

Sioċealca, 170, ir ríoċealca briaċra be ḃaoiniḃ, best spoken of men? [*O'R. has* rioċoilce, purified.]

Sioċġaoiċe, 18, fairy. Síoġaiḃe, *id.*

Siċeaṁail. Céol riċeaṁail, fairy-like music. [*O'R. has* riċeaṁail, peaceable, durable.]

Siċeal, *or* rioċal, 186, *n.* 6, a bowl.

Sloinn, 8, to give a surname to. Sloinn ḃo ċáirḃear ḃúiṁ, 84, trace back, explain your friendship for us. Sloiṁ an ḟear rin ḃúinn, 150, name that man for us.

Sluim, 172. Sluim ġalair, a fit of sickness.

Snaoiḃ, 116, whittle, chip.

Snoiḃe, 180, to whittle, *see last word,* to meander, as water, 130. [*O'R. has* rniġim, I creep, crawl, glide.]

Socaraċċ, 26, rest, easy-times. Annrin ġeoḃair coḃlaḃ rocaraċċ a'r ruaiṁnear. *O'Carolan's Ode to Whiskey.*

So-ḟuḃlaċ, 4, easily-travelled. [*Compare* ro-ḟaicreanaċ *and* ro-ċuiġreanaċ *for* roi-ḟeicce *and* ro-ċuiġce.]

Soilcaċ, 64, of 'sallow' or 'sally' wood.

Soincaṁail, *of drink,* pleasant, 190; *of people,* fortunate, happy, 196; *of satin,* handsome, shining, 168.

Sonnaċriċ, 18, a great shaking. [Cf. runn-ċaċair, a strong city; ronn-ṁarcaċ, a courier; runnġaoċ, a strong wind; *probably it is a Munsterism for* ronn-ċriċ. *See* rionna-ḃean.]

Sprealaire, 26, a good-for-nothing. An rrrealaire coire rin, that wretched pot.

Sprioránċaċċ, 20, a petty trifle.

Suanraḃaċ, 180, breathing, moving. [*It seems a combination of* uanraċċ, breathing; *and* ruan, slumber. Srannraċ, *id.*]

Súp, 94, search, range: aġ rup an ċaċa, ranging the battle (?).

C', 170, = ḃo, thy. An ġráḃ c' oiniġ.

Caıpıre, 177, loyalty. Iſ caıpıre
liom, I think it an act of friendship (?).

Ceanᵹṁáıl, 136, meeting, in the sense
of fighting. Luᴄᴄ ᴄᵲoba no
ᴄeanᵹṁála.

Ceanᵹṁaᵫ, ᵫa ᵫᴄeanᵹṁaᵫ, if there
should meet. Ceaᵹṁóᴄaᵫ, 168,
id.

Ceanᵫáıl, 160, a fire, burning; see
ᴄıneal.

Cıaᵹaᵲ, 88, perhaps the same as
ᴄéaᵹaᵲ, covering, shelter.

Cıbeᵲᵲın, 134, springing-up, welling.
Cıbıᵲ anſoᵲ a ᴄobaıᵲ, the Irish
Bible.

Cıneal, 176. Cınneál, 174, a fire;
see ᴄeanᵫáıl.

Cıneaṁlaᴄᴄ, 172, fieriness.

Cıonnᴄaıᵲe, 56, a requisite. Cᵲı
ᴄıonnᴄaıᵲe loınᵹe. [For other
forms see p. 56, n. ¹].

Coll, 32, the hind-quarters (?). Cá
ſıᴄe ſᵲeabán aᵲ a ᴄoll, aᵹuᵲ
ſıᴄe poll aᵲ a ᴄoᵲᵲ, old poem,
MS. A.D. 1763. It also means
head, but evidently not here; see
ᴄulaᵲ.

Coᵲ, also ᴄoᵲo, sometimes also moᵲo,
used with ᴄeıneaᵫ, 102, a large
fire.

Coᵲaᵫ, 20. Ᵹan ᴄoᵲaᵫ ᵹan ᴄuaᵲ-
aᵲᵹᵫáıl, without tale or tidings.
[O'R. gives ᴄóᵲaᵫ, an answer].

Cᵲeanna, 40, plur. of ᴄᵲıan, a third
part.

Cuıl, v., 84, to flood, pour like a flood.
Do ᴄuıl an ᴄonn ᵹᵲáᵫ ſo mo
ᴄᵲoıᵫe.

Cuıᵲnᵲeaᴄ, 156, they abated, ceased.
Cáᵲnaım, I lower.

Culaᵲ, 10, a head-piece, from ᴄul,
face, head; cf. ᴄul le ᴄul = vis-
à-vis.

Culᴄánᴄa, ᴄalᴄánᴄa, 18. Conveying
the idea of vigorous, vehement.
[In these cases of almost identical
adjectival repetition, the first vowel
of the first adj. is short o or u,
and that of the second a, as
boᴄóıbeaᴄ baᴄoıbeaᴄ, ſul-
ſaᵲᵲnaıᵹ aᵹuᵲ ſalſaᵲᵲnaıᵹ,
etc.]

Uᵲaᵫ, 6, also ıoᵲᵲaᵫ, apparel. O.Ir.,
eᵲᵲaᵫ.

Uᵲluıᵹeaᴄᴄ, 92, smiting, conflict.
[oᵲᵫ uᵲluıᵹe, a smiting sledge-
hammer, occurs in my MS. of
bᵲuıᵹean beaᵹ no h-Alṁu-
ınne.]

Uᵲ-Luaᴄᵲaᵫ, 112, strewing a floor
with fresh rushes.

Uᵲṁaıᵲneaᴄ, 54, 72, 148, apparently,
boldly, energetically.

Uᵲᵲaᵫnoᵲ, 6, also spelt, oᵲᵲóᵲ,
honour, reputation. [Father
O'Leary of Castlelyons tells me it
means the kind honour at present
usually called ᴄᵲeıbeaṁaınᴄ, or
influence.]

Uᵲᴄóᵹᵫáıl, 18, 24, 29, apparently,
a vigorous hoist or lift.

cRíocҺ.

IRISH TEXTS SOCIETY.

President:

DOUGLAS HYDE, LL.D., M.R.I.A.

Vice-Presidents:

THE RIGHT HON. LORD CASTLETOWN.
REV. MAXWELL CLOSE, M.A., F.G.S., M.R.I.A.
HIS EMINENCE CARDINAL GIBBONS.
JOHN KELLS INGRAM, LL.D., S.F.T.C.D.
HIS EMINENCE CARDINAL MORAN.
THE RIGHT HON. THE O'CONOR DON, D.L.
THE MOST REV. DR. O'DONNELL, Bishop of Raphoe.
THE REV. THOMAS J. SHAHAN, D.D.

Executive Committee:

Chairman—PROFESSOR F. YORK POWELL.
Vice-Chairman—GODDARD ORPEN.

F. A. FAHY.	FIONAN MACCOLLUM.
T. J. FLANNERY (T. Ó FLANNGHAILE).	DANIEL MESCAL.
GEORGE A. GREENE, M.A.	ALFRED NUTT.
JOHN P. HENRY, M.D.	J. TODHUNTER, M.D.

Hon. Gen. Sec.—ELEANOR HULL.
Hon. Sec. for Ireland—NORMA BORTHWICK.
Hon. Treas.—J. G. O'KEEFFE.

Consultative Committee:

PROFESSOR ANWYL.	PROFESSOR MACKINNON.
OSBORN BERGIN.	JOHN MACNEILL, B.A.
DAVID COMYN.	KUNO MEYER, PH.D.
T. J. FLANNERY.	REV. EUGENE O'GROWNEY, M.R.I.A.
HENRI GAIDOZ.	REV. PETER O'LEARY, P.P.
REV. PROF. RICHARD HENEBRY.	DR. HOLGER PEDERSEN.
REV. PROF. MICHAEL P. HICKEY,	PROFESSOR RHYS.
M.R.I.A., F.R.S.A.I.	PROF. DR. RUDOLPH THURNEYSEN.
DOUGLAS HYDE, LL.D., M.R.I.A.	PROFESSOR DR. H. ZIMMER.
P. W. JOYCE, LL.D., M.R.I.A.	

IRISH TEXTS SOCIETY.

THE IRISH TEXTS SOCIETY, established for the purpose of publishing texts in the Irish language, accompanied by such introductions, English translations, glossaries, and notes as might be deemed desirable, held its Inaugural Meeting on April 26th, 1898.

The idea of establishing such a Society had long been contemplated by the Irish Literary Society in London, and it is to their initiative that the scheme owes its origin. So far back as 1896, a Provisional Sub-Committee was appointed by their Committee to consider the feasibility of establishing such a Society, and a circular was sent out by Mr. T. J. Flannery (Tomás ó Flannghaile), Chairman, asking for support. The response not being considered sufficiently favourable, the matter was allowed to drop until May, 1897, when the Provisional Committee was re-formed, and a fresh circular, drawn up by them, was widely distributed both in these islands and in America. The Provisional Committee was composed of the following Members :—David Comyn, Dr. A. Colles, Frank A. Fahy, T. J. Flannery, George A. Greene, M.A., Douglas Hyde, LL.D., P. W. Joyce, LL.D., J. M'Neill, Daniel Mescal, J. G. O'Keeffe, Goddard Orpen (Chairman), Michael O'Sullivan, George Sigerson, M.D. Miss N. Borthwick and Miss Eleanor Hull acted as Hon. Secs. (*interim*), and Mr. R. A. S. Macalister as Hon. Treas. (*interim*).

At the Inaugural Meeting held in the Rooms of the Irish Literary Society in April, 1898, the Chairman was able to state that 370 applications had been received for Membership, and that over £50 had been contributed to the Editorial Fund. The Provisional Committee was then dissolved, and Officers and Committee were elected by ballot.

It is intended that the work of the Society shall be chiefly directed to the publication of texts in modern Irish. Besides the literary importance of such texts, it is hoped that they will meet the increasing need of students of the modern tongue for suitable reading-books, and will enable learners to form an Irish style upon sound literary models. While occupying themselves chiefly with the production of modern texts, the Committee, however, by no means overlook the importance of the more ancient literature; and it is proposed, when funds permit, to publish occasional extra volumes, containing earlier texts of importance. The first volume of this "Additional Mediæval Series" will be published almost immediately, and will contain the Feast of Bricriu (*Fled Bricrend*), edited, with Translation and Notes, by George Henderson, M.A., PH.D.

The Annual Subscription has been fixed at 7s. 6d., payable on January 1st of each year, on payment of which Members will be entitled to receive the Annual Volume of the Society, and any additional volumes which they may issue from time to time.

The Committee make a strong appeal to all interested in the preservation and publication of Irish Manuscripts to contribute to the funds of the Society, and especially to the Editorial Fund, which has been established for the remuneration of Editors for their arduous work.

THE ANNUAL GENERAL MEETING of the Society was held on April 26th, 1899, in the Rooms of the Irish Literary Society, 8, Adelphi Terrace, Strand, London, W.C.

On the proposal of Dr. Henry, seconded by Mr. Goddard Orpen, Mr. R. Barry O'Brien took the chair.

The following Report was read by the Honorary Secretary :—

REPORT.

It is with regret that the Committee meet their Members on this the first Annual Meeting of the Irish Texts Society without having been able to carry out their promise to produce their first volume at the date at which it was hoped that it would have been ready, namely, in March of the present year. Owing to unexpected pressure of other work, Dr. Douglas Hyde has not been able to push the volume through the press so rapidly as he had anticipated. The work is, however, well advanced, and the Committee hope to place it at an early date in the hands of their Subscribers. The volume will contain Text and Translation of two romantic tales of the 16th and 17th centuries, entitled ᵹiolla an Ⅎiuᵹa (Lad of the Ferule), and Eaċṫṗa Cloinne Ríᵹ na h-Íopuaiḃo (Adventures of the Sons of the King of Norway), with Glossaries and brief Introduction.

The Committee are glad to report that the additional volume promised this year to their Subscribers is also passing through the press, the whole of the Text and Translation being now in the printers' hands. This extra volume, which it is hoped will form the first of a series of volumes containing older texts, to be published occasionally as funds permit, will contain a revision of Dr. E. Windisch's text of the *Fled Bricrend* (Feast of Bricriu), accompanied by Translation, Glossary, and Notes. The editor is Dr. George Henderson, of Edinburgh. It is hoped that this occasional series of more ancient texts will attract the interest of scholars of the older tongue, while the ordinary volumes of the Society will, it is anticipated, prove acceptable to students of modern Irish.

Tomás ó Flannghaile reports that he is engaged upon the work of editing, with translation, beaċa Choluim-ċille, or Life of Saint Colum-kille, and that the first half of the work, to include some 150 pages of Irish text with accompanying translation, will be ready in October. This work will be edited from the autograph ꝳꞅ. in the Bodleian Library, Oxford, and will now be given to the public for the first time. The book was compiled by Maghnus ó Domhnaill (Manus O'Donnell), brother of the reigning prince of Tír-chonaill (Tyrconnell), in the early part of the 16th century.

Mr. David Comyn reports that the first volume of his complete edition of Ⅎoṛuṛ Ⅎeaṛa aṛ Eiṛinn, or History of Ireland, by Geoffrey Keating, is in active preparation, the preliminary work of investigation and comparison of ꝳꞅꞅ. being well advanced. He hopes, if so desired by the Committee, to have the work ready to go to press before the close of the year.

The Committee have received an offer of a collection of hitherto unpublished Munster Poetry, carefully chosen from manuscripts of the last two hundred years, to be accompanied by suitable translations and glossary.

They have also had an offer of a volume containing the earliest, or Book of Leinster, text of the "Fate of the Children of Uisneach," with translation and notes on the development of the story, from the time of the earliest versions to the late folk-lore forms. These offers are under the consideration of the Committee. If accepted, this latter work would form one of the "Additional Mediæval Series" of texts.

The Committee, in December of last year, appointed a special Sub-Committee to consider the possibility of drawing up a cheap, handy, pocket dictionary of Irish-English, English-Irish words for the use of students of the modern tongue. Under the active superintendence of Mr. G. A. Greene, M.A., and chiefly through his personal exertions, this work has made some progress. After careful and lengthened consideration, the Sub-Committee decided to adopt the method of compiling the existing glossaries of modern Irish words, in order to form a foundation upon which to add words gathered from other sources. Several workers at a distance are assisting the undertaking by drawing up alphabetical lists of words in common use not to be found in the existing glossaries. These words will be added to the lists already compiled.

Rev. P. O'Leary and Mr. David Comyn have kindly offered assistance in the final revision and editing of the work.

The Society now numbers 462 Members.

The Treasurer presented a Financial Statement showing the gene ral position of the Society at the date of the General Meeting.

Receipts.				Expenditure.			
	£	s.	d.		£	s.	d.
To Subscriptions, ...	... 115	10	3	By Postage and Stationery, ...	26	16	6
„ Donations,	... 94	14	9	„ Photographing 'Life of Saint Columkille' in Bodleian Library, Oxford, ...	15	0	0
				„ Remuneration to Editors, ...	15	0	0
				„ Refund of Subscription and Donation, ...	2	3	6
				„ Balance in hand, ... 151	5	0	
Total, ...	£210	5	0	Total,	£210	5	0

On the motion of Mr. G. A. Greene, seconded by Mr. Goddard Orpen, supported by Mr. Monro, the Report and Financial Statement were adopted.

On the motion of Mr. Nutt, seconded by Mr. Greene, Dr. Douglas Hyde was re-elected President of the Society.

On the motion of Mr. Orpen, seconded by the Rev. M. Moloney, the Hon. Secretaries, Miss Hull and Miss Borthwick, were re-elected.

On the motion of Mr. Greene, seconded by Dr. Henry, Mr. J. G. O'Keeffe was re-elected Hon. Treasurer to the Society.

According to Rule 6, three Members of the Executive Committee retire annually by rotation, or, in case of equality, by lot. The following Members retired in accordance with this Rule :—Professor York Powell (*Chairman*), Mr. F. A. Fahy, and Mr. M. O'Sullivan. Mr. O'Sullivan has since resigned his seat owing to absence from London ; but Professor York Powell and Mr. F. A. Fahy were re-elected at the General Meeting. Mr. F. MacCollum and Dr. Todhunter were elected to fill the vacancies caused by the resignations of Captain De La Hoyde and Mr. M. O'Sullivan.

GENERAL RULES.

OBJECTS.

1. The Society is instituted for the purpose of promoting the publication of Texts in the Irish Language, accompanied by such Introductions, English Translations, Glossaries, and Notes, as may be deemed desirable.

CONSTITUTION.

2. The Society shall consist of a President, Vice-Presidents, a Consultative Committee, an Executive Committee, and Ordinary Members.

OFFICERS.

3. The Officers of the Society shall be the President, the Honorary Secretaries, and the Honorary Treasurer.

EXECUTIVE COMMITTEE.

4. The entire management of the Society shall be entrusted to the Executive Committee, consisting of the Officers of the Society and not more than ten other Members.

5. All property of the Society shall be vested in the Executive Committee, and shall be disposed of as they shall direct by a two-thirds' majority.

6. Three Members of the Executive Committee shall retire each year by rotation at the Annual General Meeting, but shall be eligible for re-election, the Members to retire being selected according to seniority of election, or, in case of equality, by lot. The Committee shall have power to co-opt Members to fill up · sual vacancies occurring throughout the year.

CONSULTATIVE COMMITTEE.

7. The Consultative Committee, or individual Members thereof, shall give advice, when consulted by the Executive Committee, on questions relating to the Publications of the Society, but shall not be responsible for the management of the business of the Society.

MEMBERS.

8. Members may be elected either at the Annual General Meeting, or, from time to time, by the Executive Committee.

SUBSCRIPTION.

9. The Subscription for each Member of the Society shall be 7/6 per annum, entitling the Member to one copy (post free) of the volume or volumes published by the Society for the year, and giving him the right to vote on all questions submitted to the General Meetings of the Society.

10. Subscriptions shall be payable in advance on the 1st January in each year.

11. Members whose Subscriptions for the year have not been paid are not entitled to any volume published by the Society for that year, and any Member whose Subscription for the current year remains unpaid, and who receives and *retains* any publication for the year, shall be held liable for the payment of the full published price of such publication.

12. The Publications of the Society shall not be sold to persons other than Members, except at an advanced price.

13. Members whose Subscriptions for the current year have been paid shall alone have the the right of voting at the General Meetings of the Society.

14. Members wishing to resign must give notice in writing to one of the Honorary Secretaries, before the end of the year, of their intention to do so, otherwise they shall be liable for their Subscriptions for the ensuing year.

EDITORIAL FUND.

15. A fund shall be opened for the remuneration of Editors for their work in preparing Texts for publication. All subscriptions and donations to this fund shall be purely voluntary, and shall not be applicable to other purposes of the Society.

ANNUAL GENERAL MEETING.

16. A General Meeting shall be held each year in the month of April, or as soon afterwards as the Executive Committee shall determine, when the Committee shall submit their Report and the Accounts of the Society for the preceding year, and when the seats to be vacated on the Committee shall be filled up, and the ordinary business of a General Meeting shall be transacted.

AUDIT.

17. The Accounts of the Society shall be audited each year by auditors appointed at the preceding General Meeting.

CHANGES IN THESE RULES.

18. With the notice summoning the General Meeting, the Executive Committee shall give notice of any change proposed by them in these Rules. Ordinary Members proposing any change in the Rules must give notice thereof in writing to one of the Honorary Secretaries seven clear days before the date of the Annual General Meeting.

LIST OF MEMBERS.

[*An asterisk before the name denotes that the Member has contributed to the Initial
Expenses of the Society, or to the Editorial Fund.*]
[*A + denotes that the Member is deceased.*]

Abercrombie, Hon. John.
Agnew, A. L., F.S.A. (Scot.).
Ahern, James L.
Aherne, Miss M.
*Allingham, Hugh, M.R.I.A.
*Anderson, John Norrie, J.P., Provost of
  Stornoway.
Anwyl, Prof. E., M.A.

Baillies' Institution Free Library, Glas-
  gow.
Banks, John.
Barrett, S. J.
Barry, Thomas.
Beck, P.
Belfast Library and Society for Promot-
  ing Knowledge.
Bergin, Osborn J.
Berry, Captain R. G.
Berryhill, R. W.
Bigger, F. J., M.R.I.A.
Blair, Rev. Dr. Robert.
*Bolton, Miss Anna.
Borthwick, Miss N.
Boston Public Library, U.S.A.
*Boswell, C. S.
*Boyd, J. St. Clair, M D.
*Boyle, William.
Boyle, Rev. Thomas, C.C.
Brannick, L. Theobald.
*Brenan, James.
Brett, Charles H.
*Broderick, Hon. Albinia.
Brooke, Rev. Stopford A.
*Brophy, Michael M.
*Brower, John L.
*Browne, Rev. R. L., Ord. Min.
Brunskill, Rev. K. C.
Buchanan, Miss Jeannie.
*Buckley, James.

Bund, J. W. Willis, Q.C.
*Burke, Thomas.
*Burnside, W.
Byrne, Matthew J.

Calder, Rev. J.
Campbell, Lord A.
Carbray, Felix.
Carey, J.
Carmichael, Miss Ella.
Carrigan, Rev. William, C.C.
*Casey, Patrick.
Casey, Rev. Patrick.
*Castletown, Right Hon. Lord.
Cavanagh, Michael.
Clarke, Henry Wray, M.A.
Clarke, W. H., L.R.C.P. & L.R.C.S.
*Close, Rev. Maxwell H., M.R.I.A., F.G.S.
Cochrane, Robert, F.R.S.A.I., M.R.I.A.
Coffey, George, B.A., M.R.I.A.
*Colgan, Rev. William.
*Colgan, Nathaniel.
Collery, Alderman B., M.P.
Colles, Dr. Abraham.
Colles, Ramsey.
*Colman, James, M.R.S.A.I.
*Comyn, David.
Connolly, P. F.
*Conway, Rev. David.
Cooke, John.
Costello, Thomas Bodkin, M.D.
Costello, Brother Francis, O.S.F.
Cox, Michael, M.D., M.R.I.A.
Craigie, W. A.
Creighton, Dr. R. H.
Culwick, J. C., MUS.DOC.
*Cunningham, J. T.
Curran, John.
*Curren, Rev. W. H.
Cusack, Professor J.

Daly, Timothy.
Darby, Martin, M.D.
Davies, Thomas J.
*De La Hoyde, Captain Albert.
Delany, The Very Rev. Dr.
*Delany, The Very Rev. William, S.J.,
   LL.D., M.R.I.A.
Devitt, Rev. Matthew, S.J.
Dickson, Miss Edith.
Dillon, John, M.P.
Dillon, William.
*Dix, E. Reginald McC.
Dodd, Maurice J.
Dodgson, Edward Spencer.
Doherty, Anthony J.
Donelan, James, M.B.
Doody, Patrick.
Dottin, Professor Georges.
Doyle, J. J.
Doyle, J. J.
Dresden, Königliche Oeffentliche Bib-
   liothek.
Drury, Miss Edith.
Dufferin and Ava, The Most Hon. The
   Marquis of, K.P.
Duignan, W. H.
Duncan, Leland L.
Dwyer, Arthur W.

Eccles, Miss C. O'Conor.
Evans, Miss E. M.

*Fahey, Rev. J., D.D., V.G.
Fahy, Frank A.
Farquharson, J. A.
Fenton, James.
Fernan, John J.
Ferriter, P.
Fish, F. P.
Fitz Gerald, Michael J.
*Fitz Gerald Lord Walter.
*Fitzmaurice, Rev. E. B., O.S.F.
Flannery, T. J.
Forest Gate Branch of the Gaelic
   League.
Foreman, W. H.
Frazer, James, C.E.
†*Frederic, Harold.
Frost, James.

Gaidoz, Henri.
Gallagher, J. S.
Gallogly, Michael F.
Galway Branch of Gaelic League.
Gannon, John Patrick.

Gavigan, Thomas.
Geoghegan, Professor Richard H.
†Gilman, Herbert Webb, J.P.
Gleeson, Rev. Matthew C.
Glynn, John.
Glynn, J. A., B.A.
Glynn, Thomas.
Golden, Miss B.
Gonne, Miss Maud.
Gordon, Principal.
*Goudie, Robert.
*Grainger, William H., M.D.
*Graves, Alfred Percival, M.A.
*Gregory, Lady.
*Greene, George A., M.A.
*Griffin, Richard N.
*Gwynn, Edward John, M.A., F.T.C.D.,
   Todd Professor, R.I.A.
Gwynn, Stephen.

Haffenden, Mrs.
Hallissy, Miss Margaret Mary.
Hamilton, G. L.
*Hartland, E. S.
Harvard College Library, Mass.,U.S.A.
Hayde, Rev. John.
*Hayes, Cornelius J.
*Hayes, James.
Healy, Most Rev. John, D.D., LL.D.,
   Coadjutor Bishop of Clonfert.
*Healy, Maurice, M.P.
Henderson, George, M.A., PH.D.
Henchan, Martin J.
Henry, James, M.D.
Henry, John P., M.D.
*Heron, Francis, M.B.
*Hickey, Rev. M., M.R.I.A., F.R.S.A.I.
Hogan, John.
*Horsford, Miss Cornelia.
*Hull, Miss Eleanor.
Hurley, Timothy J.
*Hutton, Mrs. A. W.
Hyde, Douglas, LL.D., M.R.I.A.
Hynes, Rev. John, B.D.

*Ingram, John Kells, LL.D., S.F.T.C.D.
Inverness, Gaelic Society of.
Irving, Daniel.
*Iveagh, Right Hon. Edward Cecil,
   Baron, D.C.L.

Jack, J.
*James, W P.
Johns Hopkins University Library, Bal-
   timore, Maryland, U.S.A.

*Johnson, James Patrick, M.A.
*Jones, Bryan J.
Joyce, Patrick Weston, LL.D.
Joyce, M.A.
Joyce, William B.

Kane, Robert Romney, M.A., LL.D.,
    County Court Judge.
*Kavanagh, Rev. Brother J. C.
Keane, John.
Keating, Miss Geraldine.
*Keawell, P. J.
*Keily, Miss B.
*Kelly, John F.
Kelly, J. S.
Kent, Thomas Rice.
*Kent, Pierce.
Keohane, Miss May.
Ker, Professor W. P.
Kiely, John.
*Kiely, John M.
*Killen, William.
King's Inns, Hon. Society of, Dublin.
Kittridge, Professor G. L.
*Knox, H. P.

*La Touche, J. Digges.
Lawless, Peter.
Lawson, Dillon.
Leahy, Andrew.
*Lecky, Right Hon.W. E. H., M.P., P.C.
Lee, Mrs.
Lefroy, B. St. G.
Lehane, D.
Lewis, Sir William J. Bart.
Lillis, James T.
Limerick Free Library.
Little, Miss M.
Liverpool Public Library, per P.
    Cowell, Librarian.
Lloyd, J. H.
Lloyd, Miss M.
London Library, per C. L. Hagbert
    Wright, Librarian.
Long, W.
Longworth-Dames, Capt. M.
Loth, J., Doyen de la F. des Lettres.
*Loughran, Rev. Dr., C.C.
*Lynch, Timothy.
Lyons, Very Rev. John C., O.P.
Lyons, Patrick.

*Macalister, R. A. S.
Macbean, Edward.
M'Bride, A.

*MacBrayne, David, F.S.A. (Scot.).
M'Call, P. J.
M'Carte, Matthew.
M'Carthy, John.
M'Carthy, Justin, M.P.
*M'Clintock, H. F.
MacCollum, Fionan.
*M'Connell, James.
MacDermott, M.
MacDonagh, Frank.
MacDonagh, Michael.
Macdonald, Rev. A. J.
*M'Donald, Rev. Allen.
MacDonald, William.
MacDowell, T. B.
M'Dwyer, James.
M'Fadden, Rev. James, P.P.
MacFarlane, Malcolm.
M'Glynn, Right Rev. Monsignor, V.G.
M'Ginley, Connell.
M'Ginley, Rev. James C.
*M'Ginley, P. J.
M'Groder, John.
M'Hale, Mrs.
MacKay, A. J. J., LL.D., Sheriff of
    Fife.
*MacKay, Eric.
MacKay, J. G.
MacKay, Thomas A.
MacKay, William.
M'Keefry, Rev. Joseph, C.C.
M'Kenna, Stephen J.
MacKenzie, William.
Mackinnon, Professor Donald.
*Mackintosh, Rev. Alexander.
Mackintosh, Andrew.
Mackintosh, Duncan.
*Mackintosh, C. Frazer, LL.D.
*M'Lachlan, Rev. Hugh.
*Maclagan, R. C., M.D.
Maclean, Rev. Donald.
M'Leod, John, M.P.
Macleod, Norman.
*MacLoughlin, James L.
MacMahon, the Rev. Eugene, Adm.
†MacMahon, J. K.
MacMahon, Hugh.
*MacMahon, Rev. Thomas, P.P.
*MacManus, Miss L.
*MacManus, Patrick.
*MacMullan, Rev. A., P.P.
*MacNamara, C. V.
MacNeill, John.
*MacNeill, Patrick Charles.
*M'Nelis, Rev. A., P.P.
M'Nulty, Robert.
*M'Sweeney, Timothy.
Maffett, Rev. Richard S., B.A

Magrath, C. J. Ryland.
Maher, Rev. Br. J. R.
Manchester Free Libraries, per C. W.
Sutton, Librarian.
Mangan, D.
Manly, Miss Bridget.
*Manning, M. A.
Manning, T. F.
Marcon, Dr. P. B.
*Martin, A. W.
*Martyn, Edward.
Mathew, Frank.
Melbourne, Victoria, Public Library
and Museum of.
Merriman, P. J., B.A.
Mescal, Daniel.
Meyer, Professor Kuno.
Meyrick Library, Jesus College, Ox-
ford, per W. M. Lindsay, Librarian.
*Miller, Arthur W. K., M.A.
Milligan, T.
Mills, James.
Mitchell Library, Glasgow, per F. T.
Barrett, Librarian.
*Mockler, Rev. T. A.
Molloy, William R. J., J.P., M.R.I.A.
*Moloney, Rev. Michael.
Monro, C. H., Fellow Caius College,
Cambridge.
Moore, Rev. H. Kingsmill.
Moore, Norman, M.D.
Moran, His Eminence Patrick F.,
Cardinal, D.D., Archbishop of
Sydney (Life Member).
Moran, James.
*Moroney, P. J.
Morris, Patrick.
Morrison, Hew.
*Mount St. Joseph, The Right Rev.
The Lord Abbot of.
Mount Mellary, The Right Rev. The
Lord Abbot of.
Mulhearn, Joseph.
Murphy, Conor.
Murphy, John.
Murphy, John J.
Murphy, John W.
Murphy, J. J. Fintan.
Murphy, Michael.
Mussen, A., M.D.

Nagle, W. H.
National Library of Ireland.
Naughton, O.
*Neil, R. A.
Newark Free Public Library.
New Ireland Literary Society.

New York Philo-Celtic Society.
New York Public Library.
*Noonan, J. D.
Nottingham Free Public Library,
Borough of.
Nutt, Alfred.

O'Brien, R. Barry.
*O'Brien, Edward.
O'Brien, Michael.
*O'Byrne, M. A.
*O'Byrne, Patrick.
O'Byrne, W.
O'Callaghan, Joseph P.
O'Callaghan, J. J., Phys. and Surg.
O'Carroll, J. T.
*O'Conor Don, Right Hon. The, D.L.
O'Dea, Rev. D., C.C.
O'Doherty, The Most Rev. Dr., Lord
Bishop of Derry.
O'Donel, Manus, R.E.
*O'Donnell, The Most Rev. Dr., Lord
Bishop of Raphoe.
O'Donnell, Manus.
O'Donnell, Patrick.
O'Donoghue, D. J.
O'Donoghue, Mortimer.
†O'Donoghue, P. J.
O'Donoghue, R., M.D.
O'Dowd, Michael.
O'Driscoll, Rev. Denis, C.C.
*O'Farrell, P.
O'Gallagher, M.
O'Gorman, Thomas.
O'Grady, Standish Hayes.
O'Growney, The Rev. Eugene, M.R.I.A.
O'Hanlon, Very Rev. Canon, P.P.
*O'Hea, P.
O'Hennessy, Bartholomew.
O'Keeffe, J. G.
O'Keeffe, Michael.
O'Kieran, Rev. L., C.C.
O'Kinealy, Justin.
*O'Laverty, Rev. James, P.P., M.R.I.A.
O'Leary, Daniel.
O'Leary, Denis Augustine.
*O'Leary, James.
O'Leary, Rev. James M., C.C.
O'Leary, John.
O'Leary, Rev. P., P.P.
O'Leary, Neil.
O'Neill, Captain Francis.
O'Reilly, Miss.
*O'Reilly, Very Rev. Hugh, M.R.I.A.
O'Riordan, Rev. J.
O'Riordan, E. F.
Orpen, Goddard.
*O'Shea, P. J.

*O'Shaughnessy, R.
Ossory and Ferns, Right Rev. The
  Bishop of
O'Sullivan, D.
O'Sullivan, Daniel
O'Sullivan, Michael.
O'Sullivan, Rev. T.

Parkinson, Edward.
Pearse, P. H.
Pedersen, Dr. Holger.
Pettit, Denis.
Plummer, Rev. C.
*Powell, Professor F. York, Regius Pro-
  fessor of Modern History, Oxford.
*Power, Edward J.
Power, Rev. P.
*Power, William Aloysius Lucas.
Pratt Institute Free Library, Brooklyn,
  New York, U. S. A.
Prince, J. Dyneley, PH.D.
Purcell, Joseph.

Queen's College Library, Cork.

Raleigh, William.
Rapmund, Rev. Joseph, C.C., M.R.I.A.
Rhys, Mrs. Ernest.
*Rhys, Professor John.
Rice, Hon. Mary Spring.
*Richardson, Stephen J.
Robertson, J. L.
Robinson, Professor F. N.
Rolleston, T. W.
Rossall, John H.
Rushe, Denis Carolan, B.A.
Ryan, Andrew.
*Ryan, Mark, M.D.
*Ryan, Patrick J., M.D.
*Ryan, Rev. T. E.
Ryan, W. P.

Savage-Armstrong, G. F.
Scanlan, Joseph, M.D.
Scanlan, Rev. James, C.C.
Scott, Miss Jean MacFaelan.
*Sephton, Rev. John.
*Seymour, Rev. Robert, D.D.
Shahan, Very Rev. Thomas J., D.D.
Sharp, William.
*Shaw, W. N.
Sheehan, Daniel.
Sheil, Peter.
Shekleton, A. J.
Sheridan, Rev. Joseph, C.C.

Sheridan, J. J.
Shorten, George.
Shorter, Clement.
Sigerson, George, M.D.
Sinton, Rev. Thomas.
Smyth, F. Acheson.
Sneddon, Geo. T.
Stokes, Whitley, D.C.L.
Stoney, Bindon B., M.A., LL.D., F.R.S.
Strassburg, Kaiserlich Universitäts u.
  Landes Bibliothek.
*Sweeny, William M.

Taylor Institution, Oxford.
Tenison, E. R., M.D.
*Thompson, Miss E. Skeffington.
Thurneysen, Professor Dr. Rudolf.
Todhunter, John, M.D.
Toronto Library.
Traherne, Llewellyn E.
Trench, F. H., Fellow of All Souls,
  Oxford.
Twigg, John Hill.

Vallàck, Miss A.
Vienna, Imperial University Library.

Wallace, Colonel.
Watkinson Library, Hartford, U. S.A.
Walsh, Rev. Martin, P.P.
Walsh, Martin S.
Walsh, Most Rev. William J., D.D.,
  Lord Archbishop of Dublin.
Ward, John C.
Ward, Timothy.
*Waters, George A., M.D., Surg. R. N.
Webb, Alfred.
Weld, W. R.
Welter, Y. H.
White, Major J., J.P.
White, William Grove.
*Williams, T. W.
*Wilson, R. H.
Wilson, T. C., M.D.
Windisch, Professor Dr. Ernst.
Wood, Alexander.
Worcester Public Library, Mass.,
  U. S. A.

Yale University Library, New Haven,
  Conn., U. S. A.
Yeats, W. B.
Young, Miss Rose M.

Zimmer, Professor Dr. H.
Zupitza, Dr. E.

LIST OF IRISH TEXT SOCIETY'S PUBLICATIONS

IN HAND OR ISSUED.

1. Ꞃɩolla an Ḟɩuᵹa [The Lad of the Ferule].
   Eaċꞃa Cloinne Ríᵹ na h-Ioꞃuaɩꞅe [Adventures of
   the Children of the King of Norway].
   (16th and 17th century texts.)
   Edited by DOUGLAS HYDE, LL.D.

   _____

2. ꞃeaċa Ċoluɩm-cɩlle [Life of Columba]. By Manus
   O'Donnell, 1521.
   (From the MS. Bod. Lib.)
   Edited by Tomás Ó Ꞃlannᵹaɩle.

   _____

3. Foꞃuꞃ Feaꞃa aꞃ Éɩꞃɩnn [History of Ireland]. By
   Geoffrey Keating.
   Edited by DAVID COMYN, Esq.

   _____

4. Collection of unpublished Munster Songs and
   Poems taken from MSS. of the last 200
   years.
   Edited by REV. P. S. DINNEEN, S.J., M.A.

   _____

ADDITIONAL SERIES.

1. Fleꞅ bꞃɩcꞃenꞅ [The Feast of Bricriu].
   (From Leabhar na h-Uidhre, with conclusion from Gaelic
   MS. xl. Advocates' Lib., and variants from B. M. Egerton,
   93; T.C.D. h. 3. 17; Leyden Univ., Is Vossii lat. 4ᵃ. 7.)
   Edited by GEORGE HENDERSON, M.A., Ph.D.

IRISH-ENGLISH, ENGLISH-IRISH POCKET DICTIONARY.

A SPECIAL SUB-COMMITTEE has been appointed by the IRISH TEXTS SOCIETY to consider the possibility of publishing a handy Irish-English, English-Irish Pocket Dictionary of modern Irish for the use of students. The Committee, under the superintendence of Mr. G. A. Greene, M.A. (Chairman), is now actively engaged in this work, with the assistance of a number of workers at a distance, who are aiding them by drawing up lists of modern words from published texts and other sources. Offers of help in the compilation of this Dictionary will be gladly received by the Hon. Secs., Miss Hull and Miss Drury, Irish Literary Society, 8, Adelphi Terrace, London, W. C.

The Rev. Peter O'Leary, P.P., and Mr. David Comyn have kindly offered assistance in the final revision and editing of the work.

Full information will be given at a later date as to the publication and cost of the Dictionary.

DAVID NUTT, London.

MR. NUTT *has published in the Grimm Library the following works illustrative of Celtic Mythology and Romance :—*

THE VOYAGE OF BRAN, SON OF FEBAL, TO THE LAND OF

THE LIVING. An Old Irish Saga now first edited, with Translation, Notes, and Glossary, by KUNO MEYER. With an Essay upon the Irish Vision of the Happy Otherworld, and the Celtic Doctrine of Rebirth, by ALFRED NUTT. 2 vols.

I. THE HAPPY OTHERWORLD. Pp. xvii + 331. 10s. 6d. net.

II. THE CELTIC DOCTRINE OF REBIRTH. Pp. xii + 352. 10s. 6d. net.

SOME PRESS NOTICES.

Monsieur H. D'Arbois de Jubainville in the "Revue Celtique."—" Œuvre d'une grande valeur scientifique et d'une lecture agréable."

Monsieur H. Gaidoz in "Mélusine."—" Édition, tradition et commentaire philologique sont d'une critique irréprochable. . . . M. Nutt est bien informé: ses matériaux sont pris aux meilleures sources : son exposition est nette et précise : son livre est une œuvre d'histoire générale à la fois des croyances et des littératures."

Monsieur Gaston Paris in "Romania."—" Trés savante étude . . . qui sera lue avec grand profit par tous ceux qui s'occupent de littérature comparée ou d'histoire religieuse."

Professor Ernst Martin in the "Zeitschrift für deutsches Alterthum."—" Ueberall verwertet Nutt die besten und neuesten Hilfsmittel, aber er vermehrt auch selbstständig das Material und zieht eine Reihe von Schlüssen welche er methodisch begründet und zugleich klar und fesselnd vorträgt."

Professor F. York Powell in "Folk-Lore."—" The most valuable contribution to the history of religion and religious ideas that, so far as my knowledge goes, last year gave us."

Monsieur L. Marillier in the "Revue de l'Histoire des Religions."—" M. Nutt aura rendu un éminent service en portant à la connaissance des mythologues des documents dont beaucoup malheureusement ne sont mis à profit que dans le cercle étroit des celtisants ; il en aura rendu un plus grand encore en faisant avec tant de sureté critique et de solide érudition l'analyse et l'histoire des conceptions complexes qui y sont contenues."

Notes and Queries.—" This notable contribution to the history of Celtic myth and religion."

Manchester Guardian.—" The book is important, because it is a carefully reasoned constructive effort to get a working-theory of Aryan religious history."

Inverness Northern Chronicle.—" A reconstruction of pre-Christian Irish theology. . . . Professor Meyer's translations are admirable. . . . It is impossible to give in this notice an idea of Mr. Nutt's painstaking gathering of materials, or of the scientific use he makes of them in the work of restoration."

Modern Language Notes (Baltimore).—" The field has been thoroughly examined for material; the material has been well and clearly worked over. The statements of fact are always fair; the reasoning is usually clear, forcible, and just, and the conclusions sane."

DAVID NUTT, London.

THE CUCHULLIN SAGA IN IRISH LITERATURE. Being a Collection of Stories relating to the Hero Cuchullin, translated from the Irish by various scholars. Compiled and edited, with Introduction and Notes, by ELEANOR HULL. With Map of Heroic Ireland. Pp. lxxx + 316. 7s. 6d. net.

SOME PRESS NOTICES.

The Academy.—" The English reader could not wish for a better introduction to the wildest and most fascinating division of Irish myth."

Mr. T. W. Rolleston in the "Daily Express."—"This great Saga has many aspects—mystical, historical, ethnological, and literary. I have here touched on the latter only, but the more one reads it the deeper appears its significance and value, the fuller its interest. Every Irish reader who desires to know something, as all of us should desire, of his spiritual ancestry, should place this book on his shelves."

The Scotsman.—" A selection made and annotated with much judgment."

Northern Chronicle.—" The work of compilation has been exceedingly well done."

The Outlook.—" Miss Hull's very admirable edition of the Cuchullin Saga furnishes one of the best available examples of the character of Irish romantic legend."

The Daily Nation.—" Miss Hull's introduction is one of the most lucid and careful studies of mediæval Irish literature yet published in popular form."

THE LEGEND OF SIR GAWAIN. Studies upon its Original Scope and Significance, by JESSIE L. WESTON. Pp. xiv + 117. 4s. net.

SOME PRESS NOTICES.

Manchester Guardian.—" A careful, readable, and suggestive study which adds substantially to the results obtained by Madden's well-known book."

Academy.—" Invaluable in clearing the path for a final survey of the tangled wood of Arthurian legend."

Professor W. P. Ker in "Folk-Lore."—"A clear and interesting account of the part taken by Gawain in some of the romances, with a view to the possible interpretation of the facts in connexion with Celtic, and especially with Irish literature."

⁂ The special interest of this study to Irish readers is the clear demonstration of the parallelism between the Welsh Gawain and the Irish Cuchulainn. New proof of this parallelism is afforded in Mr. Henderson's edition of *Fled Bricrend*, the second volume of the Irish Texts Society's publications.

www.ingramcontent.com/pod-product-compliance
Lightning Source LLC
Chambersburg PA
CBHW030403270326

41926CB00009B/1238